D1553991

GIROLAMO FRESCOBALDI

Drawing of
Girolamo Frescobaldi
by Claude Mellan

GIROLAMO FRESCOBALDI

Frederick Hammond

HARVARD UNIVERSITY PRESS
Cambridge, Massachusetts, and London, England
1983

Printed in the United States of America

This publication has been supported by a subvention
from the American Musicological Society.

Designed by Victor A. Curran

Library of Congress Cataloging in Publication Data

Hammond, Frederick, 1937–
Girolamo Frescobaldi.

Bibliography: p.
Includes index.
1. Frescobaldi, Girolamo, 1583–1643. I. Title.
ML410.F85H35 1983 786.5'092'4 [B] 82–11938
ISBN 0–674–35438–9

FOR RALPH KIRKPATRICK

Non senza fatiga si giunge al fine

Preface

The seeds of this study were planted some twenty years ago, when Ralph Kirkpatrick pointed out the need for an account of Girolamo Frescobaldi's life and work. The intervening years have brought a revival of interest in Girolamo, expressed in a number of important but specialized monographs and a handful of performances and recordings. Nonetheless, the major Italian keyboard composer of the seventeenth century has remained without a comprehensive study in English and without a dependable one in any language.

From that chance observation, the topic of this book has hunted me down. My first acquaintance with Frescobaldi's music, the source of whatever subsequent understanding of it I have acquired as a performer and scholar, was made during my undergraduate studies with Kirkpatrick at Yale. A fellowship to the American Academy in Rome in 1965 brought me and a harpsichord to Italy for a year that I employed in learning and performing a significant body of Girolamo's keyboard music. The noose tightened a bit further as my interests began to center on the study and performance of seventeenth-century Italian keyboard music, and it became apparent that a detailed examination of Frescobaldi's life and work would provide an ideal focus for these interests in the context of my regular visits to Rome. A few summers later I put together a biography of Girolamo from the sources then generally available, which showed how fragmentary and uneven were the current materials for a full-scale study and prompted my final surrender to the topic as a serious project.

Succeeding visits to Italy were devoted to a minute examination of Girolamo's background and life, above all as revealed in the voluminous archival remains of his patrons in Ferrara, Mantua, Florence, and Rome. The intervening periods were employed in gathering the materials for a survey of Frescobaldi's entire production and in transcribing works otherwise unavailable: the madrigals, the sacred collection, the fugitive vocal compositions, and the two editions of the *Canzoni* in part-books. This labor was illuminated by constant study and performance of Frescobaldi, especially by the experience of recording all the toccatas of the *Libro secondo*.

The result of these coordinate efforts is a general study of Girolamo Frescobaldi and his music. It cannot pretend to be an overall history of Roman music of the period or even of Roman keyboard music, since in many areas—the polychoral mass, small sacred concertos, instrumental ensemble music, manuscript studies—the essential groundwork is still being laid. And yet a study that concentrates on Girolamo alone has at least two advantages to offer a wider public. First, it contributes to the reassessment of a great composer known to the general public, if at all, by only a few works, and most of them spurious. Second, in focusing on Frescobaldi rather than attempting a panorama the historian does no violence to the evidence. No matter how fascinating the lives of the lesser seventeenth-century Italian keyboard composers and how suggestive their works may be, the facts remain that Girolamo was the major keyboard composer of the epoch, that he was recognized as such by contemporary musicians, and that with a few exceptions the evidence that suggests their formative influence on Frescobaldi can equally well be argued in the opposite direction.

In the arrangement of this study I have hewed to the main current of Frescobaldi's career as it appears to me. He did write vocal works, and in addition to the printed collections that were issued under the composer's supervision there is a large body of manuscript keyboard music attributed to Frescobaldi. Nonetheless, it seems to me that Girolamo's significance and influence lie in the repertory of his printed instrumental works (a view shared by many of his contemporaries), and I have accordingly placed the consideration of his vocal works and of the manuscript keyboard repertory in appendices to avoid losing the thread of his development.

Just as the decision to write this book was a gradual process, so in its rewriting one theme began to emerge ever more clearly: the interaction of Girolamo's Ferrarese musical inheritance with his Roman experience. Indeed, much of the attraction of the project was the opportunity to examine my own Roman experience and to embody it in a study of the City in the seventeenth century. In a kind of double focus, the depiction of Frescobaldi's Rome, in the period of its greatest change since Augustus, has been pursued within the equally dramatic transformation of modern postwar Italy. In the course of this, many of the social and religious traditions that even twenty-five years ago provided a link with the past have disappeared, to be reestablished only with much scholarly and imaginative effort. As well as being the biography of a man and the examination of a body of music, this book has become inescapably an attempt to apprehend a place and a time.

The completion of such an attempt evokes not only the City and its remote past but the contribution of institutions and friends as well. Among the former, my greatest debts are due in Rome to the library of the American Academy, the music history section of the German Historical Institute and its director, Dr. Friedrich Lippmann, the Archivio Storico del Vicariato di Roma at San Giovanni in Laterano, the Archivio and Archivio Segreto of the Biblioteca Apostolica Vaticana, the Archivio di Stato, the Archivio Aldobrandini, the Archivio Doria-Pamphilj, the Biblioteca Casanatense, the Biblioteca del Conservatorio di Santa Cecilia, and the Biblioteca Corsiniana. Much of the musical material was examined in the rich holdings of the Civico Museo Bibliografico Musicale in Bologna, with the kind assistance of its director, Dott. Sergio Paganelli. In Ferrara I have consulted the Archivio di Stato and the Biblioteca Comunale Ariostea; in Florence, the Archivio di Stato, the Biblioteca Nazionale Centrale, the archives of Santa Croce and San Lorenzo, and the library of the Harvard Center for Renaissance Studies at Villa I Tatti; in Modena, the Archivio di Stato and the Archivio Segreto Estense; in Reggio Emilia, the Biblioteca Municipale; and in Venice, the Biblioteca Marciana and the library of the Fondazione Cini. Outside Italy, material has been furnished by the Bibliothèque Royale of Brussels; the British Library in London; the Santini Collection now in the Priesterseminar in Münster; the Bibliothèque du Conservatoire, Bibliothèque Nationale, and Ecole des Beaux Arts in Paris; and the Minoritenkonvent and Oesterreichische Nationalbibliothek in Vienna. In the United States I have consulted the New York Public Library and the Mary Flagler Cary Collection in the Pierpont Morgan Library, New York City; the Library of Congress; the Newberry Library in Chicago; the Research and Music Libraries of the University of California at Berkeley and Los Angeles; and the libraries of Yale University and the Yale School of Music. Illustrations appear here by the kind permission of the Biblioteca Apostolica Vaticana in Rome, the Soprintendenza Beni Artistici e Storici of Florence, Princess Aldobrandini (Villa Aldobrandini, Frascati), the Staatliche Museen Preussischer Kulturbesitz in Berlin, the Bibliothèque Nationale and Ecole des Beaux-Arts in Paris, the Nationalmuseum in Stockholm, the William Andrews Clark Memorial Library and the Special Collections of the Research Library of the University of California, Los Angeles, the Metropolitan Museum of Art, the Spencer Collection of the New York Public Library, and the Smithsonian Institution.

I have attempted to include the results of several recent studies on subjects touching Frescobaldi's career: Anthony Newcomb's work on the musical culture of Ferrara, his research on documents pertaining to Girolamo's earlier years, and his article on Frescobaldi in the new *Grove Dictionary;* John Harper's study of Frescobaldi's instrumental canzonas; Susan Parisi's examination of Mantuan court records; the researches of John Hill on Cardinal Montalto's musical establishment; Alexander Silbiger's work on Italian keyboard manuscripts and on Frescobaldi's pupils, and an unpublished study on tempo and time signatures in Frescobaldi's keyboard music; James Ladewig's dissertation on the *Recercari et canzoni;* and the publications of the Frescobaldi *Gesamtausgabe* now in progress. Much of this material was communicated to me before publication, for which I am especially grateful. I have profited also from the work and advice of other specialists in Italian music of the seventeenth century: the late Putnam Aldrich, Lorenzo Bianconi, Adriano Cavicchi, Etienne Darbellay, Margaret Murata, Lucy Hallman Russell, Anne Schnoebelen, and Eleanor Selfridge-Field.

Other friends have provided assistance from their profound knowledge of things Roman: Irving Lavin, Marilyn Aronberg Lavin, the late Georgina Masson. To Msgr. Charles Burns in Rome and Dott. Gino Corti in Florence I owe thanks for assistance with archival problems. Edwin Seroussi copied the music examples. Gregory Harrold has answered questions about organ terminology and history, and Professor Gerhard Croll of the Musikwissenschaftliches Institut in Salzburg provided me with a recording of a newly restored claviorganum. Eugene Walter contributed a line from his *Monkey Poems,* Marchese Ferdinando de' Frescobaldi furnished information on the Florentine Frescobaldis, and Donna Orietta and Don Frank Doria-Pamphilj gave me the opportunity of performing Frescobaldi in their Roman palace, once the home of Girolamo's patron Cardinal Pietro Aldobrandini. Donna Livia Aldobrandini Pedicone kindly assisted in gaining permission to reproduce the portrait of Cardinal Pietro. Dr. Eckhart Knab of the Albertina in Vienna provided information on Mellan's portrait of Frescobaldi. Isabel and Laurance Roberts read the typescript of this study astutely and sympathetically, and Paul Reale furnished detailed criticism of the analytical chapters. My family has provided support and encouragement. Much of my work in Europe has been facilitated by grants for research and other assistance from the University of California at Los Angeles, the UCLA Center for Medieval and Renaissance Studies, and the Gladys Krieble Delmas Foundation, as well as by fellowships and hospitality from the American Academy in Rome and the Harvard Center for Renaissance Studies at Villa I Tatti. Material employed here has appeared in more extended form in the *Journal of the American Musicological Society, Analecta Musicologica,* and the *Essays Presented to Myron P. Gilmore.*

Certain friends have contributed to this undertaking beyond all reasonable obligations. Sibyl Marcuse, not content with giving advice on musical instruments and examining the typescript carefully, has also read proofs. James Moore drew my attention to the Venice manuscripts containing attributions to Frescobaldi and provided meticulous catalogues of them. Howard Mayer Brown impelled me to rethink the musical chapters and with characteristic generosity vetted the result. To Margaretta Fulton's faith in this project and to the editorial labors of Katarina Rice I owe the happy completion of my work. Since my arrival at the American Academy in 1965, Princess Margherita Rospigliosi has been a source of constant hospitality and encouragement and a living link with the Roman past. Finally, Ralph Kirkpatrick has followed this book in its slow evolution with unfailing patience and has spurred on its completion by judiciously alternating the carrot of his approbation with the stick of well-merited criticism. It is dedicated to him because, quite simply, without him it would not exist.

F.H.
Rome

Contents

Illustrations

PART ONE

Frescobaldi's Life

1

Ferrara

The casual traveler to Italy cannot fail to visit Rome—crowded, noisy, smog-ridden, but still exasperatingly beautiful after twenty-eight centuries of recorded history. Unless he is an amateur of musical curiosities, however, he will probably overlook a modest stone tablet in the porch of a Roman basilica commemorating the death of Girolamo Frescobaldi in 1643. The proud "Ferrarese" that someone has added in pencil beside the composer's name is unlikely to impel the traveler to visit Ferrara, a city where time seems to have run down and stopped. Four centuries ago, however, Ferrara was the seat of one of the most brilliant courts of the Renaissance, while Rome was still emerging from the abandon and decay of the Middle Ages.

Another tablet—now illegible—affixed to a derelict house just off one of the main streets of Ferrara identifies the home of Frescobaldi's youth, purchased by his father in 1584. The cathedral's baptismal register shows that the infant Girolamo Alessandro, son of Filippo and Lucrezia Frescobaldi, was baptized in September 1583.[1] He was named for his paternal grandfather, his earliest recorded ancestor. Girolamo's parents also produced a daughter, Giulia, and after his mother's death his father married again and increased the family by another son and daughter. The fact that Girolamo's half-brother, Cesare, was known as a musician supports the tradition that their father was an organist.[2] Filippo Frescobaldi's property holdings and the esteem in which he was held show that he was a man of substance, but there is no evidence to connect him with the ancient Florentine noble house of Frescobaldi.[3] Certainly, in later years—even in a Florentine publication—Girolamo always pointed to his Ferrarese origin and musical training as the formative influence of his career.

Ferrara's comparative isolation has spared enough to evoke the sixteenth-century city for the modern visitor. The center of the town is still defined by two spacious streets. The Giovecca, off which the Frescobaldi house stands, marks the boundary between the medieval nucleus of Ferrara and its Renaissance enlargement; the Strada degli Angeli, crossing the Giovecca at right angles, passes the rose-and-white cathedral in which Girolamo was baptized, the palace and the massive castle of the Este dukes, and the palaces and gardens that punctuate the smaller domestic buildings. Even today, Ferrara has a unique flavor. The wide streets, the surprising extent of the small, low houses, and the prevalence of warm brick all give a neat, self-contained, and—on a gray day—almost Netherlandish air to the city. It is less than an hour's drive from Bologna, with its mountainous approach and outposts, but in its setting of flat fields planted with wheat, vines, and fruit, Ferrara belongs unmistakably to the great plain of the Po stretching north to Venice and west to Lombardy.

In the sixteenth century the duchy was one of the richest domains in Italy. Its fertile territories occupied the center of the Pianura Padana, bounded by Venice on the north, Bologna (in the hands of the papacy) on the south, and Mantua on the west. In addition to Ferrara itself, the duchy included Modena, Reggio Emilia, and the port of Comacchio. Irrigated by the Po, the Reno, and the canal of Modena, it had grain to export, wine, wood, meat, dairy products, and "sturgeon and fresh-water fish from the Po, others from the valley of Comacchio, besides salt-water fish, and in addition pheasants, partridges, quail, hare, goats, boar, and much other game."[4] These natural riches were complemented by the flourishing industry of the cannon foundries, whose products appear in the portraits of Alfonso I d'Este by Titian and the Dossi atelier.

These advantages produced an unmistakable Ferrarese character whose sybaritic tendencies sometimes grated on the sensibilities of other Italians. Writing in 1589, the Florentine resident in Ferrara found the Ferrarese lazy, vain, greedy of titles and distinctions, more martial in appearance than in fact, spendthrift, and disdainful of those "in trade" (including the Florentines). Owing to their laziness, their households contained disproportionate numbers of servants. Their former dissoluteness was now confined mostly to the Carnival season, when they took a childish delight in masking. Proud of their native city, they were polite and hospitable, their children well brought up. Their religion was not fervent, except for superstitious veneration of the dead. The men "have great inclination toward music, and are very studious of music and musical instruments," while the women "greatly delight in music and in playing various instruments, and many of them excel in this profession."[5]

Almost nothing of Frescobaldi's personality emerges from his biography, but a few incidents in his life suggest that his character resembled that of his compatriots.

Despite the surviving monuments and the contemporary accounts of Frescobaldi's native city, present-day Ferrara breathes little of the spirit that animated the duchy in its final flowering. As Girolamo himself later asserted, this was the achievement of the ruling house and above all of Alfonso II d'Este, the last legitimate duke of Ferrara. Alfonso's reign was based on practical politics—strategic marriages, maintenance of the economic health of his duchy, prudent reform—but his consuming passion was the arts. The culture of a great court is a fragile creation, however. Although isolated products of Alfonso's patronage survive, such as the poems of Guarini and Tasso and the madrigals of Luzzasco Luzzaschi, the ambience that formed them has been less fortunate. In Alfonso's court the painting, music, and poetry were permeated by the spirit of *villeggiatura,* the life of the ducal *delizie* or pleasances. There were at least nine *delizie* in Ferrara alone, comprising gardens, baths, villas, and preserves for fish and game, linked by canals whose flanking paths were screened by alleys of olives and vines.[6]

This vanished world of lawns and gardens, fountains, and superbly painted rooms was filled with music. Alfonso II's musical establishment was described in detail by the theorist Ercole Bottrigari, who lived in Ferrara from 1576 to 1587, in his *Il Desiderio* of 1594. Under the direction of Ippolito Fiorino, the Duke's *maestro di cappella,* and Luzzasco Luzzaschi, the ducal organist, the *musica* contained both Italian and Flemish musicians, singers as well as performers on cornetts, trombones, dolzaines, pipes, viols, *ribechini,* lutes, citharas, harps, and keyboards.[7] The keyboard players had at their disposal four *claviorgana,* five organs of various types, and five harpsichords, all maintained by professionals.[8] Two large rooms were set aside for the musicians, their instruments, and their music, in which they could practice at will. According to an inventory of 1625, the Duke's musical library, which passed to his Este cousins in Modena, contained some 254 items: masses, motets, madrigals, and lighter secular genres. The composers represented included not only Ferrarese musicians such as Luzzaschi and Milleville but also the Neapolitans Dentice, Stella, and Gesualdo, the Venetians Willaert and Andrea Gabrieli, and Marenzio, Rore, and Lassus.[9]

The public ensemble of the ducal musicians was the *concerto grande* under the direction of Ippolito Fiorino, which performed for "Cardinals, Dukes, Princes or other great personages" on their visits to Ferrara. This group included not only all the singers and players in the Duke's employ, but also "every Ferrarese who can sing and play well enough to be judged by Fiorino and Luzzasco good enough to participate in such a concert." The ensemble actually played "no other compositions than one or two written for this purpose only, one by the late Alfonso della Viola, the other by Luzzasco," principally because of the difficulties of intonation in an ensemble combining voices with instruments of fixed, partly variable, and variable pitch. Performers in the *concerto grande* might attract the attention of Duke Alfonso himself, who frequently attended rehearsals and offered criticism, which the musicians were expected to bear "with gracious modesty."[10]

The greatest musical jewel of Ferrara, the *concerto delle dame,* unlike the *concerto grande* and the equally famous nuns of San Vito, was not intended primarily for the public amusement of distinguished visitors but rather for the private delectation of Alfonso himself. This enjoyment had a strong proprietary note, as the Duke was jealous both of his performers and of their repertory. In the first period of its existence, from 1567 up to Alfonso's marriage with Margherita Gonzaga in 1579, the *concerto delle dame principalissime* had consisted of cultivated aristocratic amateurs supplemented by professional musicians such as Luzzaschi. After Alfonso's marriage the group was reorganized into a virtuoso chamber ensemble built around three sopranos (who also played harp, viola, and lute), a keyboard player (Luzzaschi), and a player on the archlute or pandora (Fiorino).[11] Their regular concerts, lasting from two to four hours, were probably performed for an intimate audience, judging from the tiny but exquisite room in the ducal palace that has been identified as a music room.[12]

The young Girolamo may have encountered the musical world of Ferrara through family connections. Luzzaschi stood godfather to another of Filippo Frescobaldi's children,[13] and Ippolito Fiorino was later involved in the problems surrounding Girolamo's marriage, together with a "Signor Goretti." This was presumably Antonio Goretti, a noted Ferrarese amateur, later a collaborator of Monteverdi, who maintained a large instrumentarium and music library. There, in the presence of Luzzaschi and Fiorino, Artusi heard the madrigals that prompted his attack on Monteverdi.

The earliest account of Girolamo's career, that of Agostino Superbi published in 1620, stresses his precocity: "Already in his first youth he played the most notable organs in his native city and did great things."[14] Libanori's somewhat suspect account of 1674 is more circumstantial:

> As a boy he was deemed an Angel of the heavenly Choir for the delicacy of his voice in singing, and the swiftness of his hand in playing. While still a Youth, brought through various principal Cities of Italy, with his sweet song and sound on all the Instruments of Music, both those played by the breath, and by the hand, but especially the harpsichord and Organ, he drew the ears to hear him, and the tongues of all to praise him. He touched the keys of the Organ with such art, and fine order, and quickness of hand, that he astonished those who saw and heard him.[15]

A poem in praise of Frescobaldi supports this description: "When [Frescobaldi] had scarcely attained the seventeenth year of his age the City heard him playing the organ with wondrous art, and was astounded."[16]

Under Alfonso's rule Ferrara had become "one single Academy" in which "the children of every father were almost all musicians,"[17] and it is not surprising that the young prodigy attracted Luzzaschi's attention. Girolamo became his pupil and more than once acknowledged his formative influence, the last time twenty-three years after Luzzaschi's death.

The breadth of Luzzaschi's musical experience must have made him an ideal mentor. Born sometime before 1545, he had studied with Cipriano da Rore until Rore's departure from Ferrara in 1557, after which he probably completed his training in composition with Alfonso della Viola; his organ teacher seems to have been Jacques Brumel.[18] Luzzaschi served the Ferrarese court in a variety of capacities. He was a singer in the ducal chapel from about 1563; at Brumel's death in 1564 he became first organist to Alfonso II, and by 1581 he was ranked with Giuseppe Guami and Claudio Merulo as one of the three great organists of the time; in 1582 he became organist of the cathedral as well. Since most of his keyboard works have been lost, however, Luzzaschi is now remembered as a vocal composer. By 1570 he had succeeded Alfonso della Viola as director of the Duke's *musica da camera,* a post that presumably demanded the composition of the five-part madrigals that Luzzaschi published in 1571, 1576, and 1582. Although not issued until 1601, his madrigals for solo voices and obbligato keyboard were clearly intended for the *concerto delle dame* and thus written well before Alfonso's death in 1597. In addition to his abilities as a singer, keyboard player, and composer, Luzzaschi was one of the few musicians capable not only of playing but even of composing for Nicola Vicentino's arcicembalo, a fearsomely complex harpsichord designed to produce all three of the ancient Greek genera.[19]

Girolamo's student years in Ferrara coincided with the significant musical developments of the 1580s and 1590s, in which Duke Alfonso's musical establishment played a central role. In 1571 the court ladies performed solos and duets accompanied by Luzzaschi; with the arrival of a virtuoso bass singer around 1577 this repertory was supplemented by simple genres such as the *arie da cantar sonetti,* now cultivated as occasions for florid vocal embellishment. The same years also saw a revival of interest in the polyphonic madrigal at the Ferrarese court, and these two musical trends were fused after the creation of the semiprofessional group in 1580 in the "luxuriant" madrigal. The madrigal took on something of the structural clarity and superficial ornamentation of less sophisticated genres, resulting in a texture based not upon the older ideal of equality of voices but upon a simpler homophonic texture enlivened by diminution rather than by structural counterpoint.

Although the new luxuriant madrigal was a natural development for younger composers—notably the Romans Luca Marenzio and Ruggero Giovannelli—it required a distinct effort on the part of the most distinguished senior composers of the Ferrarese circle, Luzzaschi and Wert. Luzzaschi in particular seems to have been uncomfortable with the new style; this, along with a decline in the quality of the *concerto delle dame* beginning about 1586, may account for his relatively small production in the 1580s. The turning point in the further evolution of the madrigal at Ferrara came with the advent of Don Carlo Gesualdo, Prince of Venosa, who journeyed to Ferrara early in 1594 to marry Donna Leonora d'Este, the sister of Duke Alfonso's cousin and heir, Don Cesare. The arrival of Gesualdo, accompanied by the lutenist Fabrizio Filomarino and the keyboard player and composer Scipione Stella, stimulated the ducal musicians to display their skill, and the Prince was particularly struck by Luzzaschi's performance on the organ and arcicembalo.[20] Luzzaschi's madrigal writing, however, proved to have greater influence on Gesualdo's career. Gesualdo acknowledged to Count Alfonso Fontanelli that he had "left that first style and put himself to imitate Luzzasco, highly loved and praised by him,"[21] an esteem Gesualdo demonstrated by dedicating to Luzzaschi his fourth book of madrigals, issued at Ferrara in 1596. The Prince's extended visits to Ferrara—until May 1594, and again at the end of the year for about two years—seem in return to have galvanized Luzzaschi, who issued no less than three madrigal collections between 1594 and 1596, manifestos of a stylistic counterrevolution in the direction of serious and expressive madrigal writing influential far beyond Ferrara.[22]

Some of this influence was exercised through the immediate experience of Ferrarese music, which in turn was receptive to external stimuli. Such diverse musicians as Costanzo Porta, Luca Marenzio, Claudio Merulo, and John Dowland visited Ferrara, and Giaches de Wert frequently traveled from Mantua (drawn as much by his passion for Tarquinia Molza as by the excellence of Ferrarese music). Orlando di Lasso was so impressed that he could "no longer praise my *musica*," his employer complained. Although the Ferrarese displayed little interest in monody, recitative, or opera (except for scenography), the visits of Bardi, Corsi, and Rinuccini and Giulio Caccini's close association with Ferrara in the 1580s and 1590s show that the Camerata was conversant with musical trends there.[23] Monteverdi's intention to present a manuscript collection of madrigals to Alfonso II was frustrated by the Duke's death, but in 1603 Monteverdi dedicated his fourth book of madrigals (many on texts by Ferrarese poets) to the new Ferrarese Accademia degli Intrepidi. The earlier strong Venetian influence on Ferrarese music does not seem to have extended to widespread adoption of the *stile concertato* except for an occasional polychoral mass, but works by both Luzzaschi and Frescobaldi (including a double-choir canzona) appeared in the Venetian Alessandro Raverij's *Canzoni* of 1608, together with six canzonas of Giovanni Gabrieli; and Luzzaschi's lost books of ricercars were published by Gardano of Venice.

The Ferrarese tradition of instrumental music is still unstudied, but its influence is obvious in Luzzaschi's other pupils: Girolamo Belli; Fabio Richetti, organist of the cathedral in Modena; and Carlo Mentini, called Fillago, organist of Santi Giovanni e Paolo in Venice and first organist of San Marco. The second organist of the Ferrarese court, Alessandro Milleville (d. 1589), was the teacher of Ercole Pasquini, who became organist of the Cappella Giulia at St. Peter's in Rome in October 1597.[24]

Unfortunately, only four of Luzzaschi's keyboard pieces survive, and Pasquini's works are transmitted in manuscripts often corrupt and uncertain in chronology. The sources of Ferrarese keyboard style presumably lay in the work of Brumel, whose keyboard writing balances considerations of part-writing and cantus-firmus treatment with those of freer organ sonority.[25] The wide geographical range of Alfonso's music library suggests that the important keyboard collections issued in Venice and Rome at the end of the century also were known in Ferrara, and three of Luzzaschi's extant keyboard works, a toccata and a pair of ricercars, appeared in Girolamo Diruta's *Il Transilvano* (Venice, 1593, 1609–1610) together with pieces by the two Gabrieli, Merulo, Quagliati, and Guami. The equally important tradition of southern Italian keyboard writing, presumably transmitted by the close cultural links between the Neapolitan and Ferrarese courts, was represented in person at Ferrara by Scipione Stella.[26] The works attributed to two other musicians of the court circle, the violist Orazio Bassano and the organist Vincenzo Bonizzi (d. 1630), a pupil of Merulo, suggest that ornamental diminution was as characteristic of Ferrarese instrumental style as it was of vocal music.[27]

The importance of lute music in Ferrara is evident in the careers of Leonardo Maria Piccinini and his three sons, Alessandro, Filippo, and Girolamo. From 1582 until his death (before 1597) Leonardo Maria served Duke Alfonso. Alessandro first appears on the court rolls in 1590 and his brothers in 1597.[28] After the dissolution of the court in 1597 Filippo entered the service of Cardinal Pietro Aldobrandini and deserted it—along with Giambattista Marino—to enter that of the Duke of Savoy. Girolamo accompanied Guido Bentivoglio to Flanders and died there. Alessandro became musical adviser to Enzo Bentivoglio and is known to have furnished a Ruggiero, a romanesca, a corrente, and a "toccata stupenda" for the use of Enzo's *musica* in 1609–1610,[29] but none of these can be identified with certainty in his published *Intavolatura di liuto, et di chitarrone* of 1623.

Frescobaldi's first musical experiences thus witnessed the development of the luxuriant madrigal in the 1580s and 1590s, the reciprocal influence of Gesualdo and Luzzaschi that led to the more serious and expressive madrigal after 1594, and the less clearly defined but no less important developments of Ferrarese instrumental music, as transmitted through the most celebrated composer and keyboard player of the duchy. The art of Rore and Brumel, as Girolamo received it from Luzzaschi, was a compendium of mainstream Netherlands practice and idiomatic keyboard style, but it also contained the seeds of seventeenth-century second practice, as Giulio Cesare Monteverdi indicated in naming Rore and Luzzaschi among the founders of that style. On the evidence of Luzzaschi's surviving vocal and instrumental works, Frescobaldi must have learned from him not only the rudiments of the composer's art but also Luzzaschi's contrapuntal skill, sophisticated handling of diminution, harmonic boldness, and sensitivity to texture. Like Luzzaschi, Girolamo became one of the few competent performers on the arcicembalo, a tradition he apparently transmitted to his own pupils. His later chromatic experiments within the context of more conventional tunings may also have been inspired by Luzzaschi. The course of Ferrarese music in the years 1580–1600 laid down the outlines of Frescobaldi's future career. Until 1628 he worked in the categories cultivated by his Ferrarese teacher and contemporaries: keyboard compositions in both strict and free styles, the instrumental canzona, the unaccompanied madrigal, and sacred and secular concertos for voices and continuo. He never attempted opera or oratorio, and it was only after his arrival in Florence in 1628 that he experimented extensively with affective monody.

The first record of Girolamo's musical activity occurs in a brief list compiled in 1683 of *maestri di cappella* and musicians of the Ferrarese Accademia della Morte. The Accademia, a hybrid of religious confraternity and humanistic academy, enlivened its principal functions with notable musical performances. From the 1590s its organists were Luzzaschi, Ercole Pasquini, and Frescobaldi, who apparently succeeded at the age of fourteen on Pasquini's departure in 1597. They served under a number of able *maestri di cappella:* Fiorini (1594–1597), Giulio Belli and Alessandro Grandi (1597–1604), and Paolo Isnardi (1604–1609), perhaps the son of the homonymous maestro of the Ferrara cathedral.[30]

The cultivation of music at the Ferrarese court during the last years of Alfonso II's reign reflected the withdrawal of the Duke and his entourage from increasingly menacing realities, above all the famine of 1591–1592 and the dilemma of the Este succession. The Este held Ferrara and Comacchio as a fief of the papacy passing in the legitimate male line. Despite three marriages, Alfonso had failed to produce an heir, and his nearest male kinsman, Don Cesare, was of illegitimate descent and therefore ineligible. Nonetheless, from 1590 Alfonso attempted without success to have the papacy accept Cesare as heir to Ferrara. The accession of Clement VIII Aldobrandini in 1592 revived Alfonso's hopes, but the new Pope obstinately refused the Duke's embassies. Although the Emperor invested Cesare with the imperial fiefs of Modena and Reggio, the Pope denied him succession to Ferrara and Comacchio. Perhaps impelled by supernatural warnings—noises from the tomb of the Blessed Beatrice d'Este, which traditionally heralded family disasters—Alfonso wrote and sealed his will. In October 1597 he was taken ill, and on his deathbed he ordered the document read: in defiance of the Pope and cardinals he had named Don Cesare heir to the entire duchy.

The events of the following months as narrated by Ferrarese historians are a confusion of rival claims, military expeditions, extravagant public ceremonies, and private vendettas, all culminating in the defeat of Don Cesare. His accession was at first hailed by the Ferrarese, and the Pope and cardinals failed to put up a concerted opposition. The forceful intervention of the cardinal-nephew, Pietro Aldobrandini, finally provided a plan of retaliation based on the excommunication of Cesare, a propaganda campaign to inculcate the benefits of papal rule, and the raising of an army to counter Cesare's forces, which were commanded by Marchese Ippolito Bentivoglio. Armed with the papal excommunication, Pietro set out for Ferrara at the head of some twenty-three thousand troops. The publication of the excommunication in Bologna forced Cesare to abdicate, and the reading of the bull in Ferrara threw the city into a panic in which the sack of the town by Cesare's mercenaries was narrowly averted. Making the best of a bad situation, Cesare secretly shipped the finest furnishings of the Castello to Modena and at the end of January 1598 rode out of Ferrara and Ferrarese history.[31]

Cardinal Pietro arrived to take possession of the city on the last Friday of Carnival. His entry had elements of the comic. He was confronted with three hastily erected and half-finished triumphal arches, and his imposing retinue did not blind the Ferrarese to the fact that the young prelate was short and heavily pock marked, with a scrubby red beard (see fig. 1). While the citizens—somewhat reassured by the cardinal's dismissal of many of his forces—gave themselves over to the pleasures of Carnival, Pietro set about reorganizing the city government. Pope Clement granted a jubilee absolving Ferrara and in April set off to visit his reclaimed fief with an immense retinue of cardinals, clerics, musicians, soldiers, and servants, preceded by a consecrated Host.

Whatever the feelings of the fifteen-year-old Girolamo about the annexation of his native city by the papacy, he must have relished the pomp and noise of the Sovereign Pontiff's entry: crowds of nobles, a train of cardinals in full regalia on their mules, "fifty sons of the noblest families of Ferrara, all dressed alike in white," foot- and horse-guards firing salvos of artillery. Ferrara had never fallen to a pope in battle, but Clement and his astute nephew had finally redeemed the great oath of Julius II, "Ferrara, Ferrara, corpo di Dio, ti avrò!"[32]

Guido Bentivoglio (fig. 2), to whom we owe this description of Pope Clement's entry, himself may have walked in the procession as one of the fifty noble youths: after the Este, the Bentivoglio were perhaps the greatest family in Ferrara, former lords of Bologna and connections both of the Este and of the house of Aragon. Their palace, with its flamboyant façade of martial trophies, still evokes a race of noble soldiers, diplomats, and historians whose ambitions reached beyond Ferrara to the Low Countries and even to the papal throne. The Bentivoglio maintained the division of functions characteristic of a noble Renaissance clan. The eldest son, Ippolito, was a soldier; his half-brother Enzo acted as head of the family, courtier, and diplomat; Enzo's younger brother, Guido, like many other young nobles of intellectual bent, was destined for the Church, to be

1. Cardinal Pietro Aldobrandini, portrait by Ottavio Leoni

2. Cardinal Guido Bentivoglio, portrait by Anthony Van Dyck

advanced through the ecclesiastical hierarchy with the support of the family money and prestige in hopes of a cardinalate or even the papacy, the ultimate prize. How Frescobaldi came to the notice of the Bentivoglio is unknown—perhaps through his service in the Accademia della Morte, whose rival, the Accademia dello Spirito Santo, was founded by Guido Bentivoglio in 1597.[33] Guido is Girolamo's earliest recorded patron, but it is possible that Enzo, as head of the family, first employed Frescobaldi. In any case, the influence of Casa Bentivoglio overshadowed Frescobaldi's life long after he left Guido's immediate service.

Guido Bentivoglio was six years older than Girolamo. His interest in music may have been inherited from his mother, Isabella Bendidio, sister of the more famous Lucrezia and both of them members of the first *concerto delle dame.* The family also had literary connections. Lucrezia had been an early love of Torquato Tasso, who wrote well over a hundred lyrics in her honor, and Guarini married another Bendidio sister, Taddea. Although their half-brother, Ippolito, had commanded Don Cesare's forces, Guido's own older brother, Enzo, prudently sided with the papal government. Guido initially attracted the attention of Cardinal Aldobrandini by interceding for Ippolito with the ingenuous excuse that the renegade had been trained as a soldier rather than as a theologian. Like virtually everyone else, Cardinal Pietro—only a few years older than Guido—seems to have felt the charm of the young nobleman, and Guido was promised a post as *cameriere segreto* at the papal court upon the completion of his studies at Padua.[34]

Despite the humiliation of the papal conquest, during Clement's visit Ferrara enjoyed a glow of reflected splendor, with entertainments (including at least one performance by the *concerto delle dame*), brilliant embassies, and solemn ecclesiastical ceremonies enhanced by the papal musicians and by visitors such as Giulio Caccini. The greatest of these events was the Pope's celebration of the double wedding uniting Phillip III of Spain to the Archduchess Margherita of Austria and the Archduke Albert to the Infanta Isabella, a wedding whose political consequences were to affect Guido Bentivoglio and, through him, Frescobaldi.

At the end of November 1598 Clement set out on his return to Rome. The life of Ferrara seemed to continue as before, and the Ferrarese celebrated Carnival of 1599 with the customary jousts, comedies, maskings, and music. But the final destruction of the civilization of Renaissance Ferrara had already begun. At the end of 1598 the papal government had decided to secure the allegiance of its new subjects by building a fortress in the western part of the city. This project involved the destruction of one of the most beautiful sections of Ferrara including the Belvedere, the loveliest of Alfonso's *delizie*. Most of the Duke's musical establishment had fled to Modena with Don Cesare, but the artistic patrimony of Ferrara was not safe even there: as late as 1608 Cardinal Borghese was negotiating with Cesare through Enzo Bentivoglio for the remainder of the Este collections.[35] A contemporary chronicler lamented that "the city which had been the right eye of Lombardy, the compendium of all the beauties and delights of Italy, has come to be deformed and laid waste,"[36] and the reign of the papacy is still commemorated in Ferrara with a savagery rare even in the former papal states.

The decline of Ferrara epitomizes the general decline of the smaller Italian courts as centers of cultural influence, a waning reflected in their artistic production. The musical publications of the 1580s and 1590s—including the important ones issued at Ferrara—represented above all the courtly and Renaissance art of the madrigal; the prints around the turn of the century, however, pointed in new directions: the keyboard experiments of the Neapolitans Trabaci and Mayone, the small sacred concertos of Viadana, the monodies and dramatic works of the Florentines Peri, Caccini, and Cavalieri. These all demonstrate the concentration of effective musical patronage in the larger courts: Venice, Florence, Naples, and above all Rome. Clearly, Ferrara was no longer in the mainstream of musical activity, and both its past connections with Roman musical life and the new political orientation of the city impelled Ferrarese musicians toward Rome rather than Venice.

Frescobaldi was in a position to profit from such a move. Guido Bentivoglio went to take up his post at the papal court in 1599, and in 1601 Girolamo's teacher Luzzaschi accompanied Cardinal Aldobrandini to Rome, where Luzzaschi's accompanied madrigals were published with a dedication to the Cardinal.[37] The growing prestige of the Bentivoglio family in relations with the papal government provided yet another avenue of influence. Girolamo is reported at Rome as early as 1604, and by 1607 he was established there.

The devolution of Ferrara to the papacy and the resultant absorption of its musical and artistic culture into the Roman sphere was a turning point in the life of more than one participant. For Cardinal Pietro Aldobrandini it meant the foundation of his fortune and influence. It opened to Enzo Bentivoglio the great society of Rome, in which he became an artistic arbiter. By bringing Guido Bentivoglio to the notice of the Pope and his nephew, the devolution started him on a career as courtier, diplomat, and historian that was cut off just short of the papacy. It impelled

Frescobaldi from the backwater of Ferrarese musical life into the main current of Roman activity. The strands that intertwine in Girolamo's Roman career—his study with Luzzaschi, his service with the Bentivoglio, his succession to Pasquini at St. Peter's, his years in the household of Cardinal Aldobrandini—can all be traced back to the period of Ferrara's final flowering and its Roman subjection. For all four men, the city's great gifts came as a legacy.

2

Rome and Flanders, 1607–1608

"O Roma nobilis, cunctarum orbium domina," sang the medieval pilgrim, and across the centuries Goethe answered, "Eine Welt zwar bist du, o Rom." Early seventeenth-century Rome already displayed both faces of the City: the massive ruins of the greatest empire the world had known and, rising from them, the most grandiose artistic program since the fall of that empire, the work of a Church that claimed a dominion greater even than that of the Caesars. In 1600 the City had not reached the dazzling perfection that Bernini left at his death in 1680, but much of the shambles that confronted Martin V on his return in 1420 was being transformed on the lines laid down by Sixtus V (1585–1590): restoration of the aqueducts, movement away from the center of town, and the cutting of spacious streets through the crowded medieval quarters to connect the principal pilgrimage churches. Low, undistinguished dwellings still crowded Renaissance palaces, Roman ruins scattered untended among them. The dominant accents of the City were Castel Sant'Angelo and Michelangelo's great dome of St. Peter's, the Cupolone, towering over a tide of construction that washed up to its very foundations (fig. 3).

There is no record of Girolamo's arrival in Rome. He may have accompanied Guido Bentivoglio in 1599, or he may have joined Luzzaschi and the Ferrarese lutenist Filippo Piccinini[1] in the suite of Cardinal Pietro Aldobrandini in 1601, which would fit one reading of Don Gregorio Rasi's Latin encomium (see Chapter 1, n. 16). An unverifiable source named Frescobaldi as both singer and organist in the Roman Congregation of Santa Cecilia in 1604.[2]

On Girolamo's own evidence, he was at Rome in the service of Guido Bentivoglio by 1607. In dedicating his *Fantasie* of 1608 to Francesco Borghese, brother of Paul V and General of the Church, Frescobaldi

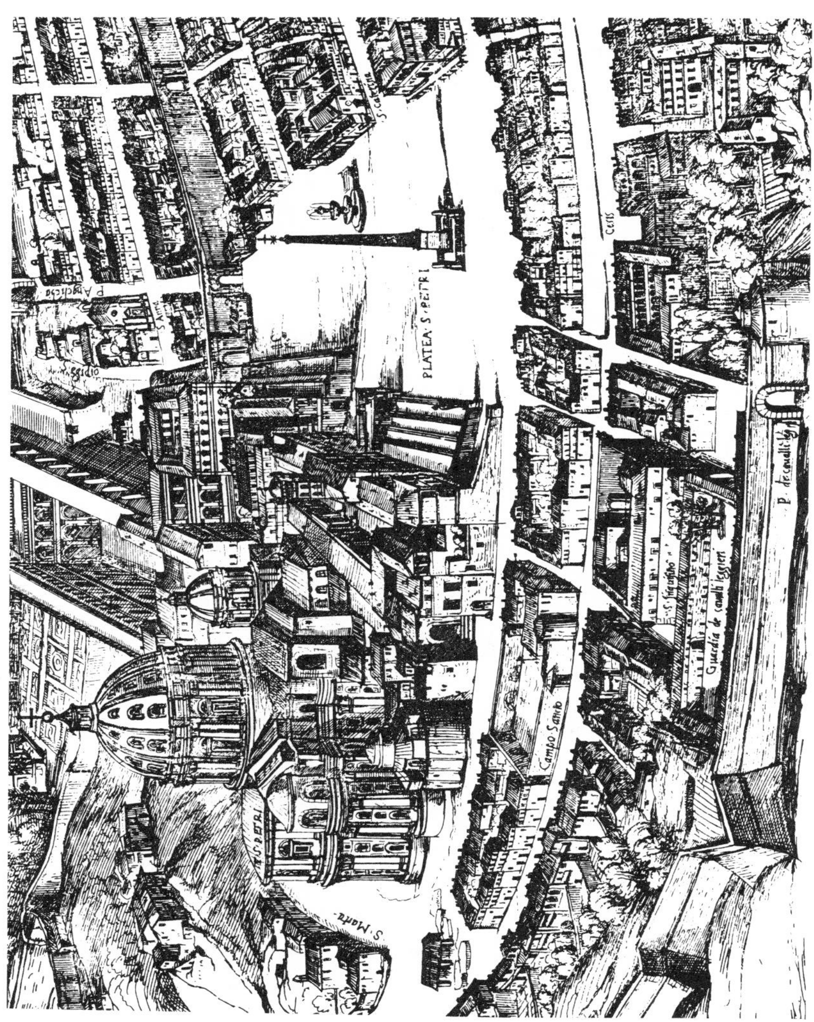

3. St. Peter's: detail of Antonio Tempesta's map of Rome in 1593/1606

recalled "that honor which your ears many times deigned to do my hand while I was staying in Rome under the aegis of Mons. the Most Illustrious Bentiuogli, Archbishop of Rhodes, when I made you hear with the sound of the keys many of these musical Fantasies which I send you, now written out in these pages."[3] This would place the performances between May of 1607, when Bentivoglio was named Archbishop of Rhodes, and June of the same year, when he left Rome for Flanders. Girolamo's documented stay in Rome may be extended back to the beginning of the year if he is to be identified with the "Girolimo Organista" (a sobriquet by which he was in fact known as late as 1627) paid by the basilica of Santa Maria in Trastevere from January through May of 1607.[4]

The conditions of Roman musical patronage were unique. The ruling class—the papal families and the hierarchy—was predominantly male, nonindigenous, and only partly hereditary. Under these circumstances, two institutions—the private *musica* and the church, represented at this stage of Frescobaldi's career by Guido Bentivoglio's musical establishment and Santa Maria in Trastevere—dominated the lives of most musicians. Like the *musica segreta* of Ferrara, the household *musica* of a great Roman ecclesiastic or nobleman was part of the state he was expected to keep, a social and political instrument as well as an artistic entertainment. (The performances Girolamo mentions in the dedication of the *Fantasie*, for example, may have been intended to ingratiate Bentivoglio, the protégé of the Aldobrandini, with the new papal family.) If its singers and instrumentalists, who were often composers as well, were sufficiently accomplished, their performances before eminent personages enhanced their patron's status, and a request for the loan of their services provided him with an effective bargaining point.

Typically, an influential patron assumed artists from his home city into his personal court, from which they could enter the mainstream of Roman patronage. The terms of this service were usually nonexclusive and the remuneration correspondingly meager, so that a young musician was free, and often obliged, to accept outside employment as well. This took the form of private pupils, occasional performances for other patrons, and casual or regular service in Roman churches. Any extended perusal of payment records and other documents of Roman musical life in the first half of the seventeenth century shows that Rome attracted a corps of competent musicians, whose careers frequently can be traced from training or service in such institutions as the German College or the Roman Seminary and whose names constantly recur in the records of the basilicas and churches of the City. It is likely, therefore, that the "Girolimo Organista" of Santa Maria in Trastevere was Frescobaldi. In any case, the archives of the basilica unfold a typical history of musical life in a great Roman church, including the role and duties of the organist.

The basilica of Santa Maria in Trastevere and its adjoining piazza are among the spots that still evoke seventeenth-century Rome, especially in the brief desertion at high summer when the noise of traffic and transistors gives way to the clang and boom of bells, the voices of nuns, the clatter of hooves and carriage-wheels, the twitter of birds, and the splash of fountains. Except for an eighteenth-century portico, the church, the piazza, and its fountain are much as they were in 1600 (fig. 4), as are the inhabitants, quintessential Romans with a succulent dialect of their own.

The interior of the basilica mixes classical and medieval remains, hieratic mosaics of the twelfth century, and more yielding work of the thirteenth, under Cardinal Aldobrandini's superb coffered ceiling enshrining Domenichino's Virgin of the Assumption. The organ and the musicians' galleries still appear as they are described in an inventory of 1624: a large organ at the side "on the Dark Street," the façade pipes in three divisions with arches, columns of gilded wood, paintings, and shutters, and a corresponding gallery on the opposite side. In addition, two platforms for musicians were placed on the pavement beside the canons' choir.[5] These arrangements suggest the performance of bichoral music, although an organ was added only later to the second upper gallery. The presence and clarity of the acoustic would have complemented both polychoral liturgical music and the smaller sacred concertos that were becoming a staple of the Roman repertory.

Before we examine the duties of "Girolimo Organista" at Santa Maria in Trastevere, it is important to recall the gap separating religious feeling and practice after the second Vatican Council from the post-Tridentine catholicism of Frescobaldi's time. The Church Girolamo served distinguished sharply between public religion and private devotion. The newer religious orders, lay confraternities, and extraliturgical cults ministered to the latter, but official public worship—the mass and offices—continued to be celebrated in uncompromising solemnity, mystery, and splendor without congregational participation. Since the most important parts of the liturgy were recited inaudibly, the attention of the congregation was focused on the visual spectacle and its musical accompaniment. The services of an important church like Santa Maria in Trastevere thus attained a degree of liturgical elaboration now lost even to the great papal functions, and the surviving records of the basilica's musical life suggest a comparable degree of musical elaboration.

4. Giovanni Falda's engraving of the Piazza Santa Maria in Trastevere

The musical establishment of the basilica was directed by a *maestro di cappella,* who supervised an organist, a choir, and eight additional musicians for festal services.[6] The principal duty of the organist was to perform at mass and vespers on Sundays and greater feasts (including Holy Week and Easter, which fell within the tenure of "Girolimo Organista"). When the liturgy was performed complete in music (whether chant, accompanied or unaccompanied *stile antico* polyphony, or accompanied *concertato* settings) solo organ music was limited to prelude, postlude, intonations, and occasional interludes. The norms for the use of the organ to replace parts of the proper and ordinary of the mass were formulated in the *Ceremoniale Episcoporum* issued by Clement VIII in 1600 and were explained and amplified for the church organist in a number of musical handbooks, notably *L'organo suonarino* (published in a variety of editions from 1605 to 1638) and the *Conclusioni* (1609) of Adriano Banchieri, the second part of Girolamo Diruta's *Il Transilvano* (1610–1611), and the *Choro et organo* (1614) of Frescobaldi's compatriot Fra Bernardino Bottazzi.

In plainsong masses the organ interludes comprised a piece for full organ (*ripieno*) at the repeat of the Introit (sometimes omitted), a *ripieno* or short *fuga* after the Epistle, a motet or ricercar at the Offertory. At the Elevation of the Host the *Ceremoniale* prescribed music "in a graver, sweeter sound," interpreted by Banchieri as a serious work "that promotes devotion." A *capriccio* or *aria alla francese,* "charming but musical," was performed after the Agnus Dei, and a short *ripieno* concluded the service. Specific feasts permitted other interpolations. At Easter, for example, it was customary to play a *battaglia,* "decent and fitting to the Holy Easter Sequence [*Victimae Paschali*]," with its image of the "wondrous battle" between life and death.[7]

In the other musical sections of the mass, the organ alternated the liturgical chant with the choir except for the Creed, where recitation of the complete text was mandatory. From Girolamo Cavazzoni's organ masses of the 1530s on, the chants selected for *alternatim* organ settings were the ordinaries of the masses for Sunday, feasts of the Apostles, and feasts of the Madonna, which in practice covered most of the liturgical year.[8]

At vespers the organist's duties were similar: a *ripieno* at the beginning and end of the service, organ interludes as substitutes for antiphons after each of the five vesper psalms, *alternatim* performance of the Office hymn, Magnificat, and Marian antiphon, and a canzona or motet after the Magnificat.[9] The *Ceremoniale* forbade "lascivious, or impure" organ music and inappropriate, profane, or theatrical melodies, which Banchieri extended to include "dances, morescas, and suchlike pieces."[10] The organ was prohibited for most of Advent, Lent, and Holy Week, and at Requiem masses it was tolerated only when played "with the principal alone, without preludes [*ingressi*] or diminutions, and with the shutters closed."[11] The performance of organ interludes at mass and vespers, together with the official limitations on their character, may have been a factor in the composition of the rather severe *Fantasie* that Girolamo dedicated to Francesco Borghese.

As for the works that Girolamo performed with the choir, enough survives of the musical library of the basilica to give some idea of its repertory. The remains dating back to Girolamo's tenure are meager, but their emphasis—as in the printed collections that the basilica began to acquire around 1614—is on functional, rather modest settings of the ordinary and proper of the mass, vespers, litanies (especially of the Virgin), and processional hymns in simple polyphony for Corpus Domini.[12] The model for this repertory was Palestrina, whose own settings constituted the nucleus of Roman church music in the first half of the seventeenth century, albeit sometimes grotesquely modernized, as in the basilica's copy of the 1646 *Missa Papae Marcelli,* where the five-part original has been rewritten for four voices and continuo.

In addition to providing solo organ works and participating as a continuo player in this simple and retrospective repertory, it is likely that Girolamo was also called upon to perform more modern works in the *concertato* idiom as well. According to Banchieri, the small sacred concertos of Viadana were particularly appropriate: works "tender, devout, pleasing, and recitative" and avoiding elaborate contrapuntal devices that obscured the words. On occasion these *concertato* pieces might employ as many as four choirs of voices, violins, viols, and a continuo section including organ, harpsichord, violone, lutes, and chitarroni, in which case the organist played an important role by adjusting his registrations and the details of his continuo-realization to the ensemble.[13] Thus a young organist in a great Roman basilica was exposed to the whole spectrum of contemporary church music: free and cantus-firmus organ works, vocal pieces in *stile antico* ranging from modest settings to the monuments of the style, and contemporary works employing recitative, concertato, and polychoral media.

The bond among the musicians who served Roman private musical establishments and churches was membership in the Congregation of Santa Cecilia. In the mid-sixteenth century the papal musicians, most of them enjoying clerical status, had constituted a closed society from which the rabble of Roman musicians was excluded. One of the notable efforts of the Counter-Reformation was the involvement of the laity in attempts toward the sanctification of their personal and professional lives beyond the formal ritual of the church, an effort epitomized in St. Philip Neri's Oratorio. The Congregation of Santa Cecilia was formed on the model of the Virtuosi del Panteon, the artists' confraternity, and was confirmed in 1585 by Sixtus V as an association of lay musicians outside the papal chapel. As such, it was bitterly opposed by the musicians of the Cappella Sistina. By 1589, nonetheless, the membership of the Congregation as represented in *Le gioie,* a collection of sacred madrigals, constituted a musical elite ranging in allegiance from the traditional citadel of St. Peter's (Palestrina, Anerio, Giovannelli, Crivelli) to the new Counter-Reformation centers allied with the Oratorio (Griffi, Quagliati) and spanning Italy from the courts of Ferrara and Florence (Marenzio, Malvezzi) to the Kingdom of Naples (Roi, Macque). Membership in the Congregation was divided into four categories: *maestri di cappella,* organists, instrumentalists, and singers. From about 1596 on, applicants had to pass an audition that included knowing how to beat time and intone for the instrumentalists and how to play figured basses ably (*correr li bassi*) for organists.[14] From its earliest years Santa Cecilia moved between the two poles of attraction of Roman musical life: St. Peter's and the Oratorio with its later offshoots.

Girolamo's tenure at Santa Maria in Trastevere was probably terminated by the new responsibilities of his patron, Guido Bentivoglio. In his *Memorie* Guido presented a vivid picture of his life at the court of Clement VIII, to which he was attached as a *cameriere segreto,* the ecclesiastical equivalent of a noble page. The unusual length of Clement's reign and the consequent scarcity of opportunities for advancement discouraged Guido from attempting a career in the Vatican, and he began instead to prepare himself for a diplomatic post abroad by the study of law, history, geography, and languages, especially Spanish.

His foresight was rewarded when the thirteen years of Clement's pontificate ended abruptly with the Pope's death in March 1605. While the daily life of the papal court witnessed the shifting of members of the reigning family and their favorites as new positions of power fell vacant, the death of a pope swept the board clean for a new game, a new set of maneuvers and alliances. Although his seven years' supremacy as the favorite nephew of Clement VIII had gained Cardinal Aldobrandini the enmity of many of his colleagues, he still commanded a bloc of votes large enough to insure the election of Leo XI Medici. Battle was again joined after the almost immediate death of the new pope, and Camillo Borghese was elected as a compromise candidate. Paul V, as he chose to be called, was the youngest of the *papabili.* His age augured a long reign; his character and that of the cardinal-nephew, Scipione Borghese Caffarelli—intelligent, vigorous, avid for power—promised a strong papacy. Neither prospect was welcome to Bentivoglio's patron, Cardinal Aldobrandini. The last straw in his deteriorating relations with the Borghese was Paul V's enforcement of the Tridentine ruling that bishops reside in their dioceses. Forced to choose between Rome and the revenues of his archdiocese of Ravenna, Cardinal Pietro left the City in May 1606, not to return until 1610.[15]

Bentivoglio's early association with the Aldobrandini did not cost him the favor of the new papal family. On the contrary, in early May of 1607 a consistory named him papal nuncio to Flanders, and a few days later the Pope confirmed the post publicly and named the new nuncio titular Archbishop of Rhodes. When Bentivoglio set out for Brussels on 11 June 1607, the twenty-four-year-old Frescobaldi presumably formed part of his imposing retinue. Girolamo had served his apprenticeship as a household musician, church organist, and composer, and had begun to frequent the great Roman families he was to serve throughout his career. His musical education was now to be completed by exposure to the Netherlandish tradition on its native soil.

Guido Bentivoglio's embassy to Flanders was typical of an age that valued the grand gesture. He traveled with a suite including the household officials, footmen, and liveried pages dear to the Ferrarese, as well as two musicians, Frescobaldi and the lutenist Girolamo Piccinini.[16] The journey was not a simple excursion across the Alps, but a semi-royal progress broken by a week's stay in Ferrara and strategic visits to important personages along the way—notably Cardinal Pietro Aldobrandini in his exile at Ravenna. After Ferrara, Bentivoglio and his retinue set off in the summer heat for Switzerland by way of Modena, Parma, and Milan, after which all the rest was "alps, crags, cliffs, precipices, one mountain on another, and St. Gothard"—still snow-covered in midsummer—"above them all."[17] They descended at Lucerne and went on to Basel, traveling about thirty miles a day. After a journey of nearly two months they reached Brussels by way of Nancy and Luxembourg.

Bentivoglio and his entourage made their formal entry into Brussels on the eve of San Lorenzo, 9 August, escorted by the court and the Spanish ambassador. To the Italians of Bentivoglio's party, Flanders must have been disconcerting. The countryside was still springlike in mid-August, by contrast with the heat and dust of the Ferrarese summer; Italian was little spoken, as the court language was Spanish; and even the familiar uses of their religion must have seemed somewhat alien in the gray Gothic churches of Brussels. Bentivoglio himself, however, felt thoroughly at home; six of his family had fought in the Spanish wars, and "it only remained for me to come here myself to become completely Flemish."[18] Indeed, Bentivoglio's affection for his adopted country shines through his accounts of the Flemish provinces, with their abundance of livestock in bright meadows, their temperate climate, and their handsome, independent inhabitants.[19]

Guido Bentivoglio's nunciature was not a post of the first rank such as those of Paris and Madrid, the primary axes of political influence in Catholic Europe. Its peculiar importance arose from the fact that the nuncio's jurisdiction included major areas of religious conflict: Belgium, the Low Countries, and Burgundy. Further, the nuncio also functioned as an agent and clearinghouse for Catholic resistance in the British Isles, the Dutch provinces, and Germany. The nuncio's diplomatic duties included regular reports to the Pope's nephew, Cardinal Scipione Borghese, on the negotiations between Catholics and Protestants that eventually resulted in the Twelve Years' Peace. His ecclesiastical responsibilities centered on the reform of the local church and the suppression of heresy especially in Antwerp, Ghent, and Brussels itself.[20]

Flanders was ruled by the Infanta Isabella of Spain and the Archduke Albert of Austria, whose wedding had been solemnized at Ferrara by Clement VIII in 1598. The Infanta, a sister of Philip III of Spain, was the nominal sovereign, but in practice she and her husband were coregents. Foreign policy was dictated by Spain, religious policy by the Jesuits. Bentivoglio's accounts of the regents' court describe a world of festivity and splendor within a context of Counter-Reformation piety. Francken and Pourbus showed Isabella and her taciturn spouse presiding over an elegant court ball; Rubens depicted her in the habit of a Franciscan nun. In the hands of the regents and their ecclesiastical mentors, the normal piety of Catholic sovereigns became an instrument of state policy, exemplified in the splendid religious processions of the Flemish court. On Corpus Domini of 1608, for example, the regents and their court followed on foot the procession in which Bentivoglio himself carried the Sacrament through most of Brussels (returning home "very tired and sweaty," he noted privately).[21]

Girolamo's journey to Flanders was something of a rite of passage. It saw his only travel outside Italy, personal contact with a non-Italian musical culture, and his first publications: a book of madrigals and three canzonas in Alessandro Raverij's *Canzoni* (Venice, 1608; see Catalogue III.A.1, II.1). Both the publications and his letters from the period show an increasing desire on Frescobaldi's part to make himself known and to compete on equal terms with established musicians. This was perhaps initiated by the death of his teacher Luzzaschi in September 1607, a month after Girolamo's arrival in Flanders. The musicians of Ferrara—some eighty in number—sang a Requiem, after which Ippolito Fiorino placed a gilded laurel wreath on Luzzaschi's coffin, "as they considered him worthy of being crowned the greatest master of his profession."[22] As the musical tradition of Renaissance Ferrara in the person of Luzzaschi was borne, laurel-garlanded, to its grave, the composer who carried that tradition into the musical culture of its Roman conquerors was preparing to submit his art "to the judgment of the World."

Most of our information about Girolamo's service in the household of Guido Bentivoglio is derived from the dedicatory letter of Frescobaldi's first published work, a collection of five-voice madrigals issued by the noted firm of Phalèse at Antwerp in 1608. The letter—Girolamo's first preserved statement—is addressed to Bentivoglio, the dedicatee, and dated from Antwerp, 13 June 1608, but it is likely that Frescobaldi was already on his way back to Italy by then.[23] "I have come to Antwerp," he states,

> with the permission of Your Illustrious Lordship to see this City, and to try out a collection of Madrigals which I have been composing in Brussels in the house of Your Illustrious Lordship since my arrival in Flanders, and I have satisfied with equal pleasure both these desires of mine; it has happened meanwhile that since these Musicians showed that they highly enjoyed my work, with great insistence they have persuaded me to consent to have it printed, whence I have chosen to obey even with some blushes, rather than to refuse with obstinate boorishness. This first work of mine will therefore appear, and as is fitting under the Name of Your Illustrious Lordship, who with infinite kindness has deigned always to favor me in the exercise of the talent, which it has pleased God to give me. In the present resolution, which I make to begin to submit my works [*le cose mie*] to the judgment of the World, I beg Your Illustrious Lordship to recognize my singular devotion to you, and my obligation as most grateful servant to your Most Illustrious House.[24]

The dedication shows that the madrigals were the direct result of Frescobaldi's service with the nuncio, who in addition to Frescobaldi and Piccinini may have employed singers for their performance. Jan Breughel's splendid *Hearing,* painted a few years later, gives some idea of music in a great Flemish household. In the background madrigals are performed by two singers, transverse flute, recorder, lute, and gamba, while in the foreground an array of these and other instruments—cornetts, a sackbut, a shawm, a rebec, a lyra, and a magnificent two-manual Flemish harpsichord—surrounds a table bearing the part-books of a madrigal collection à 6 by Peter Philips, "Organista delli serenissimi Principi Alberto et Isabella."

Frescobaldi's resolution "to begin to submit my works to the judgment of the World" was expressed in rather conservative and retrospective works. Of the nineteen madrigals in the collection, the texts so far identified include four of the Ferrarese court poet Annibale Pocaterra, two of Carlo Rinaldi, one of Horatio Ariosti (apparently first published in 1611), and five of Marino (three set as the three parts of a single madrigal). While the older authors point back to Ferrara, the number of Marino settings suggests a Roman influence, since Marino was in the service of Cardinal Pietro Aldobrandini. The style of the collection matches the amorous, pastoral character of the texts, with none of the exaggerated expressiveness of Gesualdo or the harmonic boldness and vivid pictorialism of Monteverdi.

Girolamo's interest in the local musicians at Antwerp suggests that he also investigated his peers at the court of the regents in Brussels. Their cosmopolitan musical establishment included Italian, Spanish, and English as well as native musicians. At least two of these were composers and performers of the first rank. Although few of Pierre Cornet's keyboard works survive, their size, variety, and finish establish him as the Catholic counterpart of Sweelinck. The great school of the English virginalists was represented at Brussels by Philips, who had become organist to the Archduke in 1597, sixteen years before the arrival of the better known John Bull. Philips's rich, rather Crashaw-like style attracted a Catholic compatriot to include him in the Fitzwilliam Virginal Book, but also prompted a Continental Protestant, Sweelinck, to write variations on a *Pavana Philipi.*[25]

It is sometimes assumed that Frescobaldi himself was significantly influenced by Sweelinck.[26] The young Girolamo may have journeyed to Amsterdam, like Philips in 1593, to hear the older master. On the other hand, Frescobaldi's obligations in Brussels and the shortness of his stay in Flanders—less than a year—cast doubt on this assumption, and it is known that Sweelinck never left Amsterdam for more than a few days at a time during this period. Superbi's phrase, "Then he was brought to Flanders, where he made himself talked of for many years,"[27] suggests that Girolamo was already regarded as a finished musician. In any case, the elements in Frescobaldi's style that most closely resemble Sweelinck's writing, such as his contrapuntal virtuosity and his rigor in the treatment of musical material, are the products of Girolamo's Ferrarese training and are already evident in the fantasias, which (at least in part) antedate his journey to Flanders. Moreover, nothing could be further from the ruthless consistency (and occasional monotony) of Sweelinck's figural writing than the nervous and ever-changing patterns of Frescobaldi's figuration.

Girolamo's statement that he went to Antwerp to see the city is the only interest he ever expressed in his surroundings. It must have been well worth seeing. An English visitor in 1616 described it as a city exceeding "any I ever saw any where else, for bewtie and the uniformity of buildings, heith and largeness of streets, and strength and fairness of the rampars."[28] Despite its irreversible decline as a commercial center, Antwerp still had a flourishing cultural life, about to enter its Indian summer with Rubens's return from Italy late in 1608. In addition to Pierre Phalèse and his circle, who gave Frescobaldi's madrigals so flattering a welcome, Antwerp offered another inducement to the visiting musician: the harpsichords of the Ruckers family, which were known throughout Europe and exported as far as Peru. The Ruckers made instruments in a variety of shapes, sizes, and dispositions greater than that of contemporary Italian instruments, and their rich, diffuse sound must have been a surprise to a player accustomed to the sinewy clarity of Italian harpsichords. Indeed, the Flemish harpsichord that Guido Bentivoglio sent to Cardinal Borghese became a nine days' wonder in Rome.[29]

Girolamo's visit to Antwerp probably concluded his stay in Flanders. (The assertion that he became organist at Malines and remained there for several years is unfounded.)[30] The conclusion of the dedication to the *Madrigali* suggests that Frescobaldi's service with Guido was only part of his general obligation to the Bentivoglio family. The head of the family, Enzo, was about to take up the post of Ferrarese ambassador at Rome and apparently summoned Frescobaldi to enter his service. On 9 August 1608 Guido wrote to his brother, "I will be happy that Frescobaldi come to Rome with Your Lordship for the taste you show for having him in your house."[31] (Not only did Enzo have prior claim, but Guido was hard-pressed for money to feed the "tante bocche" of his household.)[32]

Frescobaldi's first surviving personal letters date from this trip back to

Italy and already display the self-willed irresponsibility that was to characterize his relations with Enzo Bentivoglio. By late June, Frescobaldi had reached Milan, where he lodged in the monastery of Sant' Ambrogio. Instead of coming directly to Enzo in Ferrara as he had promised, Girolamo remained in Milan "to try my fortune in various parts, and also to have the opportunity of making myself known."[33] On 29 July he was still there, reiterating to Enzo his desire "to make myself known," which now included the publication of a work—the *Fantasie* issued by the firm of Tini and Lomazzo—"to fulfill the opinion of these musicians [and] . . . to give them a worthy sign of my ability." He assured Enzo that he was "making every effort to have them hurry to print this work of mine, and I will immediately be in Ferrara to execute the command of Your Most Illustrious Lordship."[34] (When the *Fantasie* in fact appeared is uncertain, since the dedication is dated 8 November 1608 from Ferrara, by which time Girolamo had been in Rome for over a week.)

The reputation Frescobaldi established in these first publications and the patronage of the Bentivoglio brought him the opportunity that was to determine his future career. On 21 July 1608 the Chapter of St. Peter's in Rome elected Frescobaldi to succeed Ercole Pasquini as organist of the Cappella Giulia. He was now provided with a regular income, a forum for performance and composition, and a secure position in the musical life of Rome.

3

Rome, 1608–1614

From the *Recercari* of 1615, Frescobaldi's publications describe him as "Organist of St. Peter's in Rome." In fact, he was attached to only one of the two musical organizations that functioned in the basilica. The first of these, the Cappella Pontificia (Cappella di Nostro Signore, Cappella Sistina), was the pope's private *musica,* which performed when the pope himself was present at a function. It employed only adult males—falsettists, later castrati, for the higher parts—without instruments, not even the organ.[1] The Cappella Giulia (so called from its original foundation by Julius II), on the other hand, was tied to the service of the basilica and churches under its jurisdiction and functioned under the immediate supervision of the Chapter of St. Peter's and the less direct authority of the Archpriest of the basilica.

The composition of the Cappella Giulia in 1608 still followed the stipulations of Sixtus V's bull of 1589. The choir consisted of four basses, four tenors, four contraltos (castrati or falsettists), and six boy sopranos. These were directed by Francesco Soriano, a former pupil of Palestrina and a member of the Congregation of Santa Cecilia, who received fifteen scudi a month. The adult singers were paid seven scudi, and the organist of the Cappella received six scudi monthly.[2]

Girolamo's appointment as organist of the Cappella Giulia is surprising in that the Chapter had no chance to interview the candidate. On 19 May 1608 they had dismissed Ercole Pasquini "for just cause" (presumably insanity), but he apparently continued to serve until the end of the month. He was replaced temporarily by Alessandro Costantini, who had been organist of Santa Maria in Trastevere in 1602. On 21 July the Chapter voted on the two candidates for the vacant post, Costantini and

Frescobaldi. Costantini received ten favorable votes, but Frescobaldi was elected with twelve positive votes and two negative ones.[3]

Letters recently discovered in the Bentivoglio archive in Ferrara reveal that the election was engineered by the Bentivoglio, and that from the first Frescobaldi treated the conditions of the post with carelessness. The pivotal role of the Bentivoglio in Girolamo's election is apparent in a letter to Enzo from Mons. Ottavio Estense Tassoni, a Ferrarese noble and member of the Chapter of the basilica, dated from Rome, 6 August 1608: "I have so much more pleasure in having promoted M. Girolamo Frescobaldi for the post of organist here at St. Peter's as I see that I have done a thing pleasing to Your Most Illustrious Lordship."[4] As another correspondent noted, by securing Girolamo's election Enzo intended to make him available for Enzo's own service in Rome: "I rejoice with him that with this opportunity he may also continue his service with Your Most Illustrious house, and particularly with the person and under the protection of Your Most Illustrious Lordship."[5]

The election was confirmed by the Chapter and accepted by Frescobaldi. He was asked to write a letter of acknowledgment, as both of Enzo's correspondents had suggested, to the Chapter and to travel to Rome with Enzo, or at least to be there in time for Enzo's arrival as Ferrarese envoy. Girolamo made no move to fulfill either condition. He stayed on in Milan, seeing the *Fantasie* through the press, although he also may have been ill and fearful of the Roman *malaria.* (Tassoni advised, "It will be well that he stay there until he is restored, since wishing to make him come now would be to put him in peril of his life.")[6] As late as October, Tassoni was still reminding Frescobaldi of the need to satisfy the canons of the basilica and to reach Rome by the time of Enzo's arrival.[7] To a Milanese envoy of Enzo, Girolamo declared flatly that he did not wish to leave Milan, despite "his word given to you and to me, not one time but several, to come to Rome with Your Most Illustrious Lordship."[8]

Finally, Enzo sent one Bernardo Bizzone to meet his reluctant servant in Florence: "I went as far as Siena, whence . . . I had to turn back, and the evening of the vigil of All Saints [31 October] I was again at Rome where with the greatest pleasure and happiness I found our Frescobaldi at my home, safe, sound, and pleased, who arrived here on the 29th."[9] Girolamo, once arrived, lost no time in taking up his post. The traditional account of his debut is that of Libanori, who asserted that "since the news had spread of this stupendous and marvelous Musician, and miraculous organist, the first time, they say, that [he played] he had more than thirty thousand hearers and the oldest and most famous organists were astonished and not a few touched by envy."[10] Bizzone's own description shows that the attendance was due less to the unheralded arrival of the new organist than to the celebration of two important feasts, All Saints (1 November) and All Souls (2 November): "The vigil of All Saints [he] took possession of the organ of S. Pietro and also played the two following feasts with great satisfaction and commendation of the Sig.ri Canons and of other *virtuosi* of the profession."[11]

Frescobaldi's association with St. Peter's lasted for the rest of his life. During those thirty-five years the building we know today largely came into existence. In 1608 a modern observer would have recognized only the east end of the church, the great piers, and the dome. The apse lacked the monumental statues in the niches, the papal tombs, a permanent high altar, the baldacchino and confessio, and the Chair of Peter. The rest of the church was a construction site in which the Constantinian nave was still being pulled down as the new façade was being built, a scene of dust, confusion, and noise. In 1611, at the height of this activity, over eight hundred men were employed, and they sometimes worked through the night by torchlight.

Notwithstanding, these first services at which Frescobaldi performed were celebrated with ceremonial and musical grandeur, since Paul V, who officiated, was knowledgeable and exacting in both areas. The singers—the Cappella Giulia supplemented by the Cappella Pontificia—were placed on temporary wooden platforms, and Frescobaldi presided not at one of the basilica's two large stationary organs but at a smaller portable instrument. In a polyphonic mass the organist's contribution was more limited than in an *alternatim* chant-mass.[12] The All Souls' mass, essentially a Requiem, would have offered even less opportunity for display.

In general, until Bernini's creation of the coordinated axial ensemble of the crossing in the 1630s, use of the immense space of St. Peter's was remarkably fluid, as witness the constant bills for moving the organ and for erecting and dismantling the platforms for the singers. The movable organ was regularly situated near the altar of Sts. Simon and Jude in the left-hand transept, later transformed into a temporary canons' chapel, but was moved, as occasion demanded, to the Cappella Gregoriana, the tribune, the choir, the sacristy, the chapels of the Sacrament, the Crucifix, the Column, and the niches in the piers (see fig. 5).[13]

Other services employed the two stationary organs of the basilica. The older of these had been commissioned by Alexander VI Borgia in 1496 and at the time of Frescobaldi's installation was placed part-way down the

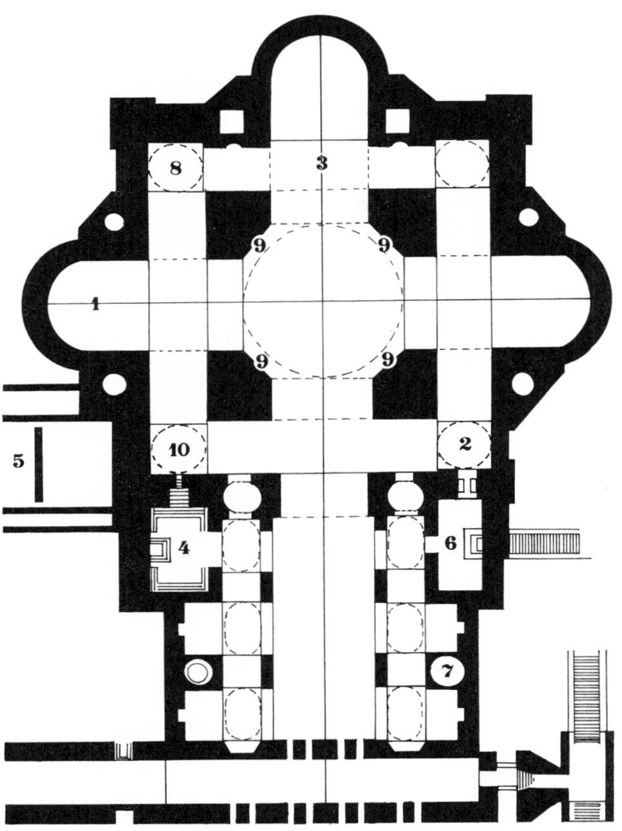

5. Location of music performances in St. Peter's: (1) Chapel of Sts. Simon and Jude; (2) Cappella Gregoriana; (3) Tribune; (4) Choir; (5) Sacristy; (6) Chapel of the Sacrament; (7) Chapel of the Crucifix; (8) Chapel of the Column; (9) Niches in piers; (10) Cappella Clementina

right-hand side of the nave. With the destruction of the old nave it was removed in 1609 to the Cappella Clementina, the northwest chapel (in liturgical orientation, since the church actually faces west) of Michelangelo's basilica, over the present sacristy door. Possibly at Frescobaldi's instigation, it was also restored by the organ builder and tuner Armodio Maccioni.[14] The second organ, whose façade is now preserved in the Chapel of the Sacrament, was built in 1580 and placed above the stair by the Cappella Gregoriana, the corresponding chapel on the southwest side of the basilica.

The busy schedule of the Cappella Giulia included not only performance of the mass and offices, as well as votive offices, in St. Peter's, but also other celebrations in churches under the jurisdiction of the Chapter throughout the City. Of the feasts kept in the basilica during this first period of Frescobaldi's tenure, two received particular musical elaboration: the feast of Sts. Peter and Paul (29 June) and the commemoration of the dedication of the original basilica in 326 A.D. (18 November). For these the singers of the Cappella Giulia were augmented by fifteen to twenty hired musicians and divided into three or four choirs placed on special platforms (see fig. 6). Frescobaldi accompanied the first choir on the portable organ; the other choirs were accompanied by hired organists on small organs rented for the occasion. Among Girolamo's colleagues at the organs we find his predecessor Alessandro Costantini, Francesco Anerio, and Prospero Santini.[15] Trombones hired from Castel Sant'Angelo probably doubled the bass line of each choir, while wind players from the Campidoglio, a violin, two cornetts, and unspecified instruments doubled other parts or played obbligati. Similar forces were employed for occasional celebrations, notably the canonization of Santa Francesca Romana in 1608 and the long-awaited canonization of Carlo Borromeo in 1610.[16]

Not all of this repertory can be identified from the surviving musical archive of the Cappella Giulia. Indeed, this contains no mass- or motet-settings for more than three choirs (usually three four-part choirs, but in one case three six-part ensembles). The nucleus of the collection consists of chant books and of polyphonic works by Palestrina, which provided settings for the proper and ordinary of both the mass and offices. The continuing use of Palestrina's music at St. Peter's is evident in the late dates of some of the manuscript copies. In medium these settings range from simple four-part works like the hymns copied part in 1582 and part in 1619, through Magnificats, Lamentations, and masses (some copied in 1607) for five and six voices, to motets and offertories for two and three four-part choirs.[17] The most grandiose of these works is a manuscript mass on *Tu es Petrus* for the feast of St. Peter attributed to Palestrina, in which the three six-part choirs seem to epitomize in music the monumental conception of the basilica and the text which the whole building proclaims: "Thou art Peter, and upon this Rock will I build my Church."[18]

Later additions to the repertory of the Cappella Giulia were frequently the work of the *maestri di cappella* under whom Frescobaldi served, notably Francesco Soriano (*maestro* 1603–1620). About the time of Girolamo's entrance into the Cappella, Soriano published a collection of masses for four to six voices, dedicated to Paul V and culminating appropriately in an

6. *Concert in Santa Maria del Popolo* by P. P. Sevin

eight-part *Missa in Papae Marcelli.* This was supplemented by a collection of *Psalmi et Mottecta* containing settings of the office and mass propers, as well as texts of special importance for the basilica, published in 1616 with a dedication to Cardinal Scipione Borghese. Newer currents in sacred music are represented by the three volumes of *Antiphonae* issued in 1613 by Giovanni Francesco Anerio, one of Frescobaldi's supplementary organists. These works, antiphons and canticles for vespers and compline throughout the year, are remarkable not only for their comprehensiveness but also for their medium: not choral polyphony but the few-voice concerto for two to four solo voices and continuo.[19]

At the time of Frescobaldi's appointment, then, the musical repertory of the Cappella Giulia was conventional and retrospective, firmly rooted in the work of Palestrina and his followers and characterized by such practices as the chanting of psalms in *falsobordone,* a conservative solution disdained by the musicians of St. Mark's in Venice, the most advanced center of liturgical composition.[20] Although newer styles and media did infiltrate the repertory of the Cappella Giulia in the second decade of the century, the *stile antico* was unswervingly maintained by the other group that performed in St. Peter's, the Cappella Sistina. The accounts of their performances in 1616 reveal a repertory still built around Palestrina and his contemporaries, and as late as 1683 Monteverdi's *stile antico* mass of 1610 was copied out for the Cappella without the brilliant concertato of its companion vesper-setting.[21]

The publication of Frescobaldi's "prime fatiche," the twelve fantasias dedicated to Francesco Borghese, apparently coincided with Girolamo's appointment to the Cappella Giulia. These works, with their rigorous contrapuntal logic and their double organization by number of subjects and modal finales, are perhaps the most cerebral of Frescobaldi's compositions. (Indeed, they seem almost a direct refutation of Antegnati's accusation in *L'arte organica,* published in the same year as the *Fantasie,* that "certain so-called modern Organists" despise the serious works of learned composers in favor of their own "improvised fantasies.") On the evidence of the dedication, it seems to have been Girolamo's custom to accumulate materials for a publication over a period of time. His next printed collections, the ricercars and first book of toccatas of 1615, thus probably show his development in the first seven years of his appointment at St. Peter's. If the musical character and requirements of the basilica seem reflected in the contrapuntal artifice of the ricercars, the brilliance of the toccatas—specifically designated for the secular harpsichord rather than the liturgical organ—points to Frescobaldi's other Roman post, his service in the household of Enzo Bentivoglio.

Enzo clearly conceived his musical establishment as a necessary part of the state he was obliged to maintain as Ferrarese ambassador in Rome, like his residence in Palazzo Sacchetti. In composition it recalled the *concerto delle dame,* comprising a "little ensemble" (*consertino*) of "two skilled ladies," Lucia and Lucrezia, augmented in February 1609 by a female harpist from Naples who received six scudi a month in addition to other perquisites. Besides Frescobaldi, the other musicians associated with Enzo's *consertino* included a certain Angiola and possibly the lutenist Alessandro Piccinini, who at any rate composed music for the "Napolitana."[22] On the evidence of other Roman musical establishments (notably that of the melomane Cardinal Montalto), the repertory of a noble *musica* was heavily influenced by Florentine monody and works such as Luzzaschi's *Madrigali* of 1601, marked by simplicity of texture, alternation of free and rhythmic passages, and vocal diminutions.

A *musica* functioned not only as a performing ensemble but also as a milieu for training its younger members. In 1615 Enzo acquired a boy soprano, Baldassare, with vocal problems and an insufficient musical background. An unspecified Nanino taught him every morning for two hours, one of singing and one of improvised counterpoint, composition, and harpsichord playing. Every afternoon he went to Frescobaldi for a harpsichord lesson. The Cavalier Cesare Marotta made Baldassare sing for him three or four times a day and composed pieces to teach to Baldassare. Marotta's wife, Cardinal Montalto's famous singer Ippolita, taught the boy to play the guitar.[23]

The progress of the *consertino,* partly under Frescobaldi's tutelage in performance and counterpoint, is described in letters written during the summer of 1609 from Enzo's household in Rome to Enzo at Ferrara: "M. Girolamo is now teaching the Neapolitan, and they expect to learn and Lucia learns from Oratietto very well, so that when Your Most Illustrious Lordship comes here these young Girls may be able to sing the notes securely; Lucia will not sing them because Your Lordship knows she has a thick skull . . . Signora Lucretia will sing the words securely because she knew a bit from madame Angiola; I don't get mixed up in the matter because m. Girolamo is teaching her."[24]

The Madame Angiola of Cosimo Bandini's letter may be identified as Angiola Zanibelli, a young woman who had originally entered the service of the Bentivoglio as a weaver or embroiderer. In 1606 she began her vocal training, and by 1608 she was sufficiently accomplished to be invited to Mantua, where she may have sung the title role in Marco da Gagliano's *La Dafne.*[25] Bentivoglio intended to bring her to Rome with him, but she demurred at teaching and suggested that the young girl Enzo proposed to engage study with her teacher. From a letter of Bandini it is apparent that Enzo's ladies, like the Ferrarese *dame*, were expected to play as well as sing: "To me it does not seem that the musical establishment makes as much progress as it did when you were here; and the cause is this, that when you were here all three played together, but since Your Most Illustrious Lordship left they have not played but once only, and Your Lordship can judge whether playing with others is the true fundamental."[26]

A letter of Frescobaldi to Enzo Bentivoglio, dated from Rome, 1 July 1609, discloses the undercurrents seething within Bentivoglio's household. Girolamo professed himself "most disgusted, having heard a certain rumor about me in the house of Your Most Illustrious Lordship about the teaching of these young ladies of yours, and having also seen from their behavior that they suspect me." He promised to acquaint Enzo with the facts of the case, resolving not to associate with them, and finally asking his release from Bentivoglio's service.[27] The situation is clarified in another—fragmentary—letter to Enzo, in which Girolamo again complained of the rumors about him and promised to marry Angiola—now revealed as their focus—with the hope of remedying his poverty by obtaining a better position for her uncle.[28]

The existence of quite another marriage proposed by the Bentivoglio for Frescobaldi is revealed in a letter of 31 July 1609 from Giulio Caccini in Florence to Enzo Bentivoglio in Rome: "As I already replied to Your Most Illustrious Lordship on the matter of the marriage which you proposed for my daughter with that young Ferrarese now Organist there at St. Peter's these Serene Highnesses do not wish to deprive themselves of this subject [the daughter], although they are content, that I find her a Husband, who is a *virtuoso,* and of her profession so that they will give the salary to both . . . She will have a dowry of one thousand scudi, and I believe that between the two the provision will be at least twenty-five scudi a month . . . in a service of little duty and less trouble."[29] Enzo had apparently planned not only to settle Frescobaldi's matrimonial future, but also to acquire a superb singer—presumably Settimia Caccini, since Francesca was already married and Dianora was not yet ten—for his *musica*; but in the event he was checkmated by the Medici counterproposal. Unwilling to lose Frescobaldi, Enzo increased the pressure to force him to marry Angiola. Ippolito Fiorini, the former *maestro di cappella* of Alfonso II, went as an intermediary to Girolamo's father:

> I have spoken with [Filippo] Frescobaldi and showed him the letter that his son wrote to Your Most Illustrious Lordship, from which he

> is half dead; I urged him to write on this matter, and he answered me that he had done it this morning and that he did not wish to write more until Saturday, and growing warm in the service of Your Most Illustrious Lordship he tells me that he does not know what to do and that he leaves thinking and the care of the matter to his son to correct the fault that he has committed in the manner that will appear best to him, feeling regret and great affliction for Your Most Illustrious Lordship's vexation, which would not have happened had his son informed him before he came to the point of promising and betrothing that young woman; now that he has gone so much further and ruled himself by his own whims let him find a remedy since he himself does not want to think about it any more.[30]

This suggests that Girolamo had consummated his betrothal with Angiola. The verbal smoke screen thrown up by his father seems to temper an aversion for the marriage with the fear of offending Enzo, Angiola's employer and Girolamo's patron. Filippo's real feelings are revealed in a letter of 29 August 1609: "Girolamo of the spinet is saying that he does not wish to marry Anzolla because his father has written him that he will give his curse to both of them . . . I went to find him in Capranica [? illegible, but Piazza Capranica is in the vicinity of Sant'Eustachio, where Frescobaldi lodged] and made great threats; he does not know what to answer but that he thought that Anzolla had a larger dowry and that her family were better. I gave him this answer and said that Your Lordship would have spoken to his father."[31]

The Bentivoglio were resolved to make an honest woman of Angiola, either by the provision of one thousand scudi as dowry, or by coercion verging on the criminal. Indeed, their anxiety has aroused the suspicion that they were using Girolamo to alleviate a scandal involving one of the family, perhaps Caterina Martinengo Bentivoglio's younger brother. Pressure was placed both on Girolamo and Filippo: "Let Your Lordship speak to him and threaten him soundly, and induce him to consent that Girolamo marry her, and let Your Lordship promise grave things and make him write him, because otherwise we will have great trouble with this fool because we are at Rome and I cannot take him by force and make him marry her . . . I cannot threaten him . . . [Let] Your Lordship convince also his father to write him that he is content because otherwise we will have vexations."[32]

The disorder that this scandal caused in Bentivoglio's household in Rome breaks out in an almost incoherent letter from Caterina to her husband:

My Lord: Your Lordship is not right to tell me that I become angry over small matters since there is nothing I can desire more than keeping your things in this absence of yours which is so long, and seeing myself bereft and not knowing the cause if it, I am afraid . . . I do not know what Your Lordship wishes me to do about this *musica* of yours, there being no other masters than Oratietto. I am not a *maestra* and cannot teach music. It has got us into trouble through your sig.r Girolamo who has put everything into confusion and then quit. Your Lordship should not complain of me, but rather of him who so tied up the mess that if Your Lordship believed me it would have been remedied and at this time the ensemble would be in good condition; but in this fashion he has taught no one but Angiola, but not music but other, merrier things, which I promise you I believe he knows backwards and forwards.[33]

The Bentivoglio continued their pressure, and Girolamo continued to refuse, citing to Enzo and Enzo's emissaries the misrepresentation of his proposed bride:

I spoke to m. Girolamo on Sunday morning at the order of the s.r Cavaliere [Enzo's brother] and the sig.ra Marchesa giving him the letter of Your Most Illustrious Lordship, since previously I had not been able to find him anywhere, and proposing to him all those considerations for which I thought to be able to persuade him to take Angiola for his wife in conformity with the promise made first to God and then to Your Most Illustrious Lordship and to these gentlemen. I found him more stubborn than ever; and because he told me that his father was not content, I showed him a letter where Your Most Illustrious Lordship wrote the s.r Cavaliere that his Father had given his word to Your Most Illustrious Lordship that he must be content with it, and must write so to him, but he answered me that his father had not written to him in this vein, but had written him that he wanted to know nothing more about it, and that if he did wrong the loss would be his, and finally he said to me that since the s.ra Marchesa had promised him that Anzola was born of honest parents, and finding her otherwise as to her mother and sisters; that he did not intend to be bound to keep his promise, if this proviso were not observed, telling me also further that he had written his opinion to Your Most Illustrious Lordship and to s.r Goretti, and that he was awaiting an answer. The s.ra Marchesa says it is not true that she had promised him anything, and adds that he made the promise freely without asking anything else, whence I have not failed to point out to the said m.

> Girolamo the harm which could befall him, whence it behooves him to consider well, since he seems unwilling to do otherwise about it.[34]

The day before Calcetto's visit, Frescobaldi had stated his position at length to Enzo:

> I believe that Your Most Illustrious Lordship will have received another letter from me, and with the present one I come to salute you and tell you at length what to my mind is involved in taking Angiola. I say to Your Most Illustrious Lordship that I have revered and esteemed the honor of Your Most Illustrious Lordship as much as my own life, that if I had not done so I believe that you would have seen signs of the results, if I had carried affection to evil or good ends. Your Most Illustrious Lordship knows that I asked to be released for this reason, then it happened that moved by compassion for her as well as that you promised me a thousand scudi as dowry I let myself be induced to do this, to betrothe her, begging Your Most Illustrious Lordship and the signora marchesa that this not be spoken of until at the coming of Your Most Illustrious Lordship to Rome we would have spoken of everything. Accordingly, if the signora marchesa knew that what I had done was done for compassion of her and that this was not a reasoned action, at least she ought to have told me about her [Angiola's] family, that they were of such reputation, which if she had done it I would have been content, but she told me the complete opposite of what I supposed, that this woman was of a quality appropriate to my honor. I tell Your Most Illustrious Lordship that after I learned this not only from my father but also from others that I would no longer bring myself to look at her let alone take her. I only beg Your Most Illustrious Lordship to take me as in truth for your true servant that I have always been to your house [and deign *canceled*] and to compose this matter for the best of one and the other parties and to consider only God.[35]

In the end, the determination of Girolamo and his father prevailed. The controversy apparently alienated Frescobaldi from the service of the Bentivoglio, and there is no further mention of his teaching the household musicians until 1612. Despite Girolamo's absence (or perhaps because of it), Enzo's musical ensemble rapidly improved, so that by the end of 1609 it was regularly visited by Cardinal Montalto and his singer, the famous Ippolita Recupito.[36] The Neapolitan eventually married "that young man who comes here to play the harpsichord," the composer Domenico Visconti, lending further prestige to the *consertino.*[37]

A series of letters from Visconti to Enzo Bentivoglio beginning in November 1611 appears at first glance to concern Frescobaldi in an all-too-familiar role. The writer is involved in a conspiracy to conceal the birth of an illegitimate child fathered by "Gironimo." The details of the case, however, show that the culprit was not Frescobaldi.[38] However, under the date 2 June 1612, the parish register of San Lorenzo in Lucina records the baptism of "Francesco the son of Girolamo Frescobaldi Ferrarese and Ursula born at Rome the daughter of Giovanni Travaglini, Milanese . . . Born the 29th day of the preceding month."[39] This time there was no escape feasible, although the union of Girolamo and Orsola was not regularized until the following year. On 18 February 1613 they were married in the sacristy of the bride's parish church, Santa Maria in Via, with only two friars of the parish as witnesses. This secrecy was probably prompted by the fact that Orsola was already pregnant with a second child, born 22 July 1613 and appropriately named Maddalena. The first of the Frescobaldi children to achieve the respectability of legitimate birth and a godparent other than a midwife was Domenico, born 8 November 1614 and held at the font of the Basilica of the Holy Twelve Apostles by Cardinal Ginnasi himself, the titular cardinal of the church.[40]

Little is known of Orsola del Pino (as she is usually called) by comparison with Girolamo's prospective brides. She was reputed to be better educated than her husband, and she brought as her dowry her family's house on Piazza Colonna, where the young couple went to live.[41]

His new responsibilities may have prompted Frescobaldi to a rapprochement with his former patrons. By the spring of 1612 Girolamo was again employed to teach the performers of Enzo Bentivoglio's household, in company with other musicians: Arrigo Vilardi, "the Hunchback," a singing teacher and perhaps composer; Ippolito Machiavelli, a musician connected with the household of Francesco Borghese; and the Cavalier Cesare Marotta, a composer employed by Prince Peretti and Cardinal Montalto.[42] The principal student of these teachers was now a certain Francesca, for whom a harpsichord was rented "because it suits her voice." "S.re Girollimo has given her lessons a few times because he is taking a purge but he told me that he has finished the purge and will give her a lesson every day."[43] Despite his promises, Girolamo continued to neglect his duties, and Vilardi took over Francesca's instruction on the harpsichord: "S.r Girolimo came here but now he does not come here at all, with all that I have been to see him many times and told him that he is wrong to treat Your Most Illustrious Lordship in this way. He always promises me to do well but the poor man is half crazy, as it seems to me. The Dwarf is satisfactory to the Cavaliere and teaches her to play the Harpsichord so that we have little need of Girolimo."[44] By the end of July 1613 Frescobaldi's break with his first patrons was complete.[45]

Despite the insinuation of mental instability, Frescobaldi may have had more cogent motives for his cavalier treatment of the Bentivoglio family. By 1615, according to his dedication of the *Recercari,* Girolamo was enrolled "among the present servants" of Cardinal Pietro Aldobrandini. Since Girolamo's associate Costantini wrote in 1622 that Frescobaldi had been in the service of the Cardinal for ten years, this would place his enlistment between 1610, the date of Aldobrandini's return from Ravenna, and 1613, the period of Girolamo's estrangement from the Bentivoglio.[46] Further, there was already a vacancy in the Cardinal's *musica* since "Filippo [Piccinini] dal liuto" had taken service with the Duke of Savoy, along with the poet Marino.[47]

Girolamo was first mentioned as a servant of Cardinal Pietro in a letter dated 1 November 1614 stating that he had an unspecified salary from the Cardinal.[48] Few details of his employment survive in the Aldobrandini papers, since servants of Frescobaldi's rank were named only in the lower reaches of the household accounts—bills (*giustificazioni*), payment orders (*mandati*), lists of those who received salaries and provisions (*salariati, companatici*)—while most of the surviving records of Cardinal Pietro's household are *libri mastri generali,* registers in which such items are entered only as lump sums. (A fire in the cardinal's household and the tangled history of the Aldobrandini inheritance may account for the disappearance of other documents.)[49]

A list of fifty-four members of the Cardinal's household who remained in Rome at his departure for Ravenna in December 1620 includes "D. Gironimo Organista."[50] Frescobaldi's service was therefore apparently limited to the cardinal's Roman residences: the palace on the Corso (now, greatly altered, Palazzo Doria) and the garden-villa at Monte Magnanapoli. Although Costantini says Girolamo was not required to follow the Cardinal to the Villa Belvedere at Frascati, on 18 June 1620 Frescobaldi was paid 24.21 scudi for seven musicians "who went to the Villa at Frascati on the occasion of the Banquet given to the Cardinal of Savoy, for the music sung by them and 3 scudi given to a Maestro who tuned the harpsichord."[51] (The guest of honor, Maurizio of Savoy, was a noted music lover and patron of Michel Angelo Rossi.) Again in September 1621 Frescobaldi was paid to tip five musicians who had performed at the last banquet; thus he must have remained in the service of the family after the death of Cardinal Pietro in February 1621.[52]

On the surface these years testify to Girolamo's increasing Romanization: his commitment to the post at St. Peter's, his difficulties with his father, his repudiation of his Ferrarese patrons in favor of one of the most powerful Roman cardinals, and his marriage to a native-born Roman. But it is perhaps a sign of the instability of his character that he was about to entertain seriously a proposal that would have meant cutting all professional ties with Rome.

4

Mantua, 1614–1615

In October 1614 Frescobaldi was approached by an agent of Ferdinando Gonzaga, Cardinal-Duke of Mantua. The Duke's emissary was Paolo Facconi, a pensioned bass-singer in the papal chapel and one of the occasional musicians hired by the Cappella Giulia, who was employed to secure Roman musicians for the Mantuan court.[1] The Duke's proposals, as transmitted by Facconi, were sufficiently enticing that by the following February Frescobaldi was willing to travel to Mantua. His reception, however, was so cold that he returned immediately to Rome, not to be tempted away from the organ of St. Peter's again for thirteen years. The narrative of this abortive venture unrolls from a correspondence preserved in the Archivio di Stato at Mantua: Facconi's letters to the Cardinal-Duke or to his secretary, Giovanni Magni, supplemented by three letters from Frescobaldi himself and by documents in the Gonzaga archive.[2]

The initiative seems to have been Ferdinando's. In the dedication of his first book of toccatas to the Duke (dated 22 December 1614) Girolamo stated that he had played for Ferdinando in Rome and that the young prelate had "deigned to prompt me to the practice of these works with frequent commands, and to show that this style of mine was not unacceptable." Since the collection marks Girolamo's first printed departure from strict contrapuntal genres into the freer world of the toccata and the variation-set, some external prompting is not unlikely, and Ferdinando's history supports Frescobaldi's ascription.

As even Giambattista Doni grudgingly admitted, Ferdinando was a "prince more than moderately informed about music."[3] He was born in 1587 to Monteverdi's patron, Vincenzo Gonzaga, and as a younger son was destined for the Church. He accepted the post of protector for Marco da Gagliano's Accademia degl'Elevati in Florence, and Gagliano's *La Dafne* was given its premiere in 1608 to celebrate Ferdinando's cardinalate.[4] Ferdinando was himself a composer and submitted his works to Gagliano and other professionals for comment and correction. According to Gagliano, three of the strongest arias in *La Dafne* were in fact the work of Ferdinando.[5] By 1610 the young Cardinal was well enough known that the singer Ippolita Recupito Marotta, an intimate of the Bentivoglio musical circle, could complain to Monteverdi that "if the Lord Cardinal Gonzaga thought as highly of me as you say, he would have favored me with some lovely aria of his, so that I could sing it."[6] In 1612 the unexpected death of his elder brother Francesco forced Ferdinando to leave Rome to take over the government of Mantua.

The musical establishment that the young dukes had inherited from Vincenzo Gonzaga was one of the richest in Europe. At this period it consisted of a *maestro di cappella;* two composers; about fourteen singers, including Adriana Basile and her two daughters, Lorenzo Sances, and Francesco Rasi; a string ensemble in which Salomone Rossi played; an organist; a harpsichordist; and two guitarists.[7] Under Monteverdi's direction the Mantuan *musica* had presented a series of dazzling performances: *L'Orfeo,* the *Ballo delle ingrate, L'Arianna,* as well as regular chamber concerts. The publication in Venice of Monteverdi's first five madrigal books, the *Scherzi,* and the 1610 mass and vespers demonstrated Mantua's importance as a center of both sacred and secular music to a wider public.[8] For reasons which have never been clarified, Francesco Gonzaga dismissed Claudio and Giulio Cesare Monteverdi shortly after his accession in 1612, replacing Monteverdi as *maestro di cappella* with the mediocre Santi Orlandi, whom he had preempted from Ferdinando's service in Rome. By the time of Ferdinando's negotiations with Frescobaldi, Monteverdi was firmly established in Venice as *maestro di cappella* of St. Mark's. Frescobaldi, as a keyboard player and instrumental composer, would not have been a direct replacement for Monteverdi (with whom the Mantuan court was still in touch), but his appointment would have restored some of the luster lost by Monteverdi's departure and enhanced the preparations for Ferdinando's wedding with Camilla Fàa. To this end the new Duke instructed Facconi to sound out Girolamo about exchanging his Roman career for service in Mantua.

Facconi's first letter to the Duke confirms Girolamo's interest in the proposal and strikes the keynote of the negotiations—Frescobaldi's new consciousness of his own worth and his unwillingness to leave the organ of St. Peter's and Rome without a post of equal importance and equivalent compensation: "I found sig. Hieronimo very disposed, who in addition to the organ of San Pietro and the provision from Aldobrandino earns 25 scudi a month. He answered me that having to leave here he will come more willingly to serve Your Highness than any other Prince; but in conclusion he does not wish to leave Rome even for an extraordinary salary, although he will decide when he will be given an equivalent living. And it must be in the form of property and his own, since he plans and wishes to establish himself."[9] In order to accomplish this, Girolamo also demanded a house for himself and his heirs in perpetuity, as Luzzaschi had received from Alfonso II.[10] From Facconi's figures it can be calculated that Frescobaldi received seventy-two scudi a year from St. Peter's, three hundred scudi a year from patrons and his "many students," and an undisclosed amount from Cardinal Aldobrandini. Girolamo's preoccupation with at least matching this annual income in Mantua is explained by the notorious financial irresponsibility of the Gonzaga family. Eight years after his dismissal Monteverdi still declared bitterly that he "would rather go begging than return to such indignity."[11]

Acting on Facconi's financial report, the Duke made Frescobaldi an offer of six hundred scudi a year. Girolamo communicated his acceptance, with the provisos that the real estate be his to bequeath and that his salary begin the day he left Rome. He further requested a house "large enough for himself and his family and his father," the loan of furnishings and utensils for two years, three portions of bread and wine a day for four months after his arrival, and an advance of three hundred scudi to cover his financial obligations. Here, for the first time, we hear of the *Toccate*: "And because the aforesaid has already begun to print a work on copper, which will cost him 500 scudi, he does not wish to leave Rome until the aforesaid work is printed which I think he intends to dedicate to Your Highness."[12]

The next matter to be settled was that of Frescobaldi's reception in Mantua. Knowing both Girolamo and the Gonzaga court, Facconi wrote to the Duke's secretary: "Let me advise Your Lordship that it is not sufficient that our master have the good intention that his foreign servants be well treated and well lodged; it is also necessary that the undertaking be in the charge of some amiable and zealous person and that he put this good will into practice. By this I mean that when this organist comes, as he will, he be recommended to someone who will treat him well, so that he has no opportunity for dissatisfaction . . . (3 December 1614)."[13] Ten days later Facconi wrote to the Duke, suggesting that Frescobaldi's contract be drawn up in Mantua "as a spur to hasten his arrival" and relaying Girolamo's request that three hundred scudi be advanced him in Rome "in respect of the great expense he has for the printing."[14] On the same day Frescobaldi wrote to the Duke, reaffirming his obligation and promising to come to Mantua as soon as he had finished the feasts of Christmas and the Epiphany at St. Peter's.[15]

A letter from Facconi to Magni, dated 17 January 1615, shows some perplexity about the real attitude of the Mantuan court:

> These words which Your Lordship writes in your last letter; I do not know what they mean, that is about the matter of the organist and they are these: Concerning the organist, His Highness will pay him what his ability deserves; and from the others he will also receive courtesy; whence Your Lordship can encourage him, and confide to him that he is well esteemed and treated. Will Your Lordship kindly favor me with a bit of gloss, since I do not understand these words well; if perhaps Your Lordship might not wish to imply that one has eaten the bread of repentance, or perhaps that this was a courtly dismissal—or better [a dismissal] *alla Mantovana;* if it were I beg Your Lordship kindly to inform me and the world of the pretext, so that both sides are satisfied: since the poor man is already well started; and immediately this work of his is printed, which he has dedicated to His Highness, he wants to come to Mantua to present it personally.[16]

Despite the date of the engraved dedication—Rome, 22 December 1614—the *Toccate* was not issued until early in 1615. The three hundred scudi promised by the Duke as a loan to pay the expenses of the printing and other obligations arrived only in late January or early February, and the actual remittance amounted to less than half the promised sum:

> When sig. Frescobaldi asked for the loan of three hundred scudi from His Highness he made this request because without this sum he could not honorably leave Rome, with the expenses of the printing and other family matters as they are. And as soon as I showed him the letter that His Highness was pleased to do him the favor of the loan, then he accommodated his creditors and all the parties concerned with this allotment. And I, in virtue of the Duke's letter, submitted, promising him what was written from Mantua. Now that he has seen that there are only one hundred forty-three and a half scudi in this remittance, and that they are not sufficient to his needs, he does not wish to leave, adducing that he has given his word to satisfy everyone and put his affairs in order before leaving Rome. But if His Highness

will favor him with the remainder, without fail he will immediately set out . . . (7 February 1615).[17]

A week later, Facconi summarized his promises and advice in a letter to the Duke written at Frescobaldi's departure. He reminded the Duke that Girolamo had left Rome contingent upon written assurances, paying his own expenses since he had not yet received the money for his trip. Facconi recommended that Ferdinando's new *virtuoso* be well lodged and that he and his family be granted tangible signs of the Duke's favor, concluding ominously, "I expect that his arrival will give a bit of displeasure to certain of Your Highness' virtuosi."[18] This letter marked the end of the negotiations. Frescobaldi set out in February, as confirmed by the records of the Cappella Giulia, which show that his salary for January and February was paid to Francesco Soriano.[19]

Girolamo's journey to Mantua coincided with a brief period of tranquillity in the recent history of the duchy. At his untimely death, Ferdinando's brother had left an infant daughter as his only heir. The child's maternal grandfather, Carlo Emanuele I of Savoy, used her as a pretext to annex Monferrato and to open war on other Mantuan territory. During the brief peace negotiated by the Treaty of Asti (December 1614 through spring 1615), Ferdinando not only engaged Frescobaldi but also attempted to obtain a dramatic work from Monteverdi.[20]

The political climate of Mantua was not the only aspect of the Gonzaga court unsettling to the seventeenth-century (as to the modern) visitor. The great sullen mass of "that immense necropolis, which is now the ex-Ducal Palace of Mantua" brooded over an expanse of malarial lagoon, and the city was notorious as one of the unhealthiest in Italy.[21] Mantuan art of the late Renaissance was marked by an element of distortion and disproportion that is still disturbing. To move from Mantegna's serene frescoes in the *Camera degli sposi,* for example, to the vast empty halls of the ducal palace with their immense gilded ceilings is to experience a disorientation that becomes nightmarish when one plunges into the gloomy, claustrophobic labyrinth at the heart of the palace, a suite of miniature rooms intended for the court dwarfs. (Piave and Verdi's change of venue for *Rigoletto,* while historically inaccurate and politically dictated, is psychologically acute.) While the great disasters of Mantua—the sale of the Gonzaga collection in 1627–1628 and the sack of the city in 1630—were still to come, the signs of decay were already visible.

Whatever Frescobaldi's expectations of the Mantuan court, there is no question about his reception there. As far away as Rome, Facconi understood that Girolamo was "very displeased," and he could not resist a bit of self-justification:

> If Your Lordship will remember, before Frescobaldi came I foresaw this whole event and told you of it, because I know both the court of Mantua and his character of an inept man outside his own house . . . Before he left here I told him that it had fortunately turned out that everything that had been promised him would be fulfilled as soon as he arrived. Now that he has arrived, I seem to understand that, from the four words that the Most Serene addressed him that first day, no one else has bothered to look at him. Let Your Lordship consider in what a state and in what misery a pilgrim must find himself, who has come at breakneck speed in the dead of winter among so much snow and mud. [14 March 1615].[22]

The Mantuan court apparently made some effort to remedy Frescobaldi's grievances, but not in time to prevent his return to his family in Rome. Girolamo did not write to the Duke again until 16 May, when he politely evaded a second attempt to lure him to Mantua: "Then, as to coming this summer with my family, I begged your Serene Highness about the difficulty of dispatching my wife and coming in good weather. Even more so now, when it would be much worse in the heat with a five-months' old baby. I regret not being single, so that I might show myself ready for the commands of your Serene Highness."[23]

Despite the expense of publishing the *Toccate* and the unhappy journey to Mantua, the venture was not a total loss for Girolamo: on 5 September he wrote to the Duke acknowledging the gift of three hundred scudi.[24] A few days later Facconi died, and with him the Mantuan project. Girolamo's reasons for not returning to Mantua were sufficient: the problems of breaking up his Roman household, the danger of travel in hot weather with an infant child. But beyond the devious courtesies of Frescobaldi's letters to the Duke one senses the hurt pride of a man who is both socially inept and a genius, and who has been snubbed.

The subsequent history of the *Toccate,* the one tangible product of the Mantuan venture and Girolamo's most important work so far, is complex. The original edition, dated 1614 in the dedication and 1615 on the title page, was almost immediately superseded by an enlarged version that retained the dedication, its date, and the date of the first title page and added "1616" to the expanded advice to the reader. Frescobaldi enlarged the variations on the Romanesca, the Ruggiero, and La Monica, and added four correnti and a set of variations on the Folia. In November 1615 Ferdinando Gonzaga resigned his cardinalate by laying his red hat at the feet of Paul V. On Epiphany Day he was installed as Duke in the cathedral of Mantua. Thus the perfected version of the work that he had in more than one sense inspired coincided with the enthronement of the last great Gonzaga duke of Mantua.

5

Rome, 1615–1628

The providential failure of Frescobaldi's Mantuan venture bound him more firmly than ever to Rome. He returned there probably in April 1615 and did not leave again until late in 1628.[1] The election to the papacy of Urban VIII Barberini (fig. 7) in 1623 shaped the history of the City for those years. Consequences of his reign—the longest of the century—were felt everywhere. A new artist, Gian Lorenzo Bernini, was given virtually unlimited control over the artistic program not only of St. Peter's but of all Rome. The outside of the basilica was completed, and at the pope's urging the crucial decisions were made for the central complex of the interior. The elevation of the Barberini clan along with Urban provided a new and seemingly inexhaustible source of artistic patronage that supported established artists, such as Carlo Maderno, and fostered younger ones, notably Bernini, Pietro da Cortona, and Andrea Sacchi. Urban and his family commissioned not only churches and palaces, with their decorations and furnishings, but more ephemeral if no less significant projects as well—jousts, religious spectacles, and above all opera. Frescobaldi entered the service of the Barberini only after his return from Florence in 1634, but the mounting artistic excitement of Roman life is mirrored in the number and quality of his publications between 1615 and 1628, the most productive period of his career: the reworking of the first book of toccatas, collections of ricercars and canzonas, capriccios, a second book of toccatas, two volumes of small sacred concertos, and a set of ensemble canzonas.

The only authenticated portraits of Frescobaldi date from these years and substantiate the impression of an artist in his prime. The original of these (see frontispiece) seems to be a drawing in black chalk (retouched for engraving) by Claude Mellan, a French artist and engraver active in Rome between 1624 and 1637. It shows a man of physical distinction with a large

7. Portrait of Urban VIII Barberini by Gian Lorenzo Bernini, engraved by Mellan

aquiline nose, heavy-lidded eyes, a rather haggard face, tousled dark hair, a wide sensitive mouth, and an alertly poised head. He is dressed soberly in a dark doublet with a plain white collar. Two engravings—both reversed—seem to stem from this original. The crude and uninformative likeness that appeared in the second book of toccatas of 1627 is attributed to "F. Io. Salianus Augustinianus" (Jean Saillant) and was engraved by "Christian*us* Sas." Mellan's own engraving, an altogether finer piece of work, modifies his original drawing by softening the prominence of the nose and the angularity of the face and by deemphasizing the generous mouth (figs. 8, 9). Both of Mellan's portraits are "speaking" likenesses in which we are confronted with a strong and perhaps not wholly sympathetic personality. The inscriptions around the frames of both engravings give the subject's age as thirty-six, which would date them as 1619—eight years before the publication of the toccatas, and five years before Mellan's arrival in Rome. A later inscription on the drawing names Girolamo as musician to the Grand Duke of Tuscany, a post he did not occupy until 1628. It is most likely that the Mellan drawing was made soon after 1624. (It is possible that a hitherto unidentified caricature by Bernini—see fig. 10—records Girolamo's appearance in his later years.)[2]

There are other evidences of Frescobaldi's growing celebrity. In 1620 Agostino Superbi included Girolamo among the "illustrious Men of the City of Ferrara" in his *Apparato:* "At present there still lives to the honor of his native city Girolamo Frescobaldi, a man of splendid talent and elevated spirit. He distinguished himself not only in music and in composition, but especially on the organ, so that he acquired a name and reputation, and belongs to the most eminent and distinguished . . . now however he resides in Rome as organist in St. Peter's, and possesses such ability that at present he must be numbered among the first organists of our time. Many of his works exist, which were printed some in Flanders, some in Milan and Rome; in addition many Madrigals and innumerable Church works, circulated in manuscript."[3] By 1624 Frescobaldi's skill as a teacher was acknowledged in print by Cesare Crivellati, whose son Domenico, thanks to Girolamo's diligence, had progressed "not badly" in singing and harpsichord playing.[4]

The little surviving evidence of Frescobaldi's private life in these years shows that circumstances and his own choice continued to weaken his ties with Ferrara and to consolidate his establishment in Rome. In November 1615 his sister Giulia was engaged to marry, and by a notary act executed in Rome Girolamo ceded to her his share of the family house in Ferrara as part of her dowry.[4] From a notary act of July 1619 we learn that Girolamo's

8. Portrait of Frescobaldi by Jean Saillant, engraved by Christianus Sas

9. Engraving by Mellan of his drawing of Frescobaldi

strongest remaining link with his native city had been broken: his half-sister, Vittoria, is called the daughter of "the late Filippo Frescobaldi."[5] Girolamo's own family continued to increase. A fourth child, Stefano, was born to Orsola del Pino in 1616 or 1617, and the last child, Caterina, arrived in September 1619 and was baptized in San Marco near Palazzo Venezia, with the Inquisitor of Malta as godfather.[6] Frescobaldi returned

10. Caricature of Frescobaldi(?) by Bernini, ca. 1640–1645

from Mantua to his wife's house in Piazza Colonna, where they remained until May 1618, when Girolamo's patron Cardinal Pietro Aldobrandini bought the property for 689.27 scudi as part of a campaign to increase his holdings across the piazza from his palace on the Corso.[7] The Frescobaldi family then moved to a house behind the Cardinal's palace in Via Santo Stefano del Cacco (so called from a statue of the god Anubis found there and mistaken for a *macacco* or baboon). According to a parish census of 1625, Girolamo's household included his wife, his children Stefano, Domenico, Caterina, and Francesco, his mother-in-law, his sister-in-law, and five lodgers, among them two Polish students, a German, and a lute player named Gaspare Rota. An account of 1627–1628 adds his wife's uncle, Ludovico, who had accompanied him to Mantua.[8]

The responsibilities of this large household must have impelled Frescobaldi to earn as much as possible. Throughout this period he performed his duties at the Vatican regularly, but this brought in only seventy-two scudi a year. Although he had given up his many students and his post with Cardinal Aldobrandini to go to Mantua, he resumed these on his return to Rome and even acepted as a pupil a boy soprano from Enzo Bentivoglio's *musica.*[9] His duties, as we have seen, included providing performers for the banquets at the Cardinal's villa in Frascati (fig. 11). It is pleasant to imagine Girolamo and his singers at the Villa Aldobrandini, their own music counterpointed by that of the water-stairs, whose torrent "rushes, cascades, hurls, jumps, dances, retreats and advances, seethes and a thousand other things" (Agucchi, 1611), or enjoying the splendid views of the Apennines, the Campagna and distant Rome, and the sea. Girolamo also performed for other patrons. Musical academies were held once or twice a week in the Roman palace of Cardinal Alessandro d'Este, and in September 1619 one of his household officials wrote to the Cardinal: "Last Thursday there were many skilled people here, and among them were Messers Catelani and Innocentio sent by Cardinal Borghese to see and play the harpsichord that Your Most Illustrious Lordship sent, which in truth is a divine thing and amazes all who hear it. In Rome there is no one who can play it save for Girolamo Frescobaldi of Ferrara, organist of St. Peter's and pupil of Luzzaschi, and even Frescobaldi does not do it except with great preparation."[10]

In 1620 Girolamo took on another post, that of organist of Santa Maria (now Santo Spirito) in Sassia. The church and its adjacent hospital are situated in Borgo Santo Spirito, a few streets from the Vatican and near the site of Luca Antonio Soldi's shop, where the 1624 *Capricci* were printed. The church is a large, oratoriolike building without transepts, richly frescoed and decorated. It still retains the façades of two sixteenth-century organs, a large instrument in a balcony halfway down the south side of the nave and a smaller one in the north side of the apse, corresponding to a *cantoria* on the opposite side.

Girolamo became organist of Santa Maria in Sassia in June 1620 and continued until mid-March of the following year. Like Ercole Pasquini, who also had served there, he was paid three scudi rather than the normal twenty-five *giuli* (sc. 2.50) per month.[11] It is difficult to understand how he reconciled the post with his duties at St. Peter's, since at Santa Maria

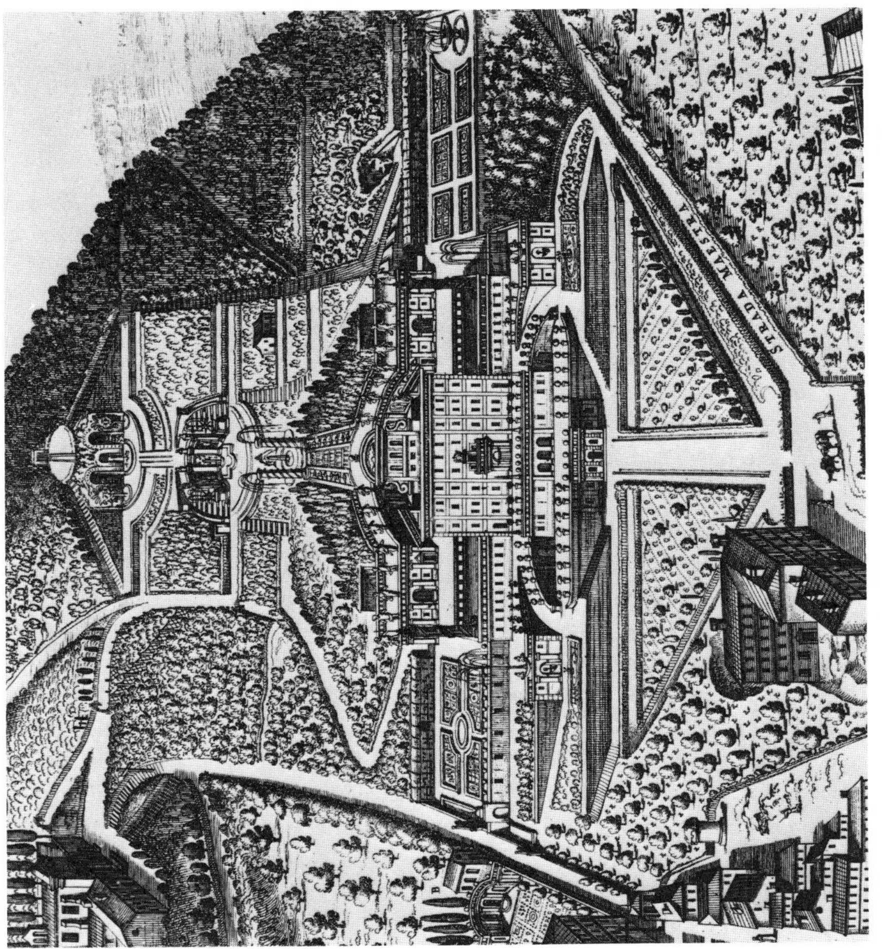

11. Engraving of Villa Aldobrandini at Frascati by Matthaüs Greuter

he was required to play mass and vespers for all feasts, as well as the Litany of the Madonna every Saturday and matins at Easter.[12] In addition, the organist was expected to play the organ of the hospital for the patients and to teach the choirboys to play the harpsichord.[13] Presumably some accommodation had been made with St. Peter's, since musicians from the basilica performed regularly at Santa Maria in Sassia. Frescobaldi himself returned from August through December of 1626 and at Pentecost of 1628 performed four services with four singers from the basilica under the direction of Paolo Agostino, *maestro di cappella* of the Cappella Giulia.

The financial records of San Luigi de' Francesi, the French national church in Rome, show that "Sr. Gironimo organista di S. Pietro" served as one of two extra organists for the church's patronal festival, 25 August, in 1625 and 1627, at a salary of two scudi. He probably also accepted other such casual employment as a member of the pool of available Roman church musicians.[14]

Frescobaldi's attempts to increase his income must be viewed against the steadily rising prices that marked the last years of the pontificate of Paul V and the economic crises under his successor. In January 1621 Paul V died unexpectedly. The Bolognese Cardinal Ludovisi was easily elected and took the name Gregory XV. His election ended the enmity between the Aldobrandini and the ruling papal family, although Girolamo's patron Pietro died too soon afterward to enjoy the amnesty. By the winter of 1621 there was a famine in the City, following by flooding of the Tiber, and in March 1622 there began a plague that lasted a year (and may have taken Girolamo's second child, Maddalena).[15] Gregory tried to offset these disasters by splendid public ceremonies, most notably the canonization in March 1622 of the great heroes of the Counter-Reformation—Ignatius Loyola, Francis Xavier, Teresa of Avila, and Philip Neri—and the triumph of the Madonna della Vittoria the following May. Nonetheless, when Gregory XV died in July 1623 the diarist Gigli observed that the Romans had been more wearied by twenty-nine months of Gregory than by nearly sixteen years of Paul.[16] The ensuing conclave consequently developed into a pitched battle between the Borghese and Ludovisi factions, prolonging the period of *sede vacante* to four weeks. Finally the summer heat and the threat of malaria compelled the cardinals to a decision, and on 5 August they elected the fifty-six-year-old Cardinal Maffeo Barberini, who took the name Urban VIII.[17]

Urban was the youngest of the candidates. In person he was handsome and dignified (except for a tendency toward fits of rage), with a cultivated intellect displayed in the composition of Latin verse, set by Kapsberger and Domenico Mazzocchi. How did the election of this amiable prelate inaugurate the golden age of seventeenth-century Rome? First, Urban's reign coincided with a remarkable flowering of artistic talent as well as with the high point of papal finances. Second, he did not so much change the traditional forms of patronage as exercise them with a logic—principally through the appointment of Bernini as chief artistic consultant—and on a scale previously unprecedented. Third, his own efforts during the first part of his reign, which centered on St. Peter's and large public enterprises, were increasingly supplemented by the patronage of his gifted nephews, more concerned with the family properties and with public spectacles. Even Paul V Borghese could quip that his brother's new palace was "too big a cage for such a bird," but the Barberini ambition was limitless. Where previous popes had generally vested access to themselves in one cardinal-nephew, Urban raised to the purple two of his nephews, Francesco and Antonio, and a brother, another Antonio. His other brother, Carlo, was named General of the Church, and his remaining nephew, Carlo's son Taddeo, was made Prince of Palestrina and Prince Prefect of Rome and was grafted on to the older Roman nobility by marriage to Anna Colonna. Previous popes had concentrated their efforts on a single religious foundation, but Urban commissioned a family chapel in Sant'Andrea della Valle, contributed to his brother's foundation of Santa Maria della Concezione, and completed St. Peter's as his principal monument. In addition to the papal residences at the Quirinal and the Vatican, the Barberini palaces eventually included Urban's original house in the Via de' Giubbonari, the palace at Palestrina, Francesco's Palazzo della Cancelleria, Palazzo Rusticucci near the Vatican, and the great new family palace at the Quattro Fontane, the work of Maderno, Bernini, and Pietro da Cortona.

Under Urban's aegis the Cappella Giulia began to reflect the growing taste for splendid polychoral church music. As early as 1616 the Gesù had presented under Anerio's direction a mass sung by "all the Singers of Rome" divided into eight choirs and placed in the balconies above the chapels of the church.[18] While not on this scale, the two principal musical celebrations of the Cappella Giulia, the feasts of St. Peter and the Dedication, regularly included extra singers (twenty-six by 1622), two and three assistant organists, and assistant conductors for the choirs.[19] The first great solemnity of Urban's reign was the celebration of the Holy Year of 1625, beginning with the unsealing of the Porta Santa of St. Peter's on Christmas Eve of 1624. On 25 March 1625 Urban canonized St. Elizabeth of Portugal in a ceremony whose decorations by Bernini included the first project for the baldacchino, the bronze for which was already being removed from the Pantheon.[20]

In 1626 Vincenzo Ugolini, *maestro* of the Cappella Giulia, was dismissed and succeeded by Paolo Agostino, a noted contrapuntist. Agostino's first year of office included an event of enormous significance. In 1626 the feast of the Dedication on 18 November was celebrated not merely as the commemoration of the Constantinian basilica but as the formal consecration of its successor by the Pope: the culmination of a project that had indirectly precipitated the Protestant Reformation and had involved the greatest Italian artists and papal patrons for well over a century. No account of the occasion describes the music in detail, but it cannot have been less splendid than the music for the anniversary of the Dedication the following year, with four choirs and instruments.[21]

The largest of these polychoral performances during the first years of Urban's reign, the music for the feast of Sts. Peter and Paul in June 1628, was also Frescobaldi's last important public appearance before his removal to Florence. At second vespers of the feast Agostino produced a work for no less than twelve choirs, in honor of the twelve Apostles. Girolamo presided at the organ amid Rome's most distinguished musicians. The castrato and composer Cavalier Loreto Vittori appeared among the three sopranos, while Stefano Landi contributed his services and those of eight additional singers; the contraltos numbered twenty, the tenors nineteen, and the basses seventeen. The accompanying instruments included five cornetts, seven violins, a contralto viola, two tenor *viole,* a *contralto di violino,* six trombones, a violone, and a bassoon. The twelve Apostolic choirs were conducted by musicians from the papal court, *maestri* in the service of Roman churches and cardinals' households (including Domenico Mazzocchi and Nicolò Borbone, the publisher of Frescobaldi's two books of toccatas), and Agostino himself. The roster of organists, headed by "Sig.re Girolamo," similarly included musicians from the most important churches of the City: Girolamo's predecessor, Costantini, and the organists of the Chiesa Nuova, the Araceli, Santa Maria in Trastevere, the Minerva, and Santo Spirito.[22] This gathering of musicians also represented the three focuses of Roman church music: St. Peter's, the Congregazione di Santa Cecilia, and the Oratorio.

Girolamo's close association with the members of Santa Cecilia renders somewhat academic the question of his own membership. In any case, his publications during these years link him publicly with the composers of the Congregazione precisely at a time when its activities affected every

Roman musician. In the early 1620s the Congregation was reorganized under Orazio Griffi, master of the papal chapel after 1623 and a priest closely associated with the Oratorian movement. Once established in the little church of San Paolino in Piazza Colonna, in the spring of 1624 the Congregation petitioned Urban VIII for what amounted to control of the musical life of Rome: the right to censor all musical publications, license schools of music, and oversee the membership of choirs. In November 1624 Urban granted Santa Cecilia supervision of musical publication and the right to license those who wished to open schools of music. When the Congregation attempted to exercise these prerogatives, however, the outcry from the papal musicians was such that two years later Urban revoked the privileges.[23]

The alliance between the Congregation of Santa Cecilia, the Oratorian movement, and the musicians associated with the Cappella Giulia is apparent in the sacred collections issued during these years. Frescobaldi published small sacred concertos in four anthologies: the *Selectae Cantiones* (1616), the *Scelta di motetti* (1618) of Alessandro Costantini's brother Fabio, the *Lilia Campi* of Giovanni Battista Robletti (1621), who printed Girolamo's *Canzoni* of 1628, and the *Sacri affetti* (1625) published by Luca Antonio Soldi, the printer of the *Capricci.* The contents of Costantini's collections seem directly associated with the Oratorio del Crocifisso, and virtually every composer in all four books was associated with both Santa Cecilia and St. Peter's; at least nine of them performed in the 1628 vespers of Sts. Peter and Paul.

The collections of secular music issued in the years between Girolamo's return to Rome and his departure for Florence in 1628 display equal vitality, together with a greater variety of expression. Fabio Costantini published two volumes of secular works, the *Ghirlandetta amorosa* of 1621 and the *Aurata Cintia* of 1622, to which Frescobaldi contributed as well as to Robletti's *Giardino musicale* (1621). A number of secular prints issued from the Florentine court, under the rule of the melomane Grand Duke Cosimo II. The publications of the Florentines Gagliano, Brunelli, Vitali, and Lorenzo Allegri were overshadowed, however, by the works of Monteverdi that appeared during these years. The epoch-making fifth book of madrigals continued to be reprinted; Book VI appeared in 1614 and Book VII in 1619, the latter followed by at least four reprints.

The musical flowering of this period is equally apparent in prints of solo and ensemble instrumental music, the area of Girolamo's principal activity. The most important solo keyboard collections issued include Trabaci's second book of ricercars (1615), Cifra's two books of ricercars and canzonas (1619) (of which the first was modeled on Frescobaldi's *Recercari et canzoni*), and Picchi's *Intavolatura di balli* (1621). In 1623 Girolamo's former associate in the Bentivoglio *musica,* Alessandro Piccinini, published his *Intavolatura di liuto.* Even more important was the first wave of collections for instrumental ensemble, which included publications by Kapsberger, Giovanni Gabrieli, Salomone Rossi, Carlo Farina, and Biagio Marini.

A rapid survey of the music produced during this period, then, shows significant productions in the fields of church music, secular vocal music, opera, solo keyboard, and instrumental ensemble music. Between 1615 and 1628 Frescobaldi published works in every one of these categories except the opera. He seems to have made his way gradually into the field of small sacred concertos by publishing single works in anthologies such as those of Costantini. His first complete volume of sacred concertos is lost, but in 1627 he issued a *Liber Secundus Diversarum Modulationum* containing thirty-two motets for one to four voices and continuo and perhaps intended for performance in St. Peter's, since it is dedicated to Cardinal Scipione Borghese, Archpriest of the basilica.[24] (Similarly, the two collections of secular vocal music Girolamo printed in Florence were heralded by the single works issued in anthologies.)[25]

Frescobaldi's major productions during this period, however, were instrumental works: the second version of the first book of toccatas (1615–1616), the ricercars and canzonas dedicated to Cardinal Aldobrandini (1615), the capriccios (1624), the second book of toccatas (1627), and a volume of canzonas for one to four instruments and continuo (1628).

In the same year Girolamo's pupil Bartolomeo Grassi, organist of Santa Maria in Aquiro near Piazza Colonna, published the canzonas in open score, together with three additional works. Grassi's extensive introduction to his edition shows that by 1628 Frescobaldi's music, especially the two books of toccatas, was considered fundamental for the keyboard player, as it was to remain for decades: "I therefore advise every student, that he provide himself with all the works of Signor Girolamo, beginning from the first book of Toccatas in Copper, & following the second now published with infinite expectation of all who profess this art, not being less worthy than the first, indeed fuller of diversity of works, as well for the Organ, as for the Harpsichord, & every keyboard player having these two books containing Toccatas, Galanteries, & responses necessary for all the needs of the Church, may deem himself content."[26] The canzonas were recommended for "liveliness, and sprightly imitative motives . . . gravity and learning," while the capriccios and ricercars supplied seriousness of style. These last works were so popular, Grassi states, that it had been necessary to reprint them three times.

Grassi's concluding paragraph raises an issue that still haunts Frescobaldi scholarship: "Signor Girolamo has made an infinite number of other volumes, & constantly goes on shaping new ones, because he is as eminent in composition as in improvisation, as Rome constantly sees, he does marvelous things; but the effort, & expense of Printing does not permit them to appear." That these survived Girolamo's death is attested by a *Nota delli musei, librerie, galerie di Roma* of 1664: "In the Frescobaldi household there are Compositions in Harpsichord tablature written by hand, and not printed by the famous Girolamo Frescobaldi father of Gio: Domenico Beneficed cleric of S. Pietro."[27] The fate of these manuscript volumes is unknown, but their existence is of central importance in evaluating the large number of works attributed to Frescobaldi in manuscript sources.

Grassi's assertions about the popularity of Girolamo's collections are confirmed by an examination of their publishing history between 1615 and 1628. The most complex is that of the first book of toccatas, issued in three versions and at least five printings in those years. For the 1628 version a new title page was engraved, the inapplicable dedication to Ferdinando Gonzaga from the 1615 and 1616 versions was deleted, and the portrait of Girolamo first published in the second book of toccatas was added.

Unlike the two books of toccatas, which were engraved on copper plates, the other two collections were printed in open score (keyboard *partitura*) from movable type, a less expensive if less elegant process. The *Recercari et canzoni,* comprising ten ricercars and five canzonas, was first issued in 1615 and reprinted in 1618. In 1624 Girolamo published his twelve capriccios on various subjects, recalling both in the dedication and in a letter to the dedicatee, Alfonso d'Este, Prince of Modena, his Ferrarese background and his studies with Luzzaschi. (The dedication was opportune, since Monteverdi noted in a letter of 2 March 1624 that the Prince of Modena was beginning to take an interest in music.)[28] In 1626 the *Capricci* (minus the variation-capriccio on "Or che noi rimena") was combined with the *Recercari,* without the dedication of either collection, and the double volume was reissued in 1628, both times by Vincenti of Venice—Girolamo's first non-Roman publication since 1608.[29]

The last new keyboard print Frescobaldi brought out before leaving Rome was the second volume of toccatas, apparently issued by Nicolò Borbone, like its predecessor. This lavish production, with its handsome title page, an engraved portrait of Frescobaldi, and the inevitable laudatory sonnet,[30] formed with the first book a compendium for the keyboard player, as Grassi noted. Perhaps modeled on the keyboard collections issued by the Neapolitans Trabaci and Mayone, it contains music for both harpsichord and organ (two pedal toccatas, two Elevation toccatas, hymns, and Magnificats for liturgical use), and ranges in genre from the toccata and canzona to lighter variation sets, dances, and the traditional gesture of an intabulated Arcadelt madrigal (*Ancidetemi pur,* also set by Mayone in his 1603 *Diversi capricci* and by Trabaci—for harp—in his second book of ricercars of 1615).

This splendid volume is dedicated to Monsignor Luigi Gallo, Bishop of Ancona and Nuncio to Savoy, the nephew of a dean of the College of Cardinals who had accompanied Clement VIII to Ferrara in 1598. Alone of Girolamo's dedicatees, Gallo was a practicing musician and perhaps Girolamo's pupil: "Having no longer been able to deny so many, who for a long time have been begging me to publish the present recent efforts of mine, I did not wish to let them appear with any other protection than that of Your Most Illustrious Lordship for the long-standing service I have with you, since the time of the Most Illustrious Cardinal your Uncle: as also since you, in addition to many other talents of yours, are so richly adorned with this of playing the Harpsichord."[31] The contents of the volume, according to Girolamo, represent a "new manner" characterized by "the novelty of the artifice with which they are loomed and woven" and to which the qualities of Gallo's playing are particularly suited—"grace, ease, variety of measure, and elegance."

The genesis of one of these publications is described in a series of letters written between October 1623 and July 1625 by Francesco Toscani in Rome to his brother-in-law, the musician Francesco Nigetti, in Florence. Toscani had been requested to send Frescobaldi's latest productions to Nigetti but found that Girolamo had printed nothing new except "four madrigals to sing with the organ, without playing, which he says is not a good thing to send out" (probably the four secular works which appeared in anthologies in 1621–1622), but that he was putting in order a book to be printed in Venice, "since these publishers here abide by a strict price."[32] Only the two printings of the combined *Recercari-Capricci* volume were in fact issued in Venice, and Toscani cannot be referring to this collection, since he states in February 1624 that Frescobaldi "says that within 10 days it will be in order," although in the event it was at the last folio in April and still incomplete in mid-May.[33] Over a year later, Toscani went to see Girolamo, who told him that the book was finished "but he could not give it to me at present."[34] Toscani finally obtained the volume with considerable effort, "since he is a man so long drawn-out in handling his affairs as you could not imagine." "This week I have been there every day. I had to stay at his house for two solid hours waiting for him to recorrect it, as you see, for the printer has made some mistakes, but they are corrected."[35] The volume arrived safely in Florence and was so successful that Toscani offered to buy further copies for Nigetti's friends.[36]

The history of this anonymous volume and Grassi's account of Frescobaldi's career show Girolamo's reputation as a keyboard virtuoso, improviser, and composer at the height of his powers. His post at the Vatican and his additional income, together with powerful patronage, enabled him between 1615 and 1628 to publish works in every genre except opera, some of them splendid and expensive productions like the two books of toccatas. Grassi and Gallo testify to the ability and admiration of his students and patrons, and the frequent reprinting of his work is evidence of his widening influence. Toscani's letters show that already by 1625 Frescobaldi's works were being disseminated in Florence. Girolamo was not in the service of the Barberini family, the ultimate accolade of a Roman artist, and was still receptive to outside offers from a court where, as in Florence, his work was known and esteemed.

6

Florence, 1628–1634

By 1628, according to Libanori, Frescobaldi had become "tired of remaining in Rome." He was forty-five years old and had been organist of the Cappella Giulia for twenty years. He had published much of his important work and was acknowledged as the leading Italian virtuoso and composer of keyboard music. In 1628 Adriano Banchieri included Frescobaldi in his *Lettere armoniche,* along with Artusi, Diruta, Guami, and Monteverdi, praising Frescobaldi's "tasteggiamento soave," and about the same time Marchese Vincenzo Giustiniani (one of the most perceptive collectors and patrons of art in seventeenth-century Rome) declared, "For Organ and Harpsichord Geronimo Frescobaldi of Ferrara carries off all the honors, both in his skill and in the agility of his hands." Girolamo's growing reputation outside Italy is apparent in the 1629 keyboard manuscript of Regina Clara Im Hoff, which includes a "Couranta Frescobaldi" from the 1627 *Toccate,* transcribed in German keyboard tablature.[1]

Frescobaldi's income seems to have been sufficient to support a large family living a relatively settled life, and the precocious literary talent of his son Domenico, which was to lead to a comfortable benefice at St. Peter's, promised a secure future for the family. Girolamo's commitment to this Roman career was not, however, proof against offers of financial advantage and artistic recognition. But after the failure of the Mantuan project, such offers had to be firmer and more attractive. By 1628 comparatively few Italian courts could provide the necessary financial and artistic cachet—principally, Venice and Florence.

There is no record of Girolamo's preliminary negotiations with the Florentine court. The grand Duke of Tuscany, the seventeen-year-old Ferdinando II, passed through Rome incognito to meet Urban VIII in March 1628, and he may have encountered Frescobaldi at St. Peter's or at one of the splendid entertainments in his honor by the Aldobrandini. The banquet "with entertainment of music and song" given at the villa in Frascati, for example, was precisely the kind of occasion for which Girolamo was employed to find singers and presumably to perform with them.[2] The dedication of the 1628 *Canzoni,* Frescobaldi's only collection of instrumental ensemble music, to the Grand Duke was apparently intended to seal the contract with Ferdinando in the same manner as the dedication of *Toccate* I to the Duke of Mantua. The Chapter of St. Peter's, meeting on 22 November 1628, gave Girolamo permission "to leave the City at the pleasure of the Chapter," and six days later he drew his salary for the rest of the year and departed, not to return to the basilica for six years.[3]

The Florence to which Frescobaldi came presented a dramatic contrast with the artistic and intellectual activity of Rome. Architecturally, the city was a perfected achievement; newer trends in the visual arts were imported from outside Florence, as in the case of Pietro da Cortona. Florence indeed produced—and valued—Galileo Galilei, the greatest scientist of the century, but otherwise the spirit of historical and philological inquiry that had led the Camerata to the creation of opera was now employed in the trifling pastime of attempting to express Galilean cosmography in verse based on classical mythology. In music, the almost painful intensity of early opera, even *La Dafne* of Marco da Gagliano, had relapsed into the pretty diversions of the older intermedio, typified in Gagliano's *La Flora* of 1628. The Florence of the seventeenth century is best sought in Pisa, which has escaped the nineteenth-century incursion of genteel Anglo-American romantics and the invasion of twentieth-century tourism. Its situation and architectural vocabulary are those of Girolamo's Florence, and it is similarly underpopulated, beautiful, and lifeless.

The daily life of the Tuscan court is recorded in pitiless detail in letters, diaries, and administrative and financial records. Like most seventeenth-century courts it was peripatetic. While Florence remained the administrative center, the Grand Duke regularly visited Pisa (the seat of his order of Santo Stefano), Livorno, Pistoia, and Siena, hunted in Impruneta, and enjoyed the countryside at the numerous Medici villas. Under the influence of the Grand Duke's widowed mother and grandmother, women remarkable chiefly for their extreme piety, the daily life of the court was regulated by the course of the Church year, with a few specifically Florentine additions such as the carnival celebration of the city's patron, St. John the Baptist, in June. This annual cycle was varied by state visits, royal births, marriages, deaths, and the natural disasters that occupy so large a place in seventeenth-century chronicles.[4]

The musical establishment that Frescobaldi joined had been formed by Ferdinando I and assumed particular prominence during the last years of Cosimo II (d. 1621), when the ailing Grand Duke heard music in his chambers nearly every day and rewarded the performers with lavish gifts.[5] The *musica,* under the general supervision of Ferdinando Saracinelli, Balí of Volterra, was composed of four groups: "singers and players for chapel or chamber or stage or other needs; women maintained for the same purposes; string players [*sonatori di viola a braccio*] for dances and entertainments or for meals, who are called the ensemble of the *franzesi;* and wind players, called the ensemble of the *franciosini,* who also play at table."[6] The chapel-music contained three male sopranos, one male alto, three tenors, and one bass, plus five women, two lutes, two theorboes, keyboard, and a harp. The *concerto di ballo* consisted of five string players; the *franciosini* numbered ten performers on loud wind instruments such as cornetts, shawms, and sackbuts. Marco da Gagliano, the leading Florentine composer, served as *maestro di cappella* at court and at the Medici church of San Lorenzo. His colleagues in the *musica* included his brother Giovanni Battista, who was a theorbist, the virtuoso singers Vittoria Archilei and Settimia Caccini Ghivizzani (perhaps Girolamo's once-intended bride), and the lutenist Lorenzo Allegri. The famous trumpeter Girolamo Fantini also served in Ferdinando's household, and his name is linked with Frescobaldi's by Mersenne: "[Bourdelorius Medicus of Rome] says that he has heard from Girolamo Fantini, the most excellent trumpet player in all Italy, that he is able to play all the notes on his trumpet, and that he has played them with the organ of Cardinal Borghese, on which Girolamo Frescobaldi, organist of the Duke of Etruria and of the church of St. Peter's in Rome, played very skillfully."[7] As was customary, additional musicians were hired from other courts to supplement the resident *musica* on important occasions such as the production of *La Flora* for the Medici-Farnese wedding of 1628, and traveling musicians regularly visited Florence to perform for the court.[8]

No evidence exists defining Frescobaldi's duties in this musical organization. He is described as "Organista del Serenissimo Granduca di Toscana" on the title page of his *Arie musicali,* published in Florence in 1630. A summary of account-rolls lists him simply as "musico" at a salary of 25 scudi a month, confirmed by an account book for 1631–1632, while in 1633 he is described as "maestro di cappella" with an increased stipend of 29 scudi per month.[9] Whatever the precise nature of his employment, Girolamo at 300 to 348 scudi per annum was the highest paid musician on the salary rolls, where the normal figure is 120 scudi a year. Although below a dignitary such as the Secretary of State, the Balí Cioli, Frescobaldi ranked with the court sculptor Pietro Tacca, an artist of international reputation.[10]

The details of Girolamo's activity are as sparse as the records of its compensation. He may not even have spent the whole period in Florence. He certainly visited Venice, since he was entrusted there with a mosaic portrait to deliver to the Grand Duke.[11] Curiously neither Frescobaldi nor his family appears in a minutely detailed census of Florence taken in 1632.[12] From the meager evidence available, Girolamo was expected to participate in the performances of the court *musica* as organist and harpsichordist and to compose vocal chamber music. Outside the court, on at least one occasion he directed and perhaps composed music for an extraordinary religious celebration, served as organist of the Baptistery (San Giovanni) for at least a year, and instructed a number of pupils. (He is also named as organist of Santa Croce and San Lorenzo, but this is not substantiated by the surviving records of those churches.)[13] The evidence for these varied activities is best considered in the larger context of Florentine music during Frescobaldi's stay.

The string and wind bands provided music for court dancing and banquets, and the chamber musicians performed in private for more select audiences. Such occasions were frequent, but Girolamo's participation is mentioned only once, during the visit of M. de Béthune, French ambassador to the Holy See, in 1630. On 29 May the *franciosini* provided music for dinner, after which "everyone retired to the chamber of the Most Serene Archduchess, and stayed to hear the castrato Domenichino and Padre Onorato [a tenor] sing and to hear Frescobaldi play."[14] Girolamo's *Arie,* published the same year, probably reflects his association with the court singers.

In April 1629 Urban VIII initiated months of festivities in Rome and Florence by canonizing the Florentine Carmelite Andrea Corsini (1301–1374), Bishop of Fiesole. The Corsini, among the wealthiest of Florentine noble families, provided lavish celebrations in Rome and underwrote similar spectacles for Florence: processions, fireworks, an elaborate temporary façade for the Carmine, where the saint's body was displayed (fig. 12). The inaugural procession began at the Duomo and wound its way with the saint's banner across the river to the Carmine, the sound of trumpets alternating with the voices of the combined musicians of the cathedral and of the Grand Duke, more than sixty singers under the direction of Marco da Gagliano. The mass was sung by four choirs, and throughout the octave of the feast, music for two choirs was performed,

12. *The Carmine Decorated for the Canonization of Sant'Andrea Corsini* by Stefano della Bella

"most beautiful, since it had been entrusted to Signor Girolamo Frescobaldi, the celebrated musician of the Most Serene Grand Duke." Gagliano may have directed the vocal music while Frescobaldi presided at the richly decorated organ of the Carmine. The provision of music for the entire octave necessitated a considerable repertory for which a number of Gagliano's works would have been appropriate. Girolamo may also have contributed, since a manuscript in St. John Lateran in Rome contains two masses for double choir attributed to Frescobaldi, one on the *Aria di Fiorenza* or *Ballo del Granduca,* the most Florentine of all tunes.[15]

The archive of the guild of the Calimala, which administered the "Temple and Oratorio of San Giovanni," the Baptistery, shows that in 1630 Frescobaldi took on a previously unsuspected responsibility. "15 October 1630 . . . since by the death of Pierantonio di Pagolo Parigi the place of organist of the oratorio of San Giovanni was vacant . . . they chose and deputed the said Messer Girolamo Frescobaldi for one year organist of San Giovanni in place of Parigi."[16]

Francesco Nigetti's interest in Frescobaldi, whetted by the volume sent him by his brother-in-law Toscani, led Nigetti to study with Girolamo soon after the latter's arrival in Florence. The twenty-one-year-old Nigetti had previously studied organ and composition with Gagliano and spent 1629 working with Frescobaldi at the organs of Santa Felicità and San Lorenzo, an education that resulted in his appointment as organist and *maestro di cappella* of the cathedral at Prato. (There is a tradition that Girolamo had a hand in designing the new organ of that church.)[17] Despite the insistence of the Florentine theorist Giovanni Battista Doni that Frescobaldi was ignorant of the subtleties of ancient musical theory, Nigetti's later invention of an *omnicordo* may derive in part from the lore of the arcicembalo transmitted from Luzzaschi through Frescobaldi. The instrument on which Girolamo played at the palace of Cardinal d'Este in 1619 was clearly no ordinary harpsichord, since Frescobaldi was the only musician in Rome who could play it, and that only "with great preparation." Such instruments were known also at the Florentine court.[18]

Girolamo's teaching was perpetuated in Tuscany by a number of other pupils as well. Bernardo Roncagli served the Signoria of Lucca as *maestro di cappella,* Filippo Bandini became "organist in several churches of Florence," and the Pistoiese Valerio Spada was first organist of the Duomo in Florence from 1645 until his death in in 1649.[19] In the preface to his *Partitura di cembalo, et organo* of 1652, Don Scipione Giovanni, organist of the Mont'Oliveto in Florence, recalled that Frescobaldi had furnished the Florentine musician and mathematician Alberto del Vivaio with manuscript works for training children in music and sight-reading. In 1640 Vivaio wrote Nigetti asking to borrow "the first book of the Toccate of Frescobaldi in the first printing of which I spoke yesterday morning to Your Lordship."[20] Don Scipione himself repeated Girolamo's instructions from the second version of *Toccate* I almost verbatim in the preface to his *Intavolatura* of 1650. About 1659, when Don Severo Bonini was writing up his *Discorsi e regole,* there was still active in Florence a talented Roman woman, Lucia Coppi, who had studied with Frescobaldi.[21] Girolamo's influence was extended to a second generation of Florentine musicians through Nigetti, who had his own pupil Giovanni Maria Casini memorize all of Frescobaldi's music in the course of Casini's studies in 1674–1680.[22]

Most of Girolamo's documented activity in Florence occurred before 1630, the year of the great plague, the *male contagioso* that by June had advanced as far down the peninsula as Bologna. Florence was cut off from the outside world, and those of the inhabitants who were not ill themselves or tending the sick flocked to the churches to avert further disaster. The Grand Duke distributed 150,000 scudi in 1631 alone and made his daily round of the stricken city on foot, as he had allowed his horses and carriages to be requisitioned. The economic life of Florence came to a complete halt for six months of 1631 and again for four months in 1633; the total of the victims has been estimated at seven thousand, more than one-tenth of the population.[23] Under such circumstances musical performances were infrequent, except for an opera during the lull in the plague early in 1633.[24] When the disease broke out again that spring, as a last resort the miraculous image of the Madonna from Impruneta was carried into Florence; "from her Coming the Illness began to recede,"[25] and within six weeks it was over. Ferdinando showed his gratitude by presenting the church in Impruneta with a silver altar-frontal, on which he is still to be seen kneeling before the Madonna, and set about trying to rebuild the Tuscan economy.

During these same years Florence was subjected to another form of attack as well: the trial of its most distinguished citizen, Galileo Galilei, by the Inquisition. The prosecution of Galileo showed the meanest side of Urban VIII's character, since it was pressed because the pope believed that Galileo had caricatured him as Simplicio in the *Dialogue on the Great World Systems.* Galileo was summoned to Rome late in 1632 and tried in April 1633 by a commission that included Cardinal Francesco Barberini and Galileo's former student Cardinal Guido Bentivoglio as Supreme Inquisitor General—neither of them unsympathetic to the great scientist. On 22 June 1633 the seventy-year-old Galileo, clad in the white habit of a penitent, knelt in the hall of Santa Maria sopra Minerva and abjured his errors and heresies, the victim of a campaign of intellectual enmity, forged evidence, and the injured pride of Urban VIII.[26]

Although they antedate the plague and the trial of Galileo, Frescobaldi's *Arie musicali* (issued by Galileo's publisher, Giovanni Battista Landini) sometimes breathe the same spirit. Along with light, dancelike works, the collection contains "spiritual sonnets" that evoke the perfervid religiosity of seventeenth-century Florence. The first of the two *Arie* volumes is dedicated to the Grand Duke (the presentation copy still exists in the Biblioteca Nazionale in Florence), the second to Roberto Obizzi, the Grand Duke's Master of the Horse, perhaps in compliment to Obizzi's elevation to the marquisate of Orciano in April 1630.[27] Obizzi was a Paduan noble from a distinguished and intellectual Ferrarese family, and in his dedicatory letter Frescobaldi alluded once again—for the last time—to his own Ferrarese birth and training.[28]

The content of the two books of *arias,* however, is an indication that Frescobaldi had traveled far from the musical tradition of Ferrara. The collection contains strophic arias and through-composed madrigals (itself a Florentine distinction), but its most striking feature is the inclusion of eleven works in *stile recitativo,* a style that Frescobaldi had avoided previously. The importance of these settings is further emphasized by their placement at the head of each book. This is all the more surprising because pure recitative was beginning to lose its popularity, even in the city of its origin.[29] The *Arie* was in fact the only collection including monodies to be published in Florence between 1619 and 1635, and when the Florentine composers took up the genre again they cultivated a markedly lighter and less declamatory style.[30] The inclusion of settings based on the Romanesca and Ruggiero seems to echo a Roman vogue of about 1615, followed by Monteverdi in the Romanesca variations in his seventh madrigal book of 1619. The *Arie* also contains settings of more recent basses, the Passacagli and Ciaccona. The presence among the texts in the *Arie* of a *lettera amorosa* and a *partenza amorosa* (both texts set by Giovanni Valentini in his *Musiche a due* of 1622) also points to the influence of Monteverdi's seventh book. The attempt to discern other possible stylistic influences through concordances is unrewarding. Only eight texts from the *Arie* are so far identified: two by Della Casa (1590), one by Desiderio Cavalcabo (1590), one by Marino, two by Girolamo Preti (1614), and two by Francesco Balducci (1630), author of two oratorio librettos, a version of one of which was set by Carissimi. Frescobaldi does not seem to have relied on the usual Florentine authors of *poesia per musica.* (Indeed, if we are to believe Doni, Girolamo's literary culture was so sketchy that his wife had to explain the more difficult words in the texts he set.)[31] At least one text, "Degnati, o gran Fernando," as well as the dedicatory sonnet, "Signor, c'ora fra gl'ostri," must have been written to order and perhaps represent early efforts of Domenico Frescobaldi, of whom there survives a volume of Latin poetry and epigrams written about 1632–1634.[32]

In the general context of Frescobaldi's work, the *Arie,* his one Florentine production, seems an anomaly occasioned by the predominance of vocal music at the Tuscan court and a lingering local tradition of *stile recitativo.* And yet this same insistence on affective declamation is fundamental to Frescobaldi's art as a keyboard composer, although there it is balanced by his remarkable contrapuntal sense. The classic expression of this fusion is Girolamo's *Fiori musicali,* the collection of three organ masses and related works published the year after the composer's return from Florence. It is tempting to regard this volume of instrumental, contrapuntal, and for the most part liturgical music as the counterpart or even the reaction to Frescobaldi's Florentine experience as embodied in the *Arie.*

By 1634 Florence had little to offer Girolamo. Its intellectual achievement had been humiliated in the person of Galileo, its population was decimated, and the Grand Duke's opportunities for patronage were exhausted by the virtual bankruptcy of the state. More important, Frescobaldi had been offered the ultimate prize of a Roman artist: the Barberini summoned him back to the City to enter their service.

7

Rome, 1634–1643

Twenty years earlier Frescobaldi had protested to the Mantuan court that he did not want to leave Rome, even for an exceptional salary. Each of his absences from the City marked some significant point in his career, and each return ushered in a new phase of development. Girolamo's return from Mantua in 1615 had opened the central Roman period of his career, the years of his establishment as a composer. On his return from Florence in 1634 he issued a series of retrospective, almost valedictory publications and devoted himself to increased activity as a teacher and performer.

In the six years of Girolamo's absence much had changed in Rome, now entering the last decade of the Barberini papacy. Two of Bernini's principal projects had been realized, the bronze baldacchino in St. Peter's and the Barberini palace at the Quattro Fontane—symbolic statements of the City's sacred and secular grandeur under Urban VIII and his nephews. A third project, the systematization of the central complex of St. Peter's, was under way as the crowning artistic effort of Urban's papacy. As the pope aged, the younger members of his family assumed greater prominence in politics and artistic patronage. The principal patrons were the first and third of Urban's three nephews. The eldest, Francesco (fig. 13), was commonly called simply "il Cardinal Barberino" as the senior cardinal of the family. His coat of arms, as it appears for example on the 1637 edition of Frescobaldi's *Toccate* I, consisted of the Barberini bees differenced by a Latin cross. Antonio, created a cardinal in 1628 over Francesco's objections, was called "il Cardinal Antonio Barberino" and bore the Barberini arms undifferenced, superposed on a cross denoting his rank as Prior of Malta, in which form it appears on the title page of the *Fiori musicali.* (His uncle Antonio, with whom he is sometimes confused, was called "il Car-

13. Cardinal Francesco Barberini, portrait by Andrea Sacchi

dinal Sant'Onofrio" and carried the family arms differenced by a Franciscan device.)[1]

Francesco had the largest income, the strongest will, and the widest intelligence of the three brothers. His immense revenues were derived from a variety of benefices: he was Vice-Chancellor of the Church, Archpriest of St. Peter's, titular Abbot of Farfa. A connoisseur of literature, sculpture, architecture, painting (one of Poussin's first Roman patrons), and music, he employed all these to enhance the glory of the Barberini.

By 1632 Bernini's work on the Palazzo Barberini was far enough advanced to permit remounting the first of Francesco's lavish opera productions, the *Sant'Alessio* of the young Pistoiese (and future pope) Giulio Rospigliosi. These presentations—Rospigliosi's texts set by Landi, Marco Marazzoli, Domenico and Virgilio Mazzocchi, Luigi Rossi, and Michel Angelo Rossi—were staged with sumptuous costumes, scenery, dances, and machines. Each Carnival season the Barberini produced a sacred opera, a comic opera, and in addition a Quarantore, or Forty Hours' Devotion, in which the Sacrament was adored in an *apparato* by artists of the caliber of Bernini and Pietro da Cortona. These annual festivities continued until the death of Urban VIII in 1644 and the Cardinals' resultant flight to France.

Francesco bore the financial brunt of these spectacles, but Antonio also underwrote some of them (probably with some assistance from his brother, who even paid for having Antonio's false teeth mended). In 1634 Antonio offered a magnificent joust in Piazza Navona for the Carnival season, an occasion that demonstrated the Ferrarese accommodation with Rome in the thirty-six years since the devolution: the text and decorations were the work of Ferrarese artists in collaboration with Enzo Bentivoglio, now artistic adviser to Taddeo Barberini; Cornelio Bentivoglio rode as champion; and Guido published an account of the event.[2] (It is tempting to link the *Capriccio sopra la battaglia,* which Frescobaldi published in the 1637 *Aggiunta* to the first book of toccatas, with such an occasion.) In 1642 Antonio undertook the production of the Rospigliosi–Luigi Rossi opera *Il palazzo incantato.*

The initiative of Girolamo's final return to Rome was taken by Cardinal Francesco Barberini, who, as both Archpriest of the Vatican and a patron of immense wealth, was in a unique position to enhance every aspect of Frescobaldi's career. Cardinal Francesco first paid Frescobaldi "sc. 100 in cash for assistance for the Journey that he must make from Florence to Rome with his family."[3] (At their return to Rome in April 1634 the family consisted of Orsola, the children Domenico, Stefano, and Caterina, Orsola's sister, and a Florentine servant.) They moved into a house near the bottom of the Salita Magnanapoli (fig. 14), the steep descent leading past Villa Aldobrandini down to the column of Trajan; for the house's rent the Cardinal paid Frescobaldi 30 scudi semiannually.[4] By August 1634 Girolamo was enrolled among the members of Cardinal Francesco's household at a monthly salary of 3.60 scudi, with additional gratuities.[5] At St. Peter's the Cardinal was responsible for a supplement of 24 scudi per annum to Frescobaldi's salary as organist, raising the total to 96 scudi a

14. Marco Sadeler, *Trajan's Column and the neighborhood of Monte Magnanapoli*

year.[6] For Girolamo's talented son Domenico, Cardinal Francesco later obtained the reversion of a benefice there and paid for the necessary documents.[7]

The payment records of the Cappella Giulia suggest that Girolamo remained in Rome during the last decade of his life, except for a possible visit to Venice for the publication by Vincenti of the *Fiori musicali,* whose dedication is dated from Venice, 20 August 1635. (Despite the dedication of the *Canzoni* from Venice, 10 January 1635, Girolamo seems to have been in Rome at the time.)[8] In 1629 Paolo Agostini had died, to be succeeded as *maestro di cappella* of the Cappella Giulia by Virgilio Mazzocchi, who later assumed the musical direction of Cardinal Francesco Barberini's household as well.[9] Under Mazzocchi's direction the services of the Cappella continued to increase in splendor, and Frescobaldi regularly participated as first organist. In 1636, for example, the feast of Peter and Paul was celebrated with vespers from five choirs and "Cornetti 3. for the Cuppula," enthusiastically described by Della Valle as "a great big piece of music . . ., I know not whether for twelve or sixteen choirs, with an echo choir at the top of the cupola, which I understand in the spaciousness of that vast temple made marvellous effects."[10] The anniversary of the Dedication was kept with six choirs, each with its own continuo organ, accompanied by pairs of violins, alto and tenor *viole,* cornetts, trombones, and theorboes, as well as three violoni and two spinets.[11]

Frescobaldi seems always to have been concerned about the condition of the instruments on which he performed, and less than a month after his return to St. Peter's extensive repairs were made to the portable organ.[12] These were apparently ineffective, however, since in March 1636 the Fabbriceria of San Pietro commissioned a new portable organ at the suggestion of Cardinal Francesco. The instrument was to be placed on a wheeled platform to facilitate the necessary moving. The construction of the organ was entrusted to Girolamo's associate Ennio Bonifatij, *maestro d'organi* of the basilica, who began work late in 1636 and finished by the spring of 1638. Despite its intended mobility, the completed instrument contained no less than fourteen registers, more than in many large stationary instruments.[13]

The careers of both the *maestro di cappella* and the organist of the Cappella Giulia, Virgilio Mazzocchi and Frescobaldi, reflect the overlapping relationships between the singers of the Cappella Sistina, the singers and instrumentalists associated with the Cappella Giulia, and the household *musiche* of the Pope and his nephews. Mazzocchi seems to have assumed the direction of Cardinal Francesco's musical establishment about

1636, and his first documented opera for the Cardinal, *Chi soffre speri,* was produced for Carnival of 1637. Mazzocchi was responsible both for these large public spectacles and for the private musical performances in the Cardinal's household. Frescobaldi's role is less certain; his name appears rarely in the Cardinal's financial records except in connection with his regular salary and rent payments. Since detailed accounts survive for many of the operatic productions, including the names of the keyboard players (many of them also employed in the Cappella Giulia), it seems probable that Girolamo did not take part in the yearly operatic spectacles.

Girolamo's receipt of a pension from Cardinal Barberini did not necessarily require regular personal attendance on the Cardinal; his status as a *straordinario* in Francesco's household resembled the *servitù particolare* of a painter or sculptor, who in return for his pension was expected only to offer his patron the first refusal of completed works.[14] Nonetheless, although there is no direct evidence to link Girolamo's service with Cardinal Francesco's household music, Frescobaldi's history as a performing musician—his keyboard performances for Francesco Borghese, Ferdinando Gonzaga, and the guests of Cardinal d'Este, his service in the *musiche* of the Bentivoglio, the Aldobrandini, and the Medici—suggests the small, aristocratic concert as a preferred milieu. Girolamo's choice of residence tends to support this. In seventeenth-century Rome the Salita Magnanapoli was about as far from St. Peter's as it was possible to live but convenient to Francesco's palace of the Cancelleria, the papal palace at the Quirinal, and the Palazzo Barberini at the Quattro Fontane. These various Barberini palaces housed a splendid collection of keyboard instruments, so that a performer in their service had a choice of organs and harpsichords in a wide spectrum of ranges, registers, types, and national styles of building.

Cardinal Franceso's *famiglia* included four resident musicians: three singers (two of them also members of the papal chapel) and a performer on plucked string instruments; Frescobaldi and Johann Hieronymus Kapsberger were nonresident musicians.[15] The household musicians formed the nucleus of Cardinal Francesco's private *musica,* which consisted of a viol consort, other instrumentalists, and singers, who performed regularly at select "academies." Their repertory included not only music by composers of the Barberini circle but also works of Nenna, Gesualdo, and Monteverdi, among others.[16] The cultivation of the consort of viols in the Cardinal's musical establishment is surprising in view of the general lack of interest in the viola da gamba in Italy and the very ambiguity of the term "viola," which was applied to members of the violin and gamba families indifferently. Nonetheless, a chest of viols formed part of the Barberini instrumentarium, and in 1632 Cherubino Waesich, who later appeared as a continuo player in Cardinal Francesco's operatic productions, published a collection of five-part canzonas "to play with the viole da gamba," followed by two concerted madrigals. The preface to Domenico Mazzocchi's important *Madrigali* of 1638, dedicated to Cardinal Francesco, specifically mentions performance at the Cardinal's academies, and the collection includes a setting of Tasso's "Chiudesti i lumi, Armida" designated "Ruggiero a 5. per le Viole." It is noteworthy, therefore, that the category Frescobaldi most enlarged in his 1634 reworking of the 1628 ensemble canzonas was the canzona for four instruments and continuo (CATB, Bc), appropriate for viol consort.

Although Frescobaldi's fame extended well beyond the boundaries of Italy in his last years, he had an articulate opponent in the Barberini household itself, the theorist Giovanni Battista Doni, Francesco's secretary. Père Marin Mersenne, in his *Harmonie universelle* of 1636–1637, had included "Fresco Baldi" with Marenzio and Monteverdi among "des autres excellens Compositeurs" not known to him personally. Even this restricted recognition drew a heated denial from Doni: "Touching the fact that you put Frescobaldi on the level of the most esteemed musicians in Italy, with Luca Marenzio and Monteverdi, you should not deceive yourself in this. For there are today at Rome a dozen musicians who are more esteemed than he. But being perhaps the most able man there is today in Italy for playing the organ and harpsichord and composing pieces for them, the ignorant deem that he has gained the farthest point of this profession." For Doni, the real musician was the *melopoios,* a theorist trained in the musical lore of classical antiquity, unlike Frescobaldi: "He is so little knowledgeable that he does not know what is a major or minor semitone and scarcely plays on the metabolic keys (which one commonly calls *chromatic*). And when he does not understand some rather unusual word in vernacular poetry, he asks his wife's opinion of it, who knows more about it than he."[17] Doni returned to the attack in another letter to Mersenne concerning musical illustrations for a treatise: "As to Frescobaldi, he is the least appropriate of all; seeing that he is a very coarse man, although he plays the organ perfectly and may be excellent for composing fantasies, dance music, and similar things; but for setting the words [*accomoder les paroles*], he is extremely ignorant and devoid of discrimination, so that one can say he has all his knowledge at the ends of his fingers. And I doubt not that he is more esteemed far from here than where he is."[18] In the treatise *On the Excellence of Ancient Music,* eventually published in 1647, Doni went so far as to declare that "a certain ragged old man" had persuaded Frescobaldi to approve the equal temperament of semitones "against the judgment of his ears" by "frequent drinking-bouts *gratis.*"[19] Doni's disciple Pietro Della Valle was moved to reply obliquely in a discourse addressed to Lelio Guidiccioni, "On the music of our times that it is not at all inferior, indeed it is better than that of the past" (1640), in which he chided that "even Your Lordship confesses [that Frescobaldi] has astonished and often moved you."[20]

In the midst of a busy performing career Girolamo found time to publish, with the financial assistance of Cardinals Francesco and Antonio, three important collections and to put the most significant portion of his earlier work in final form. The first of these publications to appear was the ensemble *Canzoni,* issued in 1634 by Vincenti of Venice with a dedication (dated 10 January 1635) to Desiderio Scaglia, Cardinal of Cremona. The collection is by no means merely a reissue of the 1628 version; additions and deletions of some works and extensive alteration of others show a continuing development of Girolamo's style as a composer of instrumental ensemble music.

The *Fiori musicali,* also published by Vincenti, represents Frescobaldi's crowning effort as a composer of liturgical organ music. This collection of three organ masses (the masses of Sunday, of the Apostles, and of the Madonna traditional since Girolamo Cavazzoni's *Intabulatura d'organo* of the 1540s) and other related works is dedicated to "Cardinal Antonio Barberino"—as the arms of the title page show, the younger Antonio, not his uncle the ascetic Capuchin monk—in a letter dated from Venice, 20 August 1635. This is a tiresome piece of official flattery, but in the chatty incoherence of the subsequent address to the reader we seem to catch the authentic tones of Girolamo's speech:

> Having always been desirous (for that talent granted me by God) to rejoice with my labors the students of the said profession, I have always shown with my Publications, in tablature, and in score of every sort of caprices and inventions a sign of my desire, that everyone seeing, and studying my works should be pleased and profited. With this book of mine I will say only that my principal end is to please Organists having made such composition in such a style of playing, that they will be able to respond at Mass [as] at Vespers, since I know that this is of much profit to them and they can also use the said Verses at their pleasure, ending in their Cadences the Canzonas and the Ricercars, when they would appear too long.

The mass-selections of the *Fiori* thus complement the music for vespers included in the second book of toccatas. The *Fiori* has the further pedagogic aim of encouraging practice in reading from open score, which "like a touchstone distinguishes and makes known the true gold of virtuous deeds from the Ignorant." The *Fiori* is the only publication Girolamo expressly dedicated to a member of the Barberini family, and the tunes of the *Bergamasca* and the *Girolmeta,* on which he based two capriccios, recur prominently in *Chi soffre speri,* one of Cardinal Francesco's operas for Carnival of 1639. The collection survives in numerous copies, although J. S. Bach's is now lost, and was successful enough to inspire almost immediate imitation. In 1642 Vincenti published Fra Antonio Croci's *Frutti musicali,* a collection of organ masses and other works intended to prepare students—beginning with those as yet unable to span an octave—to perform Frescobaldi's works. In 1645 Vincenti issued Fra G. B. Fasolo's *Annuale,* which contains organ music for both mass and vespers and concludes with four fugues on subjects prominently treated by Frescobaldi in the *Fiori* and *Capricci*: the Bergamasca, Girometta, Bassa Fiamenga, and Ut, Re, Mi, Fa, Sol, La.[21]

Girolamo's continuing concern for his earlier productions is apparent in the re-editions of his two books of toccatas issued in Rome in 1637 by the versatile Nicolò Borbone under the patronage of Cardinal Francesco Barberini. An *Aggiunta* (*Toccate* I, p. 69) comprises the last keyboard works published by Frescobaldi. (The authenticity of the posthumous canzonas that Vincenti printed in 1645 is doubtful; see Appendix I.A.) The *Aggiunta* contains balletti, correnti, passacagli, ciaccone, variations, and two programmatic capriccios on "la Battaglia" and "la Pastorale." For the sake of consistency, Girolamo removed the variations on the *Ciaccona* and on the *Passacagli* from the reprint of *Toccate* II, since the same material had received its ultimate transmutation in the *Cento partite* of the *Aggiunta.* Frescobaldi may have composed the *Aggiunta* in 1635–1636, on the evidence of the music paper supplied him from Cardinal Francesco's household expenses.[22]

The question of Frescobaldi's further development after these last publications is tantalizing. Della Valle observed in 1640 that "if today he uses another manner, with more *galanterie* in the modern style, which does not please Your Lordship so much, he must do so, because with experience he will have learned that to please everyone, this manner is more elegant, although less learned; and while it can succeed in indeed giving delight, the music and the player can demand nothing more." Unfortunately, the only evidence to document such stylistic development is to be found in manuscript works attributed to Frescobaldi, of uncertain date and questionable authenticity. Among the most significant of these are the codices now in the Chigi collection in the Vatican and an immense anthology of Italian keyboard music copied out between 1637 and 1640 in New German tablature and presented in a sumptuous format—clearly a commission from a wealthy German family, perhaps the great banking house of Fugger (see Appendix I.B and Catalogue I.B).

The manuscript circulation of both authentic and dubious works of Frescobaldi is an index of the growing celebrity that continued to bring him pupils, now from Germany as well as Italy. Most of Girolamo's pupils, like the composer Luigi Battiferri and the publisher Giovanni Angelo Muti, are known only to specialists. (There is no evidence that Michel Angelo Rossi, often described as a pupil of Frescobaldi, ever studied with him.)[23] But by 1637 Girolamo's fame in Germany was such that a young court organist, Johann Jacob Froberger, set out from Vienna in October of that year with a subsidy of two hundred florins granted by the Emperor. Froberger remained in Rome until 1641; thus his stay coincided with the years of Frescobaldi's best documented activity as a performer. (Girolamo was so highly regarded in Germany in the decades after his death that the claim to have studied with him became almost a joke, which may explain why Johann Kaspar Kerll, Heckelauer, and Franz Tunder have been mistakenly cited as pupils of Frescobaldi.)[24]

Frescobaldi's career as organist of the Cappella Giulia, household musician to the Barberini, and teacher continued the activities of his earlier years. In this last decade, however, he also entered a new field, that of the oratorio and public concert, in one of the most celebrated musical institutions of seventeenth-century Rome, the Oratorio del Crocifisso. The Arciconfraternita del Santissimo Crocifisso di San Marcello—to give it its full name—originated in devotion to a miraculous crucifix in the church of San Marcello on the Corso. A group of Roman prelates and nobles founded a society, later raised to a confraternity, of the Holy Cross, confirmed by Clement VII Medici in 1526. The organization grew rapidly in wealth and influence, and in 1562 the first stone of the present building, designed by Giacomo della Porta, was laid. The Oratorio is a large, hall-like open space, decorated with a fresco cycle depicting the history and miracles of the True Cross. The French viol player André Maugars, who published an account of his visit to Rome in 1639, described the church as being smaller than the Sainte-Chapelle in Paris: "At the end . . . there is a very spacious Gallery with an Organ of medium size very sweet and very fitting to the voices. On the two sides of the Church, there are again two other small Platforms, where there were the most excellent of the Instrumental Music."[25]

Devotional societies like the Crocifisso quite openly presented elaborate musical performances as a means of attracting crowds. While St. Philip Neri's Oratorio became a center of sacred music with Italian texts, the Crocifisso specialized in the Latin oratorio, the *concertato* motet, and instrumental music. The principal performances were presented from three to six o'clock on Friday afternoons in Lent. The best musicians in Rome were engaged (many of them from St. Peter's), and each year the governors of the Arciconfraternita selected a well-known maestro to supervise the music and celebrated preachers to deliver the sermons.[26]

The surviving records of the Crocifisso, still insufficiently studied, provide some details of these performances. The Oratorio possessed a large positive organ and owned or rented a smaller portable instrument. (The 14′ flute principal of the former was probably the reason Maugars found it "très doux et très propre pour les voix.")[27] In 1643 another small instrument was purchased from Girolamo's colleague Ennio Bonifatij, maker of the new movable organ for St. Peter's.[28] While the use of organs occasions no surprise, it is more unusual that the harpsichord formed a regular part of the instrumental ensemble at the Crocifisso as early as 1611.[29] During the years that Frescobaldi performed there—always at the harpsichord, never at the organ—two instruments were generally employed, and on occasion a *spinetta* as well. In 1641 a *spinetta* was rented from the instrument builder and tuner Boni da Cortona, who also looked after the Barberini instruments.[30] The principal harpsichord seems to have belonged to one of the officials of the Arciconfraternita, while in 1639 a second instrument was brought from the Vatican (perhaps the one that Cardinal Antonio Barberini kept there).[31]

The records of the Crocifisso are too fragmentary to provide a connected account of its musical activities and of Frescobaldi's participation in them during the last decade of his life. The only reference to music in the materials from 1635 is a bill from Bonifatij for adjusting and repairing the organ. In 1636 he rented the Crocifisso a portable organ for the Lenten music and a harpsichord was provided for a celebration of the Forty Hours.[32] In 1637 the music during Lent was directed by Orazio Benevoli, organist and *maestro di cappella* at Girolamo's former church, Santa Maria in Sassia, and Cortona was employed to tune the harpsichords.[33] Only an unitemized receipt for payment to musicians survives from 1638. The documentation for 1639, however, is unusually full: Bonifatij was paid for the transport of an organ, a *spinetta,* and two harpsichords,[34] and the performances themselves are described in a firsthand account by Maugars.

The documentation for 1640 is the most complete of the period of Girolamo's association with the Crocifisso. The most important of these records is a sheet listing the performers for each of the five Fridays in Lent. The ensemble for the first Friday consisted of four sopranos and pairs of contraltos, tenors, and basses. The two harpsichords were played by Frescobaldi (paid sc. 1.20) and "Gio: batta" (Ferrini? paid sc. 1); one of the two organists was Francesco Muti. The group was completed by three lutes, a violone, a lira, and two violins. The second Friday in Lent, at which Girolamo did not appear, featured Loreto Vittori and Marc'Antonio Pasqualini, perhaps the most famous castrati of the day, at 3.05 scudi each. With the addition of the organist of San Giovanni dei Fiorentini as second harpsichordist, the other forces duplicated those of the preceding week. The two great castrati again appeared on the third Friday, with Frescobaldi at the harpsichord. Only Pasqualini sang the fourth Friday, and neither appeared on Passion Friday. Girolamo played at all the performances.[35] No further payment records of this precision have come to light, but from the use of two harpsichords in succeeding years it seems possible that Frescobaldi continued to perform at the Crocifisso.[36]

A setting by Frescobaldi of a Lamentation for Maundy Thursday was included in a manuscript of Roman liturgical and devotional music for Holy Week, Easter, and the Easter season (Bologna Q 43; see Catalogue III.B.7). Many of the works are anonymous, but the composers named include the architect Carlo Rainaldi, Marco Marazzoli, Bonifazio Graziani, and Francesco Foggia. (Monteverdi is also included, in a contrafactum of the *Lamento di Arianna* set as a *Lamento della Madalena.*) Marazzoli's oratorios were performed at the Chiesa Nuova, but both Foggia and Graziani were associated with the Crocifisso. Foggia directed the music for Lent of 1641, and Graziani supervised the Lenten music for 1650.[37] Since the contents of the manuscript seem to date about 1640–1650, it is possible that Frescobaldi's Lamentation setting is one of his latest works and was intended for performance at the Crocifisso.

The piecemeal record of the Lenten performances is filled out by Maugars's account of the music for 1639, which names the Crocifisso as the best place to hear recitative style, "not at all in use in France." This was embodied in Latin role oratorios on subjects from the Old Testament and Gospel texts appropriate to Lent:

> The voices began with a Psalm in the form of a Motet, and then all the instruments did a very fine *symphonie.* Afterward the voices sang a Story from the Old Testament, in the form of a spiritual drama, like that of Susanna, of Judith and Holofernes, of David and Goliath. Each singer represented a character in the Story and expressed perfectly well the force of the words. Following that, one of the most celebrated preachers gave the homily. When that was finished, the Music recited the Gospel of the day, like the story of the woman of Samaria, the woman of Canaan, Lazarus, the Magdalen, and the Passion of Our Lord: the Singers imitating perfectly the various personages described by the Evangelist.[38]

These works were executed by a small group of singers, two on a part for choral passages, with extra sopranos who were apparently soloists, accompanied by two violins and a large body of continuo instruments: two harpsichords, a spinet, two organs, three lutes, a lira, a violone, and an "Arcibasso" (probably a double-bass gamba).[39] These may have been divided up and allotted to different protagonists for characterization, as in the works of Cavalieri and Monteverdi. Although Maugars simply notes that the instruments played a *symphonie,* later in his letter he describes a variety of instrumental pieces: "As to the Instrumental Ensemble, it was composed of an Organ, a large Harpsichord, a Lira, two or three Violins, and two or three Archlutes. Sometimes a Violin played alone with the Organ, and then another answered; another time all three played different parts together, and then all the instruments took up together." These instrumental interludes also included improvisations on bass patterns: "Sometimes an Archlute made a thousand variations on ten or twelve notes, each note of five or six measures; then the other played the same thing, although differently." Maugars leaves no doubt as to the identity of the principal instrumentalist: "But above all the great *Friscobaldi* made appear a thousand sorts of inventions on his Harpsichord, the Organ always holding firm."

Maugars's phrase, "l'Orgue tenant tousiours ferme," is vague, but it seems to suggest that the organ sustained the harmonies of a standard bass-chord progression while Girolamo improvised variations on the harpsichord. (There is some evidence for such a practice in connection with one pattern, the Bergamasca, which figures in another form in the *Fiori musicali*).[40] Maugars's concluding eulogy stresses Frescobaldi's brilliance as an improvisor: "It is not without cause that this famous organist of St. Peter's has acquired so much fame in Europe; because, although his printed works give sufficient witness of his ability, in order to judge his profound knowledge it is necessary to hear him improvise toccatas full of contrapuntal devices and admirable inventions. That is why he well merits your proposing him, as a model to all our organists, to make them want to come to hear him at Rome."[41]

Most of Frescobaldi's activity in his last decade—his publications and his performances at St. Peter's, in the Barberini household, and at the Crocifisso—was directly or indirectly connected with the Barberini. As these years revealed, that family's power rested on a knife-edge. Their administration of the papacy, while an artistic triumph, was a financial and political disaster compounded by bad weather, scarcity of food, high prices, floods, and epidemics. Any major challenge would uncover the maladministration of the Cardinals, and only the life of their ailing uncle stood between them and ruin. The final catastrophe was precipitated by Urban's seizure of the Farnese fief of Castro in 1641. The Duke of Parma counterattacked and advanced down the peninsula. Despite the enormous sums poured into the hands of Taddeo Barberini, Prince Prefect of the City, the papal forces—when there were any at all—were largely unarmed and unprovisioned and no match for the Duke and his army. By 1642 the situation was so far beyond control that Urban simply retired into the Vatican (which had a secret passage leading to Castel Sant'Angelo) and left the Roman people to their fate.[42]

Francesco Nigetti's nephew Hippolito described life in Rome during the siege in a series of vivid letters to his uncle in Florence. The City was overrun with soldiers, who had driven the inhabitants out of their houses, "and they have made Gates at the head of the Streets to be able to lock them all in, so that they may not go about Rome in the evening; in daytime one sees nothing but Soldiers."[43] The Prince Prefect, theoretically responsible for the defense of Rome, had hurried off to Ferrara, which the Venetians planned to flood by diverting the Po. After Urban's retirement to the Vatican the terrified citizens formed a militia: "everyone has buckled on a sword and dagger . . . everyone is afraid, and the Banks are locked and no longer pay anyone . . . they go around the City all day sounding drums to warn now this quarter, now that one."[44] By some miracle the Duke of Parma retreated from Rome, which he could easily have taken, and the citizens were spared the ultimate consequences of the mismanagement of Urban and his nephews.

The War of Castro was not the only sign that the world in which Frescobaldi lived and worked was breaking up. In 1637 Donna Olimpia Aldobrandini died, the matriarch "who in the time of her pope ruled Rome at her pleasure and was the mother of princes and cardinals." With the death of Cardinal Ippolito Aldobrandini the following year the family became extinct in the male line. Guido Bentivoglio, whose career, like Frescobaldi's, had owed much to the Aldobrandini, was moved to reflect in a long threnody that "Death mows impartially with his inexorable scythe, and brings down every human life, every earthly exaltation."[45]

Throughout this period of political upheaval Girolamo continued to perform at St. Peter's, drawing his salaries for January and February of 1643 and signing the receipts himself (fig. 15).[46] On 19 February, just before a fresh outbreak of rumors of war, he was seized with a high fever. He received the last rites and died on the night of Sunday, 1 March. Although he was resident in the parish of San Lorenzo de' Monti, his body was hurriedly carried to the basilica of the Holy Twelve Apostles, where his son Domenico had been baptized, and was buried there on Monday morning. His funeral mass was sung by "the principal musicians of this city"—perhaps his colleagues at St. Peter's or the Congregazione di Santa Cecilia.[47]

The Roman archives have so far failed to yield a will for either Girolamo or his widow. After Frescobaldi's death his family moved to Borgo Vecchio, presumably for Domenico's greater convenience to the Vatican. In 1649 Stefano Frescobaldi died, followed in 1651 by Orsola del Pino; Caterina died in 1687, apparently insane. With the death of Domenico Frescobaldi in 1688 Girolamo's posterity became extinct. Urban VIII survived Girolamo by a year, and Cardinal Bentivoglio died during the ensuing conclave, which was on the point of electing him pope.[48]

Frescobaldi's central role in the formation of seventeenth-century Italian keyboard style was recognized by his contemporaries. In his *Discorsi e regole* (ca. 1659) Don Severo Bonini asserted that Frescobaldi "had found a new manner of playing harpsichords" which was now accepted by everyone, and whoever "does not play according to his style is not esteemed."[49] Although Antimo Liberati, writing in 1684, characterized Frescobaldi as "unhappy and inept" in vocal writing, he acknowledged him "the wonder of the keyboard in our times, both with the hands, and with the pen, as so many of his written and printed works show us."[50]

Frescobaldi's keyboard music continued to exert a vital influence for over a century after his death. His immediate successors continued to compose in the genres he had rendered exemplary, a few of them even attempting the moribund ricercar, and his name was routinely attached to anonymous manuscript pieces and collections. It is in fact possible that the very respects in which this repertory differs from its Frescobaldian

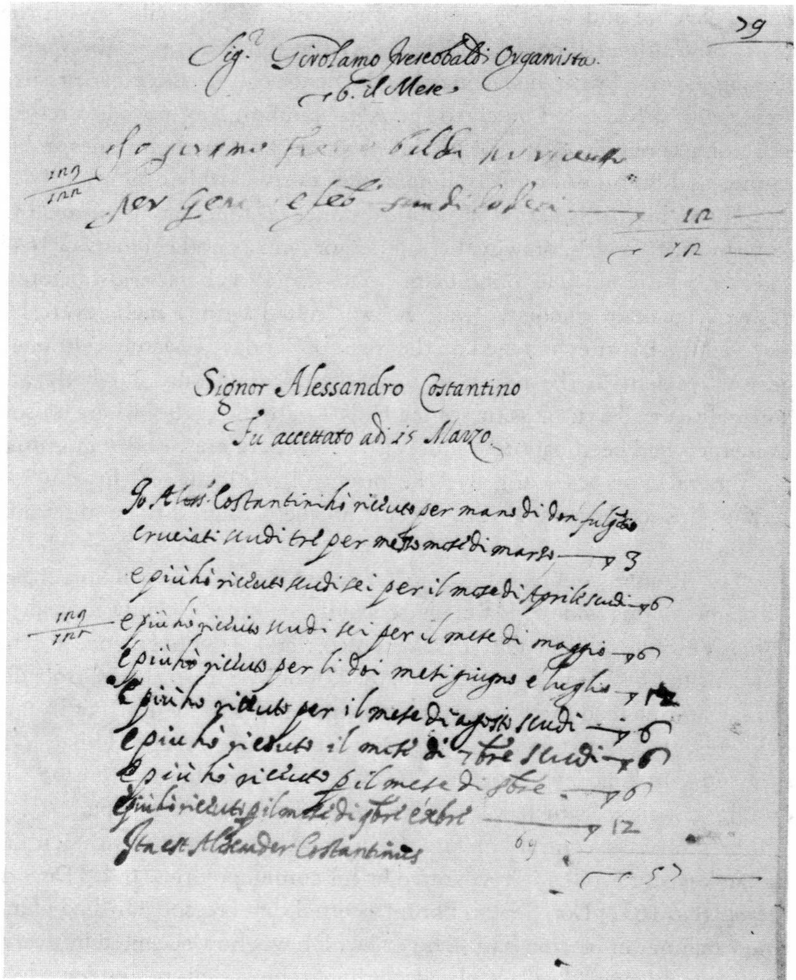
Sig.r Girolamo Frescobaldi Organista
6. il Mese

Signor Alessandro Costantino
Fu accettato adì 15 Marzo

15. Frescobaldi's last payment receipt

models—an increasing continuity and use of imitative texture in toccata writing, the tendency toward free treble- or bass-dominated textures as opposed to strict four-part writing, and the joining of single movements to form larger works (foreshadowed in the *Fiori musicali* and the *Aggiunta*)—reflects Frescobaldi's style in his last years.[51]

In the 1660s the direct influence began to wane, and Frescobaldi's authentic works began to be collected and treated as models of a historical style. As early as 1628 Grassi had recommended Frescobaldi's works as a basic model repertory for the keyboard player, and in 1642 Croci published his *Frutti* to prepare students for their study. But it was Bernardo Pasquini (whose first keyboard works are preserved in a manuscript copied in the 1660s) who elevated Frescobaldi to the rank of a pedagogical authority. Pasquini purchased a copy of the first book of *Toccate* (the 1628 edition) in 1662 and copied out for his own use the rarer *Fantasie* (see Catalogue I.A.3c and I.A.1). Pasquini's familiarity with Frescobaldi's music (and not merely the two volumes of it he is known to have possessed) sometimes resulted in virtually literal quotation in his own works. Other Italian teachers, such as Lorenzo Penna (*Li primi albori musicali,* 1684) and Pasquini's pupil Francesco Gasparini (*L'armonico pratico al cimbalo,* 1708), followed his practice of commending the study of Frescobaldi to their pupils. Since Domenico Scarlatti knew Pasquini and was an intimate of Gasparini (he may have had a hand in the composition of *L'armonico pratico*), Frescobaldi has justly been claimed as "a true spiritual ancestor of Scarlatti."[52]

In northern Europe one may distinguish broadly between the influence of Frescobaldi's printed works as compositional models and the influence of his performing style as transmitted by his contemporaries and pupils to succeeding generations. Where Frescobaldi was adopted as a model, as in the German-speaking countries, we find also the greatest number of manuscript copies and attributions. (Indeed, in Germany the copying of Frescobaldi's printed collections continued into the nineteenth century.) That many of these manuscript works are patently spurious verset-cycles still testifies that the Germans valued in Frescobaldi's work the strict four-part writing going out of fashion in Italy. The influence of Girolamo's toccatas, canzonas, and ricercars is apparent in Froberger's works, and the keyboard production of Johann Kaspar Kerll seems almost a gloss on Frescobaldi's oeuvre. Although representative selections of Frescobaldi's keyboard works were included in German instructional treatises as early as the 1670s, it was the masterful counterpoint of the *Fiori musicali* that inspired Fux in southern Germany and Johann Sebastian Bach in the north.[53]

French musicians, on the other hand, seem to have been influenced by Frescobaldi's style of playing as exemplified by Froberger; the manuscript tradition of Girolamo's works in France is virtually nonexistent, with the striking exception of a "Duresse" copied by Louis Couperin (see Catalogue I.B). A work like Louis Couperin's unmeasured prelude after a Froberger toccata, however, suggests graphically how the French perceived the freedom of Frescobaldi's style of performance (see Example 15.16).

Girolamo's music was known in England by 1627, when William Heather left to the Music School at Oxford a collection that included works of Frescobaldi; and John Blow quoted two excerpts from a Frescobaldi toccata in his own works.[54] Hawkins praised Girolamo enthusiastically, but the English so little understood the elements of his musical style that they accepted as genuine Frescobaldi the three *routinié* keyboard fugues of Gottlieb Muffat that Muzio Clementi published in the second volume of his *Practical Harmony* (1802), along with five genuine works.[55] One of these spurious works still appears in piano anthologies as a truly amazing anticipation of the Bachian keyboard fugue.

The anniversaries of Girolamo's birth and of his first publication awakened scholarly interest in his career, but the indispensable prerequisites for an understanding of his life and work, a complete critical edition of his music and a scholarly biography, have taken an additional three-quarters of a century. More important, Doni—with all his malice—grasped a fundamental truth: Frescobaldi is a composer whose art flows through the fingers; until he is performed with both historical and musical insight his work remains enigmatic and unconvincing.

8

Frescobaldi's Instruments

Girolamo Frescobaldi spent his entire documented career as a performer on the organ and harpsichord, and even his most hostile critics acknowledged his preeminence as a keyboard player and composer. No instrument on which he is known to have played has survived unaltered, but the evidence of archival materials and of extant instruments can be combined to illustrate the resources available to Frescobaldi in the successive phases of his career and his employment of them.

Italian organs were built in two main types, the large stationary instrument with a richly decorated façade that constituted a notable architectural feature of a church, and the smaller portable instrument that could be moved as required for church or domestic use. The basis of seventeenth-century Italian organ construction was a principal at eight-foot or lower pitch, upon which successive single registers built up a series of octaves and fifths, as opposed to the northern European tradition of mixtures. Both metal and wood pipes were employed. Although large instruments had a considerable variety of registers, including reeds, tremolo, *voce umana,* and incidental effects such as birdcalls, even they generally lacked the multiple keyboards and independent pedal registers of northern organs. Pedalboards, when present, generally operated pull-downs connected to the manual keys. Smaller organs were furnished with fewer registers and were in demand in Rome not only as solo instruments but also for the increasing performance of polychoral church music. In 1639 Maugars heard at Santa Maria sopra Minerva a mass for ten separate choirs, each with its portable organ, of which he estimated that there were more than two hundred in Rome, "but in Paris one could scarcely find two at the same pitch."[1]

Throughout Girolamo's tenure at St. Peter's, the instruments there consisted of two large fixed organs and a smaller portable one; of these, nothing remains except one façade. The small organ that Frescobaldi inherited on his appointment in 1608 is undocumented, and the history of the larger instruments is incomplete. The older of these, built in 1496 for Alexander VI Borgia, had a principal in the façade, a divided octave register allowing solo and accompaniment on the single keyboard, nine registers for the pieno, two ranks of flutes, and one rank of trombones.[2] Soon after Girolamo's arrival this organ was overhauled, and the renewed instrument was demonstrated in a concert for the Persian ambassador in September 1609.[3] After considerable work between 1624 and 1626 the organ was removed from its previous position above the stairway door by the altar of the Madonna to the screen between the Cappella Clementina and the new canons' choir, so that it could serve for both chapels. It was first played there on the feast of St. Gregory in March 1626, and a month later Urban VIII judged it a great success.[4]

The second organ, whose case survives, was built in 1580 by Marino and Vincenzo of Sulmona and is described as possessing a fundamental pipe of 3.30 meters, which suggests that it had a sixteen-foot principal, probably with a keyboard descending only to F rather than to C. As of 1597 its register of *tromboni* and/or *zampogne* had never played.[5] An estimate prepared in 1751 for the repair of the instrument enumerated sixteen registers: three principals (including one toward each of the two chapels), two octave registers, a "fifth register" (perhaps 2 ⅔ ′), a 2′, a 1 ⅓ ′, another six registers for the ripieno, and *ottava bassa* and quint flutes.[6] No mention was made of the *zampogna,* tremolo, or *voce umana* registers. Around 1628 the organ was placed in a position analogous to that of the older instrument, on the screen between the Cappella Gregoriana and the Cappella del Sacramento (Sagrestia Nuova).[7]

The subject of organ registration was treated at some length by Diruta and Antegnati in their instruction books. The type of instrument they presuppose was detailed by Antegnati as consisting of the usual ripieno built in fifths and octaves above an eight-foot principal, to which were added solo registers (*registri da concerto*); a principal divided so that the treble was connected to the keyboard and the bass to the pedals; flutes (4′, 2′, perhaps a 2 ⅔ ′ to be employed with the principal); a separate 1′ register which could be combined with the 4′, 4′ flute, and 1 ⅓ ′ to produce a *concerto di cornetti*; *fiffaro* or *voci umane*; and tremulant (not a separate rank).[8]

Diruta's registrations were conceived according to the affective characters of the various church modes or tones:

I: serious and pleasing: principal (8′) with 4′, flute, or 2′
II: melancholy: principal solo with tremolo, played in its natural range with sad modulation
III: conducive to lamentation: principal, 4′ flute
IV: lamenting, sad, and sorrowful: principal with tremolo, or flutes in their natural range
V: joyful, modest, and pleasing: 4′, 2′, and flute
VI: devout and serious: principal, 4′, flute
VII: happy and sweet: 4′, 2′, 1′
VIII: charming and delightful: solo flute; flute and 4′ or 2′
IX: happy, gentle, and sonorous: principal, 2′, 1′
X: somewhat sad: principal with 4′ or flute
XI: lively and full of sweetness: solo flute; flute, 2′; flute, 2′, 1′; 4′, 2′, 1′
XII: sweet and lively: flute 4′, 2′; solo flute.[9]

Antegnati's suggested registrations were based not on the mode of the piece to be played, but on the genre of the work and its liturgical context. The full ripieno (principal, 4′, 2′, 1 ⅓′, 1′, ⅔′, [½′, ⅓′]) was to be employed at the beginning of a service, for introits and intonations, and at the end (Deo Gratias) for toccatas and works with pedal. Half-ripieni were composed of principal, 4′, 1′, ⅔′ or ⅓′, 4′ flute; principal, 4′, 4′ flute; or principal, 4′ flute—the latter two useful for accompanying motets. Bright registrations (principal, 4′, 2 ⅔′ or 2′ flute; 4′, 4′ flute) were suited to diminutions and *canzoni alla francese.* The addition of the tremolo to the latter combination rendered it appropriate only to pieces without diminution, although tasteless players employed it also for diminished canzonas. Of softer combinations, the solo principal accompanied motets for few voices, and Antegnati was accustomed to play it also at the Elevation; the addition of either tremolo or *fiffaro* demanded a slow legato style without diminutions. For a dialogue effect Antegnati recommended 4′ flute plus divided principal, in which the flute sounded with the principal in the soprano of the keyboard and alone in the bass, against the principal in the pedal.[10]

Registrations could be changed only at breaks in the music where the player was free to remove one or both hands from the manual (unless an assistant drew stops for him). All the stops of the ripieno could be brought on by drawing a single lever, the *tiratutti.* Antegnati advised varying style and registration from time to time to avoid boredom. Three of Banchieri's organ pieces in *L'organo suonarino* specify register changes, and Monteverdi also indicated them in the large Magnificat of the 1610 vespers.[11]

For the performer, these seventeenth-century Italian organs differ from modern instruments in many respects. Within a consistent tonal design, they are capable of considerable variety of timbre, from the delicacy of the solo stopped flutes to the power and brilliance of the ripieno. The mechanical action permits subtler gradations of articulation than more modern systems, a distinction particularly apparent in the smaller organs. In these the case is open, and the pipes are on a level with the player's head. Since the key weight is relatively light the sensation of mechanical mediation almost disappears. These factors, together with the sustained character of organ sound, combine to produce an impression of extraordinary involvement in the music. Especially in contrapuntal textures, the player can almost feel that he is singing independent lines and not simply approximating them through a mechanism.

The large Italian harpsichord of the late sixteenth and seventeenth centuries, such as Maugars described Frescobaldi playing at the Oratorio del Crocifisso, was one of the most satisfying musical instruments ever contrived (fig. 16). Its typical form—a sharp curve in the upper bentside tapering gradually to a long, narrow tail—was the result of a wide octave span on the keyboard, a short string scale in the treble, and the maintenance of a true scale (that is, one in which the string length doubles at each descent of an octave) well down into the tenor register. The case was remarkably light and resonant. The sides (generally of cypress) were so thin that steaming or molding was unnecessary to produce the curve of the bentside; they were simply nailed and glued to a deal bottom and braced by a line of wooden knees at the join. The soundboard was made of cypress, spruce, or fir. Surviving authentic Italian harpsichords have only one keyboard and one or, more often, two sets of strings—generally 8′ × 8′ but sometimes 8′ × 4′. (However, instruments with two or three keyboards and as many as eight registers are known to have existed.)[12] The differing plucking points of two eight-foot registers would have resulted in two solo stops, one round, the other nasal in timbre. Surprisingly, this possibility seems to have been rejected: in many extant instruments it is impossible to change registers without removing the jack-rail. (Here again the evidence of existing instruments is contradicted by descriptions of mechanisms for changing registration.)[13] There is some evidence for buff and "harping" stops as well.[14]

Plectra were usually of quill, although hard leather and other materials were also employed.[15] The keyboard had box, bone, or ivory naturals with

16. Harpsichord by Girolamo Zenti, Rome, 1666

arcaded fronts and ebony sharps. The usual compass was something over four octaves, from C in the bass to c, d, e, or f''' in the treble, but a few instruments went down to GG. The lowest octave in the bass was usually short, C/E or GG/BB; complete octaves were uncommon enough to warrant the qualification "all'ottava bassa." The instrument was placed in a sturdy outer case which was painted, or covered with leather or cloth, and from which it could be withdrawn partly or entirely for playing. (Pull-down pedals like those of Italian organs were sometimes attached to the bass keys.)

The acoustical results of this arrangement are admirable. The separation of the harpsichord from its case created the ideal solution to the problem of permitting the instrument to resonate without leaving it unprotected. Although there are regional differences in the sound of Italian harpsichords—characteristically, the Venetians favored resonance, the Florentines clarity—all of them have a full, clean sound marked by a strong percussive attack and fairly rapid decay. What seem limiting factors—the single keyboard, the restricted number of registers and the difficulty of changing them—direct the player to the instrument's real strengths: clarity of contrapuntal exposition, a rich palette of articulation, and, owing to its greater dryness of sound, a wider spectrum of arpeggiation.

Smaller instruments of the harpsichord family were produced in great quantities in seventeenth-century Italy. Of the two main types, both with projecting keyboards, the virginal was rectangular in shape and the spinet pentagonal. There also existed a particularly resonant type of bentside spinet, datable from 1637 in surviving examples.[16] These were all generally single-strung, which permitted a longer scale with no increase in tension. The usual range of such instruments was four and a half octaves with a short octave in the bass.[17] Although the pentagonal spinets were less than satisfactory tonally, the Italian virginals had an excellent sound, and one quite different from that of the harpsichord. "The timbre is rounder, revealing a stronger box resonance; the bass is less hard, more 'tubby,' and the treble is purer, although less brilliant."[18] These instruments were listed in inventories as "spinetta" or "spinettina," a category which included as well instruments at higher pitch (quint or the four-foot spinets popular around the middle of the century), and perhaps small spinets strung with gut.[19]

The early history of the clavichord is traceable largely from Italian sources. By the seventeenth century, however, it seems to have fallen into disuse in Italy. It occurs rarely, if ever, in inventories of household instruments, and the instructions for tuning the clavichord given by Cima in his *Ricercari* of 1606 constitute one of the few evidences for its continued use.

Seventeenth-century inventories do attest the frequent presence of an instrument so far largely ignored in the revival of early music, the claviorganum. This combination of organ and harpsichord, in which each could be played separately or both together, was completely unstandardized. The thirty-odd surviving claviorgana join organs having wood pipes, metal pipes, and regals with spinets and wing-shaped harpsichords. The presence of register-stops on the harpsichord constituent of early claviorgana and divided organ-registers suggests that the makers aimed at the greatest possible versatility of tonal combinations.[20] The one documented use of the claviorganum was as a continuo instrument in opera.[21]

When we turn from a general consideration of seventeenth-century keyboard instruments to a detailed examination of the harpsichords and organs available to Frescobaldi in the course of his career, it becomes apparent that these few basic types—stationary and portable organs, large and small plucked keyboard instruments, and claviorgana—were realized in a wide variety of detail. The testamentary inventory of goods belonging to Alfonso II d'Este compiled in 1598 lists fourteen keyboard instruments. Of these, four are claviorgana, containing harpsichords of two and three registers. The organ of the first was pitched "alla quarta bassa," another had a register of reeds, and a third was presumably the famous "instrumento piano e forte . . . con il suo organo sotto." Among the other keyboard instruments of the Duke's collection we find a *nasino* with two registers (perhaps a high-pitched organ); a chromatic instrument (presumably of the harpsichord family) with two registers and split keys; another chromatic instrument with two keyboards, one above the other; and harpsichords of one and two registers, including one with a long octave (*ottava bassa*) in the bass.[22] The collection of Don Cesare d'Este, housed in the Palazzo dei Diamanti, contained ten organs of varying sizes, including an *organo grande,* a portable *organino,* an organ and a *regaletto* of cypress, an organ with paper pipes, and an organ used at table. The harpsichords are summarized as "twelve instruments to play, with two registers, one of various sorts."[23]

There is no surviving inventory of the household goods of Guido Bentivoglio during his nunciature in Flanders. Given Girolamo's interest in the musical life of the Spanish Provinces as demonstrated in his trip to Antwerp, it is likely, however, that he played on instruments of local manufacture. These differed markedly from their Italian counterparts both in basic principles and in outward appearance. The instrument and its outer case were combined into one heavier case. The string scaling, while longer than that of Italy, was also less true in the tenor and bass, so that the curve of the harpsichord bentside was more gradual than that of an Italian instrument. The sound of a Ruckers harpsichord has been described as having less initial impact than that of an Italian instrument, slower decay, less definition but great smoothness, and a more resonant bass.[24]

The Ruckers family, the most famous of the Antwerp makers, built instruments in a variety of types greater than that of Italian builders. They constructed one-manual harpsichords with two registers, 1 × 8′, 1 × 4′, in three sizes; a two-manual transposing instrument with the lower manual a fourth or fifth lower than the upper in pitch; two models of virginals with 1 × 8′ and various models at raised pitch; two types of virginals with 1 × 4′; and a double virginal combining an eight-foot instrument with an *ottavina* which could be played separately or placed on top of the parent to provide a four-foot register. In the smaller types a distinct difference in tone resulted from the placement of the keyboard to the right or to the left of the center. Those in which it stands toward the left "are even and playable—these are called *spinetten*." "In some the jacks stand about half way between the bridges, and these are the most common; they are called '*muselars*' "; according to another authority, they are "good in the right hand, but grunt in the bass like young pigs."[25] Nonetheless, they are ideal for some compositions, notably dance music.[26]

Enzo Bentivoglio's papers give little information about his household instruments—indeed, there may have been no harpsichord, since in 1610 the Cavalier Marotta had his own "Cimbalone" moved in for a performance, and in 1612 there was "no harpsichord until a week ago, the which harpsichord has been rented."[27]

An inventory of 1603 shows that Cardinal Aldobrandini, Girolamo's other Roman patron in his early years, possessed a rather motley array of keyboard instruments: a small cabinet-organ with three registers; two large Neapolitan harpsichords with split keys and another Neapolitan instrument in a painted case; a harpsichord of unspecified provenance with the Cardinal's arms, and an old Venetian instrument with two registers; two regals, one with wood pipes, the other with brass; and a claviorganum in bad condition.[28] Later inventories of the Cardinal's palaces after they had passed into the Pamphilj family describe additional instruments: a "*grave organo* made like a large harpsichord" and the cabinet-organ in the garden-villa at Monte Magnanapoli, and two harpsichords, one "covered with cordovan with a cover all painted with its stand painted red outlined in gold" in the villa at Frascati, where Girolamo performed. The palace on the Corso contained six harpsichords, one of three registers, two of two registers, and two of one, all richly decorated. The only maker named is Girolamo Zenti (fl. 1633–1683), to whom are attributed a *spinetta* and a *spinettina* in red cases picked out in gold. The organ room contained a handsomely decorated instrument with eight registers.[29]

There is no extant list of the instruments in the possession of the Medici court during Girolamo's stay there from 1628 to 1634. However, an inventory of 1640 presumably includes items from the previous decade, and their description is sometimes amplified in succeeding lists for 1652, 1654, and 1669.[30] Aside from a *geigenwerk,* whose progressive disintegration can be traced through the four documents, the first keyed instruments encountered are two "large and good" spinets, furnished with outer cases and having five broken semitones, which suggests the standard four-and-a-half-octave keyboard in which all the D- and G-sharps are split except for the treble G. (Despite the fact that false intonation sounds worst in the upper register, accidentals were not commonly split in the treble.)[31] The other plucked stringed keyboards in the inventories comprise a small green spinet and a Neapolitan harpsichord attributed in a later inventory to the Trasuntino family, although they worked in Venice rather than Naples; Guido Trasuntino (fl. 1560–1606) was famed for instruments which "in melody and harmony surpass all the others."[32]

The 1640 inventory of the Medici instruments lists no fewer than seven organs of widely varying specifications. "Two double enharmonic and diatonic organs, with two wooden keyboards of five feet," are qualified in 1654 as "Gromatico," made of cypress, with a double keyboard and one of them having two registers. The "two pipe organs with a principal and octave, and the other at the unison with one principal" are otherwise unspecified, but the "pipe organino of five feet with a single register" is listed in 1654 as being at the fifteenth, with partly stopped pipes. The "large pipe organ of fourteen feet" may be the "organ of cypress of 45 keys with a single register," whose range was probably C/E–c‴. Another organino combined a regal and a register of cypress flutes, with a similar compass of forty-five keys.

The Medici collection, as reflected in these inventories, was relatively small and contained keyed instruments mostly of Italian origin and pattern. On his entry into the Barberini household in 1634, Frescobaldi gained access to many more instruments, of at least two national traditions. The most fully documented instrumentarium is that of the younger Cardinal Antonio, recipient of the *Fiori musicali.* An inventory of his possessions taken in 1630–1640 lists a church organ, two claviorgana, a regal, ten harpsichords of various types, and three spinets. Two of the harpsichords are "long," indicating a long octave in the bass; two others are "spezzato con ferri," provided with split keys and pull-down pedals. Another "si suona in due persone," perhaps a Flemish "mother and child" virginal, while a "Spinet with a high keyboard inside where the strings are" suggests another Flemish model, the ottavina with a recessed keyboard.[33]

Cardinal Francesco's household inventories record only the few keyboard instruments which were prominent articles of furniture as well. A list made in 1631–1636 mentions two: an organ in the form of a cabinet with four registers, wood pipes, ivory keys, and "another similar register which are [played? *sono* = *sonò*?] the spinet"—a claviorganum; and a "Harpsichord to play with three *ordini* made by the Cortonese who resides with the Mattei." The *ordini* may have been either register-stops or the additional levels of keys in enharmonic instruments. This is perhaps identical with the instrument described in the 1649 inventory of Cardinal Francesco's possessions in the Cancelleria: "Two harpsichords together, that is one on top of the other, the one on top with three registers; that below with one register made by Gio: Batta Cortonese."[34] The builder was in any case the same, Giovanni Battista Boni da Cortona, a maker who specialized in instruments with split keys.[35] The accounts of Cardinal Francesco and of the Oratorio del Crocifisso show that Boni regularly tuned and repaired their instruments.

The other instruments enumerated in the 1649 inventory comprise "A Harpsichord made standing [clavicytherium] / a large Harpsichord with a low [long] octave, and several registers / a Harpsichord with two registers with a keyboard of mother-of-pearl, inlaid with white and black bone with a pipe organ in its painted case"—a Spanish or German claviorganum.[36] One harpsichord "with various registers" was purchased in 1628, another was bought by Cortona in 1636, and Antonio's accounts for 1639 show payments for a long harpsichord, a *graviorgano* with a harpsichord, a spinet, and a Flemish organ with lead pipes.[37]

Most of the specialized keyboards described in these inventories were probably designed to deal with the problems arising from meantone tuning (see below), but periodically instruments were constructed with the more recondite aim of producing the three ancient Greek genera by means of split keys, additional rows of keys, and multiple registers. The inventories show that such instruments occurred in the collections of Girolamo's patrons, and—despite Doni's denigrations—Frescobaldi was well acquainted with them. He was the pupil of one of the few competent performers on Vicentino's arcicembalo, he himself was reputed to be the only player in Rome capable of manipulating a similar instrument, and he seems to have transmitted this skill and interest to his Florentine pupil Francesco Nigetti. (He did not, however, petition Cardinal Barberini to construct an organ on the model of Doni's *cembalo triarmonico* built for Della Valle, as is sometimes claimed.)[38]

Two problems bedevil our understanding of seventeenth-century keyboard instruments: the questions of temperament and pitch. The problems of temperament arise, of course, from the mathematical incompatibility of a system based on a series of perfect (2:1) octaves with a system based on a series of perfect (3:2) fifths. In the most common seventeenth-century meantone tuning, octaves and selected major thirds were tuned as pure by flattening the fifths slightly, which resulted in two sizes of semitone and a "wolf" usually placed between G-sharp and E-flat. This adjustment had the desirable effect of stressing the purity of the triad and thus throwing relations of consonance and dissonance into higher relief. The varieties of meantone temperaments also made acoustical realities of the affective characters claimed for various modes or keys. The undesirable corollary was the impossibility of enharmonic equivalences: the same accidental that produced a pure A-flat against C could not function as G-sharp with E. One solution to this problem, equal temperament, was known in the seventeenth century, but principally as a compromise tuning for fretted instruments. There is no evidence that Frescobaldi was a proponent of equal temperament—even Doni's scurrilous anecdote concedes that Girolamo approved it "against the judgment of his ears."[39]

The appearance of enharmonic pairs in the same piece of music by no means demonstrates the necessity of equal temperament. Where the "bad" accidental is a passing note, the disturbance is slight; where it seems to be a calculated device (as in *Toccate* II/11, measures 63–64), the result can be hair-raisingly effective. Even if the presence of incompatible accidentals in a single piece were an indication of equal temperament, such instances are rare in Frescobaldi's early work. By 1615 Trabaci had to specify "cembalo cromatico" for some of his keyboard pieces, but as late as 1627 only the passage cited above goes beyond the limits of the normal meantone keyboard in the toccatas of Frescobaldi's second book.

The greater frequency of enharmonic pairs in the 1637 *Aggiunta* (notably in the *Cento partite*) may reflect Girolamo's increasing familiarity with the instruments of the Barberini harpsichord builder and tuner Boni da Cortona. His keyboards were furnished with split keys, which provided a short octave in the bass and G- and D-sharps in which the front half of the key produced the sharp, the rear the enharmonic flat (fig. 17). Even

a *View of the keyboard from above*

b Front view

17. Virginal by Giovanni Battista Boni da Cortona, 1617, with split keys for bass short-octave and non-enharmonic tuning

on harpsichords lacking such devices, in an age when most performers tuned their own instruments slight adjustments could have accommodated the greater number of problems arising from meantone tuning. Like all systems of temperament, it was a historical, variable solution to an eternal and insoluble problem. Even in the seventeenth century a little healthy skepticism was expressed about the finer points of tuning. "In harmonized music," declared Bontempi, "not even a Comma is perceptible, let alone a small fraction of one."[40]

The question of pitch (or pitches) to which keyboard instruments were tuned in late sixteenth- and seventeenth-century Italy needs at least to be raised, if for no other reason than the fact that present-day exponents of early music tend to impose "low" pitch (A = ca. 415) as indiscriminately as their predecessors accepted modern orchestral pitch. First, it is clear that there was no standard Italian pitch. Marco da Gagliano, writing from Florence in 1612, reported that "in Rome they sing a tone lower than here."[41] In 1627 Ennio Bonifatij was paid ten scudi for the overhaul of the portable organ in St. Peter's, including the addition of "all the Pipes to lower it a half tone or a bit less."[42] (Since an organ pipe was tuned by tapping a mandrel into the top of the pipe, organs tended inevitably to rise in pitch, and eventually an instrument was restored by moving all the pipes down and adding the necessary new ones at the top.) In 1639 Maugars did imply that there was an accepted *Roman* pitch, to which the two hundred or so small portable organs used throughout the City for polychoral works were tuned.[43] In 1640 Doni asserted that pitch rose as one ascended the peninsula: Neapolitan organs and harpsichords were tuned a semitone below those of Rome, while Florence, Lombardy (including Ferrara), and Venice were successive semitones higher than Rome. One modern authority has estimated Roman pitch in Doni's time at about A = 440, which means that the Venetian A would have been the equivalent of the modern c.[44] In the course of explaining this phenomenon (the laziness of singers, the influence of castrati, the prevalence of *bassi profondi* at Rome), Doni observed that Roman pitch had been lowered by a semitone in the last forty years, which might be another reason for the retuning of the organ at St. Peter's.[45] Antonio Barcotto confirmed in 1652 that Roman organs were among the lowest used in Italy, and Venetian instruments the highest, although portable organs in the Veneto were pitched a tone lower than stationary ones. He distinguished between the pitch-levels by assigning the lower to choirs and to high voices, the higher to low voices and to violins.[46] To summarize, it appears that Roman pitch declined during Frescobaldi's lifetime, a change perhaps reflected in one instrument under his supervision, and that by mid-century Roman pitch was standardized momentarily somewhere about the present-day level.

It is sometimes asserted that Italian keyboard music of the late sixteenth and seventeenth centuries was destined indifferently for organ or harpsichord. There was certainly a considerable degree of overlapping between the two media, but Girolamo and his contemporaries did in fact distinguish between organ and harpsichord both in repertory and in technique.[47] The repertory of the church organist was limited by the rulings of the Council of Trent and subsequent decrees, which at least in theory outlawed dances and intabulations, variations, and other works based on secular sources. Among the categories of music that the explicators of the Tridentine decrees permitted in the liturgy were versets, intonations, toccatas, the ricercar and fantasia, the capriccio, the canzona, and the generic category "sonata."

At the other end of the spectrum, collections of dances from the mid-sixteenth century through Frescobaldi's lifetime included specific designations for *arpicordo, cimbalo,* or *clavicembalo* in their titles. (Collections of other secular genres were sometimes described as "intavolatura d'organo" or "per sonar d'organo"; but the first of these, Antico's *Frottole intabulate da sonar organi* of 1517, depicts immediately under the title a musician playing the harpsichord.) Antonio Valente's *Intavolatura* of 1576, which contains ricercars, fantasias, intabulations, and variations, is designated "de cimbalo," and the preface asserts that the tablature will teach even the musically illiterate to play the harpsichord. In both his collections Trabaci advised that his works might be performed on any instrument but especially organ and harpsichord; in the 1615 volume he added that the works for harp might also be played on the harpsichord, "since the Harpsichord is Ruler of all the instruments in the world, and one can play everything on it with ease."[48]

Frescobaldi's own title pages and prefaces reflect this distinction in repertory. *Toccate* I, containing toccatas, variations, and correnti, was originally designated "d'intavolatura di cimbalo," and the directions in the 1616 preface concerning arpeggiation and repetition of chords presuppose the nonsustaining harpsichord rather than the organ. For the 1628 reprint the designation was changed to "cimbalo et organo" with no alteration of the contents, presumably to bring it into conformity with the title of *Toccate* II, which did contain organ music. The *Fiori musicali* were intended "to please the Organists," although the *Bergamasca* and *Girolmeta,* as secular tunes, were equally appropriate for the harpsichord.

Grassi's observations in the preface to his edition of the 1628 *Canzoni* suggest that *Toccate* I was intabulated by non-keyboard players for performance on their own instruments, but—surprisingly—the *Recercari* and *Capricci*, despite their publication in keyboard partitura, were "only for the use of keyboard players," whom Grassi seems to consider mainly as "sonatori di Cimbalo." Grassi's edition of the canzonas could be performed by solo keyboard or with other instruments.

At every stage of his career Frescobaldi was provided with instruments of professional caliber, in a variety that matches the variety of his keyboard production. The large organs of St. Peter's and Santa Maria in Sassia were adequate to the grandest of his pedal toccatas and were the natural medium for the liturgical organ works. Other contrapuntal genres would have been appropriate also to smaller organs or to the harpsichord. This ambiguity is not always a disadvantage. The sustained clarity of the Italian organ may make explicit the contrapuntal relations that the harpsichord can only suggest, and the crisp attack and rapid decay of the Italian harpsichord can emphasize the feeling for color and texture that pervades even Girolamo's "abstract" writing.

Of the harpsichord works, Girolamo's dances and smaller variation sets can be charming on an Italian virginal or spinet (and three works in Grassi's edition of the *Canzoni* specify *spinettina*). However, the most appropriate medium for his major harpsichord works—the toccatas and the great variation sets—is the large Italian harpsichord with one manual, two sets of strings, and little or no means of varying registration, despite the historical exceptions to each of these specifications.

One further possible performing medium remains, the claviorganum, intended to combine the incisiveness of the harpsichord with the sustaining power of the organ. On the meager evidence of the two functioning claviorgana known to me, in practice the disparity between the two tone-qualities is sometimes excessive; but if organ and harpsichord registrations are properly matched, the performance of works that require both a clear attack and a sustained sound, such as the eleventh toccata of the first book, is entirely convincing on the claviorganum.[49]

Despite the variations that contemporary organology is beginning to individuate in Italian keyboard instruments, they all display consistent characteristics exactly suited to Frescobaldi's music. They speak easily and forcefully, with a clarity of attack that encourages a wide variety of articulation. Even in the case of relatively large organs, there is a minimum of mechanical intervention and a consequent sense of direct involvement in the sound production. Both organs and harpsichords are ill-suited to rapid changes of registration, but in both the basic sound is generally so excellent that the ear does not need to be titillated by constant changes of color. This in turn frees the performer to use these instruments to their best advantage, to employ their incisiveness and clarity in realizing the vocal declamation and passionate rhetoric of Frescobaldi's music.

PART TWO

The Music

9

The Art of Counterpoint: The *Fantasie* of 1608 and the *Recercari et Canzoni* of 1615

No aspect of Frescobaldi's development has generated more speculation than the sources and formation of his keyboard style. Such speculation generally starts from a preoccupation with the most daring and experimental aspects of that style, exemplified in the toccatas and in the chromatic works; their counterpoise in the more contrapuntal genres of fantasia, ricercar, and canzona is ignored. This has led to two contrasting distortions of Girolamo's musical personality. In the first, Girolamo is presented as a unique genius with no historical antecedents, a figure of "grandezza e solitudine." In the second, the striking stylistic features are taken out of context and explained by reference to a single composer, school, or musical device, the more unlikely the better: Cabezón, Sweelinck, the Neapolitans, a shadowy north Italian school, the *inganno.*[1]

The failings of the first approach—currently out of fashion in all branches of cultural history—are obvious; those of the second school are more insidious. Clearly, in dealing with a complex period and a complex artistic personality the concept of unilateral influence as an adequate explanation of stylistic character and development is simplistic. Beyond this, however, lies concealed the fact that the available information in the form of surviving music and historical documents is insufficient in many cases to provide any answers whatever. To take a case in point, it is logical to suppose that the primary formative influences upon Frescobaldi's keyboard style were those of his Ferrarese teacher, Luzzaschi, and the Roman keyboard composers around 1600. Of Luzzaschi we have four surviving authentic keyboard works, three of them miniatures; of datable works by Roman composers we have a toccata by Quagliati and a volume of gagliarde of G. F. Anerio. In the absence of such essential material, it is unrealistic to chart unequivocal lines of stylistic tradition.

It is possible, however, to establish at least a general context for the examination of Frescobaldi's earliest keyboard publications by summarizing the most important printed collections (the dating of manuscripts is usually so uncertain as to render them useless for a chronological study) of works in strict style from the mid-sixteenth century up to 1607, when Girolamo was already at work on the *Fantasie,* and toccatas, variations, canzonas, and dances up to 1614, when *Toccate* I had been compiled in its first state and the *Recercari et canzoni* was presumably being prepared for publication (see Table 1).[2]

The places of publication for these collections indicate the most important Italian schools of keyboard composition in the late sixteenth and early seventeenth centuries. Venice was clearly preeminent, attracting not only the organists of St. Mark's and other local musicians but also composers from Ferrara, Brescia, Bologna, and other north Italian cities. The Neapolitan houses seem to have published only local composers, latterly pupils of Giovanni de Macque, whose own keyboard works survive only in manuscript. Milanese publishing was also largely parochial in character, with a preference for *partitura* or open-score format. Roman keyboard publication was almost nonexistent, except for collections printed in keyboard score (two-staff notation) from engraved copper plates rather than the more usual and less expensive technique of movable type.

The serious contrapuntal ricercar (as opposed to the earlier improvisatory type) first appeared in printed keyboard music in Girolamo Cavazzoni's *Intavolatura* of 1543. All four of Cavazzoni's ricercars are extended, carefully crafted contrapuntal works. They are based on several successive subjects, but overt sectionalization is generally avoided by elided cadences and other types of transition between sections. While the basic movement is a decorated note-against-note texture, there also occur livelier cadential ornaments and even running figuration in treble or bass against slower-moving chords. The last two ricercars contrast the prevailing duple meter with concluding triple sections, rounded off by a duple cadence.

The clarity of general conception and the flexibility in detail found in Cavazzoni's ricercars continued to characterize the genre in the hands of his successors. Perhaps the earliest ricercars of probable influence on Frescobaldi were those of Claudio Merulo, first printed in 1567 and reissued in 1605. The eight ricercars of the set follow the order of the eight modes, although a transposed C mode is substituted for the F mode without B-flat. Owing both to their length—an average of one hundred breves—and their introduction of as many as eight successive subjects, Merulo's ricercars seem deficient in motivic concentration and contrapuntal artifice.

The ricercars of Merulo's colleague Andrea Gabrieli display a variety of treatment far beyond Merulo's. Andrea is credited with raising still higher the level of an already serious genre through the systematic employment of learned devices such as inversion, augmentation, and diminution. Both of his collections of ricercars are arranged modally, the first a set of thirteen covering all twelve modes (filled out with two pieces by Giovanni Gabrieli), the second a group of six ricercars on tones I, II, V, and IX. Andrea's ricercars are written on single subjects, double subjects derived by inversion, other subject-countersubject pairs, and from two to five subjects treated successively. Except for two concluding triple sections in the first and fifth ricercars of the 1595 book, cadences are generally elided, and motion is continuous. Augmentation and diminution appear within the prevailing texture rather than defining discrete sections as they do in the works of Sweelinck. The degree of surface ornamentation varies widely. Some ricercars are completely unadorned, others set off cadences by ornamental flourishes, and some are dominated by decorative figuration.

Four keyboard works of unquestioned authenticity by Luzzaschi exist: a toccata in the first part of *Il Transilvano,* two posthumous ricercars in the second volume, and a ricercar in the Foà collection. (The surviving work of the other notable Ferrarese keyboard composer, Ercole Pasquini, is of doubtful value for stylistic comparison because Pasquini left Ferrara for Rome in 1597, and his keyboard music is transmitted only in manuscripts—often corrupt—that appear to date from well after his death.)

Luzzaschi's two ricercars in *Il Transilvano* inaugurate a series on the twelve modes by a variety of composers and follow the pattern of the other ricercar pairs as stipulated by Diruta.[3] They are complementary in length (twenty-four breves each), in the relation of their subjects—the subject of the first is inverted to produce that of the second—and in their common finalis. The higher range and clef system of the first ricercar define the authentic Dorian mode; the lower ambitus and clef-arrangement of the second, the plagal. In part owing to the external restriction of each of the twelve ricercars in the volume to a single page, both of Luzzaschi's contributions have a strong sense of harmonic architecture and motivic unity. The rhythmic writing, although devoid of ornamentation, avoids monot-

TABLE 1. Italian keyboard publications, 1567–1615

YEAR	COMPOSER	PLACE	FORMAT	CONTENTS
[1567]$_2$ =1605h	C. Merulo	V	ks	Ricercars
1575$_5$	R. Rodio	N	kp	Ricercars, cantus firmus fantasies
1576$_3$	A. Valente	N	Skt	Fantasia, ricercars, Salve Regina, intabulations, variations, gagliarde, balli
1580$_3$	A. Valente	N	kp	Organ versets
[1586]$_2$	M. Facoli	V?	ks	Passamezzo, ? (original lost)
1588$_3$	M. Facoli	V	ks	Passamezzi, saltarelli, padoane, arias
[158?]$_4$	L. Luzzaschi	V	—	At least three volumes of ricercars
1590$_5$	F. Maschera	V	kp	Keyboard versions of Maschera's first book of ensemble canzonas
1591$_3$	B. Spiridio	V	ks	Chanson intabulations
1591$_4$	B. Spiridio	V	ks	Toccatas, ricercars, canzona
1592$_7$	C. Merulo	V	ks	Canzonas
1593$_3$	G. Diruta et al. (*Il Transilvano* I)	V	ks	Toccatas by Diruta, Merulo, A. and G. Gabrieli, Luzzaschi, A. Romanini, P. Quagliati, V. Bell'haver, G. Guami
1593$_4$	A. and G. Gabrieli	V	ks	Intonations, toccatas
1595$_3$	A. and G. Gabrieli	V	ks	Ricercars
1596$_7$	A. Gabrieli	V	ks	Ricercars, fantasia, canzona, intabulations, passamezzo
1598$_9$	C. Merulo	R	ks	Toccatas
1599$_9$	V. Pellegrini	V	ks	Canzonas
1600?b	F. Rovigo, R. Trofeo	M	kp	Canzonas
1601e	G. Guami	V	kp	"Canzonette alla francese"

TABLE 1, *continued*

YEAR	COMPOSER	PLACE	FORMAT	CONTENTS
1603a	A. Banchieri	V	part-books	"Fantasie overo canzoni alla francese"
1603b	A. Mayone	N	kp	Ricercars, canzonas, intabulation, toccatas, partite
1603c	G. M. Trabaci	N	kp	Ricercars, canzonas, capriccios, canti fermi, gagliarde, partite, toccatas, intabulation
1604d	C. Merulo	R	ks	Toccatas
1604e	A. Padoano	V	ks	Toccatas, ricercars
1605a	G. D. Rognoni	M	part-books	Includes a *partito* of canzonas à 4 and à 8
1605d	A. Banchieri	V	kp	"Sonate," capriccios, liturgical works
1605f	A. Gabrieli	V	ks	Canzoni alla francese, ricercari ariosi
1605g	A. Gabrieli	V	ks	Canzoni alla francese, ricercar
1606a	G. P. Cima	M	kp	Ricercars, canzonas
1606d	C. Merulo	V	ks	Canzonas
1607l	G. F. Anerio	R	ks	Gagliarde
1608d	C. Antegnati	V	ks	Ricercars
1609f	A. Mayone	N	kp	Ricercars, canzonas, intabulation, toccatas, partite
1609–10	G. Diruta et al. (*Il Transilvano* II)	V	kp, ks	Intabulations of canzonas; ricercars of Luzzaschi, Diruta, Banchieri, Fatorini; liturgical pieces
1611b	C. Merulo	V	ks	Canzoni alla francese
1614b	B. Bottazzi	V	ks	Liturgical pieces
1615c	G. M. Trabaci	N	kp	Ricercars, versi, toccatas, gagliarde, partite

Abbreviations: M = Milan, N = Naples, R = Rome, V = Venice; kp = keyboard partitura, ks = keyboard score, Skt = Spanish keyboard tablature.

ony through syncopation and the creation of a fluid rhythmic texture. Occasionally the composer is seduced by the open-score format into voice-crossings that are more apparent to the eye than to the ear.

The Foà ricercar—twice the length of both *Transilvano* pieces combined—presumably shows Luzzaschi working free of external restrictions. It displays some of the same characteristics as the miniature pair, notably construction on two subjects related by inversion (Ex. 9.1). The overlapping sections of this large work are defined by permutations of this opening material which reveal that for Luzzaschi the "subject" is less an exact intervallic sequence than a succession of events: a step in one direction followed by a series of steps in the opposite direction (Ex. 9.2). The richness and concentration induced by the artificial format of the miniature ricercars, with their thematic and formal coherence, here expand into repetitive melodic lines and monotonous pacing. Some of the keyboard writing is awkward, but at least one passage foreshadows Frescobaldi's creation of idiomatic keyboard sound through contrapuntal materials (Ex. 9.3).

EXAMPLE 9.1 Luzzaschi, Ricercar (MS Foà 2), measures 1–7 (transcribed by James Ladewig)

EXAMPLE 9.2 Luzzaschi, Ricercar, measures 32–34

EXAMPLE 9.3 Luzzaschi, Ricercar, measures 85–89

The ricercars of the Neapolitans Mayone and Trabaci show the influence of their teacher, Giovanni de Macque, whose own manuscript set of ricercars on the twelve modes remains unpublished.[4] The four ricercars in Mayone's 1603 collection are based on double (in one case triple) subjects, of which the first tends to predominate. Virtually all of the material in the working out of each ricercar is derived from the initial motives. The twelve ricercars of Trabaci's 1603 collection follow Macque's in their arrangement by modal finales (D, E, F, G, A, C) with some transpositions. Trabaci, who was not averse to advertising his own ingenuity, indicated in the title the number of subjects (*fughe*)—from one to four—in each ricercar. In construction the subjects frequently show some reciprocal relation (a rising figure may be balanced by a descending one outlining the same interval, for example), and literal inversions (*riversi*) also appear. The subjects are introduced together at the opening of each ricercar, are employed throughout, and are usually presented simultaneously at the end. Ten of the ricercars are continuous, with no full internal cadences. The two ricercars that show clear structural divisions (VIII, on the Ruggiero, and X) add a contrasting triple section with a duple cadence; both are longer than the single-section ricercars. Ornamental figuration occurs only in these two ricercars and in the fifth one.

Trabaci calls the reader's attention to the appearance of two devices that were to become hallmarks of Frescobaldi's style. The fourth ricercar is headed "three subjects, and *inganni.*" According to Artusi, an *inganno* (deception) occurs "every time that, when one part begins a subject, the consequent one follows it not by the same intervals, but by the same names of the [hexachord] syllables."[5] In other words, new motivic materials may be derived by substituting for a note represented by a hexachord syllable the same syllable in another hexachord (Ex. 9.4). The other device is assumed in the title of the fifth ricercar, with four subjects "and notes that

EXAMPLE 9.4 a. Trabaci, *Ricercate* (1603), Quarto tono, measures 1–4

b. measures 17–18 (alto)

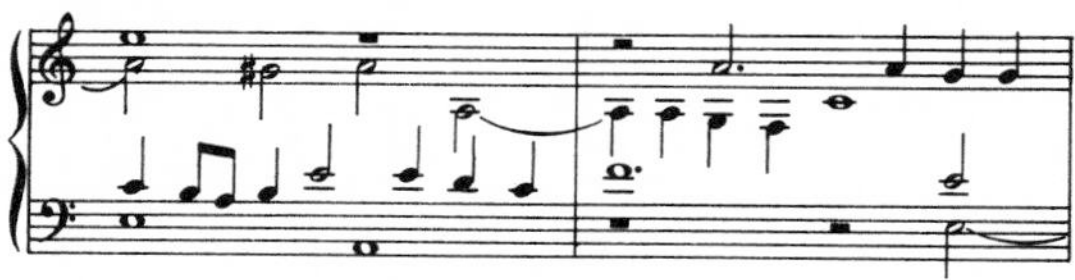

c. measure 39 (soprano)

pass as false." This constitutes an *obligo:* "a certain set condition" or subject imposed upon a contrapuntal composition.[6]

Giovanni Paolo Cima's ricercars were published just two years before Girolamo's *Fantasie* by the same firm and in the same format, and there is some evidence that Frescobaldi knew the work, since the final phrase of Cima's *Enigma musicale,* "qui non si può arrivare senza fatica," recurs at the end of Frescobaldi's ninth toccata in the 1627 set as "non senza fatiga si giunge al fine." Cima's seven ricercars do not display any obvious modal arrangement. Apel's observation that they contain two subjects, presented separately and then combined, is misleading.[7] The first subject invariably dominates each ricercar, and frequently the second is clearly derived from it by inversion. The monothematic tendency of these works is emphasized by constant motion, avoidance of cadences, and absence of figuration at structural articulations. The subject that opens Cima's sixth and seventh ricercars appears also in Frescobaldi's eleventh fantasia, and Cima's treatment of it as a tenor ostinato in a wide variety of note-values (Ricercar VII) anticipates Frescobaldi's use of ostinato.

The ricercar, the normative genre of serious contrapuntal keyboard composition, thus presented a wide spectrum of possibilities. Subjects could vary in number from one to four simultaneously and to as many as eight in succession. They could be either distinct in character or related in a variety of ways, most obviously by inversion. In character they might range from the classically profiled motto to the ornamental figure. The possibilities of structural organization consisted of everthing from monosectional works with no full internal cadences to constructions whose multiple sections were further set off by cadential ornamentation and shifts from duple to triple meter. Size could vary from the twenty-four breve miniatures of the *Transilvano* composers to the monstrous ricercars of Jacques Buus, over eleven times their length. Despite the basically contrapuntal conception of the genre, ornamental figuration was not excluded. All of the modes were employed, and modal organization of sets of ricercars was frequent. Some composers eschewed the more arcane contrapuntal devices, others employed them as an integral element in motivic development, and a few set them up as self-imposed hurdles for the greater display of compositional virtuosity.

Frescobaldi's *Fantasie* of 1608

The designation "fantasia" occurs sporadically in Italian keyboard sources, attached to everything from *cantus firmus* settings to *canzoni alla francese.* On the evidence of the twelve fantasias he published in 1608, we can conclude that Frescobaldi regarded the genre as a contrapuntal study in the tradition of the ricercar. Within this tradition Frescobaldi's fantasias do not conform to any single known model or regional school. Like the ricercars of *Il Transilvano,* Cima, and the Neapolitans, they were printed in keyboard *partitura.* Like the ricercars of Merulo, Andrea Gabrieli, Macque, Trabaci, and Antegnati, they are arranged by modes. Like Trabaci's ricercars, they are based on varying numbers of simultaneous subjects indicated in their titles, but here the arrangement is systematic: a set of three ricercars each, on one, two, three, and four subjects. In seven of the twelve fantasias Frescobaldi includes at least one triple section, like Andrea Gabrieli, Trabaci, and Antegnati, resulting in a clear three- or five-part structure. The consistent employment of augmentation and diminution suggests the influence of Andrea Gabrieli's ricercars, but unlike Andrea, Frescobaldi sometimes defines entire subsections by one device (see Table 2).

In details of structure, motivic treatment, and sectional relationships each fantasia is a unique solution. What they most clearly share is the rigor with which their composer derived each work from its initial subject at a level of concentration that he never again attempted. The subjects he invented are particularly suited to such treatment. Like those of many of

TABLE 2. The *Fantasie* of 1608

FANTASIA NUMBER	NUMBER OF SUBJECTS	FINALIS	RANGE	NUMBER OF SECTIONS (MENSURATION CHANGES)	NUMBER OF MEASURES
1	One	G (D transposed with B-flat)	G-g″	3	68
2	One	G (D transposed with B-flat)	F-d″	5	92
3	One	E	E-e″	3	85
4	Two	A (E transposed with B-flat)	E-d″	1	84
5	Two	F (no B-flat)	A-a″	3	123
6	Two	F (no B-flat)	F-f″	1	102
7	Three	G	G-g″	1	87
8	Three	G	E-f″	3	98
9	Three	A	C-a″	1	93
10	Four	A	F-e″	3	113
11	Four	F (C transposed with B-flat)	A-a″	1	99
12	Four	F (C transposed with B-flat)	E-f″	3	91

his predecessors, they usually begin by outlining some strong interval—third, fourth, fifth—in long notes that then dissolve rhythmically into scalar figures (Ex. 9.5). (In the sixth fantasia the same effect is achieved by adding an offbeat ostinato to the initial motto—Ex. 9.6.) Since Frescobaldi follows Trabaci in presenting the subjects of a multiple fantasia simultaneously, complex interrelations increase with the number of subjects. In the fantasias on two subjects the most common relation is inversion, either literal, as in the fifth fantasia, or allusive, as in the fourth (Ex. 9.7).

EXAMPLE 9.5 Frescobaldi, *Fantasie* I-V, subjects

EXAMPLE 9.6 Fantasia VI, measures 1–4

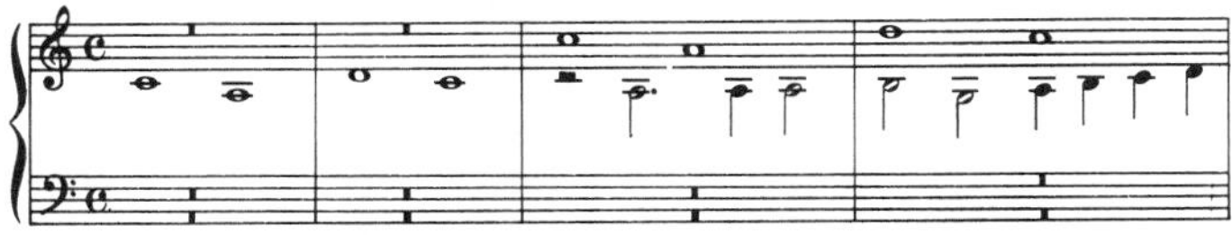

EXAMPLE 9.7 a. Fantasia, V, measures 1–4

b. Fantasia IV, measures 1–4

In the fantasias on three subjects one or two of the motives are strongly intervallic, the remainder less striking owing either to scalewise construction or to a less emphatic presentation. Frequently the subjects are related by inversion or by a stress on the same interval, as in the eighth fantasia, where all three subjects outline tetrachords, III is the inversion of I, and II is also built on the intervals of the fourth and whole tone (Ex. 9.8). In the tenth fantasia the four subjects are in fact two pairs in literal inversion (Ex. 9.9).

Like Luzzaschi, Frescobaldi regarded his subjects as a series of musical gestures rather than as a fixed interval series, and in some cases a subject may develop throughout its fantasia to emerge transformed at the end (Ex. 9.10; see also Ex. 9.8 and the analysis of Fantasia II). The most obvious

EXAMPLE 9.8 Fantasia VIII, measures 1–4

EXAMPLE 9.9 Fantasia X, measures 1–6

EXAMPLE 9.10 Fantasia VIII, measures 88–96 (see Ex. 9.8)

agents of such thematic manipulation are augmentation, diminution, and the *inganno*. The effect of regular augmentation is most apparent where repeated statements of an augmented subject are used to produce a *cantus firmus* or ostinato (Ex. 9.11). Diminution is commonly employed to generate figural material from the original subjects (Ex. 9.12). Although either technique can set the general rhythmic pace of a section, both often occur together as a means of creating a complex texture saturated with motivic material (Ex. 9.13).

The *inganno* assumes an underlying identity of hexachord syllables despite a changed intervallic sequence, and in some cases not only creates

EXAMPLE 9.11 Fantasia V, measures 80–85

EXAMPLE 9.12 Fantasia IV, measures 27–28 (see Ex. 9.7b)

EXAMPLE 9.13 Fantasia VII, measures 76–78

new figural patterns, as in measure 76 of Ex. 9.13 (derived from the first subject), but even challenges the authority of the original motif (Ex. 9.14).

Chromatic inflection of basic diatonic materials also plays an important role in Frescobaldi's motivic development, sometimes with far-reaching results. In the seventh fantasia an F is sharped at measure 26 in a statement of the first subject, answered by an inflection of C in subject III in bass and soprano; from then on, F and C are regularly sharped. The inflection moves up a fifth in measure 35, where G is sharped in a statement of subject III on D, and by measure 40 the same subject (now on B) includes G-, F-, and D-sharps. In the *Fantasie* tonal shapes are generally less important than linear counterpoint (some fantasias have no cadences on anything but the tonic), but here the harmony suggests D, A, and E major, and cadences on D.

Most of the fantasias—even those with no decisive internal cadences—have sections defined by level of rhythmic subdivision and consequent varying density of texture. (The exception is Fantasia IX, which in its poorly differentiated subjects, monotonous pacing, and occasional miscalculations of sonority is the weakest work of the set.) Frequently some detail in the preceding cadence prepares the new rate of movement, and sometimes it is reached by a rhythmic modulation (Ex. 9.15).

Frescobaldi's techniques of thematic transformation and rhythmic variation are strikingly represented in the second fantasia, "sopra un soggetto solo." Structurally, the work is laid out in six sections, two of them in triple meter (see Table 3). Section 1a is essentially an exposition in which the subject preserves its original rhythmic outline, although even

EXAMPLE 9.14 Fantasia X, measures 43–48: subject III (Ex. 9.9) as an *inganno*

EXAMPLE 9.15 Fantasia XII, measures 80–82

TABLE 3. Fantasia II

SECTION	MEASURES	CADENCES	METER
1a	1–23	Cadence on g in 23	C
1b	23–31	Cadence on D in 31	(C)
2	32–49	Cadence on G in 50	3
3	50–64	Cadence on g in 65	¢
4	65–69	Cadence on g in 70	3
5	70–76	Cadence on G in 76	C
6	76–92	Final cadence on G	(C)

here diminished versions of the subject appear as countersubjects and the second half of the subject is stated in augmentation (Ex. 9.16). After the cadence in measure 23 the subject is stated in jagged syncopations, and from then on its characteristic descending fourths and fifths permeate the texture at every rhythmic level from eighths to whole notes. The short triple section (in a rhythmically ambiguous pattern, like many in the *Fantasie*) employs both the descending fourth of the original subject and a variant derived by an *inganno* (Ex. 9.17). The texture of the following section is derived from the diminution of the subject, which also appears in its original values and in an augmentation that continues to clarify the basic descending tetrachord. This also underlies the following section (Ex. 9.18), which is reached by a rhythmic modulation (incorrectly transcribed in the Pidoux edition). The tetrachord becomes almost an ostinato in section five, whose shimmering overlapping figuration prepares the last section, in which the subject is presented in a magisterial rhythm and in its most compelling melodic form, a chromatic descending tetrachord.

EXAMPLE 9.16 Fantasia II, measures 20–22

EXAMPLE 9.17 Fantasia II, measure 32: sol fa mi re mi fa re (natural) = sol fa (natural) mi re mi fa re (soft)

EXAMPLE 9.18 Fantasia II, measures 62–64

EXAMPLE 9.19 Fantasia V, measures 43–45

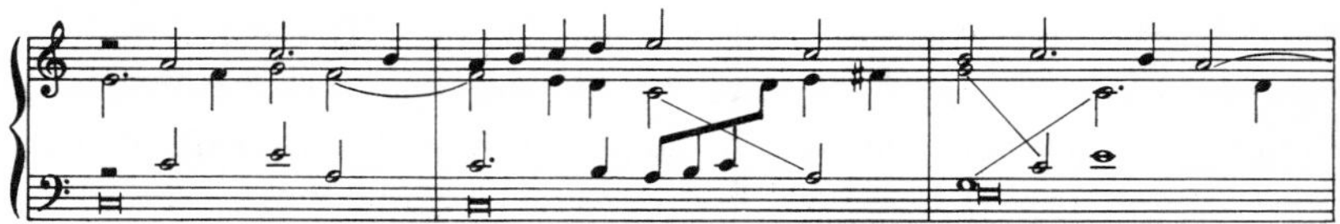

EXAMPLE 9.20 Fantasia II, measures 70–73

It is easy to give the impression that the fantasias are nothing but intellectual exercises, and certainly they are works of formidable concentration. Further, each piece is conceived essentially within the relatively limited range of three octaves around its finalis, which means that there are passages in which the clarity of the *partitura* format betrays the composer into voice-crossings unintelligible to the ear (Ex. 9.19). Nonetheless, there are also moments in which what appears to be independent part-writing in fact dissolves into an almost impressionistic keyboard sonority (Ex. 9.20).

When dealing with a group of superficially similar works in an unfamiliar style, it is easier to suggest their uniformity than to communicate their individuality. An examination of the *Fantasie* shows that within the boundaries of the genre he chose for his first keyboard publication, Frescobaldi achieved a considerable variety of formal structure and proportion, motivic structure and exploitation, rhythmic manipulation, and texture. Despite their occasional technical flaws, the fantasias display many of their young composer's gifts: a remarkable grasp of the contrapuntal potentialities of a subject and both logic and imagination in their development; a nascent sense of form and structural relationships, climax and deemphasis; and an extraordinary command of keyboard sonority within a theoretically abstract polyphonic medium.

The *Recercari et Canzoni* of 1615

The full title of Frescobaldi's next keyboard publication is *Recercari, et canzoni franzese fatte sopra diversi oblighi in partitvra.* Grammatically, only the canzonas are "made on various *oblighi,*" but in fact it is the collection of ten ricercars that is dominated by preexisting compositional requirements. Like the fantasias, the ricercars and canzonas are printed in keyboard *partitura* and are arranged modally (see Table 4). Authentic and

TABLE 4. The *Recercari* (1615)

TITLE	FINALIS	NUMBER OF MEASURES
Recerca Primo.	G (D transposed with B-flat)	82
Recercar Secondo.	G (D transposed with B-flat)	103
Recercar Terzo.	E	85
Recercar Quarto, Obligo, mi, re, fa, mi.	A (E transposed with B-flat)	90
Recercar Quinto.	F (no B-flat)	123
Recercar Sesto. Obligo fa, fa, sol, la, fa.	F (no B-flat)	76
Recercar Settimo, Obligo sol, mi, fa, la, sol.	G (C transposed)	67
Recercar Ottauo, Obligo di non [uscir] mai di grado.	G (C transposed)	70
Recercar Nono. Obligo di quattro soggetti.	A	69
Recercar Decimo, Obligo la, fa, sol, la, fa, re.	A	87

plagal ranges are denoted by *chiavette* for the higher ambitus and the usual combination of clefs for the lower range (Ex. 9.21).

The *oblighi* that govern all but two of the ricercars are of varying sorts and show the influence of a wide range of models. Recercars I and IX are closest to the southern Italian tradition, most recently expressed in Mayone's second book of *Diversi capricci* (1609). They present a cluster of subjects (three and four respectively) at the beginning, develop them jointly in the course of the work, and combine them in stretto at the end. Recercars IV, VI, VII, and X are built around solmization-ostinati, perhaps in emulation of the ostinato ricercar in Cima's 1606 volume. Recercars VIII and II have *oblighi* of external conditions: VIII that of avoiding stepwise motion, II the *obligo* of a preexisting model, Luzzaschi's Foà ricercar.[8] Like Recercar II, Recercars IV, V, IX, and X also derive from the northern Italian tradition of sectional ricercars.

These varying *oblighi* are realized in a variety of formal and musical solutions. Each of the sectional ricercars, for example, creates and employs its material in different patterns. Recercar II follows its model in defining its three sections by new material, each subject accompanied by a countersubject derived by strict inversion and resolved by cadences of increasing weight. Recercar III is additive in its treatment of its three successive subjects (A, BA, CBA). Recercar V presents its three subjects in a long opening duet, treats each of them separately in four parts, and combines them in the last section.

As one might expect from the appearance of four solmization subjects, ostinato techniques play a large part in the *Recercari.* The subject of the fourth ricercar, mi re fa mi, appears in all four voices on A (soft hexachord) or E (natural). Its first set of appearances (measures 1–28) presents it in semibreves, its second in breves, and its third in double breves. Each section has a different countersubject, the second and third freely treated in inversion as well. In the seventh ricercar, on sol mi fa la sol, the subject appears as an ostinato in tenor in the hard hexachord on D and the natural hexachord on G in semibreves and breves (or double semibreves tied across the bar) and double breves. Unlike in the fourth ricercar, the texture is continuous and is dominated throughout by a three-repeated-note figure. The ostinato la fa sol la re of the tenth ricercar appears in the other voices

EXAMPLE 9.21 Clef-arrangements in the *Recercari*

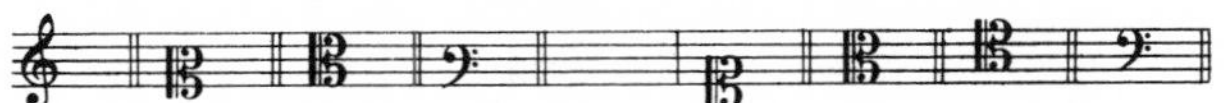

at the beginning of the work and constitutes the entire material of the soprano part in a variety of rhythmic patterns.

The sixth ricercar is a delightful study on the ostinato fa fa sol la fa. The subject has been traced to the *Dodekachordon* of Glareanus, but it is also identical with the tune "Fra Jacopino went off to Rome, a staff on his shoulder and a pilgrim's gown on his back" later employed by Frescobaldi as an ostinato in a set of variations on the Ruggiero. The tune is presented throughout in the alto on F (natural hexachord) or C (hard). It is first announced in its original rhythmic form, but its succeeding entries are in notes of equal length. The first four statements of the ostinato occur at regular intervals (measures 4, 8, 12, 16) in even whole notes. At measures 21 and 26 it appears in breves. In the first statement each breve corresponds to a measure, but the second foreshadows the approaching rhythmic delirium by splitting the breves across the bar. In measure 39 the subject appears in dotted halves against the undotted halves and quarters of the surrounding material, while in measure 45 it is stated in syncopation against the other parts. In measure 49 there begins a regular augmentation, first in dotted whole notes (always against a one-breve bar), then in dotted breves (measure 54), and finally double breves (measure 65)—see Ex. 9.22. As elsewhere in the *Recercari,* Frescobaldi develops the ostinato material in the other voices, but also invents new countersubjects.

The *obligo* of the eighth ricercar, the precondition of avoiding stepwise motion ("Obligo di non uscir mai di grado"), represents the first appearance in Frescobaldi's work of the external limitations that so stimulated his imagination. The subject matter of this ricercar—thirds, fourths, fifths, and octaves—did not encourage the definition of sections by new mate-

EXAMPLE 9.22 a. Recercar VI, measures 39–43

b. measures 45–47

c. measures 55–61

rial. Instead, Frescobaldi employed the principles of rhythmic variation from the ostinato ricercars to produce a study in changing rhythmic textures whose increasing offbeats and syncopations provide the rhythmic equivalent of a contrapuntal stretto.

By comparison with the fantasias, the ricercars show a less obsessive concentration on deriving all the motivic material of a work from a single nexus of ideas. Although most of them are organized into sections, these are now more subtly defined than in the fantasias. Unlike the wide range of rhythmic levels characteristic of the fantasias, the ricercars move in a steady minim pulse, and such obvious devices for differentiating sections as triple passages and florid decoration are totally absent. Variety is achieved more unobtrusively through manipulations of texture and the placing and relative emphasis of cadences. This is reflected in an enhanced freedom of keyboard writing; although the range of the ricercars does not exceed that of the fantasias, their part-writing generally avoids the occasional thickness and obscure voice-crossings of the earlier collection. In its imposition of *oblighi* and the variety of their treatment, the *Recercari* shows the first overt signs of two characteristics that animate much of Girolamo's later work: his predilection for self-imposed technical challenges and his musical wit in their solution.

The northern Italian keyboard canzona dates back to Marc'Antonio Cavazzoni's intabulations of four French chansons in his publication of 1523. Two decades later, his son Girolamo moved the genre a step further toward independence from vocal models by writing canzonas as paraphrases or parodies rather than simple diminutions of vocal originals, a distinction retained by Andrea Gabrieli, who titled his intabulations "canzoni" and his paraphrases "ricercari." The keyboard canzona retained close links with the instrumental canzona, so that four of Merulo's keyboard canzonas of 1592, shorn of their figuration, were printed as ensemble canzonas in Raverij's 1608 collection. Pellegrini's *Canzoni* of 1599 marks the full emergence of the independent keyboard canzona, which in the Venetian tradition is characterized by contrasts of theme and texture between clearly defined sections, often emphasized by the repetition of a section. (In M. A. Cavazzoni's canzonas the patterns ABA, AAB, and AABA occur; Cima usually repeats the closing section, ABB.) Other northern Italian composers such as Pellegrini and Cima reinforce these contrasts by inserting one or occasionally two sections of triple meter into the prevailing duple meter. Ornamental figuration appears, especially at cadences, but the conventional dactyllic themes and generally rather abstract part-writing still betray the influence of the instrumental canzona. Even in the case of canzonas derived from preexisting chansons, northern composers often added allusive family names to canzona titles.

The keyboard canzonas of the Neapolitans Trabaci and Mayone present a much livelier picture. Their figuration—less ornamental than functional—is exuberant, sometimes bizarre, and occasionally unplayable. Triple sections are a regular feature of these canzonas, and several Neapolitan works even open with chordal passages in triple meter. The subjects of the three or five sections of a typical Neapolitan canzona are generally derived from the opening material—an early instance of the variation-canzona. The subjects themselves are more varied than their northern counterparts. Two of the canzonas from Trabaci's 1603 collection state their initial subject chordally, and another subject is chromatic in outline. Unlike the northerners, Neapolitan composers did not give titles to their canzonas.

Frescobaldi's first published canzonas, the three ensemble works published in the Raverij collection, are clearly derived from the northern Italian tradition. The first, for four voices, is continuous in texture except for a coda and derives its material from the first subject and its countersubject. The second, in five parts, begins with a dactyllic theme and countersubject, subsequently simplified to an ascending and a descending scale, from which the remaining material is derived. (Luzzaschi's four-part canzona in the same collection employs similar material.) The continuous pulse and overlapped sections of the work are balanced by a variety of rhythmic surfaces. The third canzona is even more clearly Venetian, since it is set for double choir and marked by fanfare motives, alternation of the two choirs, and a sectional construction emphasized by a repeat of the second half of the work.

The five keyboard canzonas with which Frescobaldi concluded the *Recercari et canzoni* show little trace of Neapolitan influence. They all begin with imitative figures marked by the customary dactyllic patterns and repeated notes of the north Italian canzona. Each one is clearly divided into sections cadencing on the tonic or some other prominent tone of the mode (B-flat in G Dorian, for example), and the sectional organization of the canzonas is further emphasized by the inclusion of one to three passages in triple meter in each canzona (see Table 5).

TABLE 5. The *Canzoni* (1615)

TITLE	FINALIS	SECTIONS	CADENCES
Canzon Prima, Primo Tono.	G (D transposed with B-flat)	C	G
		O3	G
		C	G
		O3	D
		C	G
Canzon Seconda, Primo Tono.	G (D transposed with B-flat)	C	G
		O3	G
		C	G
		3	B-flat
		C	G
Canzon Terza. Secondo Tono.	G (D transposed with B-flat)	C	G
		O3	D
		C	D
		C3	G
		C	G
Canzon Quarta. Sesto Tono.	F	C	A
		Ͼ3	C
		C	F
		3	C
		C	F
		3	C
		C	F
Canzon Quinta. Nono Tono.	A	C	A
		Ͼ3	C
		C	A

The triple sections are continuous, but the duple ones—especially the opening sections—may be subdivided by cadences and the re-presentation of the original material, the introduction of new material, or both. In all except the first canzona, material from the opening section is brought back in the concluding one, as in ensemble canzonas. As far as thematic relations between these sections are concerned, Frescobaldi's treatment varies from new and unrelated material for each section (Canzona I) through the return of the original material or its derivatives in a concluding section (IV, V) to works in which all the major sections are based on the same material (the variation-canzonas II and III—see Ex. 9.23).

Although not a variation-canzona, Canzona IV is the largest and in some ways the most stylistically advanced of the set. Its opening section has three subdivisions: the first (measures 1–12) presents the first subject

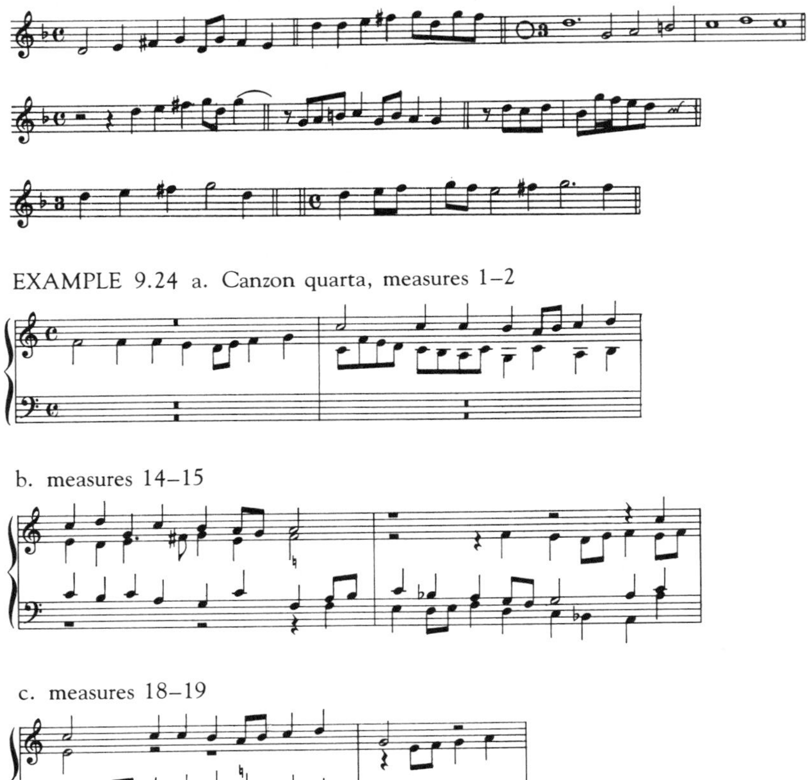

EXAMPLE 9.23 Canzona II, variations of the subject

EXAMPLE 9.24 a. Canzon quarta, measures 1–2

b. measures 14–15

c. measures 18–19

against a running countersubject; the second (measures 13–16) treats the second half of the subject as an independent figure; and the third (measures 17–25) develops the two motives together (Ex. 9.24). The short chordal triple section that follows concludes with a toccatalike flourish, a feature absent from the rather square rhythmic outline of the other canzonas. A second, more contrapuntal triple section introduces another duple passage presenting new material and cadencing into a third triple section, again concluded by a free *passaggio.* The final duple section returns to the opening subject, accompanied by a figure derived from the initial subject and developed in the second area of the opening section.

The canzonas of the 1615 collection form a pendant to the ricercars, juxtaposing sectional works in a texture marked by consistent and regular imitation (insofar as those two adjectives can be applied to any production of Frescobaldi) with the highly individual formal and textural solutions of the ricercars. In both sets of works Girolamo carries the tradition of his musical training to a logical conclusion in his mastery of formal and thematic treatment within the context of strict part-writing.

10

Songlike *Affetti* and Diversity of *Passi*: The *Toccate e Partite Libro Primo* of 1614–1616

With the publication of his first collection of toccatas, variations, and dances in 1615, Frescobaldi marked out the other half of his province as a keyboard composer. His previous works, although intended for the keyboard, grew out of the contrapuntal tradition of abstract part-writing manifest in an open-score format. The traditional concentration on motivic development dominated both form and content. Figuration was essentially motivic in origin, and structural articulations—whether unstressed, as in the fantasia, elided, as in the ricercar, or emphasized, as in the canzona—were defined by successive stages in thematic manipulation.

The historical development and compositional problems of the toccata, ostinato variation, and dance were in many respects diametrically opposed to those of the contrapuntal tradition. To begin with, they had developed as the province of the performer/improviser rather than the skilled contrapuntist. Their parameters of composition were not horizontal motives defining vertical structures but harmonic armatures—given in the variation and in some dances, contrived in the toccata—expressed by chords and by figuration in which motivic development played a negligible role. This native freedom of texture and part-writing was mirrored in the more flexible keyboard score, and dances and works based on secular materials were usually performed on the harpsichord; both facts are reflected in Frescobaldi's choice of keyboard score rather than *partitura* for the *Toccate* and its designation as *intavolatura di cimbalo.*

Frescobaldi's immediate point of departure for the most important of these genres was the Venetian toccata, as exemplified in Andrea Gabrieli's toccatas published posthumously in the 1593 *Intonazioni.* These consist of an opening in chords, perhaps enlivened with imitative figuration, and stretches of chords and scales alternating between the hands; these *passaggi* in eighths or sixteenths were sometimes relieved by a central section in undecorated contrapuntal texture. Although Gabrieli's toccatas contain in embryo all the elements of Frescobaldi's, their general impression is one of ill-defined structure and mechanical figuration. The Venetian-style toccatas published the same year in *Il Transilvano* lack even the textural contrast of Andrea's toccatas, but the two works contributed by Luzzasco Luzzaschi and Paolo Quagliati (ca. 1555–1628) are of interest as showing how the genre was treated by Frescobaldi's teacher and by an illustrious Roman contemporary. Both toccatas show a more idiomatic keyboard style, marked in Luzzaschi by impressionistic part-writing and shifts of range and in Quagliati by imaginative short imitative figures and sequences (Ex. 10.1).

It remained for another Venetian, Claudio Merulo, to reveal the latent possibilities of the toccata in his two collections of 1598 and 1604, an imposing cycle of nineteen works grouped in ten modes. Merulo's toccatas retain the external features of the Venetian toccata—chordal openings, figurally decorated harmonic successions, and contrasting contrapuntal sections—but they are constructed on a grander scale and infused with a new richness and expressiveness. This is particularly apparent

EXAMPLE 10.1 a. Luzzaschi, Toccata del quarto tuono, measures 1–8

b. Quagliati, Toccata dell'ottavo tuono, measures 14–16

EXAMPLE 10.2 Merulo, Toccata quarta, secondo tono (1598), measures 17–19

in the treatment of figuration, which replaces the mechanical scales of the Gabrieli toccata with material that is varied and unpredictable both in itself and in the changing textures it creates (Ex. 10.2). This greater freedom of texture is also apparent in the presence of contrapuntal passages not only as separate (and in fact detachable) sections but also as passing inflections of figural texture (Ex. 10.3). Merulo's expressive and sophisticated figuration, the increased subtlety of his textures, and his refinement of the conventions of the Venetian toccata raised the genre to a level where, for the first time, it was capable of revealing the full range of a composer's art.

This was not the case with the toccatas published by Trabaci and Mayone in 1603 and by Mayone in 1609, which have, in Apel's apt image, the air of plants grown in alien soil. For the most part they follow the general outlines of the Venetian toccata, with contrapuntal sections placed toward the end of a movement as well as in the middle, but their figuration is willfully erratic in design and sometimes tediously repetitious (as well as occasionally unplayable, perhaps a result of the Neapolitan

EXAMPLE 10.3 Merulo, Toccata ottava, quarto tono (1598), measures 12–14

partitura format). In Mayone's toccatas, however, the figuration sometimes achieves a compelling sequential logic (Ex. 10.4). The toccatas of Trabaci and Mayone present a few original features later taken over by Frescobaldi. One toccata in Trabaci's 1603 collection contains a section in triple meter, a feature absent from Venetian toccatas, and many of his and Mayone's toccatas employ triplet figuration. Mayone's toccatas often rein in the motion after a cadence by a shift to half-note chords, chromatically inflected with suspensions (Ex. 10.5). Nonetheless, though Frescobaldi borrowed these devices from the Neapolitans, his real forerunner was Merulo.

Six years after the appearance of Mayone's second collection, Frescobaldi's *Toccate* revealed a new world of brilliant, idiomatic, and sometimes disconcerting figured keyboard writing. The seventeenth-century player may have been as startled by these works as we are, since Girolamo felt obliged to preface the first edition with a short guide to their performance, "by means of which the works will be found easier than they appear," and to enlarge and revise these directions for the second edition (see Chapter 15).

In his second preface Frescobaldi characterizes the contents of the collection as "the manner of playing with *affetti cantabili* and diversity of *passi,*" terms whose meaning is elucidated obliquely in the two prefaces. In its narrow sense, *passi* denotes passages in consistent figuration such as eighths, sixteenths, and *passi doppi* for both hands, all of which are to be

EXAMPLE 10.4 Mayone (1609), Toccata prima, measures 27–35

EXAMPLE 10.5 Mayone (1609), Toccata quinta per il cimbalo cromatico, measures 10–14

distinguished clearly one from another in performance. More generally, *passi* are the main structural divisions of the toccatas, marked off by a minim chord in both hands (presumably on the tonic, as the preface to the *Capricci* of 1624 suggests) and sufficiently complete for the performer to end there. *Effetti* or "effects" are ornaments, such as trills and various *passaggi,* whose performance often involves rhythmic alteration of the printed text. Parallel passages in the two prefaces regarding flexibility of tempo in the toccata link the *effetto* with the *affetto,* a state of feeling like "the sense of the words" in a madrigal. The structural areas of the toccata to which Frescobaldi alludes in his prefaces are the opening in arpeggiated chordal texture, the continuation that consists of smaller *passi* forming self-sufficient units, internal "suspensions and dissonances," and cadences. The *affetti cantabili* and *diversità di passi* of the toccatas thus describe works in large sections built up of contrasting units whose articulations and contrasts are further emphasized in performance. The aesthetic that governs them is dramatic in intent and vocal in expression.

This ideal of "songlike *affetti*" completes the transformation of figural material from ornamental to affective begun by Merulo. In Frescobaldi's toccatas even the most traditional figuration is treated expressively. For example, when set against a *passaggio,* the measured trill is to be played not as written but rather as fast as possible, and the *passaggio* is to be *affettuoso* (Ex. 10.6).[1] The written-out trill, little more than an annoying mannerism in the works of Andrea Gabrieli, is fused by Frescobaldi with two vocal ornaments, Cavalieri's *zimbalo* and *trillo,* and acquires the potential energy of a coiled spring to set a static texture in motion (Ex. 10.7). In more extended linear figurations, the *passaggi* of earlier composers, Frescobaldi goes far beyond the alternations of scales and chords between the hands that were a staple of Merulo's toccatas. Even where the alternation is fairly regular, the pacing has a new urgency (Ex. 10.8). Within a single *passo* the figuration may range from relaxed scales to lines of melodic convolution and rhythmic complexity, often raised to a higher power by *passi doppi* of unprecedented rhythmic canons, cross-accents, and bold sweeps through the instrument (Ex. 10.9).

Frescobaldi's sensitivity to range and color is an important element in this new figural style. The range of an entire toccata is often laid out in the

EXAMPLE 10.6 Frescobaldi, Toccata III, measure 25

EXAMPLE 10.7 Romanesca, variation six, measure 1

EXAMPLE 10.8 Toccata VIII, measures 24–27

EXAMPLE 10.9 Toccata I, measures 16–21

opening section, and its extremes function as barriers that are reached with a sense of real physical effort; when they are shattered, as in Toccata VI, it is a musical event of calculated brutality (Ex. 10.10). This same sensitivity governs Frescobaldi's deliberately ambiguous part-writing and his bold use of octave transpositions, which translate the contrapuntal logic of the *Fantasie* and *Recercari* into a kind of fourth dimension. Changes of voice may be presented to the ear in unbroken lines (a device found in earlier Venetian toccatas), or a single line may suddenly split into two voices (Ex. 10.11). Resolutions are transferred from one voice to another or doubled in octaves, and harmonic and melodic events are underscored by dramatic shifts of register which, at their most extreme, can transform melodic and even rhythmic sequences (Ex. 10.12).

EXAMPLE 10.10 a. Toccata VI, measure 8

b. measure 11

c. measures 13–14

d. measures 34–35

EXAMPLE 10.11 Toccata VIII, measures 13–17

EXAMPLE 10.12 a. Romanesca, variation four, measures 2–3

b. Toccata VII, measure 31

c. Toccata V, measures 33–34

The "diversity of *passi*" in the toccatas is expressed as a constant variety of musical texture, the product of variations in regularity of figuration, rate of harmonic change, the shape and contrapuntal density of imitative material, and chromaticism. The short conventional rhythmic patterns that recur throughout the collection—anapests, dactyls, dotted and Lombard rhythms—are primary materials for imitative textures: not the isolated passages that appear in the toccatas of Andrea Gabrieli and Merulo (and here, in Toccatas VIII and IX) but imitations woven into the musical fabric. At the openings of the toccatas such imitations lighten the chordal structures, flickering from voice to voice (another device that Frescobaldi could have found in the toccatas of Merulo). In the course of the movement they check or impel forward motion with a subtlety unknown to Girolamo's predecessors, and the ebb and flow of intensity in the *passi* is a product of the relative saturation of the texture with these motives and the consequent complexity of their accents (Ex. 10.13). The cadences of the large sections are frequently set off by changes in texture, an

EXAMPLE 10.13 a. Toccata X, measures 1–3

b. Toccata IV, measures 30–33

c. Toccata VII, measures 35–36

EXAMPLE 10.14 a. Toccata VI, measures 8–11

b. Toccata IX, measures 16–18

intensification of short motives, a relaxation into more extended and regular *passaggi,* or—particularly in final cadences—a *passo doppio,* all emphasized by a *rallentando* (Ex. 10.14).

After these full cadences of *passi* Frescobaldi often employs one of two devices. The first, which he seems to have adopted from the Neapolitans, consists of dissonant suspensions in half-notes, which may be struck together (repeating the suspension) and reiterated "so as not to leave the instrument empty" (Ex. 10.15). The second method of creating a dramatic change in texture and character after a cadence is derived from Merulo (see

EXAMPLE 10.15 Toccata X, measures 18–19

EXAMPLE 10.16 a. Romanesca, variation eight, measure 5

b. Variation nine, measure 7

EXAMPLE 10.17 Toccata IX, measures 11–13

Ex. 10.2) and consists of an abrupt redistribution of parts into solo voice and accompaniment, the solo rising in range and usually anticipating the accompaniment—the most obviously *cantabile* of Frescobaldi's *affetti* (Ex. 10.16).

All these changing figurations and textures are firmly anchored in chords that are rarely stated as baldly as those implied by the bass, even in figured passages (Ex. 10.17). Although Frescobaldi's toccatas follow the modal arrangement of Merulo's collections and Girolamo's own *Fantasie* and *Recercari,* their harmonic structures are neither clearly modal nor clearly tonal. The strongest harmonic relationships are fourth- and fifth-related progressions in root position, colored by step-related chords or others inverted to produce stepwise motion in the bass. These progressions frequently produce smaller parenthetical events within a larger harmonic context (Ex. 10.18). The minim cadences of the large *passi* occur on the tonic or some related degree. (In general, Frescobaldi's harmonic thinking throughout his career shows less interest in varied tonal structures than many of his contemporaries had. As late as the Bergamasca in the *Fiori musicali* of 1635, five of the seven full cadences occur on the tonic, the other two on the dominant.)

EXAMPLE 10.18 Toccata IV, measures 1–7

The pivotal sections in "ligature, overo durezze" are but one example of the Neapolitan-influenced chromaticism that marks the *Toccate.* Toccata XII is in fact an essay in the Neapolitan *toccata di durezze e ligature,* handled with a surer sense of form and harmonic direction than that of its predecessors. As early as the *Fantasie* Frescobaldi had learned the directional and organizing power of a chromatic line. This device became the thread linking the harmonies of his chromatic works, often operating almost subliminally through octave-transpositions and changes of voice (Ex. 10.19). In the progressions that govern the toccatas, major and minor thirds on the same degree are interchangeable, and the Neapolitan device of flattening a previously major third is a frequent melodic inflection (Ex. 10.20).

All of these elements—chordal structures in a personal harmonic and chromatic idiom, expressive figuration, variety of texture, large sectional organization—combine to produce some general idea of the Frescobaldian toccata. An examination of Toccata I will suggest how they interact in context. The three large *passi* that make up the work are defined by minim chords: I, measures 1–16, moving from g to G; II, 16–27, G–D; III, 27–40, D–G. (Other minim cadences in measures 9, 13, and 30 are overlapped or appear temporary.) The first two measures function as the opening, the quasi-improvisatory section that states a pure tonic note or chord and moves gradually to harmonic and rhythmic exploration. Here the chordal texture is lightened by imitative anapest figures and lays out a number of harmonic and melodic alternatives even before leaving the G Dorian tonic (Ex. 10.21). The movement to the dominant, characteristically accomplished by a stepwise and chromatically inflected inter-

EXAMPLE 10.19 Toccata XII, measures 6–9

EXAMPLE 10.20 Toccata VII, measures, 1–3

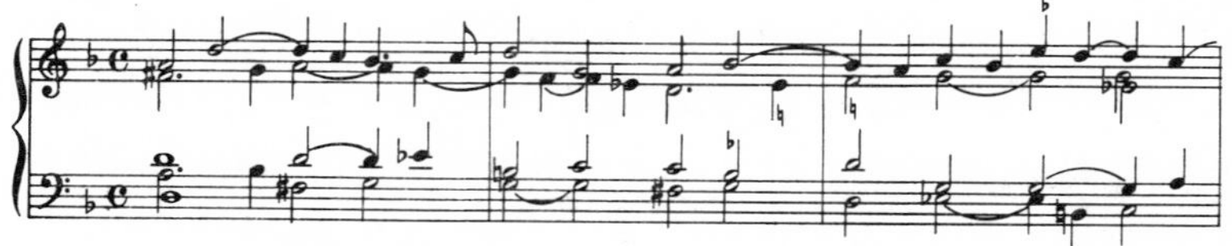

EXAMPLE 10.21 Toccata I, measures 1–2

EXAMPLE 10.22 Toccata I, measures 3–9

mediary, is accompanied by a loosening of the opening figuration into scale passages, and the establishment of V as a secondary tonic is coordinated with the establishment of the soprano A as the upper limit of the range, which is confirmed by a sweep through the entire range of the toccata (Ex. 10.22). After the momentary cadence on A as V of D, Frescobaldi explores the flat side of the mode prepared in the inflections of the opening two measures, again by fourth- and fifth-related chords and stepwise transitions (Ex. 10.23). In measure 13 the tonic cadence on D is reinterpreted as the dominant of the opening g (thus closing the harmonic parenthesis), and

EXAMPLE 10.23 Toccata I, measures 9–13

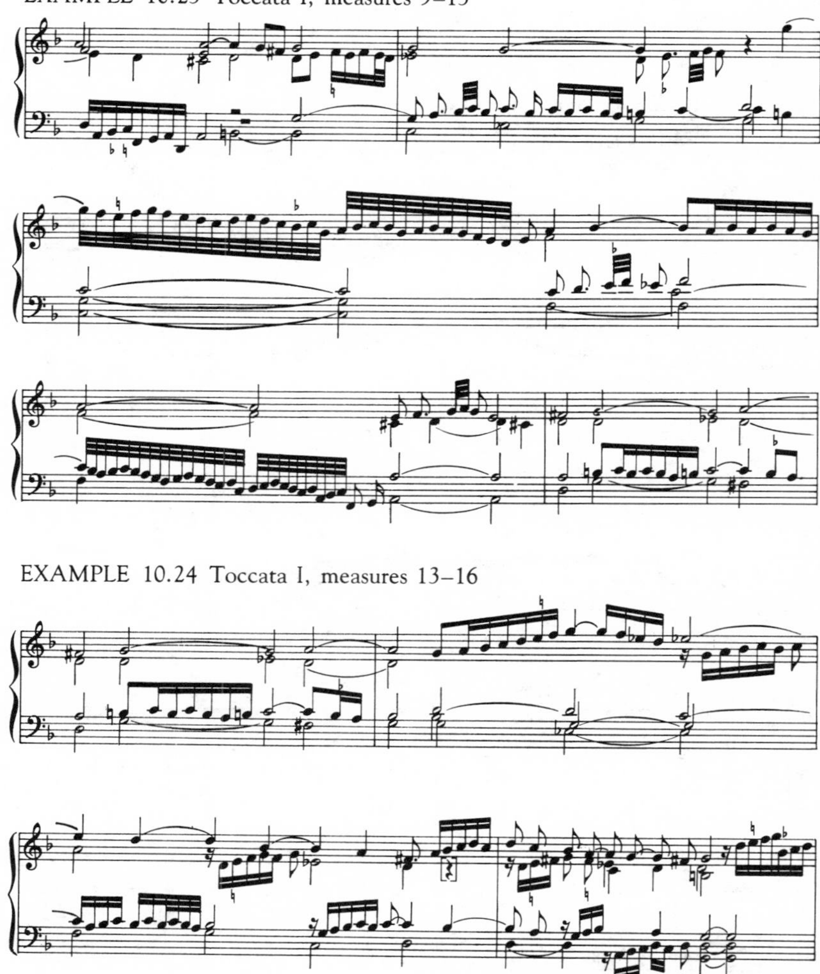

EXAMPLE 10.24 Toccata I, measures 13–16

an ever tighter imitative texture pushes toward the final cadence of the *passo* (Ex. 10.24). The second section consists of two contrasting *passi.* The first begins in long garlands of scales that gradually contract into a *passo doppio* ending on a deceptive cadence (see Ex. 10.9). The second opens with two motives in imitation dissolving into *passaggi* and reintroduces D as a second tonic (Ex. 10.25). This ambiguity is reinforced by an *affetto cantabile* that momentarily checks the forward motion of the texture to prepare the final section, an unbroken succession of harmonies stating both the flat and sharp sides of the tonic expressed in constant short imitations that broaden into rising vocal lines and a final brilliant *passo doppio* (Ex. 10.26).

The variations in the *Toccate e partite* may be divided into "large" and "small" sets—the first the extensive variations on the Ruggiero and the Romanesca, in which each partita unfolds freely and continuously without internal repetition, the second the variations on the *Aria di Monica* and the

EXAMPLE 10.25 Toccata I, measures 21–27

EXAMPLE 10.26 Toccata I, measures 35–40

six *Partite sopra Follia* added to the second edition, which retain the structural repetitions of their originals (AAB in the Monica, alternately AABB and AAB in the Follia). All of these subjects except the Monica had been treated by Neapolitan composers. The first keyboard Ruggiero was the work of Macque, and both Trabaci and Mayone published extensive variation-sets on the same material. The Romanesca was treated by Mayone in his collection of 1609, and the Follia of Girolamo's variations is a version of the Fedele, a pattern otherwise mostly cultivated by Neapolitan writers; Frescobaldi's setting also reflects the changing signatures of Trabaci's Fedele.[2]

Nonetheless, the solidity of harmonic conception and the expressiveness and variety of surface texture that characterize the toccatas of Frescobaldi's first collection also lift his variation-sets far beyond those of his predecessors. The original form of the Romanesca is preserved in Antonio de Cabezón's "Guardame las vacas" published posthumously in 1578 (Ex. 10.27). It was treated by a number of keyboard composers, and by 1589 Arbeau described it as "hackneyed and trite." It was recast—apparently by the Neapolitans—in a new form which not only prolonged its life for another quarter-century but which also illustrates vividly the difference between sixteenth- and seventeenth-century sensibilities (Ex. 10.28). Where Cabezón had followed a bass that merely defined a clear succession of chords, the Neapolitans created a line in which the original elements

EXAMPLE 10.27 Cabezón, "Guardame las vacas" (harmonic outline)

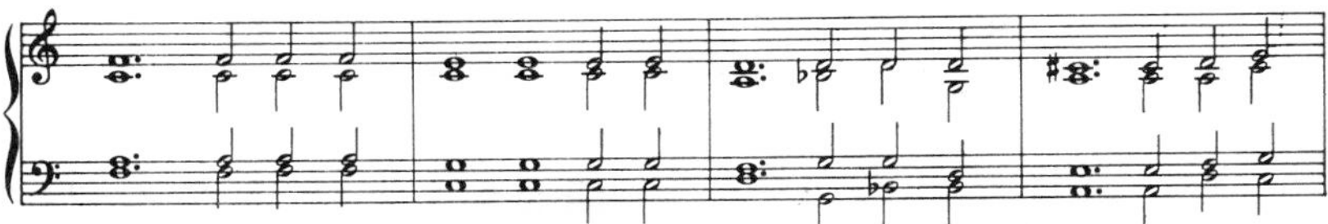

EXAMPLE 10.28 The seventeenth-century Romanesca

EXAMPLE 10.29 a. Scipione Stella (ca. 1600), Romanesca, measures 66–69

b. Mayone, Romanesca, variation one, measures 11–13

c. Frescobaldi, Romanesca, variation eight, measures 1–2

were enlarged by melodic passing-tones, each of which in turn became a potential basis for figuration. Although Stella and Mayone exploit this new musical space, nothing suggests more vividly the new scope of Frescobaldi's variation-treatment than his handling of the same material (Ex. 10.29).

In the second edition of the *Toccate e partite* the toccatas were reprinted with only minor alterations of notation, some incorporating Frescobaldi's suggestions in his prefaces. The variation-sets, however, were substantially reworked and a new one, the Follia, added. The emphasis in Girolamo's prefaces on the sectional independence of both toccatas and variations raises the question of whether they were intended as cumulative entities or were conceived as merely additive structures. The revisions of the variations do not support a clear answer. The Monica set, in which Frescobaldi rewrote the original fifth variation, discarded the sixth, and added six new variations, shows no more overall cohesion in the second version than in the first. The same is largely true of the Ruggiero, where Frescobaldi wrote a new first variation, retained only the end of the original second one, simplified the ending of variation seven, replaced variation eight, and added four new variations. These changes are largely unrelated improvements, as in the replacement of the stodgy opening variation with a richer and livelier texture and the removal of the overly emphatic closing of the seventh variation, but the last three variations show some coherence in their movement from undecorated suspensions in thirds through an imitative texture to a concluding tripla, both also in thirds.

In recasting the Romanesca set, Frescobaldi went beyond localized improvements to clarify and sharpen the continuity, structure, and dramaturgy of the cycle, at the same time enriching the cross-references among the variations. He replaced the first four sections with new *partite,* added a triple variation as number five, repeated the original variations five through eleven as six through twelve, replaced the original twelfth variation, and added two more sections at the end.

A new coherence is evident from the first variation, where the pattern of thirds and suspensions only foreshadowed in the original dominates the new variation. The alternation of decorated and undecorated variations in the first version is dropped, and the eighth-note motion at the end of variation one now flows uninterrupted into the beginning of variation two. The trill at the end of the new third variation similarly expands into the opening of the following section, the regular anapests of the original fourth variation are reserved for more telling use in the new variation thirteen, and the interpolated triple section acts as a punctuation between the first and second groups of variations.

The second group, numbers six and seven, moves from the tense reentrant figuration of the first to the more regular and brilliant writing of the second. The two following variations, presumably to be taken at a somewhat faster basic tempo since both lack *passaggi* and the first is marked ₵ rather than C, present a contrast in rhythmic texture and melodic inflection. Both are homophonic, the first largely diatonic with a few suspensions, the second highly chromatic with suspensions and passages of *affetti cantabili,* a procedure that recalls Trabaci's Fedele variations of 1603. The next three variations, ten to twelve in the new arrangement, mark the high point of the set in terms of virtuosity, culminating in the dazzling thirty-seconds of variation twelve.

In place of the original last variation with its fragmented rhythmic surface, as his concluding sections Frescobaldi presents two variations without *passaggi,* the first in even anapests, the second in half-note suspensions. On paper this seems an anticlimax. In much music of this period, however, the point of greatest intensity is reached well before the end, which functions not as a climax but as a confirmation or a transition back to the original level. Here the regular rhythm of the thirteenth variation acts as a brake on the brilliance of the preceding sections. The concluding partita is not only a schematic reduction of its predecessor, but in its persistent use of thirds it also reestablishes a link with the opening variation. Finally, by the utter sparseness of the closing Frescobaldi seems to thrust on our attention the simplicity of the foundation on which he has erected this imposing edifice.

The second edition of the *Toccate e partite* closes with four correnti, Girolamo's first printed essays in the world of the dance. Each consists of two sections, the first concise and beginning with an upbeat and a descending fourth (except for the third corrente, which begins on a downbeat with an ascending fourth) and the second more discursive rhythmically and metrically. If the writing sometimes betrays its descent from the crude chordally accompanied melodies of earlier Italian keyboard dances, it also displays refinements like the slithering hemiola suspensions of the second corrente.

Frescobaldi never surpassed the finest achievements of the first volume of *Toccate e partite.* Decades later, Bonini used "toccatas and Romanescas" of Frescobaldi to epitomize the common currency of keyboard players. Even granting all that Girolamo may have owed his predecessors in Venice and Naples, the brilliance and control of his keyboard writing seem unprecedented. It is perhaps more accurate to suggest that the technical mastery of the *Fantasie* and *Recercari* provides the foundation for the *Toccate,* and that it is upon the noble structure and lucid articulation of his earlier works that Frescobaldi spreads the shining mosaic of his toccatas and variations.

11

Various Subjects and Airs: The *Capricci* of 1624

The two versions of the *Toccate e partite* appear to have exhausted momentarily Frescobaldi's energies as a keyboard composer. After 1616 he published nothing new except a few fugitive vocal pieces until the appearance of the *Capricci* "written on various subjects, and airs" in 1624. The designation "capriccio" permitted him the unrestricted exercise of his personal fantasy since it had been attached to almost every category of keyboard composition. Trabaci and Mayone used the term generically for the contents of their collections. The two capriccios in Trabaci's 1603 volume (the only works in the four Neapolitan collections actually to bear the name) were treated as Neapolitan variation-canzonas, and the two genres were equated also in the title of Ottavio Bariola's *Capricci overo canzoni* of 1594. Macque applied the designation to pieces with named subjects in both free and imitative textures, as did Banchieri in the 1605 edition of *L'organo suonarino.* In Andrea Gabrieli's posthumously printed works the term was applied to pieces as diverse as a ricercar on the madrigal "Con lei foss'io" and a set of variations on the Passamezzo.

Most of these varieties of capriccio appear in Frescobaldi's collection. Nine of the twelve capriccios are composed on a subject identified in the title, and all of these are multisectional works resembling the canzona in structure. One of them, the "Capriccio sopra un soggetto," is a variation-canzona in subject as well as in treatment. The two capriccios whose *obligo* is a procedure rather than a subject, *durezze* and *ligature al contrario* (the resolution of dissonant suspensions upward rather than downward), instead resemble ricercars. The remaining capriccio, on the aria "Or che noi rimena," is a set of five variations that was deleted from subsequent editions of the collection.

Although Frescobaldi returned to the *partitura* format of his earlier works in the *Capricci* (partly for didactic reasons), the collection shows a new softening of his contrapuntal writing by the figural resources of the toccatas and *partite.* His preface to the collection shows him still grappling with the central problem of the *Toccate,* the construction of multisectional works whose components are governed by a variety of *affetti:*

> Since playing these works could result in much effort for some, seeing that they are of differing tempos and variations, as it also appears that the practice of the said study of score-writing is laid aside by many, I have wished to point out that in those things which do not seem governed by contrapuntal practice one must first seek the *affetto* of that passage and the goal of the Author for the delight of the ear and the way that it is sought in playing. In these Compositions entitled Capriccios I have not kept as easy a style as in my Ricercars, but one must not however judge their difficulty before putting them well in practice on the instrument, where one will know with study the *affetto* which it must have.

Girolamo's fears that the collection was discouragingly difficult were groundless since, combined with the *Recercari et canzoni,* it went through more editions in his lifetime than any of his other collections except the first volume of toccatas.

One reason for the popularity of the *Capricci* may have been the accessibility of its subjects. Many of these had a long history in vocal and instrumental composition. The ascending hexachord, the subject of the first capriccio, and the motif la sol fa re mi of the fourth (famous from its use as a *cantus firmus* by Josquin Desprez) had been treated as polyphonic instrumental works as early as Giuliano Tiburtino's *Fantasie, et recerchari* of 1549, and "lascia fare mi" continued to appear in the works of composers such as Vincenzo Ruffo (1564) and Rocco Rodio (1575). The Bassa Fiamenga and Spagnoletta, subjects of the fifth and sixth capriccios, were both familiar dance tunes from the Low Countries, perhaps reminiscences of Girolamo's brief service there with Guido Bentivoglio. The Flemish bass is derived from the allemande "Bruynsmedelijn," which appeared in a variety of lute-prints between 1569 and 1583, three of them issued by Phalèse, Frescobaldi's first publisher. The Spagnoletta tune, a variant of the Folia, according to Praetorius "Ist im Niederlande gemacht, und wird in Frankreich selten gedanzt." The Spagnoletta was widely disseminated in simple manuscript versions and was also treated by composers as diverse as Giles Farnaby and Praetorius himself. It was regarded as an exemplar of the lascivious tunes forbidden in church and reputed to induce dancing mania in the feeble-minded. The Ruggiero, the subject of the twelfth capriccio, was generally the basis of variation-sets, as in Girolamo's *Toccate,* but it was also employed as a ricercar theme by Trabaci in his 1603 collection. The aria "Or che noi rimena" is in fact another northern tune, the Dutch student song *More Palatino,* also treated by Sweelinck.[1]

The choice of several of these subjects suggests the influence of Lodovico Zacconi's second volume of the *Prattica di musica,* issued by Vincenti of Venice in 1622. Chapter 52, on composition, states that just as the first thing singers learn is the hexachord, so the first subject of the novice composer is the "Obligo di dir sempre vt, re, mi, fa, sol, la," and the subject given in the next chapter is the descending hexachord—the materials of Frescobaldi's first two capriccios. In chapters 67–68 Zacconi shows how a repeated ostinato may be combined with preexisting materials. His first example is a single repeated note, the "suono della Campana"; the second is "il canto del Cu cu" (transcribed as a falling whole tone rather than the minor third of Girolamo's capriccio).

The first two capriccios recall Luzzaschi's ricercars in *Il Transilvano,* since the ascending hexachord of the first is reversed to form the subject of the second, and the two are further complementary in that contrasting hexachords (descending in the first, ascending in the second) appear as prominent countersubjects. Both works are typical of the whole collection in infusing the contrapuntal rigor and resourcefulness of the fantasias and ricercars with the freer keyboard figuration of the toccatas and canzonas. Like the other sectional capriccios, they begin with a passage in duple meter whose straightforward counterpoint moves in a half-note pulse with quarter subdivisions and ends with a clear cadence. Duple and triple sections follow in fairly regular alternation, cadencing usually on the tonic or dominant and ending with a duple section generally more highly saturated with the subject matter of the work. The triple sections in the *Capricci* occur in a variety of mensurations—⊙3/1, O3/1, ⊙3, C3, ¢3, 3, 6/4—in values ranging from breves and whole notes to halves and quarters. Unlike virtually every other theorist and composer of the period, Girolamo states unequivocally that he does not employ these with a proportional meaning (except for the signature 6/4, which in practice is canceled by the indication 4/6). Otherwise, the longer notes are played slower, the shorter ones faster.[2]

The first capriccio is typical of the entire set in its profusion of sophisticated contrapuntal devices—diminution and ostinato (Ex. 11.1); and chromatic inflection, retrograde (Ex.11.2). These are balanced by toccatalike flourishes at cadences (Ex. 11.3). Throughout the volume, however, the technical achievement of the contrapuntal writing never obscures an infectious sense of sheer fun as the music emerges under one's fingers, an "ingenious Jesting with Art" as a later composer called it, as well as the "profound Learning" he disclaimed.

Three of the capriccios are based on ostinato treatment of their subjects: numbers three and four, on the cuckoo and la sol fa re mi, and number ten, with the *obligo* to sing the fifth part. In the capriccio on the cuckoo the soprano part consists of nothing but the cuckoo-call, the falling third D–B, and third-derived material abounds in the countersubjects as well (Ex. 11.4). Although the ostinato would tend to encourage V–I

EXAMPLE 11.1 Capriccio I, measures 25–30

EXAMPLE 11.2 Capriccio I, measures 63–66

EXAMPLE 11.3 Capriccio I, measures 84–86

EXAMPLE 11.4 a. Capriccio III, measures 1–2

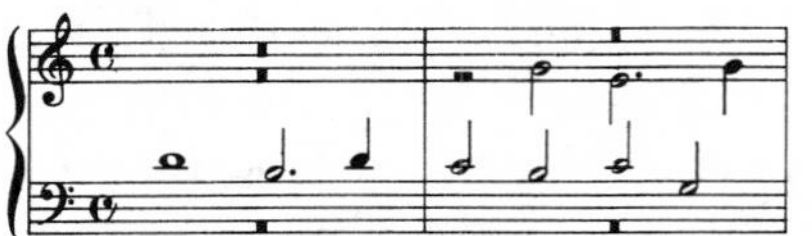

b. measures 24–25

c. measure 38

d. measures 78–79

e. measures 87–88

f. measures 142–143

cadences in G, Frescobaldi displays considerable ingenuity in avoiding these (Ex. 11.5). By contrast, its companion, the capriccio on la sol fa re mi, not only presents the subject repeatedly in the soprano but also in every other part, with an insistence reminiscent of the *Fantasie.* Unlike the

EXAMPLE 11.5 a. Capriccio III, measures 35–36

b. measures 54–55

c. measures 111–112

EXAMPLE 11.6 a. Capriccio IV, measures 32–34

b. measures 111–112

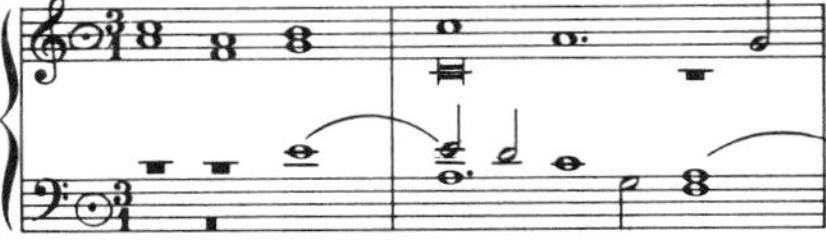

c. measures 117–119

capriccio on the cuckoo, Frescobaldi's treatment of this motif conceals rather than emphasizes the material through rhythmic transformation (Ex. 11.6).

The third ostinato capriccio has an *obligo* apparently without precedent in keyboard music: "Capriccio with the *obligo* to sing the fifth part, without playing it, always with the *obligo* of the written subject, if you wish." The subject on which the capriccio is written is given at the beginning (Ex. 11.7), and where the first hexachord syllable of the theme, re, is indicated in the tenor part, the player may add the subject as a fifth voice on either the natural or hard hexachords (and in several places not given in the Pidoux edition). In a fashion that recalls Monteverdi's "Sonata sopra sancta Maria ora pro nobis" in the 1610 vespers this ostinato is superposed on a canzonalike structure with alternations of duple and triple meter, toccatalike cadences, and extensive variation of the initial motif.

The materials of the capriccios on the Bassa Fiamenga, Spagnoletta, and Ruggiero differ from the preceding subjects in that all three are complete, preexisting melody/bass complexes rather than simple motifs. In the capriccio on the Bassa Fiamenga Frescobaldi takes two phrases from the original and treats the second as both a continuation and a countersubject of the first, in a variety of textures ranging from dense chromaticism to lively triple passages (Ex. 11.8).

EXAMPLE 11.7 Capriccio X, measures 78–81

EXAMPLE 11.8 a. Capriccio V, measures 1–3

b. measures 72–76

c. measures 85–86

EXAMPLE 11.9 a. Spagnoletta (UCLA MS 51/1, fol. 32v)

The original Spagnoletta melody consists of three sections. Frescobaldi bases the first sections of his capriccio on a subject derived from the opening of the tune, in a variety of rhythmic guises (Ex. 11.9). He then introduces a subject derived from the second phrase and develops

b. Capriccio VI, measures 1–2

c. measure 17

d. measures 52–54

EXAMPLE 11.10 Capriccio VI, measures 138–141

both with an emphasis on their common rising third. The final section of the work is marked by descending thirds that recall the last phrase of the tune (Ex. 11.10).

The "Capriccio sopra l'aria di Ruggiero" extends this technique of treating a harmonically conceived subject in a polyphonic context. Trabaci's ricercar on the Ruggiero had employed the material as the basis of a sectional contrapuntal work, but his three subjects were not quotations from the bass but free counterpoints to single phrases of it. Here, however,

Frescobaldi ignores the harmonic aspect of the original complex and divides the bass line into four phrases—presented both on G and on D—whose combination is not limited by their original succession (see Table 6). The capriccio follows the general outline of its original, with the concluding phrases dominating the final sections, as in the Spagnoletta. Frescobaldi does not intertwine the four phrases, as he did in his fantasias on four subjects, but rather states them in succession in a variety of textures. The work is further unified by the anapest figure that initially appeared as a counterpoint to all four subjects in measures 87–111; it takes over again in measure 132 to blossom into the swirling scale figures of the final section (Ex. 11.11).

TABLE 6. "Capriccio sopra l'aria di Ruggiero"

MEASURES	METER	PHRASES OF RUGGIERO
1–17	C	I, II
18–35	(C)	III, IV
36–47	⊙3	III, IV
48–64	C	I, II, III, IV
65–77	Ͼ3	II
78–86	C	II, III
87–111	(C)	I, II, III, IV
112–132	(C)	I
132–150	(C)	III, IV
151–164	(C)	III, IV

EXAMPLE 11.11 a. Capriccio XI, measures 87–88

b. measure 132

c. measures 151–152

The "Capriccio cromatico con ligature al contrario" and the "Capriccio di durezze" represent Frescobaldi's first explicit venture into the chromatic territory so long explored by his Neapolitan contemporaries, although these two works are foreshadowed in the last two toccatas of 1615, the chromatic variation of the Romanesca, and the pivotal *durezze e ligature* of the toccatas. Both are notably shorter than the other capriccios; both show less contrast in texture, without changes of meter or *passaggi* (neither goes beyond a quartering of the basic pulse); and both are chromatic, although the "Capriccio cromatico" is more highly inflected. (The repertory of chromatic tones is the same in both works: F-, C-, and G-sharp, B- and E-flat. Despite their avowed chromaticism, both works are thus playable on the ordinary meantone keyboard.)

A composition whose basic conceit was the reversal of orthodox dissonance treatment was an uncommon caprice on the part of the organist of St. Peter's, the stronghold of Palestrinian counterpoint. (It is probably no accident that its companion contains three suspensions in its first four measures, all of them now resolved conventionally.) The capriccio "al contrario" offsets the wandering tendency inherent in its *obligo* by a clear organization into three sections. The first is based on two related subjects, and in the course of the section the opening subject is transformed into a rising chromatic line leading to a cadence on A. The second section (measures 29–45), cadencing on D, is set off from the other two both by its new pair of themes and by consistently higher ranges, which, with the frequent absence of the bass, produce a brighter and more transparent texture. The third section returns to the second of the two opening subjects and in a dazzling coda presents it, its continuation, and the rising chromatic figure from the first part against the inversion of the chromatic line in the bass, with a clash of suspensions all tenaciously resolved in the wrong direction (Ex. 11.12).

The companion "Capriccio di durezze" goes far beyond the *durezze* of the Neapolitans in harmonic direction and motivic coherence. Unlike the successive enchainment of material in previous *durezze,* the capriccio presents its complete motivic repertory in the opening measures: a rising motif in the soprano, a descending line in the alto, and a descending leap

EXAMPLE 11.12 Capriccio cromatico, measures 57–62

EXAMPLE 11.13 a. Capriccio di durezze, measure 3

b. measures 30–31

of a sixth in the tenor. Even the increased rhythmic activity generated by the figure that begins in measure 30 can be traced back to the continuation of the tenor subject in measure 3 (Ex. 11.13). This motivic continuity is also reflected in the structure of the work, whose harmonic movement is interrupted only once by a cadence (measure 22) and whose rhythmic motion is continuous.

The variations on "Or che noi rimena" seem to have wandered into the *Capricci* from the world of the smaller variation-sets in the *Toccate,* perhaps to bring the contents of the volume up to the canonical number of twelve. With their removal, the *Capricci* became a coherent witness of Frescobaldi's growing ability to conceive and realize extended and variegated musical structures and to infuse them with unfailing wit and invention. The combined publication of the capriccios, canzonas, and ricercars in 1626 thus summed up Frescobaldi's development as a contrapuntal composer in a single volume.

12

A New Manner: The *Secondo Libro Di Toccate* of 1627

Frescobaldi announced his second collection of toccatas as the exemplars of a "new manner," "mounted and woven with novelty of artifice," and demanding "grace, ease, variety of measure, and elegance" in their performance. The dedicatee to whom these observations were addressed was a harpsichordist of professional caliber, and the bulk of the collection consists of genres appropriate to the harpsichord: toccatas, variations, canzonas, dances, and a madrigal intabulation. However, the volume also presents Girolamo's first published works for the organ: two pedal toccatas, two toccatas for the Elevation of the Host (a designation that had first appeared in the 1611 edition of Banchieri's *L'organo suonarino*),[1] and versets for vespers comprising four hymns and three Magnificat settings.

This *opera omnia* format is one example of the Neapolitan influence on Frescobaldi's second toccata collection. The inclusion of an intabulation of Arcadelt's madrigal "Ancidetemi pur," set also by Mayone (1603) and Trabaci (1615), is perhaps not so much an imitation as a challenge, but the presence of a toccata "di durezze e ligature" and the appearance of canzonas that open with chordal passages in triple meter unequivocally echo Neapolitan practices. Since Frescobaldi's collection was issued twelve years after the last significant Neapolitan publication, however, the influence is a case of conscious artistic choice rather than automatic imitation and expresses everywhere Frescobaldi's own musical personality. The organ toccatas over pedal-points, for example (a north Italian device that first appeared in print in Annibale Padovano's posthumous *Toccate* of 1604), evoke in their great washes of color not the intricacy of the Neapolitan Baroque but the as yet undecorated vastness of St. Peter's. The Elevation toccatas are unparalleled elsewhere, as are the cross-pollination of genres in the *Frescobalda* variations and the introduction of the ciaccona and passacagli from the guitar repertory.

The toccatas of the 1627 collection fall into three groups: harpsichord toccatas that developed from the toccatas of the 1615 collection, numbers I, II, VII, IX, X, and XI; the two pedal toccatas for organ, V and VI; and the Elevation toccatas, III and IV, with Toccata VIII, "di durezze e ligature." In the 1615 toccatas Frescobaldi had achieved musical unity in works of large primary sections and ambiguously defined smaller ones through free figuration and no metrical contrast; this balancing act he does not seem to have been inclined to repeat in 1627. The tendency of the 1627 toccatas is toward more clearly defined subsections marked by motivic consistency within and metric and textural contrast without. This development is perhaps least apparent in the opening sections of the later toccatas, since they were the most clearly delineated divisions of the earlier ones. They continue to define the initial tonality through arpeggiated chords enlivened by imitation, and to outline the effective range of the work, often in gestures of expansive sweep (Ex. 12.1). The most adventurous of these openings is that of Toccata XI. Harmonically, it proceeds to a cadence not on a degree closely related to the finalis (I, IV, V, V of V), but on VI established as V of v of v. Frescobaldi's constant sense of significant detail is evident in the preparation of this cadence as early as measure 5, and an increased capacity for large-scale harmonic planning is apparent in the delay of the cadence for sixteen measures after its preparation (Ex. 12.2). The same technique of reinterpreting harmonically a melodic arrival is employed as a transition from the cadence of the opening section in Toccatas I and II (Ex. 12.3).

EXAMPLE 12.1 Toccata II, measures 4–7

EXAMPLE 12.2 a. Toccata XI, measure 5

b. measures 14–15

c. measures 20–21

EXAMPLE 12.3 a. Toccata I, measures 14–15

b. Toccata II, measures 15–17

The closing passages of the 1627 toccatas are more clearly defined than those of the 1615 collection. Figuration, whether linear or imitative, is consistent over a longer span, and harmonic expectancy is increased by slowing the rate of harmonic change. What was a passing ripple on the surface of an earlier toccata is employed here with exaggerated logic to define the cadence (Ex. 12.4). The most dramatic emphasis of the con-

EXAMPLE 12.4 Toccata X, measures 66–74 (see Ex. 10.12c)

EXAMPLE 12.5 Toccata I, measures 57–63

cluding section occurs in Toccata I, which shifts to a 12/8 proportion where the triplets gradually permeate the texture and are then pulled back to permit a dramatic rhythmic acceleration (Ex. 12.5). This increased definition is most apparent in the central area of the toccatas, above all in the insertion of sections in triple or compound meter (I, IX, X, and XI), a feature that had previously appeared only rarely in the toccatas of the Neapolitans and never in those of Frescobaldi. The crisp rhythmic definition of these sections is one example of what is perceived as a "focused" texture, if we define focus as the consistent use of one or more elements of musical coherence such as sequential figuration, repeated rhythmic patterns, regular imitation, consecutive harmonic motion, and structural parallelism or repetition. The divergence between focused and unfocused sections is an important aspect of the new formal definition in the 1627 toccatas. Often this is expressed as abrupt juxtapositions of contrasting textures, but Frescobaldi's skill at motivic manipulation also creates modulations of textures that seem to grow under the player's fingers (Ex. 12.6).

The full range of effects in these toccatas is exploited in Toccata IX, to which its composer added the apt judgment, "Non senza fatiga si giunge al fine" (Not without effort does one reach the end). Here the opening is not chordal but rather is an expansion of the opening triad through two and a half octaves (Ex. 12.7). The range widens further, until within two measures the functional boundaries are touched: the low E recurs at strategic points and is always emphasized by a change of register (Ex. 12.8). The sections that follow are relatively short and set off by frequent minim

EXAMPLE 12.6 a. Toccata II, measures 30–31

b. measure 36

c. measure 40

EXAMPLE 12.7 Toccata IX, measures 1–4

EXAMPLE 12.8 a. Toccata IX, measures 7–9

b. measures 23–24

c. measures 49–50

d. measure 55

chords, with abrupt contrasts of textures and a variety of three-against-two rhythmic patterns, often linked by reinterpretations of cadences (Ex. 12.9). In the middle of the toccata, Frescobaldi creates a metric modulation rivaling those of his English predecessors (Ex. 12.10).[2] Focused and unfocused passages are joined with abandon (Ex. 12.11). Frescobaldi reserves his most dazzling rhythmic effects for the final cadence, an apotheosis of the preceding rhythmic clashes (Ex. 12.12). Such characteristic

EXAMPLE 12.9 a. Toccata IX, measures 12–13

b. measures 21–22

c. measures 26–27

d. measures 36–37

EXAMPLE 12.10 Toccata IX, measures 31–32

devices as the internal pedal-points and the grinding combinations of trills and *passi* embody the fancy in conception and extended logic in execution characteristic of Baroque art.

Toccatas V and VI are subtitled "Sopra i pedali per l'organo, e senza." Despite this ambiguous designation, these carefully planned pedal-points are indispensable in that they delimit the great blocks of sound, inflected by changing harmonies and modes and animated by constantly varied figuration, which make up these works. The pedal bass of Toccata V presents two rising fourths (G, C, F) and two falling fifths (A, D, G) linked by a mediant relationship. Toccata VI employs a cycle of fifths, F, C, G, D, A, which leads—again by a mediant—into the final C–F cadence. Both works thus display a harmonic outline that reaches a high point of intensity—in Toccata V the longest of the pedal-points, in VI an intensification of the longest pedal—from which it moves by a pivot to a clear cadence.

EXAMPLE 12.11 Toccata IX, measures 51–55

EXAMPLE 12.12 Toccata IX, measures 65–66

Although the figuration of the pedal toccatas is more obviously decorative in its relation to the underlying harmonic structure, which is not merely suggested—as in the harpsichord toccatas—but unequivocally present in every measure, its luxuriance is not random. In Toccata V virtually all of the figuration is derived from or stresses the interval of a fourth, contracted into a chromatic third above the penultimate pedal. In Toccata VI the upbeat scale pattern that begins in measure 6 is continued inexorably for nine measures, presented in alternation between the hands, in imitation, or in dialogue, and frequently encompassing those sweeps through the range of the instrument that characterize Frescobaldi at his most exuberant (Ex. 12.13).

If these two works display the most dazzling and public aspects of Frescobaldi's art, the three remaining toccatas of the 1627 collection—III, IV, and VIII—show him at his most private and, at times, his most enigmatic. Toccata III, the first of the Elevation toccatas, is written in the second tone, which Diruta says is to be played on the principal with the tremolo or on some register of flutes, "at the elevation of the Most Holy Body and Blood of Our Savior Jesus Christ, imitating in the playing the hard and harsh torments of the Passion."[3] Toccata IV, the other Elevation, is written not in tone four—Diruta's alternate suggestion—but in tone ten, which is appropriately played on the principal with an octave or flute and "renders the harmony somewhat sad."

These toccatas are puzzling to player and listener alike on first encounter. While their rhetoric is obviously high and passionate and the logic of isolated elements is perceptible, there is little initial feeling of overall structure or destination. Indeed, this sensation of timeless contemplation is one of the aims of the Elevation, the musical creation of a kind of eternal

EXAMPLE 12.13 Toccata VI, measures 6–9

present. In fact, however, the underlying harmonic structures of these works are more direct even than those of the pedal toccatas: in Toccata III, measures 1–13, D–A; 13–19, A–E; 20–33, (E)–E; 33–46, D–D; 46–66, D–D; in Toccata IV, measures 1–24, A–D; 25–44, D–A; 45–58, D–A.

The next level in the hierarchy that begins with these clear sectional divisions is that of the rate of harmonic change within the sections, which in both works is generally regulated by a steady half-note pulse. Beyond this rhythmic level we enter an area where the unexpected is more important than the sequential and the expected, or at any rate where the unexpected can be explained only after its appearance. For example, the fourth toccata is permeated by anticipated functional downbeats recognized as such only when they begin to move. In measures 9–10 alone this device occurs four times (Ex. 12.14). The resolution of the alto is echoed an octave higher by an anticipated downbeat in the soprano that becomes a suspension, as does the alto, and moves downward against an imitative motif that is derived from the opening (as is the decorated F-sharp in the tenor of measure 9). The ambiguity of the voice-leading is compounded by the scale descent apparently crossing from soprano to an anticipated downbeat in the alto, followed by another in the soprano.

Both toccatas are remarkable for their extended unbroken sections, and it is profitable to examine the longest of these, the opening of Toccata IV, to understand how Frescobaldi achieves this continuity. Although it would be impossible to transcribe the Elevations into four distinct and coherent voices, much of their internal logic is revealed when they are examined as impressionistic realizations of a four-voice ideal. In the beginning of Toccata IV all four voices are sounding by the second half of the first measure, but the entrance in measure 3 has nonetheless the force of a bass entry in a four-part exposition. Some of this remarkable extension is achieved by illogic, as in the constant preparation and subsequent sidestepping of full cadences either by deceptive cadences or by chromatic alteration (for example, the lowered C and F in the general A-major context of measures 14–17). Rising scale figures are an easily perceived unifying device and are variously employed, ascending regularly through

EXAMPLE 12.14 Toccata IV, measures 9–10

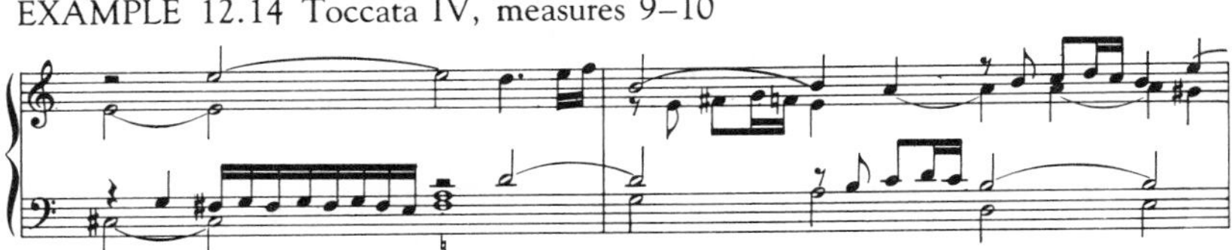

the chordal texture (measures 11–13) or declaiming against a slower version of the figure in thirds (measures 17–18). To conclude the first section of the toccata the upbeat rising figure is reversed to become a descent from a downbeat, and the remaining measures are built around falls from ever greater heights (Ex. 12.15).

If Frescobaldi is a master of strategic delay in the Elevations, he is no less capable of strongly directed motion. This may be achieved by a simple acceleration of note-values or harmonic movement, by melodic and/or rhythmic sequence, or by something as simple as repetition of a note (see

EXAMPLE 12.15 a. Toccata IV, measures 2–3

measures 14–16). Perhaps the best example of this control is the concluding portion of Toccata IV. Its rhythmic patterns, especially the Lombard rhythm, are consistent over relatively long spans. The harmony changes regularly every quarter-note, frequently a chromatic inflection of a more basic change on the half-note, and the bass is firmly marked. The logic of linear construction—which is not necessarily the logic of part-writing—is adamant and lends a peculiar urgency to the figural patterns derived from the previous sections of the toccata.

The remaining contents of the 1627 *Toccate* are a heterogeneous assemblage. The six canzonas fit neatly into Frescobaldi's continuing exploration of the genre. The first three and the last continue the development of the variation-canzona, a procedure most strikingly exemplified in the descending chromatic subject of Canzona III. The inclusion of free figural writing in sectional contrapuntal works, which Girolamo began in the capriccios, is now integrated seamlessly into the texture, so that sections regularly begin with the energy of canzona-motifs and dissolve into brilliant figuration. The repetition of the opening section in Canzona IV adopts a common Venetian practice, as does the return of opening material at the end of Canzona VI, but the triple meters of the last two canzonas and the chordal opening and refrain of Canzona V are imaginative developments of Neapolitan conventions.

A growing interest in dance rhythms is apparent in the collection's five gagliarde, six correnti, and variations on the "Aria detto Balletto" (*More Palatino*) and "Aria detta la Frescobalda." Neither dance type is fully stylized. The gagliarde consist of two or three sections beginning on a downbeat; their rhythmic concision recalls the Neapolitan ensemble galliard.[4] Each corrente contains three sections starting with an upbeat and marked by the 3/2–6/4 contrasts usually associated with the French courante. The second corrente is provided with another feature later adopted by the French, a written-out figural variation or *double.* The combination of dance and variation procedures is carried a step further in the two variation-sets, which include dancelike sections. These are identified as Gagliarda and Corrente in the *Frescobalda,* which is thus the first variation-suite and presumably the model for Froberger's amalgamation of the variation and the dance-suite in his *Mayerin.*

The organ-versets for vespers are a new genre only in their appearance in print, since Frescobaldi, like any other seventeenth-century Italian organist, improvised their equivalents every working day of his life.[5] The versets are designed for *alternatim* performances of the Magnificat and the hymns for the principal occasions of the liturgical year: Sunday (*Lucis*

Creator Optime), feasts of the Apostles (*Exultet Celum Laudibus*; *Exultet Orbis Gaudiis* in Urban VIII's breviary of 1632), and feasts of the Virgin Mary (*Ave Maris Stella*). In their clear sense of direction and eminently satisfying economy the versets recall the liturgical organ music of Cabezón. The chant materials are treated as long-note *cantus firmi* in one or more voices, paraphrased, or divided up to provide subjects for imitative treatment or tripla variations.

The currents of the past and the future are defined most sharply in the intabulation and the bass variations. Arcadelt's "Ancidetemi pur" belongs to the most classic of his madrigal collections, the first book of four-part madrigals, which went through some forty-three editions between 1539 and 1654 (including one by Monteverdi in 1627). Nothing could be farther from the Renaissance intabulation than Frescobaldi's realization of this suave, chaste work with its clear AAB structure as a continuous, passionately declaimed toccata (Ex. 12.16).

The inclusion of variations on the Ciaccona and Passacagli, by contrast, begins a process of creating large musical structures from common and ill-defined elements, rather than the radical reinterpretation of an existing work of art. The ciaccona was originally a lively dance, the passacaglia a ritornello, and both were developed in the musically marginal world of the guitar tablature. When Frescobaldi took up these patterns they were still evolving, although the ciaccona had settled on the major and had developed a typical rhythmic pattern in triple meter; the passacaglia could be in major or minor. The short repeated phrases of both patterns had a potential for chains of continuous variations strikingly different from the articulated, closed structures of earlier variation materials.[6] If Girolamo's intabulation is of interest as the last flower of a dying tradition, his treatment of the ciaccona and passacaglia in the 1627 book is above all the

EXAMPLE 12.16 a. Arcadelt, "Ancidetemi pur," measures 1–5

b. Frescobaldi, "Ancidetemi pur," measures 1–10

preparation for the *Cento partite sopra passacagli* in the 1637 *Aggiunta* to *Toccate* I, in favor of which both of the present sets were removed from the 1637 reprint of *Toccate* II. In both of the 1627 sets the identity of the two-measure pattern is rigidly maintained, figuration is conventional, and chromatic interest is rare. Although the guitar tablatures present both patterns in a variety of keys, Frescobaldi maintains the original tonality throughout each set.

The central achievement of this volume is its repertory of toccatas, which attain an unprecedented grandeur, richness, and expressiveness of declamation, now channeled and organized by clear and yet subtle structural principles. Equally striking in the dances and organ-versets of the collection is Girolamo's command of the epigrammatic statement. These two principles—grandiose rhetoric and the irreducible minimum of conciseness—reach out in opposite directions, finally to meet in the *Fiori musicali.*

13

A Variety of Inventions: The *Canzoni* of 1628 and 1634

Musicological interest has long focused on the development of the sonata, above all the solo and trio sonatas. This emphasis has led to the neglect and undervaluation of genres and instrumental combinations that do not apparently feed into this retrospectively defined mainstream. In fact, however, instrumental music for a variety of media in a fundamentally conservative idiom was an important part of Italian musical production past the middle of the seventeenth century, as witness the instrumental works published by Cavalli in 1656, many of which might have been composed half a century earlier as far as their outward style is concerned. It is characteristic of Frescobaldi that he chose to continue to cultivate the canzona in ensemble as well as keyboard music, and that he defined the merit of his 1628 collection as "the variety of the inventions" with which he "considered the convenience of various instruments" in nine combinations, fashionable, unfashionable, and idiosyncratic.

Three editions of Frescobaldi's *Canzoni* exist: Girolamo's set of part-books and his student Bartolomeo Grassi's version in score, published in Rome in 1628 by Robletti and Masotti respectively, and the composer's revised part-book version issued in Venice by Vincenti, of which the title page is dated 1634 and the dedicatory letter 10 January 1635.[1] Since neither of the 1628 editions is more precisely dated, their priority is unclear. In favor of Grassi's edition are its careful preparation and precise alignment (a rarity in *partitura* publications, as he points out), the greater accuracy of its text, the inclusion of three additional works (a toccata for spinettina and violin, and a toccata and canzona for spinettina), and a lack of reference to any preexisting edition in the informative preface. Frescobaldi's part-books evince haste and carelessness in their preparation, and it seems likely that he threw the collection together to provide a work to dedicate to his prospective patron, the Grand Duke of Tuscany. (The names appended to the canzonas in Grassi's volume commemorate his patrons, friends, and citizens of his native Lucca and have nothing to do with Frescobaldi.) On the other hand, if Girolamo had "an infinite number of volumes" of unpublished works, as Grassi asserted, it seems strange that he would bother to republish a collection already in print in another format. The possible priority of Girolamo's version is strengthened by details of Grassi's edition which suggest that he was working from Frescobaldi's part-books. Grassi's occasional omission of ties, for example, points to unbarred printed parts rather than a barred manuscript score as an ultimate source. Further, although Grassi opens his collection with an extra canzona not published by Frescobaldi himself until the 1634 volume, he still numbers a later piece "Canzona terza," as it appears in Frescobaldi's 1628 part-books, rather than the correct "Canzona quarta."

In both Frescobaldi's and Grassi's editions of 1628 the canzonas are arranged according to medium with similar but not identical repertories (see Table 7). In medium, the canzonas combine the older tradition of the ensemble canzona (CATB/bc) with the newer solo and trio textures of Frescobaldi's contemporaries such as Biagio Marini and Dario Castello (C/bc, CB/bc, CC/bc, CCB/bc) as well as original solutions (B/bc, BB/bc, CBB/bc, CCBB/bc). One legacy of the older ensemble canzona is the anomalous role of the obligato bass throughout the *Canzoni.* Even where it is the only solo part, it generally follows the continuo line (or rather the continuo is a reduction of the bass line) and rarely engages in independent figuration. Where two basses are employed, they frequently alternate with each other. Thus the canzonas for canto solo, CB, and CBB are subdivisions of the same medium, as are those for CC, CCB, and CCBB. (In the canzonas for a single canto, however, only those without bass employ *passaggi.*)

The instrumentation of the indicated voices is rarely specified. In the part-books the basso continuo is allotted to the organ, and of the first four canzonas for canto solo and continuo, three are assigned to violin or cornett, the fourth to violin. The bass parts of the fourth canzona in four parts are marked "Tiorba" and "Violino," which recalls a direction of Girolamo's colleague Johann Hieronymus Kapsberger in the preface to his *Sinfonie* of 1615: "For first and second bass is understood whatever instru-

TABLE 7. The *Canzoni* prints of 1628

GRASSI 1628	EQUIVALENT IN FRESCOBALDI 1628
Canzona prima (C/bc)	
Canzona 2a	Canzon prima (C/bc)
	(Canzon 2a)
Canzona 3a	Canzon 4a
Canzona 3a [*sic*]	Canzon 3a
Canzona 5a (B/bc)	Canzon 1a (B/bc)
Canzona 6a	Canzon 3a
Canzona 7a	Canzon 4a
Canzona 8a	Canzon 2a
Canzona 9a (CC/bc)	Canzon prima (CC/bc)
Canzona 10a	Canzon 2a
Canzona 11a	Canzon 3a
Canzona 12a	Canzon 4a
Canzona 13a	Canzon 5a
Canzona 14a (BB/bc)	Canzon prima (BB/bc)
Canzona 15a	Canzon 2a
Canzona 16a	Canzon 3a
Canzona 17a	Canzon 4a
Canzona 18a (CB/bc)	Canzon prima (CB/bc)
Canzona 19a	Canzon 2a
Canzona 20a	Canzon 3a
Canzona 21a	Canzon 4a
Canzona 22a	Canzon 5a
Canzona 23a	Canzon 6a
Canzona 24a (CBB/bc)	Canzon prima (CBB/bc)
Canzona 25a	Canzon 2a
Canzona 26a	Canzon 3a
Canzona 27a	Canzon 4a
Canzona 28a (CCB/bc)	Canzon 5a (CCB/bc)
Canzona 29a	Canzon 6a
Canzona 30a (CCBB/bc)	Canzon prima a quattro (CCBB/bc)
Canzona 31a	Canzon 2a
Canzona 32a	Canzon 4a
Canzona 33a	Canzon 5a
Canzona 34a	

TABLE 7, *continued*

GRASSI 1628	EQUIVALENT IN FRESCOBALDI 1628
Canzona 35a (CATB/bc)	Canzon 3a (CATB/bc)
Canzona 36a	Canzon 6a
Canzona 37a	
Toccata per spinettina e violino	
Toccata per spinettina sola, over liuto	
Canzona per spinettina sola detta la Vittoria	

ment that may play chords [*in consonanza*] such as lute, chitarrone, cembalo, harp, and the like. For first and second canto, violin, cornett, and the like."[2]

The general formal outline of these ensemble canzonas follows the expanded framework of the keyboard canzonas in the 1627 collection. They begin either directly with imitative material (often the stereotyped dactyllic canzona-motif) or with a chordal introduction in duple or sometimes in triple meter, and proceed in a series of contrasting sections each defined by a cadence on the tonic or a related degree. Variation techniques are the basis of thematic manipulation in these canzonas, and many of them are strict variation-canzonas in which the material of all the component sections is derived from the opening subject.

Other aspects of the *Canzoni*, however, show the influence of contemporary instrumental publications. Tempo indications occur here for the first time in Frescobaldi's works, "adagio" for a cadence or a free transitional section like the pivotal passages in the toccatas, followed by "alegro" to indicate a return to the original sprightly tempo of the canzona. Dynamic indications—*forte* and *piano* echo effects—occur frequently, as they do in the 1621 sonatas of Dario Castello. The number and variety of sections are greater than those of the keyboard canzonas, and where repetitions are indicated they show less stereotyped patterns.

Within the boundaries of the genre, the canzonas for each of the various combinations of parts differ in detail from each other. Grassi's second canzona (= the first in Frescobaldi's 1628 print) for canto solo shows how Frescobaldi treated the solo medium. The work consists of eight sections in contrasting meters and tempos (see Table 8). The list of cadences shows that the first three sections make up a larger organization ending on the tonic A, from which the other two imitative sections also

TABLE 8. Canzona for canto solo (Grassi 2)

SECTION	MEASURES	SIGNATURE	TEMPO	CADENCE
1	1–10	C		C
2	10–13	(C)	Adagio (1634)	E
3	14–22	(C)	Alegro (1634); 35–36	
			Adagio (1634bc)	A
4	23–32	C3 (Grassi) ⊙3/2 (1628) C·3/2 (1634)	Alegro (1634bc)	C (into 33)
5	33	C	Adagio (1634bc)	C (into 34)
6	34–51	3	Alegro (1634bc)	C (into 52)
7	52–56	C	Adagio	e
8	57–83	(C)	Alegro	a

start out, thus creating tonal contrast within a context of overall balances that is characteristic of the collection. (The emphasis on a tonic and a clearly defined series of relationships around it does not force Girolamo to forgo harmonic richness and ambiguity: as in the toccatas, he can inflect scales either tonally or modally and treat any degree as either major or minor.) All of the allegro sections are imitative in texture, all of the adagios free and more or less ornamental. The imitative material of the four allegros is all derived from the opening motto of a descending fourth and its tonal answer, a descending fifth, followed by a leap of a third and stepwise movement (Ex. 13.1). The chromatic inflections of the inverted subject at the opening of the last section are balanced by a sequential passage that would be unusual in the keyboard canzonas, and by a de-

EXAMPLE 13.1 a. Canzona prima, C/bc (Grassi 2), measures 1–2

b. measures 14–15

lightful echo coda ending *piano* (Ex. 13.2). Structurally, the canzonas for CB/bc and CBB/bc follow the same general outline, but their texture is occasionally enriched by independent bass writing (Ex. 13.3).

The canzonas for two cantos, CCB/bc and CCBB/bc, whose medium

EXAMPLE 13.3 Canzona 2a, CBB/bc (Grassi 19), measures 5–8

of two dominant upper parts and continuo was well established by 1628, display the repertory of accepted devices for works featuring two treble instruments—alternation of subject and countersubject between the two solo parts, suspensions, echo effects, and virtuosic cadential *passaggi*—within the general structural framework of the variation-canzona. In the CCBB/bc canzonas the two basses alternate in doubling the continuo line and presenting independent material.

Frescobaldi was the first composer to publish canzonas for solo bass and continuo, and he produced more than half of the surviving canzonas for combinations—BB/bc, CBB/bc—involving two basses. In these works the coalescence of the various bass lines is most emphasized; this may have been mitigated in performance by a continuo realization that took an active part in the development of motivic material. (The fact that many canzonas begin with the continuo alone in an upper register, after which it enters in the bass, suggests that the opening line may have been continued as a polyphonic counterpoint.)

Perhaps owing to the experimental nature of the medium, the canzonas for bass solo rely less on variation techniques than on the juxtaposition of a number of contrasting sections. These include extended free sections, interspersed passages in triple and compound meters, and soloistic improvisatory *passaggi* (Ex. 13.4). In the canzonas for two basses and continuo the outlines of the bass and continuo are similar, and the alternation of the two solos again often reduces the texture to a single line. Here the interest centers on Frescobaldi's manipulation of the relation

EXAMPLE 13.4 a. Canzona 4a, B/bc (Grassi 7), measures 31–35

between the two soloists, the length and speed of their alternations. In the fourth canzona for two basses, for example, after the first imitative section the second bass presents a long, almost recitativelike phrase, answered by the first. As they dialogue the phrases alternate more rapidly, and finally the two parts intertwine at the cadence (Ex. 13.5). This dialogue recurs

EXAMPLE 13.5 a. Canzona 4a, BB/bc (Grassi 17), measures 29–34

b. measures 40–45

twice again in the canzona, finally emerging to dominate the last section, an extended passage in consistent figuration.

Grassi's and Frescobaldi's editions of 1628 generally coincide except for details of the canzonas in four parts (CCBB/bc, CATB/bc), where divergences are wider. To begin with, Grassi includes eight four-part canzonas, while Frescobaldi's edition contains only six, omitting Grassi's numbers 34 and 37. (Number 34 was reinstated in the 1634 collection.) In the works common to the two 1628 editions there are notable textual differences. In the second canzona, for example, Grassi's version consists of an opening section, repeated, followed by sections two to five, repeated as a unit. Frescobaldi's version adds new sections between one and two and between three and four and suppresses the repeat. Grassi's number 34, when it turns up in the 1634 volume, is identical with Frescobaldi's version only for the first thirty-two measures.

Perhaps because they are closest in medium to the keyboard canzona, in which Girolamo had worked for over a decade, Frescobaldi's four-part CATB canzonas as a group show a firm touch in combining striking effects for the upper parts with significant participation in the musical fabric for all the voices. The texture of these works is imitative, and they are more tightly contrapuntal than the other canzonas. All of them are variation-canzonas, and in Grassi's version none has more than one section in triple meter.

The thirty-sixth canzona of Grassi's collection represents an appar-

EXAMPLE 13.6 a. Canzona terza (1615), measures 1–2

b. measures 17–20

c. measure 31

ently unique connection between the ensemble canzona and its keyboard counterpart, since its opening thirty-three measures reproduce the beginning of the Canzon terza from the 1615 collection of ricercars and canzonas. A comparison of the two works reveals Frescobaldi's development in the thirteen years separating the two works. The 1615 canzona is a strict variation-canzona, laid out in regular alternation of duple and triple meter sections, in all of which the subject is clearly recognizable (Ex. 13.6). Even though some of these close on D rather than on the tonic G, the latter is immediately reestablished. The revised canzona contains only three sections, the second in triple meter and cadencing on B-flat, reached from the quoted material by a transition that effects a real modulation (Ex. 13.7). The material is more subtly derived from the initial motif, internal divisions are overlapped, and a short hocketing coda forms an idiomatic close (Ex. 13.8).

The three works that Grassi added to his edition of the *Canzoni* are largely of extramusical interest. They all specify the spinettina (or lute as an alternative)—perhaps an instrument at higher pitch, quint or four-foot, or a small gut-strung harpsichord. Agazzari includes the spinetto among ornamental rather than fundamental instruments, and Frescobaldi treats it as a melody instrument in both hands above a basso continuo. These works represent Frescobaldi's first tentative experiments in the juxtaposition of free and contrapuntal genres which he later pursued in the

EXAMPLE 13.7 Canzona 6a, CATB/bc (Grassi 36), measures 33–37

EXAMPLE 13.8 Canzona 6a, measures 74–77

* Frescobaldi interpolates a tripla here; small notes show Frescobaldi variants

Fiori musicali. The toccata for spinettina and violin is a canzona preceded by a rhapsodic section that functions like the introductory toccata of the spinettina pieces.

Although little is known of Frescobaldi's musical activities in Florence between 1628 and 1634, he was clearly impelled to a drastic revision of the *Canzoni.* A comparison of the 1634 edition with those of 1628 shows far-reaching alterations in virtually every category. Some groups of canzonas, like those involving canto solo, escaped relatively unscathed. In other categories, a number of the original canzonas were replaced by new ones or revised (see Table 9). The relations between the 1628 and 1634

TABLE 9. Comparison of the 1634 and 1628 canzona repertories

SCORING	1634	1628 (PARTS)	1628 (SCORE)	TOTAL
C/bc	4	4	4	5
B/bc	3	4	4	4 (+ 3r)
CC/bc	4	5	5	5 (+ 3r)
BB/bc	4	4	4	4 (+ 4r)
CB/bc	6	6	6	6
CBB/bc	4	3	3	5 (+ 2r)
CCB/bc	5	3	3	5 (+ 1r)
CCBB/bc	4	4	5	6 (+ 2r)
CATB/bc	6	2	3	8 (+ 1r)

Note: r = revision.
SOURCE: John Harper, "The Instrumental Canzonas of Girolamo Frescobaldi: A Comparative Edition and Introductory Study" (Ph.D. dissertation, University of Birmingham, England, 1973), p. 106.

TABLE 10. The 1634 canzonas and the 1628 prints

SCORING	TRANSFERRED	REVISED	NEW	TOTAL	OMITTED
C/bc	4	–	–	4	(1)
B/bc	–	3	–	3	(1)
CC/bc	1	3	–	4	(1)
BB/bc	–	4	–	4	–
CB/bc	6	–	–	6	–
CBB/bc	–	2	2	4	(1)
CCB/bc	2	1	2	5	–
CCBB/bc	1	2	1	4	(2)
CATB/bc	–	1	5	6	(2)
Total	14	16	10	40	(8)

SOURCE: Harper, "The Instrumental Canzonas of Girolamo Frescobaldi," p. 107.

collections range from transfer, essentially unaltered, through more or less extensive revision, to suppression of previous canzonas in favor of new ones (see Table 10). Comparison of a 1628 canzona with its later reworking shows how complex these revisions are. The last of the bass canzonas (number 8 in Grassi, Canzona terza in the 1634 print) is longer by three sections in its second version, and much of what survives from its earlier state is considerably altered. Frescobaldi replaced the original adagio introduction by a new one of the same length, but changed only the final chord of the ensuing allegro. The original triple section that followed and its replacement are both based on the allegro material. The rhapsodic *passaggi* of the first version were replaced by a straightforward adagio, followed by an interpolated 6/4 allegro and an adagio and concluded by the last six measures of the allegro that they replace. The next adagio of the original is expanded from six breves to ten, and instead of the passage-work that concludes the first version there are two new sections, an allegro and a tripla. In general, these revised works contain much less of the expressive instrumental declamation evident in the earlier versions. The number of sections per canzona tends to increase, especially the adagio sections. The same is true of the revisions in the canzonas for two basses, although some of the rewriting, as in the tightened opening section of Grassi's number 14 (Canzona prima in 1634), has a clearer rationale.

The most obvious alterations in the canzonas for two cantos consist in the elimination of the dramatic *forte-piano* contrasts of the first versions. In the canzonas for canto and two basses, on the other hand, the alternations between homophony and counterpoint in the revised first canzona, the chromatic adagio of the new third, and the processional opening and echo effects of the new fourth all increase the sensuous effect of the works.

The CATB canzonas played a small role in the 1628 prints (three in Grassi, two in Frescobaldi), but in preparing the 1634 volume Frescobaldi added five new works in this medium and completely revised the one he retained from the earlier collection, perhaps with Cardinal Francesco Barberini's viol consort in mind. This group of six four-part canzonas opens with two works built on bass patterns, the only works of this type in the

EXAMPLE 13.9 Canzon prima sopra Rugier, measures 1–6

three versions of the *Canzoni.* The basses chosen are the subjects of Frescobaldi's largest variation-sets in the 1615 *Toccate,* the Ruggiero and the

EXAMPLE 13.10 Canzon prima sopra Rugier, measures 55–69

Romanesca. Here they are treated as canzona-variations: the preexisting material is stated in the bass, and each statement forms one section of the canzona. The basso continuo has the original version of the bass line, and the instrumental bass participates in the web of short imitative patterns woven by the upper parts while maintaining the outlines of the original pattern under the decoration (Ex. 13.9). Unlike the keyboard capriccio on the Ruggiero, here the material in the upper parts is not derived from the bass, with one striking exception. The Ruggiero canzona consists of five sections (C, O3/1, C, 3, C), each corresponding with a statement of the bass until the end of the fourth section, when the seemingly inevitable cadence on G is wrenched around to C and the alto plays, as a kind of *cantus firmus,* the last phrase of the Ruggiero, now transposed to C. This dislocation is finally remedied by the bass, which finishes the canzona by completing the original interrupted cadence (Ex. 13.10).

The remaining four canzonas are among the most successful works in the collection. Like the two on bass patterns, they are tightly woven contrapuntal works that develop one or a pair of motives imitatively in a series of closed sections. While these sections may contrast greatly in character, much of the thematic material is consistent, notably a penchant on the part of the composer for quartal themes. Some, like Canzona III and Canzona VI, are variation-canzonas. In others, thematic opposition is created, as in the fourth canzona, where Frescobaldi introduces a narrow chromatic motif in the last section as a foil to the open fourths and fifths of the opening two sections. The third, fifth, and sixth canzonas all contain passages of extensive syncopation and rich dissonance. The third and fifth canzonas open with chordal passages rather than the usual imitation, and all except the last contain passages in which a full chordal texture is presented as a contrast to the prevailing imitative one. Unlike earlier canzonas, no sections are repeated, and no tempo alterations are indicated (although the fourth and fifth canzonas contain sections that suggest an adagio marking). In general, these last four-part canzonas and many of the revisions of the other canzonas show Frescobaldi moving away from the more obvious effects of contemporary instrumental music to a renewed concern with concision without shortness of breath and extension without prolixity, which foreshadows the achievements of his last years.

14

Last Works: The *Fiori Musicali* of 1635 and the *Aggiunta* to *Toccate* I of 1637

Titles such as *Fiori musicali, Sacri fiori,* and even *Sudori musicali* were commonplaces of seventeenth-century music printing. Nonetheless, Frescobaldi's *Fiori,* the last complete collection he issued, does in fact represent a final flowering in its summary of the genres Girolamo had cultivated throughout his career—the toccata, canzona, capriccio, ricercar, and organ-verset—and in its integration of the two contrasting strains in his work, Renaissance counterpoint and Baroque keyboard virtuosity. The choice of three organ masses (Sundays, feasts of the Apostles, feasts of the Virgin Mary) carried on the learned tradition reaching back to Girolamo Cavazzoni and the composers of the Castel d'Arquato manuscript.[1] The contrapuntal and didactic conception of the *Fiori* is emphasized by its presentation in keyboard *partitura.* Despite this intention, however, Girolamo's preface also insists that the *Fiori* are to be played with the same concern for *affetti* and expressive, flexible execution as the toccatas.

The traditional Italian organ mass consisted of keyboard settings of alternate sections of all five parts of the mass ordinary: Kyrie, Gloria, Creed (omitted in the mass of the BVM, and in all three after the Council of Trent), Sanctus, and Agnus Dei. The unset portions of the chant were to be performed by the choir. The organ could be played at the beginning of the service and at the end and substituted for items of the proper of the mass during the service: the Gradual after the Epistle, the Offertory after the Creed, the Elevation of the Host (not a separate item of the proper), and the Post-Communion (see Chapter 2).

Frescobaldi's three masses (see Table 11) differ somewhat in their provisions for the ordinary and proper. The contents of the *Fiori* provide music for all the items of the mass proper, but of the ordinary Frescobaldi set only the Kyrie. The Creed was customarily omitted, and at a silent low mass the music at the Offertory might have extended to the consecration, where the Elevation would replace the Sanctus and Agnus Dei; but the omission of the Gloria is surprising. Both Croci (1641) and Fasolo (1645) provided settings for all four movements.

TABLE 11. The contents of the *Fiori musicali*

SUNDAY	APOSTLES	MADONNA
Toccata avanti la Messa	Toccata avanti la Messa	Toccata avanti la Messa
KYRIE	KYRIE	KYRIE
KYRIE	KYRIE	KYRIE
CHRISTE	CHRISTE	CHRISTE
CHRISTE alio modo	CHRISTE	CHRISTE
CHRISTE alio modo		
CHRISTE alio modo		
KYRIE alio modo	KYRIE	KYRIE
KYRIE alio modo	KYRIE	KYRIE
KYRIE alio modo	KYRIE	
KYRIE ultimo		
KYRIE alio modo		
KYRIE alio modo		
Canzon dopo la Pistola	Canzon dopo la Pistola	Canzon dopo la Pistola
Ricercar dopo il Credo	Toccata avanti il Recercar	Recercar dopo il Credo
Alio modo, si placet	Recercar cromaticho post il Credo	
	Altro recercar	Toccata avanti il Ricercar
		Recercar
Toccata cromaticha per la levatione	Toccata per le levatione	Toccata per le levatione
Canzon post il Comune	Ricercar con obligo del basso	Bergamasca
Alio modo, si placet	Canzon quarti toni dopo il Post Comune	Capriccio sopra la Girolmeta

Note: Words in capital letters indicate items of the mass ordinary.

The toccatas that preface the three masses employ a repertory of gestures that is clearly related to the 1627 *Toccate* but the form is now realized on a tighter scale (the longest occupies only ten breves) with all the conciseness of the liturgical versets in the earlier collection. Owing in part to the firm control of the bass line, these epigrammatic miniatures compress an astonishing variety of figuration and affect into their small compass (Ex. 14.1).

An examination of the Kyrie-settings (see Table 12) raises the question of their performance in terms of the relation between the original chant and the organ-versets, which varies among the three masses. The standard *alternatim* performance of the Kyrie began with the organ and alternated the sections regularly with the choir, so that two organ settings of both Kyries and one of the Christe would be necessary.[2] *Alternatim* performance suits Frescobaldi's setting of the Sunday mass best, despite the five settings of a chant phrase that occurs only once in the original. In the mass of the Apostles one organ verse would be superfluous in each section of an *alternatim* performance, and a similar presentation of the Marian mass would not only eliminate three of Frescobaldi's versets but also leave the final chant section unset.

The twenty-six Kyrie/Christe versets, like the versets of *Toccate* II, treat the chant material in three ways: as a *cantus firmus*—often in long note-values—in any one voice; as a clear melodic shape in two or three voices against other material; and as a source of motives for points of imitation. The first and fifth versets of the Sunday Kyrie, for example, both employ the chant as a soprano *cantus firmus,* but in one setting it is accompanied by a short imitation in duple meter, in the other it is treated as a tripla of almost dancelike character. The last two versets of the Marian mass employ their respective chants to provide imitative material, but one

EXAMPLE 14.1 Toccata avanti la Messa della Domenica, measures 1–4

TABLE 12. Chant-setting in the *Fiori*

CHANT STRUCTURE	FIORI
Sunday (Mass XI, *Orbis Factor*)	
Kyrie: AAA	Kyrie: A
	Kyrie: A
Christe: BBB	Christe: B
	Christe alio modo: B
	Christe alio modo: B
	Christe alio modo: B
Kyrie: AAC	Kyrie alio modo: A
	Kyrie alio modo: C
	Kyrie alio modo: C
	Kyrie ultimo: C
	Kyrie alio modo: C
	Kyrie alio modo: C
Apostles (Mass IV, *Cunctipotens Genitor*)	
Kyrie: AAA	Kyrie: A
	Kyrie: A
	Kyrie: A
Christe: BBB	Christe: B
	Christe: B
Kyrie: CCC_1 (extended ending)	Kyrie: C
	Kyrie: C
	Kyrie: C_1
Madonna (Mass IX, *in festis BMV 1*)	
Kyrie: ABA	Kyrie: A
	Kyrie: B
Christe: CDC	Christe: C
	Christe: D
Kyrie: EDE_1 (extended ending)	Kyrie: E
	Kyrie: D

creates a regular nonfigural rhythmic surface while the other is permeated by syncopations, suspensions, and incisive rhythmic patterns. This variety of character is emphasized by Girolamo's direction that "among the Kyries some can be played with a fast tempo, and others with a slow one."

The five Gradual and Post-Communion canzonas of the *Fiori* are Frescobaldi's last essays in a genre that had engaged him throughout his career. These are all imitative, multisectional canzonas based on motto themes, but rigid sectionalization is avoided by the use of free passages, often marked "adasio" and sometimes of considerable figural elaboration, as a foil to the imitative sections (often indicated by "alegro" after an adagio). If the toccatas of the *Fiori* can be said to show the influence of contrapuntal and motivic economy on a figural and discursive genre, the canzonas of the collection show how keyboard figuration could soften the somewhat rigid outlines of the canzona.

All five canzonas can be described as variation-canzonas insofar as the opening material forms the basis of each succeeding section. The simplest instance is the Gradual canzona from the mass of the Madonna, nothing more than a duple and a triple statement of the subject (the Bassa Fiammengha) separated by a free adagio. The Gradual canzona of the mass of the Apostles varies the usual procedure by presenting the subject first in a chordal introduction before its appearance in imitation. In the Post-Communion of the Sunday mass the structure is enriched by an "alio modo" section based on a new subject against which the original material is placed as a countersubject. The remaining two canzonas, the Gradual from the Sunday mass and the Post-Communion from the mass of the Apostles, transform rather than merely vary their original material. In the Gradual the three statements of the subject (which outlines the initial third of the last chant Kyrie) are radically different (Ex. 14.2). The Post-Communion, somewhat more varied in structure through the employment of three adagio sections, not only alters the rhythmic shape and melodic contour of the original material but also introduces it in long notes against its own transformation (Ex. 14.3).

The six ricercars (one for the Post-Communion, five for the Offertory) return to a more severe style, mitigated in two cases by brief but expressive

EXAMPLE 14.2 a. Messa della Domenica, Canzon dopo l'Epistola, measure 1

b. measure 17

c. measures 39–40

EXAMPLE 14.3 a. Messa delli Apostoli, Canzon quarti toni, measures 1–2

b. measures 17–18

c. measures 21–24

d. measure 36

introductory toccatas—only the second occurrence of this pairing in Frescobaldi's printed works. They are organized in from two to four large sections set off by coronas where the organist could end the work if convenient. As we would expect, the ricercars are relatively unadorned in figural character, clear in overall tonal organization, and steady in rhythmic pulse. As befits a "serious" genre, two of the six ricercars are based on chromatic subjects and two others show a strong chromatic inflection.

As in the 1615 collection, Frescobaldi organizes ricercars by the use of ostinato techniques. The ricercar after the Creed in the Lady-mass has no designated ostinato, but its two sections are dominated by a single subject. In the first section, except for the cadence some portion of the subject appears in all but one of the twenty-four measures; in the second section it appears in augmentation in all four voices, unmistakable in its poignant opening leap and chromatic ascent (Ex. 14.4).

The third ricercar in the mass of the Apostles defines its ostinato as the "*obligo* of the Bass as it appears." The subject—a five-note motto—is employed motivically in the upper parts, but its appearances in the bass chart the tonal course of the work. It first outlines a circle of fifths (statements on C, G, D, A, E/ D, G), then, returning to C, a circle of fourths (F, B-flat, E-flat/ F, C). The procedure recalls that of an English hexachord fantasy, and this harmonic freedom is underscored by the fact that Frescobaldi—like the English—exceeds the bounds of the meantone keyboard.

In the second ricercar of the Messa della Madonna, Girolamo repeats the flashiest of his inventions in the *Capricci,* the "*obligo* of singing the fifth part without playing it." As in the capriccio, the *quinta parte* not only serves as ostinato but also generates the motivic material of the four written voices. Frescobaldi carries his original conceit a step further here: the first appearance of the subject in the soprano is accompanied by a quotation from Petrarch, "Intendomi chi può che m'intend'io" (Understand me who can for I understand myself),[3] indicating that the player is not given cues for the entrances of the *quinta parte,* as in the capriccio, but must seek them out himself.

The canzonas, performed at the Gradual and the Post-Communion, are the lightest in style of the contents of the *Fiori.* The ricercars for the Offertory, the beginning of the sacrificial portion of the liturgy, are more solemn in character. With the toccatas for the Elevation of the Host, we reach, both liturgically and musically, the center of gravity of the mass. The Elevations of the *Fiori* are shorter than the two Elevation toccatas of the 1627 volume and lack their almost hallucinatory timelessness, but they

EXAMPLE 14.4 Messa della Madonna, Recercar dopo il Credo, measures 24–28

display the chromaticism, expressive figuration and vocal inflection, and dramatic and declamatory rhythmic character of their predecessors. The Elevations from the masses of the Apostles and of the Madonna show this derivation most clearly, including the extent to which they too resist description and analysis. As in the earlier Elevations, a steady half-note pulse anchors the nervous and irregular rhythmic surface of the works to the basic rate of harmonic change. Internal cadences are generally avoided, and sequence is also employed as a unifying factor—sometimes unsystematically, as in the way the Lombard rhythm spreads through the texture in the closing section of the Madonna Elevation.

The Elevation from the Sunday mass, written—like the other two Elevations—in the traditional E mode, has as its analogue not the 1627 Elevations but the toccata "di durezze e ligature" of the same collection. Like its predecessor, the present work is based on a chromatic subject and eschews internal cadences and figural breaking of the basic half-note pulse. Formally, the work consists of a chordal introduction (headed "adasio"—the only case in the *Fiori* in which this indication seems to govern an entire work) whose highly inflected chromaticism prepares the descending chromatic lines that dominate the succeeding imitative texture.

Instead of the ricercar and canzonas that close the first two masses, the Messa della Madonna ends with two capriccios technically inadmissible for liturgical use as defined by the Council of Trent, since both are based on secular tunes, the Bergamasca and the Girolmeta (although Bonini complained of organists who play *ariette* "similar to the spagnoletta, or the Romanesca").[4] And indeed their texts, as quoted in the Mazzocchi-Marazzoli *Chi soffre speri* presented in Carnival of 1639 by Cardinal Francesco Barberini, are hardly elevating: "Franceschina pleases me" and "Who made you the fine shoes that suit you so well, Girometta?" The Bergamasca was set by Farnaby, Scheidt, Sweelinck, Salomone Rossi, and Viadana, and Floriano Canale's canzona "La Stella" seems to quote the Girolmeta, but Frescobaldi's settings are apparently the first Italian keyboard versions of both tunes.[5]

Despite their unprepossessing sources, these two capriccios are among the most extended and masterful items in the *Fiori musicali,* confirming Girolamo's assertion, "Chi questa Bergamasca sonara, non pocho Imparera" (Who will play this Bergamasca, will learn not a little). Like the 1624 capriccios, these works comprise a number of sections all treating the original subject but contrasting in meter, texture, figuration, and occasionally cadence:

Bergamasca

I. mm. 1–17, C, cadence on G
II. 18–40, 6/4, D
III. 41–53, C, D
IV. 54–86, C3, G
V. 87–100, C, G
VI. 101–107, C (with triplets), G
VII. 108–123, (C), G

Girolmeta

I. mm. 1–33, C, G
II. 33–49, 6/4, G
III. 50–71, C, C
IV. Alio modo, 72–95, (C), G

(The fact that the third section of the Girolmeta cadences on C rather than on G, the tonic of the rest of the piece, implies that at least here the ensuing "alio modo" is not an alternative but a necessity.)

Frescobaldi here displays with joyful abandon all the resources of his art. The dazzling cadence in the second section of the Girolmeta and the brilliant triplets in the sixth part of the Bergamasca recall the pyrotechnics of the "non senza fatiga" toccata (Ex. 14.5). Frescobaldi's resource in inventing countersubjects to the two tunes ranges from the deliberately neutral figures in the last section of the Bergamasca and in the *alio modo* of the Girolmeta to the serpentine chromaticism of sections V and III in the sister works. And it is precisely the everyday character of the two themes that prompts this show of virtuosity, a delight in the transfiguration of the banal that finds its ultimate expression the Quodlibet of J. S. Bach's Goldberg Variations.

Indeed, in considering Girolamo's last keyboard collection it is difficult to resist the obvious parallels with Bach's final works. Not even the most prejudiced enthusiast would contend that the *Fiori musicali* matches the scope of the *Clavierübung,* but the two collections share an avowed didactic aim and a valedictory summation of previous work in a variety of genres. The German "Organ Mass" in Part III of the *Clavierübung* is the Protestant counterpart of the liturgical cycles in the *Fiori musicali,* and the quotation of the Bergamasca as "Kraut and Rüben" in the Goldberg Quod-

EXAMPLE 14.5 Bergamasca, measures 105–106

libet is, as it were, a blossom plucked from the *Fiori.* The deepest relations between the two collections, however, are those of analogy rather than those of imitation. In both we find a mastery of technique so complete that the conflicting demands of concision and expression are reciprocally satisfied, and the commonplace becomes the touchstone for the transmuting power of the composer's art.

The reedition of Frescobaldi's first book of toccatas published in 1637 under the patronage of Cardinal Francesco Barberini added to the original an *Aggiunta* containing nine new works, the last to be printed during Girolamo's lifetime: three balletti; the *Cento partite sopra passacagli,* which superseded the variations on the ciaccona and the passacagli in *Toccate* II; a variation-capriccio on the Ruggiero; a capriccio on *la Battaglia;* two dance pairs, a balletto and ciaccona and a corrente and ciaccona; and a "Capriccio pastorale" for organ with pedals.

The quality of these last works is uneven. The Pastorale is interesting chiefly as an early example of the pastoral in which pedal-points imitate the sound of bagpipes, a genre that may have originated in Naples, the land of the Christmas *presepio,* or in Rome, where *pifferari* and *zampognari* still come down from the Abruzzi to serenade the Madonna and Child.[6] The Battaglia (qualified as "navale" in one copy), except for its exploitation of harpsichord sound-effects, is without doubt the weakest piece of music Girolamo ever published. The Ruggiero, with its sly quotation of the tune "Fra Jacopino" which harks back to the sixth ricercar of the 1615 collection, is a charming example of Frescobaldi's small variation-sets. The remaining works exemplify in one way or another Girolamo's increased interest in the continuous ostinato variation, an interest perhaps stimulated by his own public improvisations and by the employment of improvised passacaglias in the Barberini operas of the 1630s.[7]

The three balletti are miniature dance-suites, each opening with a two-part balletto in duple meter followed by a two-part corrente (thematically related to the balletto in the first two sets) in compound meter and concluding—in sets one and three—with passacagli. The same bass underlies both passacagli sections, stated in the minor on E in the first and both in the major, on B-flat, and in the minor, on G, in the second (Ex. 14.6). The other combinations of dance and ostinato do not shed much

EXAMPLE 14.6 Passacagli basses

additional light on the distinction between passacagli and ciaccona, since the bass of the first ciaccona, in major, is closely related to the passacagli, and the second is little more than a modulating cadential progression (Ex. 14.7).

In all these works the dance movements display the straightforward vigor and metrical subtlety we have come to expect from Frescobaldi's dance writing. The ostinato movements—especially the passacaglias of the balletti—have a new quicksilver variety of constantly changing register, chromatic inflection, and play with symmetry and asymmetry so idiomatic to the keyboard that they seem written-out improvisations. Indeed, two seventeenth-century manuscripts of keyboard music that present passacaglias in every possible key, including the equivalents of E-flat major and c minor, f minor, A major, and E major, seem to provide models for such improvisation, but it is impossible to decide whether they foreshadow or reflect Frescobaldi's own performances and publications.[8]

Girolamo's new mastery of continuous keyboard textures in the decade between 1627 and 1637 was hard-won. The Ciaccona and Passacagli variations from the 1627 book are surprisingly limited in comparison with the rich variety of their companion toccatas. In both sets of variations the two-measure module of the original is rigidly maintained, and since both patterns begin on I and end on V, each new variation starts with a monotonously predictable tonic cadence on the downbeat. The texture of the Ciaccona in particular accentuates this, since almost invariably figuration in one hand is accompanied by chords in the other, and the variations tend to be paired, one hand picking up the figural material of the other from the previous variation. Perhaps the most obvious features of the Ciaccona set taken over into later works are the frequent addition of 4 to V^5 chords, the minor inflection of the third, and a sense of contrasting textures (Ex. 14.8).

The Passacagli variations, twice the length of those on the Ciaccona (a phenomenon visible also in guitar variations), show a greater awareness

EXAMPLE 14.7 Ciaccona basses

EXAMPLE 14.8 a. Partite sopra ciaccona (1627), measures 20–22

b. measures 25–26

EXAMPLE 14.9 Partite sopra passacagli (1627), measures 1–11

of keyboard space and an attempt to link single variations into larger groupings (Ex. 14.9). Among the other devices retained in later treatments of the same material are the pedal-point trill and an *alio modo* section, here a change of meter rather than of tonic.

The next stage in Girolamo's development of these two patterns appears in the *Arie musicali* of 1630 in the form of an Aria di Passacaglia, "Cosi me disprezzate," and a Ceccona, "Deh, vien da me." Here Frescobaldi avoids the rigid sectionalization of the 1627 keyboard variations by alternating sections in free recitative style and duple meter with triple-meter sections based on the ostinati. Further, the ostinati themselves are treated with greater freedom. The Passacaglia outlines a descending tetrachord and can be realized in a variety of figurations, sometimes with extensive substitutions (Ex. 14.10). The Ciaccona is again a cadential figure (Ex. 14.11). Most important, both patterns are now permitted to modulate, and this combines with the overlapping of bass phrases by the vocal lines to break up completely the static periodicity of the 1627

EXAMPLE 14.10 a. Aria di passacaglia, measures 1–3

b. measures 7–8

EXAMPLE 14.11 Ceccona a due tenori, measures 1–3 (original notation)

keyboard settings. Both tonally and texturally the result is a new freedom and flexibility.

The passacagli, ciaccona, and dance attain their apotheosis in the *Cento partite sopra passacagli.* The problems posed by this work begin with the title. Typographically, the "Cento" appears to be an afterthought, and in fact there are seventy-seven variations on the Passacagli, plus forty-one more on the Ciaccona. The index of the volume compounds the confusion by ending the *Cento partite* at the Corrente and listing the remainder of the work as *Corrente e passachagli* and *Ciaccone e passachagli.* This suggestion of a complex evolution for the work is confirmed by the alteration of page numbers on the original plates.[9] Frescobaldi's note added in 1637 to the 1616 preface states that "the Passacagli can be played separately, as one prefers, with the adjustment of the tempo of one part and another; so with the Ciaccone." One glance at the music, which employs seven different triple mensurations and sixteen changes of mensuration, raises the question of what role these symbols play in "the adjustment of the tempo of one part and another."

The materials for an answer should first be sought in an examination of Frescobaldi's use of triple mensurations. (The only variation in his employment of duple meter is the occasional replacement of C by ₵, which probably indicated a faster tempo; see Chapter 15.) Unfortunately, a survey of triple mensurations in Frescobaldi's work does not seem to reveal either a consistent doctrine or even a consistent evolution, particularly in regard to proportional relationships. The only unequivocal proportional signs indicate relationships between duple and triple meters, not between two triple mensurations. These unequivocal indications are 12/8, canceled by 8/12, and (except at the beginning of a work) 6/4 canceled by 4/6 or, in later works, by C. Outside of the *Aggiunta* two triple signs in succession virtually never occur, which casts further doubt on their proportional interpretation in the *Aggiunta.* The greatest variety of triple signs appears—not surprisingly—in the mixed contents of *Toccate* II and in the other genres that employ contrasting triple sections: capriccios and canzonas. In addition, single collections seem to display common notational features. The more archaic signs—those involving ⊙ or O and black notation—tend to disappear from later works, but the 1634 *Canzoni* are a striking exception. The most common ternary sign in the instrumental works is Ͼ3 (but Ͼ3/2 in the 1634 *Canzoni*), which does not appear at all in the near-contemporary *Arie.* There the sign (C)3 appears to indicate a reduction in note-values. In the madrigal "Bella tiranna," for example, the same material is presented as C3, 6/4, and 3. (This example also shows that an indication such as C added to another sign—in this case 3—at the beginning of a work is a general indication concerning perfection and imperfection; the 3 that appears later on has the same meaning as the opening C3.) Similarly, the sign Ͼ3/2 in the *Canzoni* governs both 3/2–6/4 and 3/1–6/2 passages, the latter perhaps also reduced in performance. Finally, in his later works Frescobaldi occasionally used signs (3/2, 6/4) in their modern signification of groupings rather than as proportions; the most obvious case is 6/4 placed at the beginning of a work, where it cannot refer to a preceding C.

The mensural indications in the predecessors of the *Cento partite* scarcely foreshadow the intricacy of the later work. The 1627 Ciaccona is notated throughout in Ͼ3, barred as 3/2 and 6/2. The Passacagli set is similar until the *alio modo,* where Ͼ3 (= 3/2) is replaced by C6/4 apparently indicating a different grouping of the same note-values. (The procedure is reversed in the Passacagli of the third balletto from the *Aggiunta,* where 6/4 becomes Ͼ = 3/2.) In the Aria di Passacaglia from the *Arie,* the passacaglia sections are written in C3 (afterward 3) = 3/1–6/2 or 3/2. Allowing for some freedom in the recitative sections (in C) and the reduction of 3 to 3/2, the piece supports a proportional interpretation in which 𝅝. in 3 equals 𝅗𝅥 in C. In the Ceccona, the ciaccona sections are notated C3, 3, and 6/4. (The intervening recitatives are all in C.) Although the change from 3 to 6/4 is inexplicable musically, at any rate it leaves no doubt as to the reduction of 3 (Ex. 14.12). Here again, a proportional relation between triple and duple sections makes musical sense.

With these observations in mind we may turn to the *Cento partite* (see Table 13). It opens in 6/4 (the C preceding the 6/4 merely indicates that the rules of perfection and imperfection do not apply; it disappears in the subsequent recurrences of 6/4), and the sign thus indicates not a proportion but a grouping. As employed here, its distinguishing feature is its rhythmic flexibility: not only 3 × 2 or 2 × 3, but also 12/8 (4 × 3), as in *Toccate* II/9. In fact, 6/4 still obtains in the following corrente, so the changed designation 3/2 probably reflects the new title, although 3 is more frequently used in Girolamo's other correnti. The sign 3/2 appears relatively late in Frescobaldi's works and, as in its other appearances in the *Cento partite,* may govern either 3/2 or 6/4 groupings. Both Ͼ3/2 and C3/2, on the other hand, show only 3/2 patterns. In at least one case it is clear that Ͼ3/2 and 6/4 measures differ only in their grouping of notes, and that 6/4

EXAMPLE 14.12 Ceccona a due tenori, measures 26–29 (original notation)

EXAMPLE 14.13 a. Cento partite, measures 89–90

b. measures 96–97

TABLE 13. The *Cento partite sopra Passacagli*

MEASURES	DESIGNATION (TEXT)	DESIGNATION (INDEX)	TONAL CENTER	MENSURATION
1–41	*Cento* PARTITE SOPRA PAS-SACAGLI	Partite cento sopra il Passachagli	d	C6/4
41–52	Corrente	Corrente e Passachagli	d	3/2
53–88	Passacagli		d	Ͼ3/2
89–102			d	6/4
103–110			d–F	Ͼ3/2
111–131	Altro Tono		F	[Ͼ3/2]
132–139	Ciaccona	Ciaccona e Passachagli	F	O3
140–151			F–C	Ͼ3
152–163	Passacagli		C	3
164–173			C	6/4
174–197	Ciaccona		C–a	3/2
198–217	Passacagli		a	Ͼ3
218–237	Ciaccona		a–d	3/2
238–255	Altro Tono		d	[3/2]
256–267	Passacagli Altro Tono		d	C3/2
268–279			d	3
280–283			d	6/4
284–314	Altro Tono, measures 285, 308		d–a, a–e	3 (6/4 and 3/4 bars)
315–326			e	Ͼ3

Note: Lines show major structural divisions as indicated by coronas and breve cadences.

groupings can vary down to the eighth note (Ex. 14.13). The same appears to be true of the relation between 3 and 6/4 (Ex. 14.14).

Of the other mensurations in the *Partite,* 3 indicates variously 3/2, bars of mixed 6/4 and 3/4 (measures 284, 290), or 3/4 alone (measure 268). The sign Ͼ3, which governs a passage alternating between 3/2 and 6/4 groupings at measure 140 and sections in unequivocal 3/2 (or 3/2 × 2) at measures 198 and 315, probably has its original meaning of a ternary division at one level and a binary division at another. In most other music of this period, the mensuration O3 = 3/1, which occurs at the first ciaccona, would imply a proportional reduction. However, this is explicitly contradicted by Frescobaldi's preface to the *Capricci.*

There seems no direct evidence, therefore, for a solution of the mensural problems of the *Cento partite* by treating the changing signatures as proportional manipulations of a constant tactus, but there is a certain amount of evidence for considering them as appropriate groupings and subdivisions of a constant semiminim beat and therefore a flexible tactus— in effect, no tactus at all.[10] This interpretation is at least consistent with Frescobaldi's few remarks on the subject and tends to be confirmed by his notational practice in other late works. Finally, it produces a performance that can be made to yield musical sense. This may leave Girolamo's direction to adjust the tempos of sections to each other still unexplained, but it is worth noting that he makes it in the context of excerpting the passacagli or the ciaccone for performance separately, not for the performance of the entire piece.

The basic material of the *Cento partite* is the same as that of the earlier sets: a descending tetrachord for the passacagli and a cadential I–V–vi–I^3–IV–V progression for the ciaccona. The tonal freedom first essayed in the *Arie* settings is here expanded to stable tonal areas on d, F, c/C, a, and an eventual close in e. These modulations are accomplished by two cadential relations: a rise of a minor third, from minor to relative major, or the reverse; and a rise of a fifth by what we would describe as a V of V progression. The lowered third and V^5_4 chords of the 1627 passacagli are now employed dynamically as agents of these modulations (Ex. 14.15).

The richness of Frescobaldi's invention seems inexhaustible. The con-

EXAMPLE 14.14 Cento partite, measures 163–164

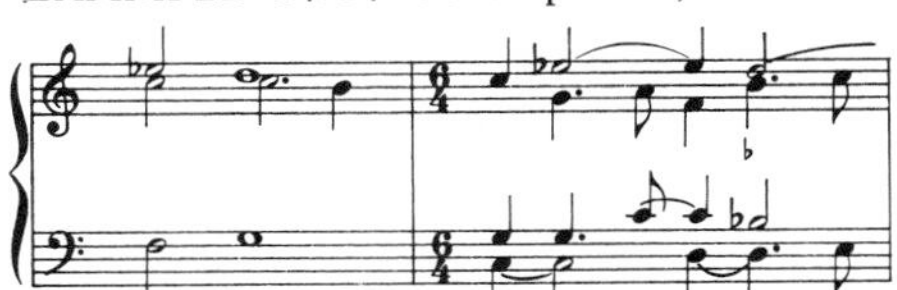

EXAMPLE 14.15 Cento partite, measures 107–111

EXAMPLE 14.16 Cento partite, measures 301–305

EXAMPLE 14.17 Cento partite, measures 315–326

trasts of texture, chromatic decoration, internal trills, sudden bursts of rhythmic activity and moments of repose, and chains of brilliant figuration produce a constantly varied surface. But these do not occur at random, as in the 1627 sets (which are perhaps closer to actual improvisation). Rather, they are placed so as to define the larger structures of the work and create its moments of greatest intensity, the last of which traverses a space of three and a half octaves in as many measures (Ex. 14.16). The work concludes in a manner that recalls the last variations of the Romanesca set. The range gradually telescopes, the saraband rhythms of the passacaglia dissolve into even quarters under a series of languorous descending pedal-points, and like a slowly rotating crystal the work circles to a halt (Ex. 14.17). As much as anything in his production, Girolamo's last great creation leaves us with a sense of both wonder and fulfillment: "Intendomi chi può che m'intend'io."

15

The Performance of Frescobaldi's Keyboard Music

Frescobaldi may have been as Doni depicted him, an unlettered and uncultivated craftsman, skilled only in the composition and performance of keyboard music. Nonetheless, Girolamo's fugitive observations on his own works echo the language and reflect the criteria of his more sophisticated contemporaries in poetry and the visual arts. The qualities of *maniera* ("style" in the abstract), *novità* (freshness or innovation), and *meraviglia* (surprise and delight without violence to tradition) mark Frescobaldi's music and his statements about it as deeply as they mark the poetry of Marino, the architecture of Borromini, or anything from the hand of Bernini. Novelty of artifice, variety, grace, elegance, virtuoso display—and what terms could better describe the art of seventeenth-century Rome?—were cited explicitly by Frescobaldi as the hallmarks of the style he created and bequeathed as a model to his successors.

Girolamo's art was "at the ends of his fingers" at least in the sense that his style was as much one of execution as of composition. Traditionally, such personal styles had been transmitted in the contact between teacher and pupil. Where music that depended on its manner of execution for its full effect was addressed to performers outside the immediate circle of the composer, some description of this style was necessary. Giulio Caccini, for example, felt his method of singing important enough to the understanding of his music to preface the *Nuove musiche* with an extensive introduction on performance, and Frescobaldi was the first keyboard composer to follow suit in his own publications. The examination of Girolamo's prefaces and their meaning, then, is a completion of the performing text, only a portion of which is provided by the note-picture. Little serious attention has been paid Frescobaldi's directions for performance.[1] They have been cited frequently, but generally out of context and often with fundamental flaws in translation and interpretation. In any case, they must be considered not in isolation but in the larger framework of musical practice in late sixteenth- and seventeenth-century Italy.

Frescobaldi presented indications for performance in the prefatory material to four keyboard collections: the two versions of the first book of toccatas (1615, 1616), the *Capricci* (1624), and the *Fiori musicali* (1635). For the purposes of this discussion it will be assumed that these are expressions—admittedly fragmentary and sometimes erratic—of a single coherent conception of performance, and that where seeming contradictions occur they are the products of differing contexts or interpretations: no one familiar with Girolamo's letters could claim that he was an impeccable prose stylist.

For an understanding of the musical milieu in which Frescobaldi's style developed there is a rich variety of sources. The treatises of Diruta and Banchieri elucidate the basic principles of Italian keyboard technique, and further technical and interpretive information is scattered in the writings and music of Girolamo's contemporaries, notably Antegnati, Trabaci, Mayone, Bottazzi, Grassi, Maugars, Fasolo, Scipione Giovanni, and Bonini. The background and context of solo keyboard music are illuminated by accounts of continuo practice (Viadana, Agazzari, Cavalieri), instrumental tutòrs, vocal and instrumental ornamentation treatises, and the writings of the Florentine monodists. Ancillary evidence from outside Italy is provided in Thomás de Sancta Maria's discussions of keyboard fingering, rhythm, and ornamentation, and in Michael Praetorius' encyclopedic account of instruments and performance practice.

This whole body of material must be brought to bear in examining the two kinds of questions that are the legitimate concerns of the study of performance. The first category is that of *Aufführungspraxis* in the strict sense: matters such as text and notation, instrumentation, and methods and conventions of performance, which can be examined on the basis of historical evidence. The second surveys the broader field of interpretation and is concerned with such things as articulation, tempo, form, and expressive content. Contrary to the prevailing assumption, answers to questions in the first category cannot be accepted as solutions to problems in the second; but the consideration of specific areas of performance practice can lead to more general observations about interpretation.

Tempo and Rhythm

In all four of Frescobaldi's prefatory statements, questions of tempo and rhythm predominate, "since the perfection of playing consists principally in understanding the tempi" (1615). Specific tempo indications did not occur in Girolamo's instrumental works until relatively late in his career, with the markings "adagio" and "alegro" of the 1628 ensemble canzonas and the *Fiori musicali.* As in their infrequent appearance elsewhere in the music of this period, these terms seem to indicate deviations from a normal moderate tempo. This norm is certainly a survival of the Renaissance tactus, but only in very strictly defined cases can a proportional interpretation of Frescobaldi's notation be advanced (see the discussion of the *Cento partite* in Chapter 14).

The observations of Girolamo's contemporaries indicate that there existed some consensus of opinion about the performing tempos of certain genres. Canzonas were taken at a lively pace—"in haste," according to Antegnati—to emphasize their "vivacity and *motivi allegri,*" such as Grassi found in Frescobaldi's canzonas.[2] Ricercars were played more slowly, as Banchieri implied in prefacing a collection of *canzoni alla francese* (*Moderna armonia,* 1612) with the direction that repeated sections "must be played *adagio* the first time as a ricercar, and in the repeat quickly."[3] Fasolo (1645) specified that canzonas were to be played with flexible tempos within a basic moderate beat, articulating the subject to make it stand out. Ricercars began slowly but speeded up somewhat if there were contrasting sections. In liturgical organ music, masses were to be played gravely, hymns gravely but with spirit, and Elevations very gravely, sustaining the suspensions beyond their written value.[4] According to Michele Pesenti and Frescobaldi's emulator Scipione Giovanni, balli, correnti, ciaccone, and passacaglias were all taken allegro.[5]

Frescobaldi's own prefaces are less concerned with such basic tempos than with the clear definition of the individual sections that make up the toccatas, variations, capriccios, and much of the contents of the *Fiori.* These sections are generally defined by a minim chord in both hands and are sufficiently independent to end a toccata (1616), capriccio (1624), or canzona or ricercar (1635), assuming that the final chord is in the correct key (1624, 1635).

Two terms are essential to Frescobaldi's own conception of these sections: *affetti* and *effetti.* Although his employment of these seems idiosyncratic and sometimes inconsistent, in fact it follows the usage of his contemporaries, notably Caccini in the preface to the *Nuove musiche.*[6] The primary meaning of *affetto* was a passion of the soul, for Frescobaldi the essential expressive meaning of a section: "In those things that do not seem governed by contrapuntal practice one must first seek the *affetto* of that passage and the goal of the Author for the delight of the ear and the way it is sought in playing" (1624).The *affetti* of instrumental music are analogous to the words of a madrigal text: "This manner of playing must not be subject to a beat, as we see practiced in modern madrigals, which however difficult are facilitated by means of the beat, conducting it now slow, now rapid, and even [*etiandio*] suspending it in the air, according to their *affetti*, or sense of the words" (1616). They are not, however, simple instrumental equivalences to verbal expression. For one thing, they are to be discovered only in performance, by putting the music "well in practice on the instrument, where the *affetto* it must have will with study be known" (1624). Rather, Frescobaldi has created a parallel world of *affetti*, of gesture and rhetoric conceived in specifically musical terms, in which his characters declaim in a manner at once unequivocal and untranslatable.

The *effetti*, on the other hand, are the individual rhetorical devices of this musical declamation such as ornaments—"trills and other *effetti*"—"which appear by playing" (1615). Like Caccini and other contemporaries, Frescobaldi sometimes calls these *affetti*—"songlike *affetti* and diversity of passages" (1616).[7] (Indeed, in string music the direction *affetti* denoted the improvisation of *effetti*.)[8]

All the prefaces agree that toccatas and capriccios should begin slowly, the long chords of the toccatas arpeggiated on the harpsichord—"with gravity and without *passaggi*, but not without *affetti*," as Durante put it.[9] After this initial free tempo, within a single *partita* or a section of a larger work, Frescobaldi counsels a basic tempo chosen according to the *affetto* of the section as expressed in its *effetti*:

> In the partite let a just tempo be taken, and in proportion, and because in some there are rapid sections begin with a comfortable beat, since it is not suitable to begin rapidly and continue slowly; but they want to be taken entire with the same tempo. (1615)
>
> In the Partite when *passaggi* will be found, and *affetti* it will be well to take a broad tempo; which will also be observed in the toccatas. The other ones without *passaggi* can be played somewhat allegro as to beat, referring the conduct of the tempo to the good taste and fine judgment of the player. (1616)
>
> In the Kyries some can be played with a rapid beat, and others with a slow one. (1635)

Frescobaldi does not advocate taking an entire variation-set at a constant tactus, a frequent misinterpretation of the first statement that would contravene his doctrine of flexibility according to the *affetti;* it is the single variation that is to be taken at a consistent tempo throughout.

Structural cadences, no matter what values are employed to notate them, are to be held, and the tempo is gradually slowed in approaching the end of *passaggi* or cadences (1615, 1616). (This was presumably general practice, since Trabaci also recommended broadening the tempo at cadences.)[10] In the same way, it is appropriate to stop on the last note of a trill or other *effetti* such as *passaggi* in leaps or stepwise motion (1615, 1616). The 1615 preface says of double passages (ones with sixteenths in both hands) that they be taken adagio, the last note before a falling leap being "resolute and fast," which seems explained by the 1616 direction to stop at the note preceding the passage even if it is short and then to proceed resolutely, the better to show off the agility of the hand.

Frescobaldi's repertory of mensurations contains C, ₵, and a wide variety of triple measures (see Table 13 in Chapter 14). The symbol C is Frescobaldi's usual indication of duple meter. (Like his contemporaries, he also employed it for the ternary groupings of the Romanesca.) At this period the sign ₵, *tempus imperfectum diminutum,* could denote its original proportional meaning of twice the speed of a preceding C, an undefined acceleration (in his *Ricercate* of 1615 Trabaci indicated "battuta stretta" for both ₵ and Ø), or no change in tempo at all. Since Frescobaldi replaced the previous C indication of the Romanesca variations with the sign ₵ for a section without *passaggi,* for him this probably signified the second alternative, "somewhat allegro as to beat."

Girolamo's employment of unequivocal proportions is sparing. The notational evidence of his music leaves no doubt that 6/4 (canceled by 4/6) and 12/8 (canceled by 8/12) are proportional equivalents to a preceding or simultaneous C, and in some instances 3/2 also seems to be proportional.[11] Yet he himself says only that in 6/4 the tempo "be given making the beat move rapidly" (1624) and does not mention the other proportions.

In the preface to the *Capricci* Frescobaldi flatly contradicted his contemporaries' proportional understanding of triple mensurations, where notation in breves, semibreves, and minims indicated a rapid tempo. "In the triplas, or sesquialteras, if they are major [for example, 3/2] let them be played slowly, if minor [3/2] somewhat more rapidly, if of three semiminims, [3] more rapidly" (1624).[12] He did, however, occasionally retain the convention of perfection in notating such triple meters (as in the opening of *Iste Confessor*); otherwise he added dots.

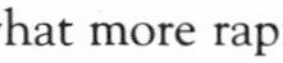

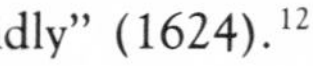

He applied coloration not only to sesquialtera, but also to major and minor hemiola: and . Reverse hemiola (white notation) also occurs, as in Canzona II of *Toccate* II.

In its untidy assimilation of certain proportional devices and its general repudiation of proportional tempo relationships Frescobaldi's practice reflects the contemporary breakdown of Renaissance notational principles. The features he did retain, however, are employed to create one of his most dramatic effects, the clash of two against three. It has been asserted that all such passages must be "assimilated," that is, that the duple divisions must be rewritten to conform to the prevailing triple subdivision.[13] As the preface to the *Capricci* demonstrates, reference to general practice is no sure guide to laying down rules for the performance of Frescobaldi's music. Beyond that, the doctrine of assimilation ignores historical, notational, and musical evidence. Renaissance notation abounded in devices for producing simultaneous congruent duple and triple subdivisions, and a glance at the enchained mensurations of *Toccate* II/9 will show that Frescobaldi was fully aware of such possibilities. The doctrine is somewhat strained by measures 11–13 of that work, where the same dotted figure has to be assimilated both to a single sixteenth sextuplet and to a triplet eighth (Ex. 15.1). It fails completely in *Toccate* II/11, where the dotted figure is counted out over eight bars as a measured sixteenth (Ex. 15.2). Two bars later it must suddenly assimilate itself as an eighth-note triplet (Ex. 15.3). The fact is that Frescobaldi possessed the equipment to notate assimilation, and when he wanted it, he did so (Ex. 15.4).

Similarly, where he wanted rhythmic alteration of the printed text, Frescobaldi specified it in his prefatory material (see also the discussion of fingering). Two *effetti* are described as demanding such alteration. Where

EXAMPLE 15.1 *Toccate* II/9, measures 11–13

EXAMPLE 15.2 *Toccate* II/11, measures 51–59

EXAMPLE 15.3 *Toccate* II/11, measure 60

EXAMPLE 15.4 *Toccate* II/11, measure 22

one finds a (written-out) trill in one hand against a *passaggio* in the other, the two are not to be divided note for note, but the trill is to be played rapidly and the *passaggio* more slowly and *affettuoso* (1616); in the toccatas of the *Fiori,* "trills, or *affettuoso* passages" are to be played more adagio, "slowing the beat." *Passaggi* for both hands where eighths and sixteenths occur together should not be taken too fast, and the sixteenths written as even should be played in Lombard rhythm, with every second one dotted (1616). Thus, a passage notated as in Ex. 15.5a should be played as in Ex. 15.5b. (Fasolo recommended playing eighths and sixteenths "as if they were half dotted" in allegro movements).[14]

EXAMPLE 15.5 *Toccate* I/5, measure 33

a. as written

b. as played

EXAMPLE 15.6 *Toccate* II/6, measures 65–68

EXAMPLE 15.7 Partite sopra la monica, variation eleven, measures 4–6

A few rhythmic alterations depended on convention. A dotted pattern beginning with a rest and a note of equal value was played in conformity with the pattern (see Ex. 13.5b). Dotted figures were also continued in contexts where the absence of double dots made their notation impossible (Ex. 15.6). Frescobaldi and his contemporaries did not always notate dotted rhythms consistently after their first appearance, and there are places in Girolamo's music where logic suggests the continuation of a dotted figure; the same is true of the occasional addition of ties (Ex. 15.7).

Frescobaldi's most idiomatic keyboard writing is animated by a seemingly endless variety of rhythmic invention. The two-against-three patterns of *Toccate* II/9, for example, occur in a dazzling succession of per-

mutations whose changing or recurrent densities of texture both vary and unite the work (Ex. 15.8). Another of Girolamo's effects is the placement of rhythmic phrases so that they overlap changes of hand position or other types of physical articulation, and the challenge to the performer is to prepare the phrase so that it moves over, and not between the physical obstacles (Ex. 15.9). Excitement may also be generated by the combination of a number of rhythmic units having nonsimultaneous downbeats, ranging from meteor-showers of tiny imitations to the convoluted cross-accents of *passi doppi* (Ex. 15.10).

In his treatment of Frescobaldi's rhythms the performer cannot content himself with reproducing their notational outline; he must first understand the sources and direction of their energy. Unfortunately, the whole concept of a rhythmic phrase, a unit accumulating intensity toward a functional downbeat or dissipating energy from it, is too often replaced by

EXAMPLE 15.9 Romanesca, variation eleven, measures 2–4

EXAMPLE 15.10 *Toccate* II/7, measures 36–39

regular stressed downbeats as indicated by barlines. (It is perhaps unnecessary to point out that downbeats are as perceptible on "nonaccentual" instruments such as the harpsichord and organ as they are on ones capable of dynamic contrast.) What appear at first to be technical problems in Frescobaldi (and elsewhere) are often musical ones, and frequently spring from faulty perception of the functional downbeat of a phrase in terms of what prepares and follows it, or from the attempt to jam more than one downbeat into a single phrase. How many performances of galliards are hamstrung by the player's inability to perceive that the first measure is an upbeat, and that no downbeat occurs until the second bar of the phrase (an observation confirmed by seventeenth-century choreography and vocal settings).[15]

Frescobaldi gave to the formulas of his predecessors a new rhetorical, expressive content, to which an understanding of rhythmic direction is essential. The combined trill and turn which is the most annoying keyboard cliché of Andrea Gabrieli and Merulo achieves an expressive urgency when conceived as the gradual accumulation of energy to explode in a downbeat and performed as an acceleration (Ex. 15.11). Unfortunately, this intensity is often vitiated by the performer's insensitivity to the declamatory possibilities of the figure (Ex. 15.12). These may seem small and relatively trivial details, but it is the essence of a rhetorical style

EXAMPLE 15.11 Trill/turn, gradual acceleration

EXAMPLE 15.12 Trill/turn, conventional execution

in any of the arts that no gesture be unimportant, haphazard, or meaningless.

Fingering and Articulation

Despite Libanori's assertion that Frescobaldi sight-read the most difficult works with his hands reversed, "that is, with the palms turned upwards"—a party-trick that is still with us—we may assume that Girolamo usually followed more conventional habits of keyboard playing as transmitted by Diruta and Banchieri. The player is to sit at the middle of the keyboard, to keep his head and body erect and quiet, to let the arm guide the hand, and to keep the hand aligned with the arm both vertically and horizontally. The fingers are to lie in line with the keyboard, slightly curved, and the cupped hand is to rest lightly on the keys for agility and ease. Sixteenth-century Italian portraits show that the placement of the thumb and fifth finger determined the position of the hand, with the longer fingers curved to accommodate them. The fingers should press the keys rather than strike them and are raised as the keys rise. For Diruta the norm of organ playing was a legato style, and he ridiculed organists who "take their hands off the keyboard so that they make the Organ remain without sound for the space of half a beat, and often a whole beat, which seems that they are playing plucked instruments." Frescobaldi's one reference to fingering suggests that he shared something of this legato ideal: "In the *Canti fermi* although they are tied[,] in order not to impede the hands they can be untied for greater convenience" (1635). (In fact, the only long ties in the Kyries are not in the chants themselves but in pedal-points, which therefore would sometimes necessitate finger substitutions in order to be performed legato as written.)

A percussive touch is appropriate to the harpsichord "by reason of the jacks, and the plectra that they may play better," and in dance music Diruta allows a detached style, "leaping with the hand to give grace, and air to their dances."[16] A certain amount of common sense is required in the interpretation of this passage. The resistance of harpsichord action, unlike that of the piano or the clavichord, is greatest in the middle of the stroke, at the point where the plectrum passes the string; beyond that, no more weight is required than what is necessary to hold the key down. Diruta presupposes a strongly quilled instrument playing dance music, in which the maintenance of rhythmic vitality is the primary consideration—indeed, an occasional thump or two is sometimes an aid to dancers. To extrapolate from his sensible suggestion a general harpsichord technique in which unnecessary weight is slammed to the bottom of the key dip is unwarranted by the historical evidence and condemned by the musical results.

Fundamental to seventeenth-century Italian descriptions of keyboard fingering is the concept of "good" (*buone*) and "bad" (*cattive*) notes—that is, notes falling on strong or weak beats or subdivisions (a distinction paralleled by the placement of up- and down-bows in seventeenth-century string playing). For Diruta, who furnishes detailed examples, in passages of notes in equal value the notes begin with a good one and alternate regularly with bad ones; an initial rest (of the same value as the notes) or a dot on the first note does not affect the succession. Where the initial rest or note is twice the value of the notes in the remainder of the passage it counts as both a good and a bad note, and the succession continues with a good one. In general (see the section on ornamentation for exceptional fingerings), the good and bad notes are assigned to good and bad fingers; in both hands the bad fingers are 1, 3, and 5, the good, 2 and 4. A good finger may be repeated on two successive good notes. Diruta's scale-fingerings bear out his observations that 2, 3, and 4 do the work in *passaggi* (*note negre,* not to be confused with *tasti negri* or black keys), and that 3 is pivotal.[17] Diruta admits that "many worthy men" employ another fingering for scales in the left hand—2, 1 ascending, 3, 4 descending—but contends that this has the disadvantages of landing the thumb on a black key when the signature has a B-flat and of placing undue stress on the weak fourth finger of the left hand.[18] Banchieri contents himself with fingerings for right- and left-hand scales that seem to follow more general practice (confirmed by Lorenzo Penna in *Li primi albori musicali* of 1672 and Bartolomeo BisMantova, *Compendio musicale,* 1677) in treating 3 as the principal good finger in both hands (Ex. 15.13).[19]

A *salto cattivo* is a leap after a good note, a *salto buono* a leap after a bad one. The fingerings given by Banchieri and Diruta for intervals show that 1 and 5 were used where appropriate (Ex. 15.14).[20] The principal distinction between these systems and modern fingering is of course the

EXAMPLE 15.13 Seventeenth-century Italian scale fingerings
a. Right hand: Diruta, fol. 6; Banchieri (1605), p. [42]

b. Left hand: Diruta, fol. 6v; Banchieri, p. [42]

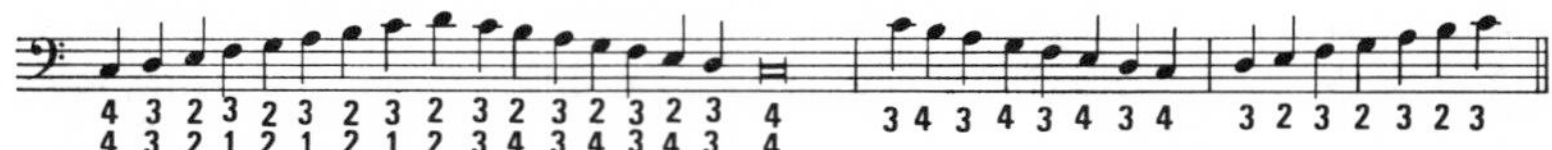

EXAMPLE 15.14 Interval fingerings: Banchieri, p. [42]

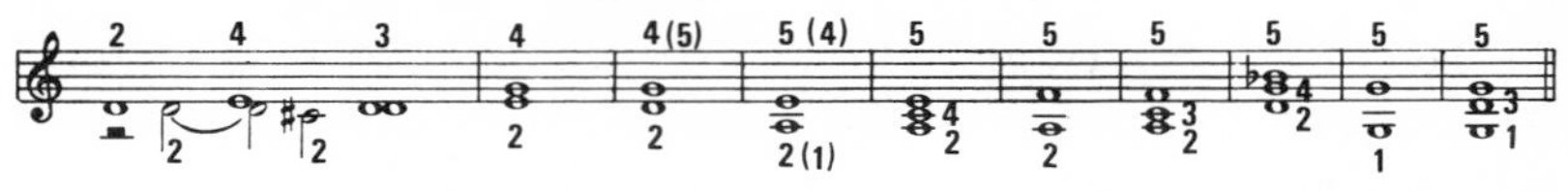

practice of passing a long finger over a short one (or even the reverse, as in Diruta's left-hand scale), as opposed to the modern system of passing the thumb under. Since the publication in 1915 of Arnold Dolmetsch's *The Interpretation of the Music of the XVIIth and XVIIIth Centuries* the study of early fingerings has tended to emphasize the long-over-short pattern and to draw from it a doctrine of pervasive long-short, two-note slurs. This overlooks the distinction between abstract and expressive fingerings (the treatises provide only the former) and is contradicted by the very sources of these fingerings. As early as 1565 Thomás de Sancta Maria provided a variety of highly sophisticated fingerings and possible unequal realizations of equal notes: not only long-short, but short-long, and short-short-short-long. He stated, however, that in touching the keys of the clavichord "the finger which touches the first is always lifted before the one that immediately follows it is touched."[21] Diruta himself noted that in playing diminutions "the next key is not struck until the finger is removed from the first."[22]

Early fingerings do not therefore demand slurs corresponding to successive pairs of fingers. A skilled keyboard player with experience in early fingerings can learn to play as rapidly, as brilliantly, and as evenly with them as with present-day fingerings, and presumably the great virtuosi of the seventeenth century were no less capable. Evenness and fineness of execution were no less prized then than now, and the mechanical grouping of scale-figures in pairs would have seemed as insensitive as does the undifferentiated clatter of modern fingerings. The investigation of historical performance practice is worse than useless if it is employed not to enlarge technical capability and musical sensitivity but to confirm technical failings by canonizing them as "authentic." Perhaps the last word should be left to Girolamo's contemporary, Michael Praetorius: "Some persons get special notions about such things, and wish to despise Organists who are not accustomed to this or that fingering. But this, it seems to me, is not worth discussing. Let one run up or down [the keyboard] with the first, middle, or last finger, and even with his nose if it helps, for as long as what he plays sounds fine and pure, and is correct and pleasant to the ear, it is not very important how one accomplishes it."[23]

The real value of earlier fingerings lies in another direction. Since they are less capable of unlimited extension—or at least less concerned with it—they force the performer to consider smaller units of meaning and their relation one to another. The study of seventeenth-century fingerings is thus perhaps the simplest (but by no means the only) way to bring the keyboard player up against the question of articulation, which his instrument poses only indirectly. The instrumental and vocal tutors of the sixteenth and seventeenth centuries demonstrate the central importance of articulation by their extended considerations of breathing, tonguing, fingering, and bowing. Serious organists and harpsichordists may profit by their example to move beyond the nineteenth-century concept of "touch" as a blanket articulation—legato, staccato, half-staccato—applied to a given passage like paint from a roller. Not only are the spaces between the notes in a sense as important as the notes themselves, but the variety and richness in the articulation of those spaces possible on historical instruments and the best modern reproductions are still incompletely explored.

One external key to the articulation of Frescobaldi's two books of toccatas has been proposed, the notation of the original engraved editions.[24] That is, the beaming of notes in the original would indicate groupings conceived and to be executed as a unit, and division of notes that might be beamed would show that they are to be separated. The engraving of the two books is certainly of a precision capable of such distinctions, extending even to precise alignment in the two-against-three passages of *Toccate* II/9. But the proposal raises a number of questions. First, if the beaming was intended as a guide to articulation, why does Frescobaldi not point this out, as Grassi called attention to the care he had taken in aligning the voices in the *Canzoni* score. Second, the idea was suggested by a similar practice in late eighteenth- and nineteenth-century

German music printing; but St. Lambert, a source nearer Frescobaldi in time if not in place, specifically denied such an interpretation of printed texts.[25] Finally, there are passages in which such a reading seems contrary to musical logic (Ex. 15.15). In any case, this notational convention—if it existed—is valid as an indication of articulation only at the primary level of groupings; it cannot indicate relations within a unit or between larger units, for which it is necessary to consider the nature of articulation.

Any musical composition is a constantly shifting web of relationships—formal, tonal, melodic, harmonic, motivic—and articulation, the movement from one note to the next in a specific context, is a response to all of these factors. Keyed instruments, especially the harpsichord, have always evoked experiences whose physical reality is beyond the capacities of performer and instrument: the human voice, other instruments, the dance. Keyboard articulation has as its source vocal inflection both in its delineation of melody and in the wide spectrum of vowel and consonant color and definition, enriched by the analogues of breathing and bowing in instrumental music. Beyond this, the player must also bring to bear, in dealing with Frescobaldi, an awareness of the elements that formed his keyboard style: the contrapuntal tradition of the late Renaissance, the resources of affective declamation, and the continuo player's sense of underlying harmonic structure and inflection.

In some cases, as in Frescobaldi's variation-sets, a clear and repeated harmonic structure is the given of the work, which becomes an interplay between a constantly varied figural surface and a clearly articulated harmonic armature. In other instances a work may seem to evolve so organically that its structural coherence is apparent only in retrospect. Yet beneath the surface of even the most arbitrary succession of musical events in Frescobaldi there is a logic that serves to guide the articulation of notes within the musical structure. Especially in the preceding analysis of the toccatas we have seen the role played by significant detail, the raw material of articulation, in such evolutions, where a pebble dislodged at the beginning of a work precipitates an avalanche further on. Let us take as a case in point the opening of the ubiquitous ninth toccata from Book II (see Ex.

EXAMPLE 15.15 "Ancidetemi pur," measures 81–82

12.7). Although virtually every rhythmic and harmonic destination in the excerpt is reached by the same cadential figure, in each context it acquires a different meaning. The soprano D in measure 1 is the first departure from the F triad; the alto A in the same measure is an indecisive confirmation of the triad; and the jagged descending bass entrance in measures 1–2 sets the whole harmonic fabric in motion. The high F at the end of the third measure juxtaposed with the low F in the bass outlines the range that dominates the remainder of the toccata.

The communication of these musical facts in performance is dependent on the articulation of the notes—their preparation and spacing, guided by vocal and harmonic feeling in terms of their contexts. Clearly the E-flat in measure 5, the pivot away from F major, demands a preparation different form the assertive F-major triad that precedes it, just as the comparative rhythmic regularity of measure 7 and its upbeat requires an articulation that outlines the basic interval of each figure. Measures 20–24 make these points even more clearly (see Ex. 12.8, 12.9). Measure 20 and mm. 21–22 are related in their presentation of rising figures against a pedal-point and in their rhythmic sequences, but every unit of each passage and both as a whole are differentiated by varying degrees of melodic and harmonic stability. No musical repetition can ever be exact; even if the context remains unchanged, every repeat is either an intensification or a relaxation of the original. Thus the appoggiatura ostinato in measure 20 must be articulated differently in each new harmonic context.

Measure 23 epitomizes one of the most difficult tasks in performing these works: the perception and communication of simultaneous rhythmic motion on levels ranging from that of the fundamental harmonic movement to that of the most intimate details of its superficial ornamentation. Functionally, the measure is merely a prolongation of the dominant pedal at the end of measure 22, but it moves harmonically at the levels of the whole note, quarter, and eighth, melodically at the level of the sixteenth note, and rhythmically at all of these in addition to the unmeasured pedal-point trill. Further, such passages must be played in relation to notes that are decaying, have ceased to sound, or may not have been stated explicitly at all (see the implied pedal-point on A in measure 23).

The phenomenon of decay is particularly characteristic of Italian harpsichords and both demands and facilitates a wide vocabulary of arpeggiations. In the arpeggiated openings of Frescobaldi's toccatas the varied speed and patterns of the arpeggios can reveal the relations of harmonic intensity between the chords or *botte ferme,* as in Louis Couperin's prelude in imitation of the first toccata of Froberger, with its rich arpeggiation, interpolated passing-tones and ornaments (Ex. 15.16). Seventeenth-century Italian performers made a habit of dwelling on the expressive dissonance of suspensions.[26] Frescobaldi recommended arpeggiating "suspensions, or dissonances, as also in the middle of the work they will be struck together, so as not to leave the Instrument empty, which striking will be repeated at the pleasure of the player" (1616). It is appropriate "in certain dissonances to stop, arpeggiating them, so that the following section comes out more spirited" (1624).

The injunction "not to leave the Instrument empty," which was repeated by Frescobaldi's successors,[27] has wider applications than arpeggiation or repetition of chords. Otherwise well-intentioned performances of Girolamo's works are often marred by miscalculations of timing and ugly breaks in the line, the result of insensitivity to the decay of harpsichord sound. The harpsichord, in general, has a curious power of projection, of shouting on the housetops what is whispered in the ear. Unfortunately, what it projects most clearly is the performer's failure to conceive and prepare a passage adequately. One way around the emptiness of cadences on an Italian harpsichord is the shaping of what precedes the cadence so that, even if it is a full chord after an open texture, its arrival is perceived as a point of repose. As a physical analogy, one might suggest

EXAMPLE 15.16 a. J. J. Froberger, Toccata I, measures 1–3

b. Louis Couperin, Prelude à l'imitation de Mr. de Froberger

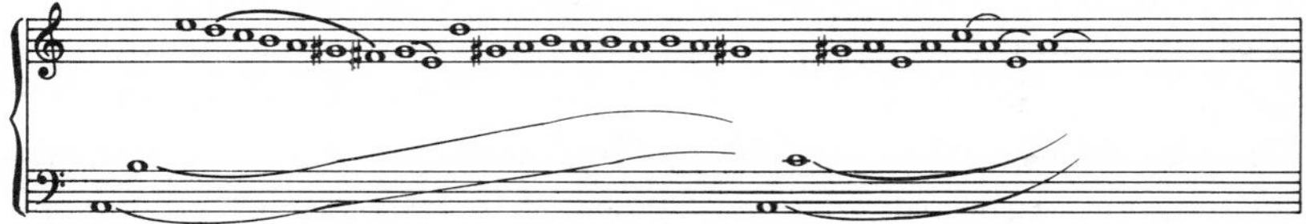

a dance phrase ended on the toes, with the head erect, as opposed to a round-shouldered, flat-heeled thump (accompanied by an almost audible sigh of relief).

Ornaments and Ornamentation

The continuing controversies about the minutiae of ornamentation have tended to obscure its essential character in the sixteenth and seventeenth centuries. It was not a cerebral attempt to realize a historical imperative but a natural expression of technical skill and musical imagination grounded in the conviction that any precious object, whether a piece of music, a jewel, or an ancient building, could be rendered more beautiful by embellishment. In practice, ornamentation was neither a totally free improvisation nor the laborious recombination of textbook formulas, but rather an individual response, conditioned by training and experience, to certain conventional stimuli.

The literature on the practice of ornamentation relevant to Frescobaldi's keyboard music covers over a century, from Thomás de Sancta Maria's *Arte de tañer fantasia* of 1565 to Bartolomeo BisMantova's *Compendio musicale* of 1677, and embraces encyclopedic works, diminution treatises, instrumental tutors, and collections of music. The performing media encompass voice, keyboard, and wind and string instruments.[28] The size of this body of information should not blind us to the fact that, in the last analysis, it is all a commentary on existing, audible musical practice, irretrievably lost to us. If one imagines trying to reconstruct the style of Art Tatum from reviews, a jazz textbook, a collection of finger exercises, and the sheet music for "Sweet Georgia Brown," that will give a fair idea of the difficulties involved in recreating an Arcadelt madrigal as embellished by a virtuoso around 1600.

Late Renaissance embellishment moved in a more or less continuous spectrum from simple conventionalized ornaments through more elaborate and extended decoration to diminutions of a preexisting model, such as the *quinta voz* settings of Diego Ortiz, which were in effect new works. Such embellishments were to be added in performance, either worked out beforehand (especially in ensemble music) or improvised. Such improvisations were not completely free, however, since the literature provided the musician with literally hundreds of formulas for each musical situation, which were employed as modules, and models for their combination in more extended diminution. The prevalence of intabulations, performed at the tempos of their undecorated models, shows that late Renaissance embellishment was above all light, brilliant, and decorative in intention.

The primary innovators of the early seventeenth century, the composers of the Florentine Camerata, did not so much invent new forms of embellishment as change the spirit in which it was employed. Many of their ornaments were in fact taken over from Renaissance practice, but they were now intended for expression as well as for decoration, to enhance the affective, rhetorical style of Florentine monody. Their employment at the pleasure of the performer was also considerably curtailed.

Keyboard music, true to its homogeneous background, both cultivated its own repertory of ornaments and drew upon the resources of vocal and instrumental embellishments. The influence of Florentine expressive ornamentation can be traced in such works as the second part of Diruta's *Transilvano,* and in Frescobaldi's reference to "modern madrigals" (which doubtless included the solo settings Caccini published with that designation) as models for the performance of his toccatas.

The Repertory of Ornaments

Italian practice distinguished two types of ornament, the smaller localized decoration (*effetto, accento*) and the extended virtuoso *passaggio* or *gorgia,* applied in varying degrees to both vocal and instrumental music. *Effetti* could be written out, indicated by a conventional sign, or added freely by the performer; *passaggi,* except at cadences, were provided most often by the composer.

For convenience, the general repertory of late sixteenth- and seventeenth-century ornaments can be organized by a combination of shape and function into melodic, repercussive, and compound (usually cadential) ornaments. The simplest melodic ornaments decorated single intervals, both ascending and descending, in a wide variety of rhythmic patterns that included both on-beat and pre-beat forms (Ex. 15.17). These could also be applied on a wider scale (Ex. 15.18). Repercussive orna-

EXAMPLE 15.17 a. Zacconi (1592), fol. 56: ornament and pre-beat interpretation

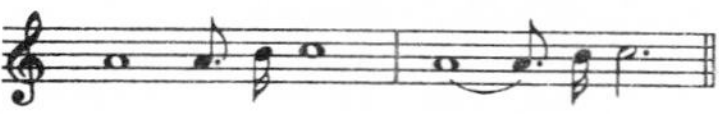

b. Bovicelli (1594), pp. 17–19: on-beat and pre-beat ornaments

c. Banchieri, *Cartella* (1601), p. 50: accenti

d. Rognoni (1620), fol. 1: "beginning under the note"

e. Rognoni, accenti

EXAMPLE 15.18 Rogniono (1592), interval-decorations

EXAMPLE 15.19 a. Cavalieri (1600): monachina; trillo; zimbelo

b. Caccini (1602): trillo; ribattuta di gola

c. Praetorius, *Syntagma* III (1619), p. 237: trillo

d. Rognoni (1620), fol. l: tremolo in due modi; gruppo semplice; gruppo doppio; tremolo alle note di semibreve; trillo sopra la minima; trillo sopra la semibreve primo modo; secondo modo

e. J. H. Kapsberger (1640), trillo

EXAMPLE 15.20 Bovicelli (1594), p. 13: accenti sopra le minime (^ = tremolo formato); accenti sopra alle semiminime (^ = tremolo non formato)

EXAMPLE 15.21 a. Dalla Casa (1584), p. 5: tremolo groppizato de semibreve; p. 6: tremolo groppizato de minima

b. Dalla Casa: groppo battuto de semibreve; groppo battuto de minima

c. Zacconi (1592), fol 61v: cadenza

d. Conforti, p. 25: groppo di sopra; mezzo groppo; trillo

e. Conforti, mezzo [trillo]; groppo di sotto; mezzo [groppo di sotto]

ments, either alone or combined with turns, are found in both vocal and instrumental sources, either as repeated notes or as oscillations between the main note and upper or—more rarely—lower auxiliary (Ex. 15.19). Repercussive ornaments were also employed to enliven more extensive embellishments (Ex. 15.20). It is not always possible to distinguish between purely repercussive and repercussive-cadential figures, since cadences were more complex in construction, drew upon a variety of patterns, and often tended toward the more extended *passaggio* (Ex. 15.21).

f. Conforti, groppo; mezzo [groppo]; [ ]
g. Conforti, groppo; trillo; mezzo [trillo]
h. Bovicelli, p. 12: groppetti
i. Cavalieri, groppolo
j. Virgiliano (ca. 1600), p. [34]: cadences
k. Banchieri (1601), p. 50: fioretti
l. Banchieri, bass cadences
m. Caccini, gruppo; cascata doppia

n. Praetorius, pp. 238–239: trilli, accenti, gruppi

o. Rognoni (1620), fol. 1: gruppo semplice; gruppo doppio

EXAMPLE 15.22 Fantini (1638), p. 11: accelerating cadence

Some notational evidence suggests that these cadential ornaments were not taken in strict tempo but accelerated gradually (Ex. 15.22).

These same general types can be distinguished in the ornaments described in keyboard treatises. Stepwise melodic embellishments were employed both before and on the beat to decorate single notes or intervals (Ex. 15.23). From the mid-sixteenth century, keyboard repercussive ornaments had employed the lower as well as the upper auxiliary (Ex. 15.24), although the upper was regarded as preferable. The main-note trill seems

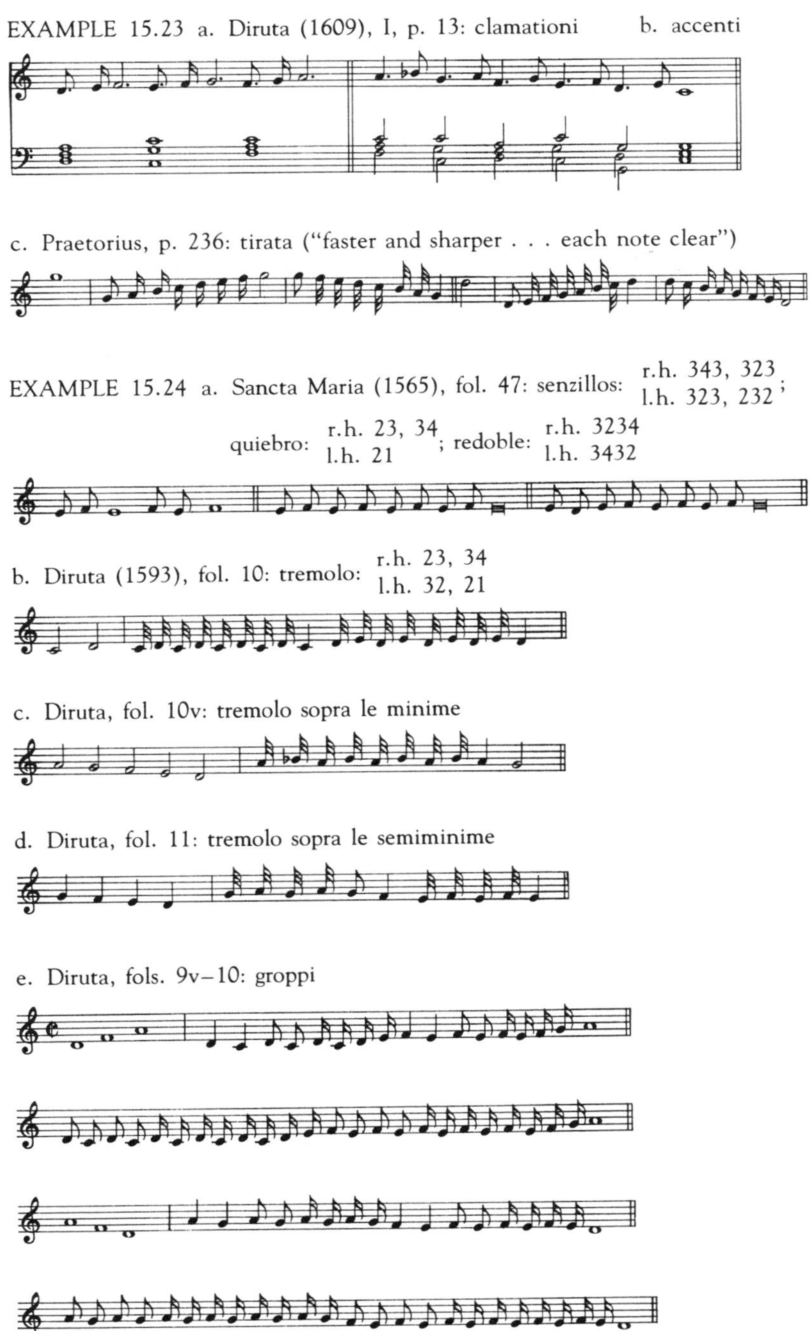

EXAMPLE 15.23 a. Diruta (1609), I, p. 13: clamationi b. accenti

c. Praetorius, p. 236: tirata ("faster and sharper . . . each note clear")

EXAMPLE 15.24 a. Sancta Maria (1565), fol. 47: senzillos: r.h. 343, 323; l.h. 323, 232; quiebro: r.h. 23, 34; l.h. 21; redoble: r.h. 3234; l.h. 3432

b. Diruta (1593), fol. 10: tremolo: r.h. 23, 34; l.h. 32, 21

c. Diruta, fol. 10v: tremolo sopra le minime

d. Diruta, fol. 11: tremolo sopra le semiminime

e. Diruta, fols. 9v–10: groppi

f. Diruta, fol. 11: tremoletti

g. Praetorius, p. 235: tremulus ascendens; tremulus descendens

h. Praetorius, p. 236: groppi ("must be played sharper than the tremoli")

i. Praetorius, p. 235: tremoletti

EXAMPLE 15.25 Mayone (1609), trills

to have taken on some of the expressive rhythmic character of Florentine vocal ornamentation (Ex. 15.25). As in general practice, keyboard compound-cadential ornaments were more extended in length and included trill-plus-turn patterns beginning both on the main note and on the upper auxiliary (Ex. 15.26). Some were performed in strict rhythm, others were accelerated gradually (Ex. 15.27). Although the repeated-note trill does not seem to have been a staple of keyboard embellishment, it appears in at least one late source as part of a cadential ornament (Ex. 15.28).

EXAMPLE 15.26 a. Diruta (1593), fols. 9v–10: groppi in accadentia: r.h. 43 l.h. 23, 12

b. Macque, Capriccio sopra re fa mi sol, measure 60

c. Diruta (1609), I, p. 13: groppi sopra l'accadenze

EXAMPLE 15.27 Mayone (1609), Canzona francese terza, measures 87–88

EXAMPLE 15.28 a. Penna (1672), p. 152: prattica con la sinistra

b. Penna, prattica con la destra

EXAMPLE 15.29 Trabaci (1615), p. 126: trillo doppio

Ornamental Signs

The one conventional sign that appears in Frescobaldi's printed keyboard works is the letter "t." As an indication of an unspecified ornament it had been employed in Italian keyboard music as early as 1576, in the *Intavolatura de cimbalo* of Antonio Valente. Diruta interpreted "t" as *tremolo,* Cavalieri as *trillo.* For both it denoted a trill beginning on the main note, alternating with the upper auxiliary, and occupying half the value of the principal note (assuming that a tie is to be added to Cavalieri's example); Diruta and Praetorius, however, confirm that keyboard players also interpreted the sign as a mordent or lower-note trill. Trabaci (1603) employed "T." to mean *trillo,* but from the context it appears that he intended a cadential trill with some kind of turn, alternating with the upper auxiliary and beginning on either the main or upper note (Neapolitan practice seems to have been flexible on this point), the *groppo/groppolo* of Diruta and Cavalieri. Durante (1608) indicated by "t" a trill that could be added to a written-out trill or *groppetto.* In his collection of 1615 Trabaci introduced the sign "T+" for a cadential trill (*trillo doppio*) beginning on the lower third (Ex. 15.29).

Diminution treatises and written-out examples show cadential trills beginning on the upper note, but Diruta's preference for interpreting "t" as a main-note trill rather than a mordent is confirmed in the teaching of Bottazzi (1614), Penna (1672), who also gives trills beginning on the upper note, and BisMantova (1677). Frescobaldi's employment of the "t" sign is consistent with this tradition. When he wrote out the ornament—which he called *trillo*—he interpreted it as Diruta's *tremolo,* a trill beginning on the principal note and alternating with the upper auxiliary (Ex. 15.30). Frescobaldi's cadential *groppi,* the most frequent written-out ornament in his keyboard works, begin on the lower note except for an occasional suspension. His employment of the *ribattuta di gola* or *zimbelo* shows the influence of vocal ornamentation.

The Performance of Ornaments

The history of embellishment practice in seventeenth-century Italy indicates that the kind and degree of improvised ornament varied with time, place, medium, and genre, and that Roman keyboard music of Frescobaldi's time was inherently conservative in this respect, unlike Roman sacred vocal music. In no genre does the addition of improvised *passaggi* seem to have been contemplated, except perhaps at otherwise undecorated cadences. On the evidence of Frescobaldi's own embellished corrente in *Toccate* II and a manuscript variation of one of his balletti, dances were the keyboard genre most appropriate for decoration. The ornamentation of contrapuntal genres, on the other hand, was restricted. Zacconi stipulated that embellishments were to be omitted entirely when singing "any sort of imitations, or fantasie."[29] Although Diruta observed that the *tremolo* was to be employed "at the beginning of a Ricercare, or

EXAMPLE 15.30 a. Cento partite, measure 39

b. measures 252–253

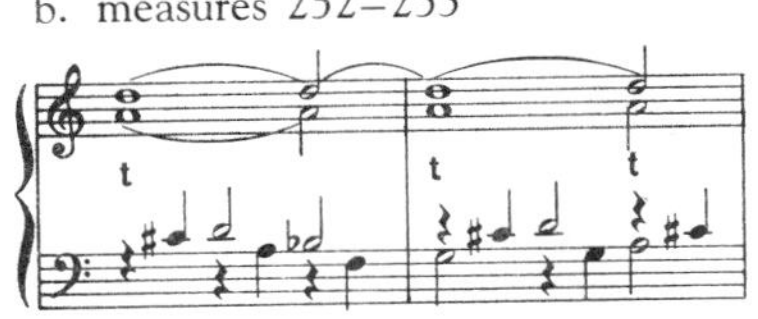

EXAMPLE 15.31 *Toccate* II/11, measures 1–2

Canzone, or any other composition and again when one hand plays several parts and the other only one," he later stated that in canzonas with small note-values and strict imitations only *tremoli* and *groppi* could be added.[30] For Bottazzi, trills were to be played "at the beginning of any sonata, and when it will seem expedient to the Organist, but the aforesaid trill must be done with grace, so that the harmony is lively, and gay."[31]

Frescobaldi's incorporation of embellishments into his keyboard style is evident in his expressive use of ornamental figures in the Florentine tradition, his extravagant pedal-point trills, and in passages such as the opening trills of *Toccate* II/11, which tempt the player to sharpen their harmonic bite by interpreting them as lower-note ornaments (Ex. 15.31; this excerpt also suggests the addition of ornaments by analogy).

The manuscript Vatican Mus. 559 contains two pieces that demonstrate how Frescobaldi's music was embellished by a contemporary and colleague, Giovanni Battista Ferrini, who played second harpsichord with Girolamo at the Oratorio del Crocifisso. The original version of the balletto from the *Aggiunta* to *Toccate* I is decorated with a number of trills, usually underlining a rhythmic stress, and a modest cadential ornament. The written-out variation confines its embellishment to the soprano part except where it dialogues with the bass and employs filled intervals, afterbeats, and the generally more continuous rhythmic surface of Frescobaldi's own varied corrente (Ex. 15.32).

This chapter is in no sense a blueprint for the interpretation of Frescobaldi's keyboard music; rather, it is a collection of information and observations that may enable a performer to encounter Girolamo's work sufficiently prepared to employ his own musical resources efficiently and imaginatively. After the player has tried to comprehend both physically and intellectually the musical organism confronting him, his final task—beyond any verbal or musical analysis—is to embody this understanding in a performance where, if he is fortunate, the heavenly lightning will kindle the tinder he has patiently assembled, and we will experience in all their pristine freshness and delight Frescobaldi's "illogic sorceries of logic floral fire."

EXAMPLE 15.32 Frescobaldi, Balletto; G. B. Ferrini Balletto 2.o (Rome, Biblioteca Apostolica Vaticana, Vat. mus. 569, fols. 18–19v)

Appendix I

Other Keyboard Works Attributed to Frescobaldi

A. THE *CANZONI* OF 1645

In 1645 Alessandro Vincenti, Girolamo's Venetian printer, issued a volume of eleven *canzoni alla francese* as "libro quarto," the fourth volume of Frescobaldi's works to come from his presses (if the 1626 *Capricci* and its 1642 reprint are considered a single opus). In a dedicatory letter dated 15 December 1644 Vincenti described the canzonas as "jewels already issued forth from the quarries of the lively talent of the most celebrated Frescobaldi, and reaching me now only after his death." Even if Vincenti received them directly from Frescobaldi's heirs, the canzonas hardly exhausted the mass of unprinted material still in Domenico Frescobaldi's hands in the 1660s. Indeed, the authenticity of the entire collection has been questioned, and certainly the titles attached to the canzonas, which refer to Vincenti himself (Canzona VIII, "detta la Vincenti"), composers in his catalogue, and other Venetian figures, have no connection with Girolamo, who never followed the northern Italian practice of naming canzonas.[1] On the other hand, it is unlikely that an important publisher like Vincenti would issue a fraudulent collection under the name of one of his principal composers so soon after the putative author's death—all the more so if there were a corpus of authentic works prepared for publication. Nor does the assumption of sharp practice square with what is known of Vincenti's character as a publisher. In 1650 he himself edited a posthumous collection by an even more famous composer, Claudio Monteverdi. Vincenti's attributions of these items have never been questioned, and the work he included that was not by Monteverdi, a Cavalli Magnificat, was labeled as such.

Nothing in the 1645 *Canzoni* absolutely precludes its ascription to Frescobaldi, and the presentation of the canzonas in keyboard *partitura* perhaps argues for it. The repertory of triple mensurations employed is consistent with Girolamo's usage (**C** 3/2 = 3/2; 3 = 6/2; 3 = 3/2, and 6/4; black 3 = 6/4; 6/4 = **C**, not 4/6)(although **O**3 and **ₑ** 3/2 do not occur). The absence of *tempus perfectum* and the cancellation of 6/4 by **C** rather than 4/6 follows Girolamo's practice in the keyboard publications after *Toccate* II.

The 1645 canzonas display a number of features in common. All eleven are variation-canzonas and have strongly profiled subjects—a descending fifth in numbers I, VII, VIII; an ascending fourth in II, IV, V, IX, and XI; a descending fourth in X; and an ascending third in III and VI. Their range in variety and complexity of texture is considerable. Canzona III, for example, has no internal divisions, treats its subject unaltered throughout, and employs no passage-work or regular figuration smaller than the eighth-note. Canzona X has a concluding toccata-like *passaggio,* while Canzonas V, VII, and XI balance their lack of *passaggi* by contrasting sections in triple meter. The remaining canzonas—I, II, IV, VI, VIII, and IX—employ both sections in triple meter and florid cadential figuration.

The closest parallel to Vincenti's canzonas is the group of six canzonas published in *Toccate* II. The 1615 canzonas already display the interest in variation procedures characteristic of Frescobaldi's later handling of the form, but they still employ *tempus perfectum* indications and their contrapuntal texture is rather stiff, owing to the general absence of free figural *passaggi.* All five canzonas of the 1635 *Fiori musicali* are variation-canzonas but are more epigrammatic in their development of material and more flexible in their rhythmic patterns, so that *passaggi* are largely unnecessary. Their repertory of triple signs also differs from that of other collections in several instances.

Of the six 1627 canzonas, the last two are entirely in triple meters and thus inappropriate for purposes of comparison. Both the 1627 and 1645 canzonas frequently employ passages in free figuration (indeed, the fourth canzona of *Toccate* II seems almost like a toccata in its figural texture). Except for the triple-meter canzonas of *Toccate* II, neither set uses *tempus perfectum.* With the exception of the chromatic subject in the third canzona from the *Toccate,* both collections show a preference for strongly intervallic subjects. The general proportions of the overall works and of their component sections are commensurate in the 1627 and 1645 canzonas. Finally, the four canzonas of the *Toccate,* like the contents of the 1645 sets, are variation-canzonas, although the later publication treats the device in a more straightforward and perhaps less imaginative fashion.

There are, however, some anomalies in the 1645 *Canzoni*. Although the tonalities—transposed Dorian, F, A, G—are unexceptionable, one of the canzonas on F is written without B-flat, a situation that does not occur in the 1627 book except in the explicitly modal context of the Magnificat Primi Toni. Exceptionally, the fourth of the 1645 canzonas, which is nearly twenty measures longer than any of the 1627 works, is written on F but cadences finally on C. The third canzona is in fact a monothematic ricercar with no ornamental figuration, no full internal cadences, and a considerable degree of chromatic inflection. Perhaps owing to their score format, the 1645 canzonas do not lie as easily under the hand as the 1627 works and present instances of awkward voice-crossings and difficult extensions. Only one manuscript concordance with this collection is given by Silbiger (Verona MCXXIX, dated 1703), unlike the numerous manuscript concordances with all of Frescobaldi's keyboard prints after the *Fantasie.*

There thus seems nothing in the 1645 *Canzoni* to which one can point as conclusive evidence of misattribution, and there are many characteristically Frescobaldian points. Certainly there is little of the stylistic incompatibility with Girolamo's authentic works that leaps to the ear and eye from most of the works attributed to him in manuscript. This, coupled with the evidence of Vincenti, which certainly cannot be ignored, suggests a cautious confirmation of the authenticity of the 1645 *Canzoni,* albeit with editorial interference in the addition of titles and perhaps other details. They may be best considered Apocrypha in the Frescobaldian canon, to be read for instruction but not applied "to establish any doctrine."

B. MANUSCRIPT WORKS

Keyboard works are attributed to Frescobaldi in a wide variety of manuscript sources of both Italian and foreign provenance, and these attributions have generally been accepted at face value. Since Alexander Silbiger's notable study of Italian manuscript sources of seventeenth-century keyboard music, however, such a position is no longer tenable. Silbiger makes a fundamental distinction in pointing out from a thorough survey of both printed and manuscript sources that the manuscript tradition is not a continuation of the printed materials but a complement to them. The printed collections—surprisingly few of which appear to have been lost—in general present highly finished productions by professional composers for accomplished performers, but the manuscript volumes are usually didactic in purpose and often amateurish both in the general musical level of their contents and in their technical requirements.

Frescobaldi dominated Italian keyboard composition and performance during his lifetime, and his influence continued well after his death. His name was thus a focus for the attribution of anonymous works or works by less celebrated authors. Subjecting these attributions to stringent criteria for credibility of transmission and stylistic congruity, Silbiger comes to the conclusion that few of the manuscript works are acceptable on historical grounds, and of those works that might conceivably be authentic a number show significant stylistic divergences from Girolamo's known productions. Of the manuscript repertory as a whole, he concludes that "there is not a single work in it whose association with the composer can be established beyond a reasonable doubt."[2]

Nonetheless, in the manuscript corpus described by Grassi and still in the possession of Domenico Frescobaldi in the 1660s we have a repertory with a past but no ascertained future, while the present manuscripts generally lack a documented provenance; the temptation to relate the two is obvious. Grassi's remarks, however, imply a body of work substantially prepared for printing, which would fit few of the doubtful keyboard works except the 1645 canzonas and the nine toccatas of the Foà manuscript. On the other hand, the manuscript works cannot be rejected solely on the grounds of quality, as opposed to demonstrable stylistic inconsistency. The three additional pieces that Grassi added to his edition of the *Canzoni* of 1628 come from Girolamo's immediate circle, and the two capriccios of the 1637 *Aggiunta* have an unimpeachable pedigree, but none of them rises above the mediocre. The manuscript collection was clearly a cherished possession of Domenico Frescobaldi, although it does not appear in his hastily drawn-up will of 1688. Perhaps the attic of some Roman palazzo still guards a repertory of unknown Frescobaldi works in Girolamo's own hand.[3]

The manuscripts containing works attributed to Frescobaldi differ widely in date, contents, and reliability. (For the individual manuscripts and their contents, see the Catalogue I.B, which summarizes the findings of Silbiger and other scholars.) Since that is the case, it is possible only to consider a few of the most important sources here. Perhaps the earliest of these is the manuscript Ravenna, Classense 545, which Silbiger dates in the late 1620s or 1630s. Contrary to his assertion, however, there is a link between Frescobaldi and Ravenna, in the person of Girolamo's patron Cardinal Pietro Aldobrandini, who was Archbishop of the city. The works attributed to Frescobaldi in this manuscript—two capriccios (in fact, variation-canzonas) and a verso—display a number of features, enumerated by Silbiger,[4] that belie their ascription to Girolamo.

A manuscript now in the Bodmer collection in Geneva has twice been reproduced as an autograph of Frescobaldi—along with Haberl's lost manuscript of the *In Te Domine Speravi,* the only source for which that distinction has been claimed. This contains *Toccate* II minus the liturgical works, two toccatas from *Toccate* I, and four additional works designated as toccatas, of which the last two are canzonas (and the second canzona is designated "Piua"). Darbellay's careful examination of the manuscript shows that it was in fact copied ca. 1670 from printed sources of the authentic works, and that the attribution of the additional works to Frescobaldi is unreliable.[5]

The most important collection of manuscripts containing works ascribed to Frescobaldi forms part of the Chigi collection in the Biblioteca Apostolica Vaticana. Chigi Q.IV.24, 25, and 27 are keyboard manuscripts in Italian format, while Chigi Q.IV.205–206 are miscellaneous collections. The keyboard volumes appear to have been compiled ca. 1630–1650 and apparently originated in the Chigi circle. Silbiger suggests that they may have been the property of Virginia Chigi-Borghese, who studied with Alessandro Costantini, Frescobaldi's predecessor and successor at St. Peter's.[6] Chigi Q.IV.24 assigns to "Fr" or "G . . ." a canzona, a *fuga* (a term never employed in Frescobaldi's authentic works), and a toccata. The flyleaf of Chigi Q.IV.25 contains an inscription in a different hand, but apparently roughly contemporary with the manuscript, that names Frescobaldi as the composer of the entire volume. The contents comprise three partitas on the Aria di Fiorenza; two pedal toccatas, each followed by a contrapuntal work (canzona or capriccio); two capriccios, one a toccata followed by a kind of variation-canzona and the other on the cuckoo call; two toccatas, one for organ without pedal; a canzona and two ricercars, one of them chromatic; and a set of three toccatas numbered separately. In addition to dances copied from *Toccate* II, Chigi Q.IV.27 contains a toccata that quotes two passages from *Toccate* I/5 and a corrente, both attributed to Frescobaldi, and sets of anonymous variations on bass patterns, of which those on a descending tetrachord are often related to passages in the *Cento partite.*[7] In a closely reasoned analysis of the genesis of the *Cento partite* Darbellay has argued that the parallels between Chigi Q.IV.27 and the *Partite* suggest a dating of 1627–1637 for the manuscript (see Chapter 14, n.9). Chigi Q.IV.205–206 includes *Toccate* II/1, 5, 6, and a portion of 9; *Pasagalli* which contain material from the *Cento partite;* and a toccata, Ruggiero, and four hymns otherwise unknown.

Several factors seem to militate against the blanket attribution of the most important of these volumes, Chigi Q.IV.25, to Frescobaldi. The variations on the Aria di Firenze with which it opens present a tune that was widely associated with Frescobaldi, but never in a source of unimpeachable authority. The pairing in this manuscript of a toccata with a contrapuntal work—a procedure that occurs only three times in Girolamo's authentic works—and *a fortiori* the confusion of the two styles in the capriccio on fol. 19 contradict the evidence of the printed collections. Much of the writing in the opening toccatas of the manuscripts proceeds in parallel sixths and tenths rather than in the dense rhythmic polyphony of the authentic pedal toccatas. The harmonic schemes of these toccatas, as indicated by their pedal-points, lack the clear definition of the two pedal works in *Toccate* II. The set of three toccatas is of such higher quality than the remainder of the collection that they have been ascribed to another hand. Unfortunately, this is probably not Frescobaldi's. The signature 6/4 for passages in 12/8, which occurs in the first and third toccatas of the set, is found only in the *Cento partite* in Frescobaldi's authentic work. Twice-transposed Dorian, with a signature of B-flat and recurrent E-, A-, and D-flats, in which the third toccata of the set is written, never occurs in Girolamo's printed corpus, although it is suggested in two variations of the *Cento partite,* whose influence is apparent in many of the Chigi manuscript works.

A comparison between the manuscript and printed capriccios on the cuckoo call highlights the difference between dubious and authentic Frescobaldi. The Chigi capriccio is built in closed *parti* like a variation-set, each ending with a full cadence or at most eliding a V into the I of the following section. The sections are of roughly equivalent lengths, and the harmonic vocabulary submits to the V–I progression underlying the ostinato. In the printed capriccio Girolamo writes sections of widely varying lengths, elides them in a variety of ways (including deceptive cadences under the ostinato), provides a wide range of figuration, and adds free non-ostinato passages.

Two of the four sets of hymn-versets in Chigi Q.IV.205 employ chants also set by Frescobaldi in *Toccate* II: Lucis Creator, the hymn for Sundays, and Exsultet Celum, the hymn for the Apostles. All four settings are of a poverty incompatible with the rich compression of Frescobaldi's own works. Even where these seem to have provided a model, as in the opening verset of the Sunday hymn, the manuscript version is a pale reflection of its original. Not surprisingly, the triple sections that vary the mood of Girolamo's versets are not even attempted here.

Even at their best, the contents of the Chigi manuscripts give the impression of works by composers saturated in the Frescobaldian idiom, who quote it literally, emulate it with far weaker powers of invention, or—as in the Ruggiero variations—exaggerate single elements of Frescobaldi's style to the point of mannerism.

To the same period as the Chigi manuscripts belong the sixteen volumes of keyboard music copied out between 1637 and 1640, now housed in the Biblioteca Nazionale of Turin in the Giordano and Foà collections. Despite the inclusion of a large body of Italian music the collection is transcribed in New German tablature. In addition to selections from Girolamo's published works—some of them grotesquely dismembered to accommodate the compiler's principle of organizing the volumes according to musical genres—the first volume includes nine unpublished toccatas attributed to Frescobaldi and the fourteenth contains three correnti. Stylistically, the Foà toccatas are closer than the Chigi ones to authentic Frescobaldi works, specifically *Toccate* I. With the exception of two short passages in 3 in the eighth Foà toccata and a 12/8 section in the ninth, they are in duple meter throughout, and most of them are continuous without a decisive internal cadence in both hands. Although they display a fair amount of Venetian-style alternation of scale and chord passages between the hands, they also show considerable and constant variety of figuration, and much more genuinely polyrhythmic figural writing than the Chigi toccatas. Dissonant ostinati recall the second book of toccatas. The structure of the pedal toccata, number nine (pedals on D, A, F, C, G, D), resembles the cycle of fifths in the pedals of *Toccate* II/6. The Foà correnti, on the other hand, are aimless and repetitive and completely lack Girolamo's sense of shaping a dance phrase.

The largest number of previously unknown works attributed to Frescobaldi is contained in the manuscript Venice, Biblioteca Nazionale Marciana, Cod. It. IV 1299. The collection is written in what appears to be a nineteenth-century hand and consists of excerpts from the printed works "ridotte ad una moderna e facile lettura" by transcription into piano score and occasional reduction of note-values, among which the compiler has interspersed ten gagliarde, two spagnolette, seventeen correnti, one each of folia, ciaccona, passaggio, and volta, six toccatas, three canzonas, three capriccios (one on the Bergamasca and one on Ruggiero), five balli or balletti, and eight versetti. The dubious provenance of the manuscript renders it useless for consideration in establishing a Frescobaldi canon, and in any case most of the repertory of original items it contains fails to rise above the mediocre level of authentic seventeenth-century aria and ballo collections.

The eight versets on the church modes in the Venice manuscript represent the only occurrence in an Italian manuscript of a genre widespread in German sources. (See Catalogue, I.B.) It would be fascinating to unravel how and why Frescobaldi's name was so persistently attached to these sets of organ-versets in Germany and Austria, but since at present there is no evidence for their authenticity they cannot change significantly our understanding of his work.

Indeed, despite the general fascination of the manuscript materials purporting to contain unpublished works of Girolamo, the final result of the labors of scholars such as Silbiger and Darbellay has been to confirm that Frescobaldi's oeuvre as published under his supervision contains most of what he wished to preserve for posterity. And, after all, he must be allowed some voice in the matter.

Appendix II

Vocal Works

A. SECULAR WORKS

1. The *Madrigali* of 1608

The volume of five-part madrigals that Frescobaldi published with Phalèse of Antwerp in 1608 does not seem to have excited much interest. It was never reprinted, and in the course of time the altus part-book of the collection now in the Bodleian Library at Oxford was lost, while the only surviving complete copy, the property of Mme de Chambure, has only recently become generally available in the Bibliothèque Nationale in Paris.

The collection begins the series of Frescobaldi's carefully considered publications and is the first evidence of his desire to make himself known. Its contents, however, are not avant-garde in medium or expression but represent one of the last offshoots of the Ferrarese madrigal school of the 1590s—the years of Luzzaschi's late works and the productions of Fontanelli and Gesualdo—and their publication just after Luzzaschi's death marks an end of this tradition. Ten of the texts have been identified:[1]

"Amor ti chiam'il mondo": Annibale Pocaterra, *Due dialoghi* (Reggio: Flauio, & Flamminio Bartholi, 1607), pp. 24–25.

"Come perder poss'io": *Delle rime di Cesare Rinaldi Bolognese Parte Terza* (Bologna: V. Benacci, 1590), p. 105.

"Da qual sfera": Pocaterra, *Dialoghi,* p. 37; *Le cento donne di Casale Monferrato. Cantate da Horatio Navazzotti, L'Asciutto, Academico Desioso* (Pavia: G. Bartolini, 1591), p. 56.

"Ecco l'hora" (2a parte): Giovanni Battista Marino, *Della lira del Cavalier Marino* I–III (Venice: Per il Baba, I–II dated 1653), II, madrigali XCIX–CI.

"Giunt'è pur Lidia" (1a parte): Marino.

"Lidia ti lasso" (3a parte): Marino.

"Perche fuggi tra salci": Marino, *Lira* II, madrigale XVIII.

"S'a la gelata mia": Pocaterra, *Dialoghi,* p. 22.

"Se la doglia e'l martire": Marino, *Lira* II, madrigale XCVIII.

"Se lontana voi sete": Horatio Ariosti, in *Il gareggiamento poetico del Confuso Accademico Ordito. Madrigali amorosi gravi, e piacevoli* . . . (Venice: B. Barezzi, [1611]), V, fol. 133v.

"S'io miro in te": Rinaldi, *Rime,* p. 207.

"Tu pur mi fuggi": Pocaterra, *Dialoghi,* p. 25.

It is conceivable that some of the unidentified texts may have been the work of Guido Bentivoglio, to whom some *poesie per musica* are attributed.[2] Frescobaldi's choice of texts reflects the Janus-like character of his first publication. The poems of Rinaldi and Pocaterra, a Ferrarese court poet (d. 1593) whose texts were set by Gesualdo, Fontanelli, and Milleville, suggest Girolamo's Ferrarese training, but his acquaintance with the work of Marino may date from his first years in Rome, where Marino served in the household of Cardinal Pietro Aldobrandini.[3]

The collection contains in all nineteen madrigals, one of them (Marino's "Giunt'è pur Lidia") in three sections. In general, the opening and closing sections are the most clearly organized. The beginning of the third madrigal, "Se la doglia e'l martire," for example, is built by a favorite device in these works, the juxtaposition of contrasting motives derived from the first two phrases of the text. While the texture is punctuated by the anapests of the second phrase, the long line of the structure is maintained by the appearance of the opening phrase in one voice or another. The following sections show careful alternation between homophonic and contrapuntal textures (a characteristic of these works) and the repetition of phrases, originally presented by a few voices and reorchestrated as a *tutti* (another hallmark of the collection). The expressive fifth- and octave-leaps of "dite" show Girolamo's clear, albeit restrained, sensitivity to the declamation of his text. Another Ferrarese trait appears in the cadence on "l'hore," where the texture is lightened by the omission of voices before the conclusion. The last section, beginning at "Mille volte morir," is built in a Monteverdian fashion on two contrasting motives, one, "to die a thousand times," the other, "but in your arms."

Frescobaldi treats the openings and closings of the madrigals, the most clearly defined sections, in a variety of ways. In many cases the ending is stressed by sheer weight, the repetition of the last phrase. On the other hand, Girolamo sometimes takes advantage of a surprise ending in the text to reflect it in the music, as in the concluding "io ardo" of "S'a la gelata mia timida lingua" with its unexpected chromatic inflection, or the swift antithesis at the end of "Vessosissima Filli." The three sections of "Giunt'è pur Lidia" are unified by the quotation of the same interval at the beginning of each part, and the final cadence is emphasized by close stretto writing. In "Se lontana" the opening octave depicting "lontana" (distant) is repeated with musical if not pictorial justification at the end of the madrigal.

Nothing in Frescobaldi's representation of his texts, either in isolated madrigalian images or affective harmonic progressions, approaches the boldness of Gesualdo or even of their common mentor, Luzzaschi. The word "funeste" in "Ahi bella si" is registered only in a few perfunctory *note nere.* The text of "Amor ti chiama il mondo" is built on the paradox that Amor is such in name only, and the line "Tu crud'empio tiranno" prompts Frescobaldi to suspensions and some clashing seconds, the most extreme affective devices in his madrigalian vocabulary, as the little melisma on "ira" is one of the few decorated passages in the whole collection. The word "tormento" is set expressively, but the same musical pattern continues on through the word "dolore"; one cannot imagine the mature Gesualdo passing up the chance to underline their contrast. Frescobaldi seems to enjoy combining contradictory *affetti,* as in the opening of "Cor mio" or the antitheses of "S'io miro in te"—"io moro," "tu ridi"; "gioia," "noia"; "ucciso," "riso"—a text that comes dangerously close to self-parody.

In general, the *Madrigali* shows Frescobaldi as a highly competent product of the late Ferrarese madrigal school. Both in the choice of texts and in their musical realization he avoids the deeply emotional, preferring to produce works that charm by their craftsmanship rather than impress by their depth. Openings are never composed to rivet the listeners' attention. The rhythmic and harmonic vocabulary is generally bland, and contrapuntal complexity is rare. One has only to compare Girolamo's setting of a phrase like "Lasso io languisco e moro" with what Gesualdo made of "Moro lasso" to realize the restriction of Frescobaldi's expressive range. On the credit side, in his manipulation of the formal clichés characteristic of the late madrigal he displays a sensitivity to text-declamation and a concern for clarity of musical structure. But Frescobaldi's very real sense of drama was not stimulated by literary texts, and these works show no trace of the striking innovations in Monteverdi's fifth book of madrigals, published in 1605 but already in circulation in Ferrara by 1600. After this bow to Ferrarese tradition, it seems that Girolamo preferred to retire from a field in which he had talent but not genius.

2. The *Arie Musicali* of 1630

Between the *Madrigali* and the publication of the two books of *Arie* in 1630 Girolamo printed only three secular vocal works, two strophic settings for voice and continuo and one through-composed madrigal for two voices and continuo issued in anthologies. In the first of these, "Alla gloria alli honori," Adriano Cavicchi sees a paraphrase of Luzzaschi's "O Primavera" (*Madrigali,* 1601) at the words "ecco la primavera." "Era l'anima mia," published in Fabio Costantini's *L'aurata Cintia* of 1622, sets a poem of Guarini (*Madrigali,* 1598, p. 92), also set by Monteverdi in his fifth book of madrigals (see Catalogue III.A.2, 3, 4).

The two volumes of *Arie musicali,* on the other hand, present a considerable variety of poets, media, and genres. Fewer than one-fifth of the texts can be identified:

"Ben veggio, donna, homai": Monsignor della Casa, in *Il secondo volume delle rime scelte di diversi autori . . .* (Venice: Giolitti, 1590), p. 607; *Rime di M. Giacomo Marmitta Parmeggiano* (Parma: S. Viotto, 1564), p. 60.

"Donna siam rei di morte": Marino, *Lira* III, p. 3.

"Dopo si lungo error": Della Casa, *Rime,* Sonnet LXXI.

"La mia pallida faccia": *Le rime del sig.* [*Francesco*] *Balducci* (Rome: G. Facciotti, 1630), p. 143.

"Oscure selve": Desiderio Cavalcabo, in *Il secondo volume . . .*, p. 597.

"Ti lascio anima mia": *Idilli, e rime di Girolamo Preti . . .* (Venice: T. Bortoloti, 1614), p. 87: "Partenza. Per una musica."

"Vanne o carta amorosa": *Idilli . . . di Girolamo Preti,* p. 53.

"Voi partite mio sole": *Le rime del sig. Balducci,* p. 31.

In view of Doni's account of Frescobaldi's meager literary culture it is not surprising to find Girolamo resorting to an anthology or to standard poets such as Marino and Della Casa, but his choice of two texts by Francesco Balducci is more interesting. Balducci (1579–1642) was a Palermitan living in Rome, a favorite of the Barberini circle and the author of two oratorio libretti. Frescobaldi must have known his work in manuscript, since it was printed in the same year as the *Arie.* [4] This in turn suggests that some of the works in the *Arie* may predate Frescobaldi's journey to Florence, which may explain the striking absence of the standard Florentine authors of *poesia per musica* from the *Arie.*

Despite the scarcity of identifiable texts in the *Arie,* the collection reflects the influence of contemporary models of vocal chamber music. The dedicatory poem was a standard genre, such as the setting "Serenissima donna" of 1590[5] or the address to the Mantuan rulers in Monteverdi's *Ballo delle Ingrate.* Frescobaldi's setting of a sonnet on the Magdalen at the foot of the Cross may have been inspired by the "Maddalena chiedendo a pié del duro legno" (1618) of Andrea Falconieri. The heroic bass aria, which seems to have had a special attraction for Roman composers, judging from Stefano Landi's setting of Petrarch's "Superbi colli" and Caccini's "Chi mi comfort'ahime" from the *Nuove musiche* (albeit by a Roman working in Florence), is exemplified here by "Donna siam rei di morte," a text that evoked a particularly personal expression from Sigismondo d'India (*Musiche* III, 1618). The vogue of the *lettera amorosa,* crystallized as a poetic genre by Marino (madrigals CVI, CVII) and as a musical type by Monteverdi and d'India, is reflected in Biagio Marini's "Le carte in ch'io" (*Madrigali,* 1618) and in settings of Preti's *lettera* by Valentini (*Musiche à due,* 1622) and Frescobaldi.

Of the forty-three works in the *Arie* (one occurs twice), twenty-seven are scored for solo voice (canto, tenor, or bass) and continuo, ten are duets (two cantos, two tenors, or canto and tenor), and six are trios (canto, alto, tenor, or tenor, alto, bass). Despite the multiplicity of designations such as sonetto, canto, canzona, and aria, the contents of the *Arie* fall into four main categories: works in continuous recitative style; arias entirely in melodic style (either strophic or with written-out varied stanzas); works mixing the two styles; and settings on bass-patterns.

In view of the fact that no other works of Frescobaldi in unmixed recitative style survive, the inclusion of no less than twenty recitative settings in the *Arie* suggests some strong external influence. The sonetto spirituale, "Maddalena alla Croce" (perhaps a delicate compliment to the Archduchess Maria Maddalena), exemplifies Girolamo's treatment of the recitative style. The rhythm of the music follows closely that of the text; important words are emphasized by setting them to higher pitches; and unusually affective words of phrases receive expressive melodic or harmonic inflections, as in the phrase, "l'anima unita ho teco (il sai, mio Redentor, mio Dio)"—my soul is united to You (You know, my Redeemer, my God)—where within the space of four measures the music moves from F major to F-sharp major by a brutal diminished seventh in the bass. The only exception to the unadorned declamation of these works and their general avoidance of organizing elements like sequence and repetition is the virtuoso bass *sonetto,* "Donna, siam rei."

The arias are the most numerous genre in the collection, consisting of some fifteen strophic settings, three settings in which the variations are written out (not including the works on bass patterns), and three mixed settings employing elements of recitative style as well. The simplest have a unified rhythmic character; others incorporate changes of meter into the setting of the strophe.

Some works in the *Arie* seem almost to foreshadow the cantata in their combination of declamatory sections and passages in the regular rhythmic writing of the arias. The most successful of these are the duets, which often incorporate changes of meter and quasi-recitatives (as for example "Se m'amate," "Dove ne vai," "Eri già," "Bella tiranna," and, of the trios, "Quanto più sorda" and "O dolore").

The bass variations comprise one setting each on the Romanesca, the Ruggiero, the Passacagli, and the "Ceccona." The Romanesca and Ruggiero settings, whose originals are closed structures, both consist of four variations over the bass. The settings based on the passacaglia and ciaccona, on the other hand, show that these were still regarded as motivic-harmonic materials without built-in structural connotations. Despite the preexisting materials, both works are treated as free alternations of the bass patterns (which can modulate) and recitative sections (See chapter 14).

The general stylistic orientation of the *Arie musicali* is difficult to explain satisfactorily. It seems simplest to attribute it to the musical taste of the Florentine court, but the next published collection of Florentine court music, Domenico Anglesi's *Arie* of 1635, seems in its avoidance of recitative and its reliance on saraband rhythms to belong to another generation. In addition to local Florentine influences and the models of Girolamo's Roman contemporaries exemplified in the collections of the 1620s it is possible to hypothesize also the influence of Claudio Monteverdi as displayed in his seventh book of madrigals, published at Venice in 1619 and reprinted in 1622, 1623, 1627, and 1628, as well as that of the *Lamento d'Arianna . . . con due lettere amorose* (1623). The text "Eri già," set by Frescobaldi in the *Arie,* also appeared in Monteverdi's *Scherzi* of 1632. Although the settings for two voices are not the most numerous items in Frescobaldi's collection, they are among the most successful, and it is precisely this combination that forms the basis of Monteverdi's Book VII. Further clear parallels include the presentation of a Romanesca setting and a *lettera amorosa* in both collections, and Frescobaldi's ciaccona for two tenors seems a forerunner of the brilliant "Zefiro torna" of the 1632 *Scherzi*. It is just this coincidence, however, that highlights the difference between the two composers. While Frescobaldi is by no means insensitive to his text in terms of affective inflections, he is not inspired to the brilliant dramatization in Monteverdi's duet and to the extravagance of his great contemporary's vocal writing.

B. SACRED WORKS

1. Small Sacred Concertos and the *Liber Secundus Diversarum Modulationum* of 1627

Girolamo's settings of sacred Latin texts were roundly attacked by Antimo Liberati in 1684:

> And therefore few Musicians are capable of this science of vocal harmony, nor is it known who may teach it, more so since a great part of the Maestri di Cappella, and Composers are so ignorant of letters, that they hardly know how to spell their own name; and so much the less do they know this vocal harmony, those who have learned to compose by the sound of the keyboard or other instruments, having gained their experience and habit in composing Ricercari, in this same manner they also compose for the vocal style, which is very different from the other, which truth is proved by the example of Girolamo Frescobaldi, who having been the wonder of our times for the keyboard, both with the hands, and with the pen, as so many of his writings and his publications show us, was to the same degree unhappy and quite inept in vocal composition, as have been, and are also at present many other Players; . . . And in truth we know not who may teach this science, if not his own taste, the knowledge of the Latin language, and the long experience and application of the Composer.[6]

The ground of Liberati's criticism is unclear, since of the few composers that he commends—Giovanni Valentini, Giovanni Salvatore, and Francesco Turini—the surviving sacred production is insufficient to permit a judgment.

Roman sacred music of the earlier seventeenth century may be divided into three categories: settings for one to five voices and continuo of liturgical or paraliturgical texts; single-chorus settings, with or without continuo, for liturgical performance (such as vesper psalms and Magnificats); and choral liturgical settings for one, two, three, or more choirs of the ordinary of the mass and standard texts from the office.

Works are attributed to Frescobaldi in the first and third categories, but the small sacred concerto seems to have engaged his attention most consistently. Beginning in 1616 he published four sacred concertos in anthologies dominated by the composers of the Congregazione di Santa Cecilia (Catalogue III.B.1–4), and a fifth work—a Tenebrae lesson—survives in a manuscript in Bologna (see Catalogue III.B.7). The *Liber Secundus Diversarum Modulationum* (Catalogue III.B.5) is his one surviving sacred collection, but its title indicates the existence of a previous volume now lost. The second book contains thirty-two small sacred concertos for from one to four voices and continuo. Published at Rome by the printer Andrea Fei, the collection is dedicated in a letter dated 1 June 1627 to Cardinal Scipione Borghese, nephew of the late Pope Paul V and, as

TABLE 14. The contents of the *Liber Secundus Diversarum Modulationum*

TITLE	VOICES	LITURGICAL USE	SOURCE
1. Aspice Domine	C	Magnificat ant., I Vespers second Sunday of November	LU 996
2. Ipsi sum desponsata	C	St. Agnes	Anerio, *Antiphonae*
3. Deus noster refugium	C		Ps. 46
4. Exultavit cor meum	T	Magnificat ant., I Vespers Immaculate Heart of Mary	LU 1612[3]
5. O Iesu mi dulcissime	T	[Feasts of Our Lord]	
6. Vidi speciosam sicut	C, C+	[BVM]	
7. De ore prudentis	C, C+	[Saint in Eastertide]	
8. Sicut mater consolatur	C, C+		
9. Beatus vir qui suffert	C, B	[Male saint]	
10. O mors illa quam amara	C, B	[Sacred Heart]	
11. Benedicta tu Mater	C, B	[BVM]	

TABLE 14, *continued*

TITLE	VOICES	LITURGICAL USE	SOURCE
12. Viri sancti	T, T	[Male martyrs]	
13. Tempus est	A, T	[Ascension]	Cf. John 16
14. Benedicite Deum	T, T	Ps. ant., II Vespers of St. Raphael, Archangel	LU 1701
15. Tota pulcra es amica mea	C, T+	Ps. ant., I Vespers of the Assumption (St. Mark's, Venice)	
16. Decantabat populus Israel	C, T	[Easter?]	
17. Exurge Domine	B, B		
18. Reminiscere	B, B	[Lent]	
19. O bone Iesu	C, T+		
20. O Sacrum Conuiuium	C, C, T+	Magnificat ant., II Vespers Corpus Christi	LU 959
21. Vox dilecti mei pulsantis (prima pars)	C, C+, T		Song of Songs
22. Quam pulchra es, & speciosa (seconda pars)			
23. Sic amantem diligite	A, T+, T		
24. Ego flos Campi	C, C, B+	[BVM]	
25. Iesu Rex admirabilis	C, C, T+		
26. Exaudi nos Deus	A, T+, B		
27. Ego clamaui	C, A, T+, B		
28. Ciuitas Hierusalem noli	C, A, T+, T		
29. Ego sum qui sum	C, A, T+, B	Easter	Ugolini, *Motecta*
30. Corona aurea super caput	C, A, T+, B	[Saint in Easter]	
31. Jesu flos mater Virginis	C, A, T+, B		
32. Ave Virgo gloriosa	C, A, T, B	[BVM]	

Note: + = missing part; LU = *Liber Usualis.* The motets are numbered according to the index of the basso-continuo part-book.

Archpriest of the Vatican Basilica, Frescobaldi's ultimate superior. The lost first book seems to have been issued shortly before the present volume, to judge from Girolamo's reference to the "Sacred measures recently printed publicly by me for the harmony of the Church and the use of piety." From the dedication it seems possible that the collection was intended for performance at St. Peter's.

Unfortunately, the second part-book, which contains the parts for Cantus II and Altus, is missing from the only known copy of the volume, so that only fourteen of the thirty-two concertos can be transcribed in their entirety. The collection does not seem to have been selected or arranged on any very clear liturgical principle, unlike those of Girolamo's contemporaries at St. Peter's (see Table 14). In addition to texts for a few specific liturgical occasions, the settings of the collection provide motets for feasts of Our Lord, the Virgin Mary, the Sacred Heart, the Ascension, martyrs, and male and female saints, some with additional alleluias for Eastertide. A comparison of the *Liber Secundus* with the paradigm of the small sacred concerto, Viadana's *Cento concerti ecclesiastici* of 1602, indicates that Frescobaldi gathered his texts from a wider, less strictly liturgical body of sources, and in some cases it is impossible to ascertain the precise destination (if any) of these works.

Five of the motets are scored for solo voice (canto or tenor) and continuo, seven for three voices of various ranges, and six for four voices (usually canto, alto, tenor, and bass); these are far outnumbered by the fourteen settings for two voices of varying ranges and continuo. The motets for solo voice generally show a relatively rapid ornamental vocal line deployed over a slower-moving bass and often working in syncopation against it. Each setting contains a brief section in triple meter more or less prompted by some aspect of the text. Despite Liberati's strictures, Girolamo does attempt to portray the emotions of the text, as witness the suspensions on "tristitia" or the melisma on "qui consoletur" in "Aspice Domine."

The duet settings, like many of Girolamo's instrumental canzonas, are characterized by a somewhat regressive treatment of the bass. The lower voice of the duet is not an independent line but an embellishment—sometimes highly ornamented—of the continuo bass (or the continuo is a reduction of the lowest vocal line). In the triple sections that occur also in these works the correspondence is especially close.

Although the trios and quartets of the *Liber Secundus* are incomplete, some idea of his treatment of the three-voice medium can be gained from his earlier occasional publications, and one item of the *Liber Secundus* can be recovered, since the incomplete "Iesu rex admirabilis" was issued two years earlier in the collection *Sacri affetti.* These three-voice works—"Iesu rex," "Ego sum panis," and "Peccavi super numerum"—show many of the characteristics of the *Liber Secundus* motets: relatively slow harmonic motion, highly ornamented melodic lines, and a lowest voice which outlines the continuo bass. Perhaps because of the serious nature of the texts, however, only "Iesu rex" employs a triple section. The larger number of voices permits a greater variety of texture without breaking the continuity of the musical fabric. The gradual rhythmic crescendo (a textural one as well, from complete homophony to syncopated imitation) in the second half of "Ego sum" is longer and more controlled than anything in the earlier portions of the *Liber Secundus.*

The Lamentation for Holy Week preserved in the Bologna manuscript Q 43, a collection probably made in Rome about the middle of the seventeenth century, would seem on the evidence of its companion works to be one of the latest of Frescobaldi's sacred settings. It is a dignified and expressive account of its moving text and at least partly refutes Liberati's blanket condemnation of Frescobaldi as a composer of sacred vocal music.

2. Polychoral Sacred Music

The polychoral sacred music attributed to Frescobaldi is of doubtful authenticity and generally mediocre musical quality. As with the lost keyboard manuscripts, there is a persistent tradition of manuscript sacred works by Frescobaldi. As early as 1620 Superbi asserted that Girolamo had composed "endless Church works, which circulate in manuscript."[7] An inventory of Schloss Ambras at Innsbruck made in 1665 includes under "allerlay Cantiones mit Generalbass" a "Magnificat a 4 Chori del 2.0 tono di Girolimo Frescobaldi auf blossen Papier geschrieben," part of a collection acquired from the Goretti family of Ferrara.[8] Padre Martini found that Frescobaldi "had also composed compositions for church and in particular a motet *Misericordias Domini* &c. a 18. and another a 12. *Plaudite Jubilate Deo.*"[9] (The recently published index to Padre Martini's letters contains tantalizing references to unspecified compositions and volumes by Frescobaldi.)[10] None of these polychoral works appears to survive.

In 1933 Raffaele Casimiri published the results of his examination of manuscripts in the musical archive at San Giovanni in Laterano. Among the contents of the collection he found a group of masses for eight voices in two choirs, identified in the part-books as masses "sopra l'aria della Monaca," "sopra l'aria di Fiorenza"; one on the first (corrected to eighth) tone; a "Missa Portae Nitent Margaritis" datable before 1643 according to the editors of the Frescobaldi masses but in fact possibly earlier, since Urban VIII's *Breviarium,* whose version of the hymn "Urbs Beata Ierusalem" it incorporates, was published in 1632; and a "Missa a 8."[11] The first two masses are copied in a single fascicle in each of the eight part-books and presumably belong together. The organ part-book identifies the first work with the additional letters "G. F.di," which Casimiri interpreted as "Girolamo Frescobaldi." (The third mass bears the suprascription "di P.T.," which Casimiri read as "Paolo Tarditi.") As Casimiri noted, the ascriptions are not more fanciful than others in Roman manuscripts, including *unica* accepted as genuine works of Palestrina. The manuscripts are not dated, but the most likely time for Frescobaldi to have written works on the Aria di Fiorenza (the Ballo del Granduca) would have been during his service at the Tuscan court in 1628–1634. It has been objected, however, that the persistent attributions of works on the Aria di Fiorenza to Frescobaldi do not withstand careful scrutiny, although he did compose a set of keyboard variations on the Monica tune.[12]

Certain formal procedures are common to both masses. The first Kyrie is set in eight parts, the Christe in four, and the concluding Kyrie again in eight, in triple meter. In both Glorias the rapid alternation of phrases in the text is mirrored by the alternation of the two choirs. In the settings of the Credo, the Crucifixus of the Fiorenza mass and the Et Incarnatus and Crucifixus of the Monica setting are allotted to a single choir, and in both the Et Resurrexit prompts a change to triple meter. In both masses the Sanctus and Agnus Dei movements are shortened, in the first case by setting only the text up to the first Osanna, in the second by setting only the first of the three invocations.

The principal interest of the two masses lies in the composer's manipulation of the given musical material, and in his alternation and combination of the two choirs. The basic material of the two masses differs widely. The Monica is a monophonic, widely disseminated tune, whose original words (later replaced by sacred texts on occasion) make it highly inappropriate for a sacred setting: "Mother, don't make me a nun / for I don't want to be; / don't cut me a habit / for I don't want to wear it. // All day in choir / at vespers and mass, / and the mother abbess / does nothing but scream. // She should drop dead." While more decorous in tone, the Ballo del Granduca is scarcely more appropriate, since its original, the ballo "O che nuovo miracolo" written by Emilio de' Cavalieri for the intermedi of *La Pellegrina* in 1589, recounts the descent of the Olympian gods to earth in celebration of the marriage of Ferdinando I of Tuscany with Christine of Lorraine. While the Monica provides a tune, the Fiorenza material comprises a melody and bass, resultant harmonic skeleton, and even an integral rhythmic pattern.

The treatments of the two originals may almost be distinguished as paraphrase and parody. Although the mass on the Monica employs harmonic progressions drawn from the original, in general the two sections of the tune are more important as sources of thematic material for a predominantly imitative texture. The Fiorenza mass quotes larger segments of its model, the six harmonic phrases that constitute the refrain of the ballo, but it is perhaps significant that the composer largely ignores the most striking progression of the original, ii–I, which he usually alters to a blandly tonal II–I.

One other sacred work is attributed to Frescobaldi, a bichoral setting in eight parts of Psalm 30, vs. 1–6, *In Te Domine Speravi* (Catalogue III.B.8). The work currently survives in a recent copy lacking the Bassus ad organum, presumably made for a performance at Ferrara in 1908. The original manuscript belonged to Franz Xaver Haberl, who considered it to be an autograph—if so, the only known music in Girolamo's hand. The work displays all the qualities of liturgical *Gebrauchsmusik*—regular overlapped alternation of the two choirs, continuous rhythmic texture, competence without excitement. Beside a work like Monteverdi's setting of *Nisi Dominus* from the 1610 vespers, composed for the same medium in the same conventions, the *In Te Domine* almost justifies Liberati's polemic.

Catalogue of Works

I. Keyboard Works
  A. Printed Sources
  B. Manuscript Sources
II. Other Instrumental works
III. Vocal Works
  A. Works with Italian Text
  B. Works with Latin Text
IV. Doubtful, Lost, and Spurious Works

Volumes of printed instrumental music are identified by their numbers in Claudio Sartori, *Bibliografia della musica strumentale italiana.* Collections of vocal and instrumental music by a single composer are identified also according to the RISM volume A/I/3, *Einzeldrücke vor 1800.* Miscellaneous collections are identified according to RISM B/I/1, *Recueils imprimés 16e–17e siècles.* Secular vocal collections are identified according to Emil Vogel, *Bibliothek der gedruckten weltlichen Vocalmusik Italiens,* other vocal works according to the revised edition, *Bibliografia della musica italiana vocale profana.* In any case where I have been able to examine a print personally, these indications have been verified and amplified. Manuscripts are listed alphabetically according to the city of their present location.

I. KEYBOARD WORKS

A. Printed Sources

1. 1608i: IL PRIMO LIBRO / DELLE FANTASIE / A QUATTRO, / DI GERONIMO FRESCOBALDI / Ferrarese, Organista. / NOVAMENTE DATE IN LUCE. / [printer's ornament] / IN MILANO, per l'herede di Simon Tini, & Filippo Lomazzo. 1608.

   Oblong quarto, 75 pp., 4-voice keyboard *partitura* across opening. On the verso of the title page the dedication to Francesco Borghese, Duca di Regnano, dated Ferrara, 8 November 1608. Index on p. 75:

Tauola di questo Libro.

IL FINE.

RISM F 1855.

Bologna, Civico Museo Bibliografico Musicale.

Modern editions: Girolamo Frescobaldi, *Fantaisies,* ed. Norbert Dufourcq (Paris: Schola Cantorum, 1956–1957, 2 fascicles) and *Girolamo Frescobaldi: Orgel- und Klavierwerke,* ed. Pierre Pidoux, 5 vols. (Kassel: Bärenreiter, 1957–1963), I. Although not reprinted, the *Fantasie* was circulated in manuscript copies, one a complete copy by Bernardo Pasquini (see O. Deffner, "Ueber die Entwicklung der Fantasie für Tasteninstrumente," Kiel diss., 1927), Berlin, Deutsche Staatsbibliothek, Mus. ms. L 121. The first three fantasies and the opening 58 measures of the fourth fantasia, the fifth fantasia, and the first 61 measures of the sixth are copied in the manuscript Paris, Bibliothèque Nationale, Mus., Rés. Vma. ms. 965, fols. 67v–70v, 77v–79v, a seventeenth-century manuscript bearing the designation "Ad usum Augustini Bonaventure Coletti," formerly in the collections of Henry Prunières and the Comtesse de Chambure.

2. 1615a: TOCCATE E PARTITE / D'INTAVOLATVRA DI CIMBALO / DI GIROLAMO FRESCOBALDI / ORGANISTA / DI S. PIETRO DI ROMA / Nuouamente da lui date in luce, & / con ogni diligenza corrette / LIBRO PRIMO / [arms of the Cardinal-Duke of Mantua] / In Roma da Nicolò Borboni. / 1615. / Con licenza de Superiori.

Small folio engraved on copper, 4 unnumbered folios + 58 pp., keyboard score. On p. (iii) the dedication to Ferdinando Gonzaga, "Di Roma. XXII. Decembre. M.D.C.XIV."; p. (v) "AL LETTORE." No index. Contents:

RISM F 1856.

Bologna, Civico Museo Bibliografico Musicale; Rome, Biblioteca Casanatense (title page of the 1637 edition, signed "Al'vso Di sor Maria Gratia in S.ta Cat.na di Siena," followed by the first six folios of 1615a, the remainder of 1637; on p. 89 "Nauale" has been added to the *Capriccio sopra la Battaglia*); Rome, Cappella Giulia.

Modern edition of the three partite in *Girolamo Frescobaldi: Keyboard Compositions Preserved in Manuscripts* (Corpus of Early Keyboard Music, 30), ed. W. R. Shindle, 3 vols. (American Institute of Musicology, 1968), III. Complete edition in *Girolamo Frescobaldi: Il primo libro di toccate* (*Opere complete,* II), ed. Etienne Darbellay (Milan: Suvini Zerboni, 1977). For facsimile material from this collection see I.A.8. Sartori and RISM notwithstanding, the Deutsche Staatsbibliothek in Berlin does not possess this edition (see Riedel, "Einfluss," p. 23, n. 31), nor does the Bibliothèque Nationale in Paris or the Library of Congress in Washington, D.C.

[1615a *bis*: Paris, Bibliothèque Nationale Vm^{7} 1809 (1), the single source of this item, has been reassigned to 1616f.]

3. 1615–1616b: TOCCATE E PARTITE / D'INTAVOLATVRA DI CIMBALO / DI GIROLAMO FRESCOBALDI / ORGANISTA / DI S. PIETRO DI ROMA / Nuouamente da lui date in luce, & / con ogni diligenza corrette / LIBRO PRIMO / [arms of the Cardinal-Duke of Mantua] / Con licenza delli Superiori 1615 / In Roma da Nicoló Borboni.

Small folio engraved on copper, 3 unnumbered folios + 68 pp., keyboard score. On p. (iii) the dedication, dated Rome, 22 December 1614; p. (v) the expanded "AL LETTORE," at the end "Christophorus Blancus sculpsit 1616." No index. Contains Toccatas I–XII as in 1615a, followed by:

PARTITE SOPRA L'ARIA / DELLA ROMANESCA	41
Parte sopra lamonicha	51
PARTITE SOPRA RVGGIERO	56
PARTITE SOPRA FOLIA.	63
Corrente Prima	66
Corrente seconda	66
Corrente Terza	67
Corrente Quarta	68

RISM F 1857.

Paris, Bibliothèque Nationale; Washington, D.C., Library of Congress (someone has added the principal bass notes of the first two toccatas an octave lower).

This edition, issued so soon after 1615a, seems to reflect either the exhaustion of that publication or an attempt to supplant it. The dedication remains the same, except for the addition of the dedicatee's name, but the advice to the reader is altered and expanded. The variation-sets are also likewise altered, and the three correnti are a new addition. The more elegant engraving of the initial material is the work of Cristoforo Bianchi, an engraver working in Milan and Rome ca. 1610–1612 (Thieme-Becker, *Lexikon,* 3, 581).

3a. 1616f: TOCCATE E PARTITE / D'INTAVOLATVRA / DI CIMBALO / DI GIROLAMO FRESCOBALDI / ORGANISTA / IN S. PIETRO DI ROMA / LIBRO PRIMO / [Gonzaga arms] / Con licenza de Superiori / In Roma appresso Nicolo Borboni.

Dedication dated 1614, preface dated 1616.

An undated reprint of 3.

RISM F 1857

Berlin, Deutsche Staatsbibliothek; Ferrara, Biblioteca Comunale Ariostea; London, British Library; Paris, Bibliothèque Nationale; Venice, Biblioteca Nazionale Marciana.

The Venice copy, dated in ink "Adi 14 Giugno 1682 In Venetia" and apparently once a part of the Contarini collection, contains on its inside cover a list of thirty-one "originali di opere Cantate" acquired for the collection between 1681 and 1683 (see Jane Glover, *Cavalli,* New York: St. Martin's Press, 1978, pp. 67–68, 117). A "Toccata Prima" and the first page of a "Toccata Seconda" from Georg Muffat's *Apparatus Musico-Organisticus* (1650) have been bound in at the end.

3b. 1628k: IL PRIMO LIBRO / D'INTAVOLATVRA / DI TOCCATE / DI CIMBALO / ET ORGANO / PARTITE SOPRA L'ARIE / DI ROMANESCA / RVGGIERO / MONICA / FOLLIE / E CORRENTI / DI GIROLAMO / FRESCOBALDI / ORGANISTA IN / S. PIETRO DI ROMA / RISTAMPATO L' ANNO M.D.CXXVIII / Per Nicolo Borbone in Roma con licenza de Superiori.

Small folio engraved on copper, 2 unnumbered folios + 68 pp. Dedication omitted, preface = 3; on p. (iv) the portrait and sonnet from 1627b.

RISM F 1858.

Brussels, Bibliothèque du Conservatoire (on the title page: "Bernardo Pasquini 11 Nouembre 1662"); Glasgow, Euing Music Library; Oxford, Bodleian Library; Wolfenbüttel, Herzog August Bibliothek.

Modern edition of the various versions of 3 in *Opere complete,* II. On the editions of both toccatas, see Claudio Sartori, "Le 7 edizioni delle *Toccate* di Girolamo Frescobaldi," *La Bibliofilia* 50 (1948), 198–214. John Blow quotes two excerpts from *Toccate* I: mm. 1–9 of Blow's Voluntary II are an ornamented version of Frescobaldi's Toccata XII, mm. 1–9 (Br. Mus. Add. MSS. 31468, fol. 9v; 31446, fol. 41; 34695, fol. 53v). Blow's Voluntary XXIX, Add. MS. 34695, fol. 10v, "A Double Vers.," in mm. 45–57 cites mm. 18–24 of *Toccata* VIII (see *John Blow: Complete Organ Works,* ed. Watkins Shaw, London, 1958).

4. 1615g: RECERCARI, / ET CANZONI / FRANZESE / FATTE SOPRA DIVERSI OBLIGHI / IN PARTITVRA / DA GIROLAMO / FRESCOBALDI / Organista di San Pietro / di Roma, / LIBRO PRIMO. / [Arms of Cardinal Pietro Aldobrandini] / IN ROMA, / Appresso Bartolomeo Zannetti. MDCXV. / CON LICENZA DE' SVPERIORI.

Small folio, 59 pp. (pp. 17–20 numbered 5–8), keyboard *partitura.* Dedication to Cardinal [Pietro] Aldobrandino, Chamberlain of the Church, on p. (3) (undated). Index on the verso of p. 59:

TAVOLA DE' RECERCARI
DEL SIGNOR GIROLAMO
FRESCOBALDI.

[printer's mark, "Franciscus Zanetti"] / IN ROMA, / Appresso Bartolomeo Zannetti. MDCXV. / CON LICENZA DE' SVPERIORI.

RISM F 1860.

Berlin, Deutsche Staatsbibliothek; Cambridge, King's College; Paris, Bibliothèque du Conservatoire (incomplete); Rome, Cappella Giulia (on the flyleaf the note, "Comprato adi 29 Ottobre 1732 f. 10 da Matteo Regattiere"); Washington, D.C., Library of Congress.

Facsimile edition by Gregg International Publishers, Westmead, 1967.

The first 48 measures of the eighth recercar appear in Paris, Bibliothèque Nationale, Rés. 819–2, a manuscript copied in Germany after 1661 (Gustafson, vol. 1, p. 22).

4a. 1618g: RECERCARI, / ET CANZONI / FRANZESE / FATTE SOPRA DIVERSI OBLIGHI / IN PARTITVRA / DA GIROLAMO / FRESCOBALDI / Organista in San Pietro / di Roma. / LIBRO PRIMO. / [arms] / IN ROMA, / Appresso Bartolomeo Zannetti. M.DC.XVIII.

Dedication = 4, without signature and *imprimatur.* Index on verso of p. 59 = 4.

RISM F 1861.

London, British Library.

5. 1624b: IL PRIMO LIBRO / DI CAPRICCI / FATTI SOPRA / DIVERSI SOGGETTI, ET / ARIE IN PARTITVRA DI / GIROLAMO / FRESCOBALDI / ORGANISTA IN S. PIETRO DI ROMA / [Este arms] / IN ROMA. / Appresso Luca Antonio Soldi M.D.C. XX.IIII. / CON LICENTIA DE SVPERIORI

Small folio, 95 pp. numbered regularly to 56, then 52–61, then without numeration, keyboard *partitura*. Dedication to Alfonso d'Este, Prince of Modena, dated Rome, 12 April 1624, and *imprimatur* on p. (2), "A GLI STVDIOSI / DELL'OPERA" on p. (3). On p. (96) the index:

TAVOLA.
DELLI CAPRICCI.

PRimo v̂t, re, mi, fa, sol, la.	4
Secondo la, sol, fa, mi, re, vt.	14
Terzo sopra il Cucho	23
Quarto la, sol, fa, re mi.	31
Quinto sopra la bassa fiammenga.	40
Sesto sopra la Spagnoletta,	47
Settimo sopra or che noi rimena.	50
Ottauo Cromatico di ligature al contrario.	57
Nono di durezze.	61
Decimo Obligo di cantare la quinta parte, senza toccarla, / sempre di Obligo del sogetto scritto.*	63
Vndecimo sopra vn sogetto.	72
Duodecimo sopra l'Aria di Rugiero.	80

IL FINE.

RISM F 1862.

Bergamo, Biblioteca dell'Istituto Musicale; Berlin, Deutsche Staatsbibliothek; Bologna, Civico Museo Bibliografico Musicale; London, British Library (2 copies); Paris, Bibliothèque du Conservatoire; Rome, Biblioteca Casanatense (manuscript corrections in ink, perhaps by Baini, the donor of the volume); Washington, D.C., Library of Congress (the entrances of the ostinato have been supplemented by the indication "re" in ink on pp. 79 [mm. 1, 16] and 80 [second system, m. 4]).

5a. 1626i: IL PRIMO LIBRO / DI CAPRICCI / CANZON FRANCESE, / E RECERCARI / FATTI SOPRA DIVERSI SOGGETTI, ET ARIE / IN PARTITVRA. / DI GIROLAMO FRESCOBALDI / ORGANISTA IN SAN PIETRO / DI ROMA, / NO-

* The tenth and eleventh capriccios are printed in reverse order in the text.

VAMENTE RISTAMPATI / CON PRIVILEGIO / [printer's mark] / IN VENETIA. / APPRESSO ALESSANDRO VINCENTI. / MDCXXVI.

Large folio, no dedication, 169 pp. (86–87 numbered 88–89, 136 numbered 138), keyboard *partitura.* On the verso of the title page the advice to the reader = 5, beginning BErche . . . instead of PER che. On the verso of p. 169 the index:

TAVOLA
DELLI CAPRICCI
CANZON FRANCESE, RECERCARI
DI GIROLAMO FRESCOBALDI
ORGANISTA IN SAN PIETRO DI ROMA.

IL FINE.

RISM F 1863.

Assisi, Biblioteca Municipale; Berlin, Deutsche Staatsbibliothek; Bologna, Civico Museo Bibliografico Musicale; The Hague, Gemeentemuseum (incomplete); London, British Library; Wolfenbüttel, Herzog August Bibliothek.

Modern editions: *Vijf Capricen, vier Canzonen en acht Ricercaren,* ed. J. B. Litzau (Rotterdam: Alsbach, 1873); *Vier Capricen, een Canzon en twee Ricercaren,* ed. Litzau (Rotterdam, 1874); *Quindici Capricci,* ed. Felice Boghen (Florence: Casa Editrice Musicale Italiana [1919]); *XVI Ricercari,* ed. Boghen (Paris: Senart, n.d.); Pidoux, II.

Material from this edition appears in the manuscript Paris, Bibliothèque Nationale, Mus., Rés. Vma. ms. 965, fols. 29–67v (see I.A.1).

5b. 1628l: IL PRIMO LIBRO / DI CAPRICCI / CANZON FRANCESE, / E RECERCARI / FATTI SOPRA DIVERSI SOGGETTI ET ARIE / IN PARTITVRA. / DI GIROLAMO FRESCOBALDI / ORGANISTA IN SAN PIETRO / DI ROMA, / NOVAMENTE RISTAMPATI / CON PRIVILEGIO / [printer's mark] / IN VENETIA. / APPRESSO ALESSANDRO VINCENTI / MDCXXVIII.

Small folio, 169 numbered pp., without dedication; = 5.

RISM F 1864.

Berkeley, University of California; The Hague, Gemeentemuseum (incomplete); Paris, Collection André Meyer; Reggio Emilia, Biblioteca Municipale; Venice, Biblioteca del Conservatorio (fondo Giustinian); Vienna, Minoritenkonvent; Wroclaw, University Library.

5c. 1642h: IL PRIMO LIBRO / DI CAPRICCI / CANZON FRANCESE / E RECERCARI / FATTI SOPRA DIVERSI SOGGETTI, ET ARIE / IN PARTITVRA / DI GIROLAMO FRESCOBALDI / ORGANISTA IN SAN PIETRO / DI ROMA. / NOVAMENTE RISTAMPATI / CON PRIVILEGIO. / [printer's mark] / IN VENETIA, / APPRESSO ALESSANDRO VINCENTI. / MDCXXXXII.

Folio, one unnumbered folio + 169 pp., p. 46 numbered 50. Without dedication = 5a; advice on verso of title page = 5.

RISM F 1865.

Bologna, Civico Museo Bibliografico Musicale; Ferrara, Biblioteca Comunale; Montecassino, Abbey Library; Munich, Bayerische Staatsbibliothek ("Monasterij B.mae Mariae in Diessen."); Venice, Biblioteca Nazionale Marciana; Vienna, Oesterreichische Nationalbibliothek.

There are some minor discrepancies in typography between this and earlier editions.

6. 1627b: IL SECONDO LIBRO / DI TOCCATE, CANZONE / VERSI D'HINNI MAGNIFICAT / GAGLIARDE, CORRENTI / ET ALTRE PARTITE / D'INTAVOLATVRA / DI CIMBALO ET ORGANO / DI GIROLAMO FRESCOBALDI / ORGANISTA / IN S. PIETRO DI ROMA / [arms of Mons. Luigi Gallo, Bishop of Ancona].

Folio engraved on copper, 2 unnumbered folios + 90 pp. On p. (iii) the dedication to Mons. Gallo, dated 15 January 1627; on p. (iv) a portrait of Frescobaldi with the legend: "HIERONYM' FRESCOBALDVS FERRARIEN. ORGANISTA ECCLESIAE D. PETRI IN VATICANO AET. SVAE 36." and underneath, "F. Io. Salianus Augustinianus deliniabat + Christian' Sas Sculpsit." (See fig. 8.) The richly decorated page also includes a laudatory sonnet by Pier Francesco Paoli of Pesaro. Keyboard score. The musical text begins on p. 1. No index. Contents of the volume:

RISM F 1866.

Berlin, Deutsche Staatsbibliothek; Chicago, Newberry Library (not the 1637 edition; the date on the dedication has been corrected to 1628 in ink); Paris, Bibliothèque Nationale (Capponi arms on binding); Paris, Collection André Meyer; Wolfenbüttel, Herzog August Bibliothek.

Modern edition of the Ciaccona and Passacagli in Shindle, III, 44–49.

Verse I of the *Hinno della Domenica* and verse IV of *Iste Confessor* appear, with some ornamentation and unattributed, in the manuscript British Library Add. 31403 (ca. 1700), fol. 65 (see Hodge, "A New Frescobaldi Attribution").

6a. 1637g: IL SECONDO LIBRO / DI TOCCATE, CANZONE / VERSI D'HINNI MAGNIFICAT / GAGLIARDE, CORRENTI / ET ALTRE PARTITE / D'INTAVOLATVRA / DI CIMBALO ET ORGANO / DI GIROLAMO FRESCOBALDI / ORGANISTA / IN S. PIETRO DI ROMA / Con priuilegio. / [arms of Mons. Gallo] / In Roma con licenza de Superiori 1637 Da Nicoló Borbone.

Folio, 2 unnumbered folios + 86 pp., verso of title page blank or containing preface of 3. On recto of second folio the dedication (= 6), on verso the portrait of Frescobaldi and Paoli's sonnet. The volume is a reprint of 6 without the last four pages, the variations on Ciaccona and Passacagli. No index.

RISM F 1867.

Ann Arbor, Mich., General Library; Bergamo, Biblioteca dell'Istituto; Berkeley, University of California; Berlin, Deutsche Staatsbibliothek; Bologna, Civico Museo Bibliografico Musicale; Brno, Moravské Múzeum; Brussels, Bibliothèque Royale (Fonds Fétis); Cambridge, Mass., Harvard University Music Library; Einsiedeln, Abbey Library; Ferrara,

Biblioteca Comunale; Florence, Biblioteca del Conservatorio (damaged); Glasgow, Euing Music Library (incomplete); The Hague, Gemeentemuseum (2 copies); Haslemere, Carl Dolmetsch Library; London, British Library (3 copies); London, Royal College of Music; London, Trinity College (incomplete); Montecassino, Abbey Library; Munich, Bayerische Staatsbibliothek; Naples, Biblioteca del Conservatorio; New Haven, Library of the Yale School of Music: "Ex libris mōrij S. Bernardi de Vrbe ad Thermas Anno 1668"; Oxford, Bodleian Library; Paris, Bibliothèque du Conservatoire (incomplete); Paris, Bibliothèque Nationale; Paris, Collection André Meyer; Perugia, Biblioteca Dominicini; Rochester, Eastman School of Music, Sibley Music Library; Rome, Biblioteca Casanatense; Rome, Biblioteca del Conservatorio di Santa Cecilia; Rome, Biblioteca Corsiniana; Rostock, Universitätsbibliothek; Siena, Accademia Chigiana; Toronto, University Faculty of Music; Venice, Biblioteca Nazionale Marciana (2 copies); Vicenza, Biblioteca Comunale; Vienna, Oesterreichische Nationalbibliothek; Washington, D.C., Library of Congress.

Facsimile edition, ed. Laura Alvini, *Archivum Musicum: Collana di testi rari,* Studio per Edizioni Scelte, Florence, 1978, vol. 4 (includes the 1627 partite on Ciaccona, Passacagli); modern edition in Pidoux, IV; Schola Cantorum, Paris, 1959; both volumes ed. Kenneth Gilbert (Padua: Zanibon, 1978).

7. 1635a: FIORI MVSICALI / DI / DIVERSE COMPOSITIONI / TOCCATE, KIRIE, CANZONI / CAPRICCI, E RECERCARI / IN PARTITVRA A QVATTRO / VTILI PER SONATORI / AVTORE / GIROLAMO FRESCOBALDI / ORGANISTA DI SAN PIETRO / DI ROMA. / OPERA DVODECIMA. / CON PRIVILEGIO. / [arms of Cardinal Antonio Barberini the younger] / IN VENETIA, / Appresso Alessandro Vincenti. MDCXXXV.

Folio, 2 unnumbered folios + 103 pp. On the recto of the second folio the dedication to Cardinal Antonio Barberini, dated Venice, 20 August 1635, on the verso "AL LETTORE"; keyboard *partitura.* Index on the verso of p. 103:

TAVOLA DELLI FIORI MVSICALI
DI GIROLAMO FRESCOBALDI

Tocata Auanti la Messa Della Domenica	1
Kirie Della Domenica	2
kirie	3
Christe	4
Christe Alio modo	5

Capricio sopra la Girolmeta. 96

IL FINE.

RISM F 1871.

Berkeley, University of California; Berlin, Deutsche Staatsbibliothek; Bologna, Civico Museo Bibliografico Musicale; Ferrara, Biblioteca Comunale; Glasgow, Euing Music Library; The Hague, Gemeentemuseum; London, British Library (King's Music Library; incomplete); Montecassino, Abbey Library; Munich, Bayerische Staatsbibliothek ("Monasterij B. V. Mariae in Diessen. 1653"); Paris, Bibliothèque Nationale; Reggio Emilia, Biblioteca Municipale; Urbana, Ill., Collection Dragan Plamenac*; Vienna, Minoritenkonvent; Vienna, Oesterreichische Nationalbibliothek; Wolfenbüttel, Herzog August Bibliothek; Wroclaw, University Library.

Modern editions: Jos. Bonnet (Paris: Senart, n.d.); Herman Keller (Leipzig: Peters, n.d.); Fernando Germani (Rome: de Santis, 1936); *I grandi organisti,* ed. Sandro Dalla Libera (Vicenza, 1957); Pidoux, V.

The designation "Opera duodecima" is obtained by counting all of Frescobaldi's published collections from the 1608 madrigals on, considering reprints as duplications of the originals, the 1634 *Canzoni* as a new publication, and including both volumes of *Diversarum Modulationum.* A manuscript copy of the *Fiori* (Dresden, Sächische Landesbibliothek, Mus. 1/B/98) was made in 1718 by Jan Dismas Zelenka (Schierning, p. 55, n. 66). A nineteenth-century copy, once the property of J. A. Fuller-Maitland and apparently prepared for publication, is found in the Special Collections of the Research Library of the University of California at Los Angeles. Material from the *Fiori* appears in Paris, B. N., Mus., Rés. Vma. ms. 965, fols. 1–28v, 71–77v (see I.A.1.)

8. 1637f: TOCCATE D'INTAVOLATVRA / DI CIMBALO ET ORGANO / PARTITE DI DIVERSE ARIE ET COR- / RENTE, BALLETTI, CIAC- / CONE, PASSACHAGLI. / DI / GIROLAMO FRESCOBALDI / ORGANISTA IN S. PIETRO DI ROMA. / Libro P.o / [arms of Cardinal Francesco Barberini] / STAMPATO L'ANNO M.D.C.XXXVII / Per Nicolo Borbone in Roma Con licenza de Superiori.

Folio, engraved on copper, 2 unnumbered folios + 95 pp. No dedication, portrait of Frescobaldi and sonnet on recto of second folio, "AL LETTORE" (= 3) on verso with the addition of "Li Passachagli . . . Ciaccone." Signed "Christophorus Blancus sculpsit 1616." Keyboard score. Index following p. 94:

* The Plamenac Collection has gone to the Yale School of Music Library.

TAVOLA

Toccate dodeci.	
Partite 14. sopra l'Aria di Romanesca.	a. cart. 41.
Partite ij. sopra l'Aria di Monicha.	a. cart. 51.
Partite 12. sopra l'Aria di Ruggiero.	a. cart. 56.
Partite 6. sopra l'Aria di Follia.	a. cart. 63.
Côrente quattro.	a. cart. 66.
[At the end of p. 68: FINIS. On p. 69: AGGIUNTA.]	
Balletto e Corrente.	a. cart. 67. [*recte* 69.]
Passachagli e Balletto.	a. cart. 70.
Balletto e Corrente.	a. cart. 71
Passachagli	a. cart. 72.
Partite cento sopra il Passachagli.	a. cart. 74.
Corrente e Passachagli.	a. cart. 76.
Ciaccone e Passachagli.	a. cart. 79.
Capriccio Fra Iacopino sopra l'Aria di Ruggiero.	85. partite. 6
Capriccio sopra la Battaglia.	a. cart. 89.
Balletto e Ciaccone.	a. cart. 91.
Corrente e Ciaccone.	a. cart. 92.
Capriccio fatto sopra la Pastorale.	a. cart. 93.

FINIS.

RISM F 1859.

Bergamo, Biblioteca dell'Istituto Musicale; Berlin, Deutsche Staatsbibliothek; Bologna, Civico Museo Bibliografico Musicale; Brno, Moravské Múzeum; Brussels, Bibliothèque Royale (fonds Fétis); Cambridge, Mass., Houghton Library, Harvard University; Chicago, Newberry Library; Einsiedeln, Stiftsbibliothek; Ferrara, Biblioteca Comunale; Florence, Biblioteca del Conservatorio (damaged); Glasgow, Euing Music Library (incomplete); The Hague, Gemeentemuseum; Haslemere, Carl Dolmetsch Library; London, British Library (3 copies); London, Royal College of Music; London, Trinity College (incomplete); Montecassino, Abbey Library; Munich, Bayerische Staatsbibliothek; Naples, Biblioteca del Conservatorio; Oxford, Bodleian Library (incomplete); Paris, Bibliothèque du Conservatoire (2 copies); Paris, Collection André Meyer; Perugia, Biblioteca Dominicini; Reggio Emilia, Biblioteca Municipale; Rochester, Eastman School of Music; Rome, Biblioteca Casanatense (begins on p. 1); Rome, Biblioteca del Conservatorio di Santa Cecilia (first 20 pp. missing); Rostock, Universitätsbibliothek; Siena, Accademia Chigiana; Toronto, Royal Conservatory; Toronto, University Library; Venice, Biblioteca Nazionale Marciana; Vicenza, Biblioteca Comunale; Vienna, Oesterreichische Nationalbibliothek; Washington, D.C., Library of Congress.

Facsimile edition ed. Laura Alvini, including prefatory material and original versions of Ruggiero and Romanesca, *Archivum Musicum: Collana di testi rari,* Studio per Edizioni Scelte, vol. 3 (Florence, 1978). Modern editions: *Douze toccatas,* ed. G. Sazerac de Forge (Paris: Schola Cantorum, 2 fasc., 1955, 1960); Pidoux, III; Darbellay (see I.A.2); Gilbert (see I.A.6a); on dances and variations from *Toccate* I–II copied in Trent, Biblioteca Comunale M 1092, see C. Lunelli, "Una raccolta manoscritta seicentesca," *L'Organo* 16 (1978), 55–75.

9. 1645a: CANZONI / ALLA FRANCESE / IN PARTITVRA / DEL SIGNOR / GIROLAMO FRESCOBALDI / ORGANISTA DI S. PIETRO DI ROMA / RACCOLTE / DALLESSANDRO VINCENTI / DEDICATE / Al molto Illustre, & Reuerendissimo P.D. / GIOVANNI POZZO / ABBATE DEGNISSIMO DI S. SALVATORE / DI VENETIA / NUOVAMENTE POSTI IN LUCE / CON LICENZA DI SUPERIORI. ET. PRIVILEGIO / LIBRO QUARTO / [printer's mark] / IN VENETIA / Appresso Alessandro Vincenti. MDCXXXXV.

Folio, 55 pp. On p. 1 the dedication, dated Venice, 15 December 1644. Keyboard *partitura.* Index on the verso of p. 55:

TAVOLA

Canzon Prima detta la Rouetta	3
Canzon Seconda detta la Sabatina.	8
Canzon Terza detta la Criuelli.	15
Canzon Quarta detta la Scacchi.	18
Canzon Quinta detta la Bellerofonte.	23
Canzon Sesta detta la Pesenti.	27
Canzon Settima detta la Tarditi.	30
Canzon Ottaua detta la Vincenti.	35
Canzon Nona detta la Querina.	39
Canzon Decima detta la Paulini.	46
Canzon Undecima detta la Gardana.	50

IL FINE.

RISM F 1872.

Ferrara, Biblioteca Comunale; London, British Library (2 copies); Montecassino, Abbey Library; Reggio Emilia, Biblioteca Municipale; Urbana, Ill., Plamenac Collection.

Modern editions: *25 Canzoni per cembalo ed organo,* ed. Felice Boghen (Milan: Ricordi, [1922]); Pidoux, I.

B. Manuscript Sources

An exhaustive survey and assessment of manuscripts containing works attributed to Frescobaldi is beyond the scope of this catalogue; a comprehensive listing and examination of such manuscripts in terms of their contents and historical context would constitute a formidable volume in itself. On the evidence of Alexander Silbiger's study, *Italian Manuscript Sources of 17th Century Keyboard Music,* it appears that the bulk of such manuscript attributions is in any case unreliable. In listing manuscripts of Italian origin I have therefore given a conspectus of the principal sources and added comments or amplifications of Silbiger's catalogue where appropriate. Information on works attributed to Frescobaldi in French manuscripts is provided by Bruce Gustafson's *French Harpsichord Music of the 17th Century.* In dealing with manuscript copies of printed works I have included only copies of special interest (those by Pasquini and Zelenka, for example) in the notes to the relevant collection in I.A (see Silbiger, pp. 50–51, for a conspectus of print/manuscript concordances). Copies of single works in miscellaneous collections have been included where it seemed appropriate. (For a list of printed works of Frescobaldi copied in German manuscripts, see Lydia Schierning, *Die Ueberlieferung der deutschen Orgel- und Klaviermusik aus der ersten Hälfte des 17. Jahrhunderts,* p. 55, n. 66, which needs some revision.)

Berlin, Deutsche Staatsbibliothek, Ms. 6612

A nineteenth-century manuscript of thirty-nine ricercars attributed to Frescobaldi, of which nos. 1–7 (in two parts) and 8–27 (in three parts) are unidentified and nos. 28–34 and 39 = *Recercari* (1615), 2–9, and 35–37 = the *Capricci* 1, 7, 10.

Berlin, Deutsche Staatsbibliothek, Ms. 40316

fol. 1: Partite sopra un aria Romana detta la Manista Girolamo Frescobaldi.

fol. 35: Toccada Girolamo Frescobaldi (not in Schierning).

fol. 71: Gironimo Frescobaldi Sopra il Gu Gu.

Lost during World War II; photostat in the Isham Library, Harvard University.

Literature: Schierning, pp. 84–86.

Modern edition: Shindle, I, 86–87; II, 73–77; III, 19–23.

Berlin, Deutsche Staatsbibliothek, Ms. 40615

fol. 179: Fuga supra Gu Gu.

fol. 181: Can: 2: To: Aut: Girolam:

Modern edition: Shindle, II, 46–49 (cf. Munich 5368); 73–77 (cf. Munich 1581).

Berlin, Staatliche Hochschule für Musik
fol. 17v: Toccate (= *Toccate* I/3)
fol. 20v: Toccata di Frescobaldi
fol. 24v: Canzon di Frescobaldi

Bologna, Civico Museo Bibliografico Musicale, Ms. AA/360
fols. 54v–55: L'Aria del Gran Ducha—del Freschobaldi.
Literature: Warren Kirkendale, *L'Aria di Fiorenza, id est il Ballo del Gran Duca* (Florence: Olschki, 1972), pp. 28, 71–72, where he notes that this is one of the two settings which are not in G major, and that it otherwise deviates from the original. Silbiger, pp. 94–96, 154, 158, 165.

Bologna, Civico Museo Bibliografico Musicale, Ms. DD/53
fols. 1–3: Toccata p[a]—Del Sig. Frescobaldi
Literature: Silbiger, pp. 96–99, 154, 158, who assigns the manuscript to the 1720s. The repertory is predominantly of the seventeenth century, and the toccata attributed to Frescobaldi is in fact by Johann Kaspar Kerll.
Modern edition: Luigi Ferdinando Tagliavini, "Un' importante fonte per la musica di J. K. Kerll," *Collectanea Historiae Musicae* 4 (Florence, 1966), pp. 283–293.

Brussels, Bibliothèque Royale II. 3908
A nineteenth-century manuscript containing the same repertory as Berlin, Deutsche Staatsbibliothek, Ms. 6612

Florence, Biblioteca del Conservatorio, Ms. D. 2358
The entire collection, which appears to date from the late seventeenth century, is attributed to "Frescobaldi (1583–1644)" on the flyleaf, but the inscription seems to date from this century.
Literature: Silbiger, pp. 104–105, 154, 158–159.

Geneva, Biblioteca Bodmeriana, Musik T.II.1
Attributed to Frescobaldi on manuscript case.
fol. 3: "Al Lettore" from *Toccate* I.
fols. 1–77: an almost complete copy of *Toccate* II, minus the liturgical works.
fols. 78–79: Prima toccata
fols. 79v–80v: Seconda.
fols. 81–83v: Terza Tocc. odi Canzone
fols. 83v–85: Piva/Quarto. Tocc.:
fols. 86–94v: *Toccate* I/1, 6.

Despite the publication of photographs of this manuscript as an autograph of Frescobaldi by Abbiati and Reimann, the investigations of Silbiger and Darbellay show that the authentic works of Frescobaldi which it contains were copied ca. 1670 from the printed editions and that for a variety of reasons the attributions of unprinted works are unreliable.

Literature: Silbiger, pp. 84, 154, 156; Darbellay, "Un manuscrit frescobaldien à Genève," *L'Organo* 13 (1975), 49–69.

London, British Library, Add. Ms. 23623

Contains one work attributed to "Hieronimo Ferabosco" but possibly by Frescobaldi.

fol. 9b: Toccata di Roma (Sexti toni).

London, British Library, Add. Ms. 34003

The works rather vaguely described in Hughes-Hughes, *Catalogue of Manuscript Music in the British Museum* (London: British Museum, 1906–1909), as for lute and organ (fols. 36–37) are the extra works included by Grassi in his edition of the 1628 *Canzoni,* of which this manuscript seems to be a copy.

London, British Library, Add. Ms. 36661

fol. 26: Del Sig. Freses Baldi. Canzona

fol. 28v: Del Sig. Freses Baldi. Toccata

fol. 31v: Del Sig. Freses Baldi. Toccata

fol. 34: Del Sig. Freses Baldi. Canzona

fol. 37: Del Sig. Freses Baldi. Toccata

A manuscript of doubtful authenticity, probably written by an Englishman "not before the late seventeenth century." The closing section of the first work has concordances in the Canzona sesta and the Canzona nona of Add. Ms. 40080.

Literature: Silbiger, pp. 66–70, 157.

Modern edition: Shindle, I, 75–85; II, 34–41.

London, British Library, Add. Ms. 40080

fol. [i]: Fioretti di Frescobaldi.

fols. 1–35: Canzona prima . . . Canzona undecima

Internal evidence makes it unlikely that these works are to be attributed to Frescobaldi in their present form; the manuscript is not in Italian format, and the blanket attribution is in a hand different from the rest of the work.

Literature: Silbiger, pp. 92, 154, 156–158.

London, manuscript in the collection of Guy Oldham

Contains an unidentified "Duresse de frescobaldi pria" (no. 66a) between works dated October 1650 and 1651 in the hand of Louis Couperin.

Literature: Oldham, "Louis Couperin," *Recherches*, 1960, 51–59; Gustafson, vol. 2, pp. 267–284.

Munich, Bayerische Staatsbibliothek, Mus. Ms. 1581

no. 127: Tertii toni [no attribution]

no. 141, nos. 144–149: copies of printed canzonas, ricercars, toccata.

no. 159: Canzon Frescobaldi

no. 160: Canzon Frescobaldi [*Capricci*]

no. 167: Fuga Fresgobalti

no. 174: Canzon Frescobalti

no. 175: Canzon Frescobaldi

no. 176: Canzon Frescobaldi

no. 177: Canzon Frescobaldi

no. 178: Canzon Frescobaldi

no. 179: Canzon Frescobaldi

no. 180: Fuga Frescobaldi gù gù

no. 181: Altro modo.

The works are copied in New German organ tablature.

Literature: Schierning, pp. 59–60.

Modern edition: Shindle, II, 49–73.

Munich, Bayerische Staatsbibliothek, Mus. Ms. 5368: "In vsum F.F. Neresheimensium 1661 11 Martij" "Anno 1682 finitum."

fol. 3V: Fuga imi toni Frescobaldi.

fol. 22: Canzon 2di Toni Frescobaldi (cf. Berlin 40615)

fol. 146: Verso primo. Octavi toni

Literature: Hans Schmid, "Una nuova fonte di musica organistica del secolo XVII," *L'Organo* 1 (1960), 107–113.

Modern edition: Shindle, II, 41–49, 79.

Naples, Biblioteca del Conservatorio, Ms. Mus. str. 73 (*olim* 34.5.28): listed by Apel as containing two unpublished works of Frescobaldi, but these are canzonas copied from printed editions (Silbiger, pp. 109–110).

New York City[?], formerly Collection of Carlo Giorgio Garofalo; contains nineteen canzonas with a blanket attribution to Frescobaldi, of which no. 12 is the Capriccio sopra un soggetto (*Capricci,* 1626) and nos. 14 and 19 are nos. 2 and 11 from the 1645 *Canzoni*.

Literature: C. G. Garofalo, "Una scoperta importante di musiche inedite e ignorate," *Rivista Nazionale di Musica* 3 (1922), 307–309; Silbiger, p. 147.

Nuremberg, Germanisches Nationalmuseum, Ms. 33748-V

Eight separately bound manuscripts, of which vol. V contains six dances concordant with works in the two books of toccatas, in somewhat altered versions; the remaining contents are mostly arie settings, probably originating in northern Italy, ca. 1640–1660.

Literature: Silbiger, pp. 84–85.

Oxford, Christ Church 1113

Contains one work attributed to "Frisco Baldy."

Literature: Silbiger, "Roman Frescobaldi Tradition," p. 77.

Paris, Bibliothèque Nationale, rés. Vm^7 675 (ms. Bauyn)

fol. 95: Capriccio del Seignor Girolamo frescobaldi Pria.

fol. 95v: Capricio del Seignor Girolamo frescobaldi—Pria.

fol. 96: Trio de Frescobaldi

fol. 108: Fantaisie du Seig.r Hierosme frescobaldi

Literature: Silbiger, *Sources,* p. 194, n. 4, where he identifies the "Trio" as a portion of *Toccate* I/12 with the inner voice transcribed an octave higher; Shindle (II, 28–31) prints the two capriccios as one work; see Gustafson, vol. 2, 314–428.

Ravenna, Biblioteca Comunale Classense, Ms. Classense 545

fols. 37–39: Capriccio di G.F.

fols. 39v–42: Capriccio di G.F.

fols. 60v–64: Canzon di Girolamo Frescobaldi.

fol. 64v: Verso di G.F.

This manuscript, the "Libro di fra Gioseffo da Ravenna. Opere di diversi Autori, di / Girolamo Frescobaldi, d'Ercol Pasquino, Cesare Argentini, Incert' Autore," was probably compiled in the later 1620s or 1630s. In addition to the unpublished works attributed to Frescobaldi, it also contains three works from *Toccate* I, two from the *Capricci,* and one from *Toccate* II.

Literature: Silbiger, pp. 111–112, 154, 159–160.

Modern edition: Shindle, II, 17–28; III, 6.

Rome, Biblioteca Apostolica Vaticana, Ms. Chigi Q.IV.24

fols. 51–52: Canzona D. Fr.

fols. 52v–54: Fuga D. Fr.

fols. 54v–56: Tocata di G . . . (?)

In Silbiger's view there is nothing to militate against the presence of authentic unprinted works of Frescobaldi in these manuscripts, which apparently come from the Chigi circle in Rome ca. 1630–1650, except the works themselves, which he describes as "simpler and more predictable" than the printed works. He also notes that the designation "fuga" does not occur in any uncontestably authentic work of Frescobaldi.

Literature: Silbiger, pp. 116–123, 155, 160–164; Harry B. Lincoln, "I manoscritti chigiani di musica organo-cembalistica della Biblioteca Apostolica Vaticana," *L'Organo* 5 (1967), 63–82; this and Lincoln's edition of works from the Chigi manuscripts are to be used with caution, as they contain errors and inconsistencies.

Rome, Biblioteca Apostolica Vaticana, Ms. Chigi Q.IV.25: "Sonate d'Intauolatura del Sig. Girolamo Frescobaldi"

fols. 1–5: Partita P.a sopra l'aria di Fiorenza (3 partite)
fols. 5v–8v: Toccata Per organo (with pedal)
fols. 8v–12v: Canzona che segue alla Toccata
fols. 13–14: Toccata per organo ("Capriccio sopra Vestiva i Colli" crossed out)
fols. 14v–18v: (untitled: second half of preceding)
fols. 19–23v: Capriccio
fols. 24–30v: Capriccio Fatto sopra il Cucchù
fols. 31–32: Toccata Per organo con Pedali.
fols. 32–34v: Canzona, doppo la Toccata.
fols. 35–36v: Toccata
fols. 37–40: Toccata per organo.
fols. 40v–42v: Canzona.
fols. 42v–45: Recercare.
fols. 45v–47v: Recercare cromatico.
fols. 48–50: blank.
fols. 51–55v: Toccata P.
fols. 56–62v: Toccata 2.a
fols. 63–69v: Toccata 3.a

The inscription on the flyleaf ascribing the entire collection to Frescobaldi is written in a hand different from that of the text (although apparently roughly contemporary with it). Silbiger suggests that the attribution may be based on the opening Fiorenza, a tune often connected with Frescobaldi even though there is no demonstrably authentic setting of it by him. The three pedal toccatas differ in important respects from Girolamo's printed works in this genre, and the pairing of free and contrapuntal works characteristic of this manuscript occurs in printed collections only in Grassi's edition of the *Canzoni* and the two toccata/ricercar pairs in the *Fiori.* The correction of "Vestiva" is accurate, since Silbiger shows that material from Palestrina's madrigal in fact occurs in the following capriccio. Gustav Leonhardt has suggested that the third of the numbered toccatas, which are notably superior to the other contents of the volume, may be the work of Froberger.

Literature: Silbiger, pp. 66, 123–125, 155, 160–164; Gustav Leonhardt, "Johann Jacob Froberger and His Music," *L'Organo* 6 (1968), 15–40; Lincoln, "Manoscritti," p. 69.

Modern editions: P. O. Santini, ed., G. *Frescobaldi: XIV composizioni inedite* (Rome: Psalterium, 1940; rev. ed. 1955); Shindle, I, 1–33; II, 1–16; III, 6–9; works by composers other than Frescobaldi, ed. Harry B. Lincoln, *Corpus of Early Keyboard Music* 32 (3 vols., 1968).

Rome, Biblioteca Apostolica Vaticana, Ms. Chigi Q.IV.27

fols. 63v–64: Corrente (= *Toccate* II, Corrente prima)

fol. 64v: Gagliarda del Frescobaldi (= ibid., Gagliarda Seconda)

fols. 70v–74v: Toc. del Signor Gierolamo Frescobaldi

fols. 75–76: Corrente del Signor Ger. F. B.

fols. 76v–77: Corrente (= *Toccate* II, Corrente Sesta)

fols. 77v–78: Corrente (= ibid., Corrente Quarta)

fols. 78v–79: [Corrente] (= ibid., Corrente Prima)

Folios 1–61 of this manuscript contain sets of variations in triple meter on a descending tetrachord or in duple meter on a descending scale figure, both with extensive employment of V^5_4 chords. The forty-four sets appear in both major and minor and on every tonic except F- and G-sharp. The sets in triple meter show considerable similarities to other passacagli in Chigi 26 and 28 and to Frescobaldi's *Cento partite*. A striking concordance with a *passacaille* of D'Anglebert suggests Italo-French influence, perhaps by way of Luigi Rossi or Froberger. Silbiger notes that copies of printed works by Frescobaldi in this manuscript are not always exact. The toccata on fol. 70v quotes two passages from *Toccate* I/5: mm. 26–28 (= mm. 6–12 of the manuscript) and m. 7 (= mm. 19–20).

Literature: Silbiger, pp. 65–66, 125–127, 155, 160–164; Lincoln, pp. 70–72.

Modern edition: Shindle, I, 34–38; III, 49–50.

Rome, Biblioteca Apostolica Vaticana, Ms. Chigi Q.VIII.205–206

fols. 54–58: Toccada Prima del 2° Libro di Intavolatura di Geronimo Frescobaldi

fols. 58v–61v: Quinta Toccata sopra i Pedali per l'Organo e senza del 2° libro di G.F.

fols. 62–67v: Toccata 6a per l'Organo sopra i Pedali e senza del 2do Libro d'Intavolatura di G.F.

fols. 70–72v: Di Frescobaldi Toccata

fols. 83–84v: Rugier del Signor Frescobaldi

fols. 95–98v: Pasagalli

fols. 103–104v: mm. 43 to the end of *Toccate* II/9

fols. 105–106: Hinno per le Domeniche di tutto l'anno. Lucis creator optime G.F.B.

fols. 106–107: Hinno della Pentecoste. Veni Creator Spiritus.

fols. 107–108v: Hinno delli Apostoli. G.F.B.

fols. 108v–110: Hinno di Natale G.F.B.

This is a miscellany made up of the items otherwise unplaceable in the systematization of the Chigi manuscripts. The Pasagalli contain quotations from the *Cento partite* (variations 1–3, 5–6, and the first Corrente of the manuscript version = 1–4, 27, 21 of the printed text).

Literature: Silbiger, pp. 132–134, 155; Lincoln, pp. 75–80.

Modern edition: Shindle, I, 38–44; III, 1–5, 10–18.

Rome, Biblioteca Apostolica Vaticana, Ms. Vat. mus. 569

fol. 1: Virginius Mutius sonabat / Año Dñi / 1661

fol. 2: Liber Virginij Mutij J.V.D. Discipulij D. Bonauenturę Mini, et Fabritij Fontanę respectiuè 1663

fols. 18–19v: the first Balletto from *Toccate* I, *Aggiunta,* with a variation by Gio. Batta Ferrini (see Ex. 15.32).

Literature: Silbiger, pp. 51, 135–139, who lists two concordances with the *Aggiunta*.

Rome, Biblioteca Doria-Pamphilj, Ms. 250 B

fol. 33v: Corrente del Sig. Girolamo (= Chigi 205–206, fol. 137v, Ravenna 545, fol. 89, "d'Hercol Pasquini")

Literature: Silbiger, pp. 114, 154.

Modern edition: Shindle, *Pasquini,* p. 28.

Rome, Conservatorio di Musica Santa Cecilia, Ms. A/400

fol. 74v: Primo ballo di Fresco baldi

fol. 75: Corrente del ballo del medesimo

fol. 75v: Secondo Ballo di Fresco baldi

fol. 76: Corrente del ballo del medesimo

These four works are accurate copies from the 1637 *Aggiunta.* Folios 40–60 of this manuscript, apparently written some time after 1715, contain French keyboard music; on fols. 61–74 are works attributed to Ercole Pasquini and Alessandro Stradella.

Literature: Silbiger, pp. 51, 140–141.

Turin, Biblioteca Nazionale, Raccolte Giordano, Foà: intavolature

Volume I (Giordano I)

fols. 33–34v: Toccata del Sig^r Frescobaldi.

fols. 35–36v: Toccata del Frescobaldi.

fols. 38v–39v: Toccata del Sig.[r] Frescobaldi.
fols. 39v–41: Toccata F. Baldi.
fols. 41–42v: Toccata del Sig.[r] Frescobaldi.
fols. 42v–44: Toccata F[o] Baldi.
fols. 44–46: Toccata di Frescobaldi.
fols. 46–46v: Toccata del Sig.[r] Frescobaldi
fols. 46v–47v: Toccata per l'Organo col contra basso overo Pedale. di Frescobaldi.
fols. 47v–128 include the toccatas from the *Fiori musicali* and *Toccate* I and II, with the indication (fol. 128), "Finis del libro di Frescobal:".

These sixteen volumes of Italian keyboard music were transcribed in New German keyboard tablature between 1637 and 1640. The size and sumptuousness of the collection show that, unlike Italian keyboard manuscripts, it was copied as a comprehensive anthology for a wealthy patron, probably a member of the Fugger family. The collection is organized rigidly by genre—so much so that imitative sections are removed from toccatas and placed with other genres in imitative texture.

Volume III (Giordano III, 1639)
fols. 98v–114 present the hymns and Magnificat verses from *Toccate* II and the masses for Sunday and the Apostles from the *Fiori.*

Volume VI (Giordano VI, 1637)
fols. 132v–141v are copies of the six ricercars from the *Fiori*.

Volume IX (Foà II, 1639)
fols. 104v–162v contain copies of the ricercars and capriccios from the 1626 collection. Of the ricercars, the first, fifth, seventh, and ninth are transposed down a fourth. The first three capriccios and the seventh, ninth, and tenth are similarly transposed. The contents of this volume are also included in the manuscript, Berlin, Deutsche Staatsbibliothek (deposited in the University Library at Tübingen), Mus. Ms. 40 615.

Volume X (Foà I, 1639)
fols. 1–10 contain the five canzonas of the 1626 *Recercari.*

Volume XIV (Foà VI, 1640)
fols. 31–31v: Corrente di G.F.
fols. 31v–32: Corrente di G.F.
fols. 32–32v: Corrente di G.F.
fols. 34v–39 present the correnti from *Toccate* I and II and the fifth variation (Corrente) from La Frescobalda.

Volume XV (Foà VII, 1639)
fols. 77–79 are copies of the five gagliarde of *Toccate* II.

Volume XVI (Foà VIII, 1640)

fols. 102v–132 transmit *partite* from *Toccate* I and II (Romanesca, Monica—the second variation omitted, Ruggiero, Folia, Passacagli, and Ciaccona), the Girolmeta and Bergamasca from the *Fiori,* and the Frescobalda from *Toccate* II.

Literature: Oscar Mischiati, "L'intavolatura d'organo tedesca della Biblioteca Nazionale di Torino," *L'Organo* 4 (1963), 1–154.

Modern editions: the nine toccatas of Volume I are printed in Shindle, I, 42–74, and the correnti of Volume XIV in III, 51–56. The toccatas have also been edited by Sandro Dalla Libera, *Girolamo Frescobaldi: Nove toccate inedite* (Brescia: L'Organo, 1962).

Venice, Biblioteca Nazionale Marciana, Cod. It. IV-1299 (Ms. 11068)

This manuscript bears the note "Acquisto Canal 1928" and is titled "Canzoni, Capricci, Toccate, Ricercate, ed altre Suonate per l'Organo, e / Clavicembalo del celebre Sig.r Geronimo Fresco Baldi / Organista della Pontifizia Basilica / di S. Pietro in Vaticano di Roma. / ridotte ad una moderna, e facile lettura da Bernardo Mantuaner." on f. [i] and "Suonate / Girolamo / Fresco Baldi / II" on the cover. The "modern, and easy reading" of the title describes the transcription into modern keyboard notation and the reduction of some note values. The collection contains 116 pieces comprising virtually the entire contents of *Toccate* I with its Aggiunta, *Toccate* II, the *Capricci,* and the *Fiori musicali.* These are presented in no particular order and are interspersed with unprinted works. Since the handwriting points to a nineteenth-century origin for the manuscript, its authority is debatable, to say the least.

p. 1 No. 1. Canzon (*Fiori,* Domenica, post il comune)
p. 3 No. 2. Canzon (*Fiori,* Domenica, dopo la pistola)
p. 4 No. 3. Capriccio Pastorale (Aggiunta)
p. 6 No. 4. Passacaglio (Cento Partite, Aggiunta)
p. 8 No. 5. Corrente (*Toccate* I)
p. 9 No. 6. Gagliarda
p. 9 No. 7. Spagnoletta
p. 10 No. 8. Ballo del Gran Duca "G. Fresco Baldi"
p. 11 No. 9. Toccata (I/2)
p. 14 No. 10. Ricercata (*Recercari,* 8)
p. 15 No. 11. Canzon (*Fiori,* Apostoli, dopo la pistola)
p. 17 No. 12. Capriccio sopra il Cucco (*Capricci*)
p. 20 No. 13. Corrente
p. 21 No. 14. Spagnoletta
p. 21 No. 15. Follia
p. 22 No. 16. Ciaccona

p. 22 No. 17. Gagliarda
p. 23 No. 18. Toccata (I/4)
p. 25 No. 19. Aria detta Fresco Balda (*Toccate* I)
p. 27 No. 20. Canzon (*Toccate* II/1)
p. 30 No. 21. Corrente
p. 30 No. 22. Balletto (Aggiunta)
p. 31 No. 23. Passacaglio (Aggiunta)
p. 32 No. 24. Toccata
p. 32 No. 25. Capriccio sopra l'Aria di Ruggiero (*Capricci*)
p. 36 No. 26. Altro Capriccio sopra Ruggiero
p. 38 No. 27. Canzon del sesto Tuono (*Toccate* II/4)
p. 40 No. 28. Toccata
p. 41 No. 29. Corrente
p. 42 No. 30. Cappriccio sopra la Battaglia (Aggiunta)
p. 43 No. 31. Balletto (Aggiunta)
p. 44 No. 32. Corrente del Balletto (ibid.)
p. 44 No. 33. Canzon del secondo Tuono (*Recercari,* 3)
p. 47 No. 34. Corrente—La Spensierata
p. 47 No. 35. Toccata
p. 48 No. 36. Canzon
p. 50 No. 37. Toccata (I/3)
p. 51 No. 38. Balletto (Aggiunta)
p. 51 No. 39. Corrente del Balletto (ibid.)
p. 52 No. 40. Canzon (*Toccate* I/5)
p. 53 No. 41. Corrente (*Cento partite*)
p. 54 No. 42. Toccata (II/1)
p. 56 No. 43. Balletto (Aggiunta, Balletto and Ciaccona)
p. 56 No. 44. Ciaconna (ibid.)
p. 57 No. 45. Canzon (*Toccate* II/6)
p. 58 No. 46. Corrente (Aggiunta, Corrente and Ciacona)
p. 59 No. 47. Ciaccona (ibid.)
p. 59 No. 48. Toccata
p. 61 No. 49. Capriccio sopra la Bergamasca
p. 62 No. 50. Toccata dell'ottavo Tuono
p. 63 No. 51. Canzon
p. 64 No. 52. Passacaglio (Aggiunta)
p. 65 No. 53. Corrente
p. 65 No. 54. Toccata (I/7)
p. 68 No. 55. Canzon del sesto Tuono (*Capricci,* 4a)
p. 70 No. 56. Toccata (*Fiori,* Madonna)
p. 71 No. 57. Capriccio
p. 72 No. 58. Canzon (*Capricci,* 2a)
p. 74 No. 59. Capriccio sopra la Spagnoletta (*Capricci*)

p. 79 No. 60. Toccata (I/9)
p. 81 No. 61. Corrente
p. 82 No. 62. Capriccio di durezze (*Capricci*)
p. 84 No. 63. Passaggio
p. 84 No. 64. Ricercata (*Ricercari,* 3)
p. 87 No. 65. Corrente (Aggiunta, 4a)
p. 88 No. 66. Ballo Todesco
p. 88 No. 67. Toccata (*Fiori,* Domenica)
p. 89 No. 68. Capriccio sopra la Sol, fâ, re, mi (*Capricci*)
p. 93 No. 69. Ricercata con quattro soggetti (*Ricercari,* 9)
p. 94 No. 70. Toccata (*Fiori,* Madonna, avanti il ricercar)
p. 95 No. 71. Capriccio sopra la Girometa (*Fiori*)
p. 98 No. 72. Canzon
p. 99 No. 73. Ricercata (*Recercari,* 5)
p. 102 No. 74. Toccata (*Fiori,* Madonna, levatione)
p. 102 No. 75. Bergamasca (*Fiori*)
p. 106 No. 76. Ricercata (*Recercari,* 2)
p. 108 No. 77. Gagliarda
p. 109 No. 78. Toccata (*Fiori,* Apostoli)
p. 109 No. 79. Volta Francese
p. 110 No. 80. Corrente
p. 111 No. 81. Gagliarda
p. 111 No. 82. Aria di Firenze osia Ballo del Duca
p. 114 No. 83. Toccata (*Fiori,* Apostoli, avanti il ricercar)
p. 114 No. 84. Gagliarda
p. 115 No. 85. Corrente
p. 115 No. 86. Balletto
p. 116 No. 87. Toccata (*Fiori,* Apostoli, levatione)
p. 117 No. 88. Gagliarda
p. 117 No. 89. Balletto (Aggiunta)
p. 117 No. 90. Corrente
p. 118 No. 91. Toccata chromatica (*Fiori,* Domenica, levatione)
p. 119 No. 92. Gagliarda
p. 120 No. 93. Balletto
p. 121 No. 94. Corrente (Aggiunta)
p. 121 No. 95. Ricercata (*Fiori,* Domenica, dopo il Credo)
p. 123 No. 96. Gagliarda
p. 123 No. 97. Corrente (= No. 80)
p. 124 No. 98. Ricercata cromatica (*Fiori,* Apostoli, post il Credo)
p. 126 No. 99. Gagliarda
p. 126 No. 100. Corrente
p. 127 No. 101. Ricercata (*Fiori,* Apostoli, altro)
p. 129 No. 102. Gagliarda

p. 130 No. 103. Corrente
p. 130 No. 104. Toccata (I/10)
p. 133 No. 105. Corrente
p. 133 No. 106. Ricercata con obbligo del Basso (*Fiori,* Apostoli)
p. 135 No. 107. Canzon del Quarto Tuono (*Fiori,* Apostoli)
p. 137 No. 108. Corrente
p. 137 No. 109. Toccata (II/2)
p. 139 No. 110. Ricercata (*Fiori,* Madonna, dopo il Credo)
p. 140 No. 111. Canzon (*Fiori,* Madonna, dopo la pistola)
p. 142 No. 112. Corrente
p. 142 No. 113. Toccata (II/3)
p. 145 No. 114. Ricercata (*Fiori,* Madonna, obligo di cantare)
p. 147 No. 115. Toccata
p. 147 No. 116. Corrente
p. 148 No. 117. Balletto
p. 149 No. 118. Toccata (II/4)
p. 151 No. 119. Kyrie de Dominica (*Fiori*)
p. 151 No. 120. Kirie (*Fiori,* Domenica, as are the following through No. 130)
p. 152 No. 121. Christe
p. 152 No. 122. Christe alio modo
p. 153 No. 123. Christe alio modo
p. 153 No. 124. Christe alio modo
p. 153 No. 125. Kirie
p. 154 No. 126. Kirie alio modo
p. 154 No. 127. Kirie alio modo
p. 155 No. 128. Kirie alio modo
p. 156 No. 129. Kyrie alio modo
p. 156 No. 130. Kirie alio modo
p. 156 No. 131. Kirie degli Appostoli (*Fiori,* Apostoli, through No. 138)
p. 157 No. 132. Kirie
p. 157 No. 133. Kirie
p. 158 No. 134. Christe
p. 158 No. 135. Christe
p. 159 No. 136. Kirie
p. 159 No. 137. Kirie
p. 160 No. 138. Kirie
p. 160 No. 139. Kirie della Madonna (through No. 143)
p. 161 No. 140. Kirie
p. 161 No. 141. Christe
p. 162 No. 142. Christe
p. 162 No. 143. Kirie
p. 162 [Kyrie]

p. 163 No. 144. Versetto del Pm̄o Tuono
p. 163 No. 145. Versetto del 2do Tuono
p. 163 No. 146. del 3z̄o Tuono
p. 163 No. 147. 4t̄o Tuono
p. 164 No. 148. 5.to Tuono
p. 164 No. 149. del 6to Tuono
p. 164 No. 150. del 8vo Tuono
p. 165 No. 151. del Pm̄o Tuono
p. 165 No. 152. Inno della Domenica (*Toccate* II, through No. 158)
p. 166 No. 153. Inno degli Apostoli
p. 167 No. 154. Inno de' Confessori
p. 169 No. 155. Inno Ave Maris Stella
p. 170 No. 156. Magnificat del Pm̃o Tuono
p. 171 No. 157. Magnificat del 2do Tuono
p. 172 No. 158. Magnificat del Sesto Tuono
p. 174 No. 159. Corrente
p. 174 No. 160. Corrente
Fine delle Suonate Fresco Baldi
p. 175 Avvertimenti from the second version of *Toccate* I and an index of some items from the *Fiori musicali.*

Literature: Silbiger, pp. 144–145, 164–165.

Venice, Biblioteca Nazionale Marciana, Cod. It. IV–1727 (Ms. 11425)

Folios 1–16v contain copies of the toccatas of *Toccate* I with the end of I/9 and mm. 1–4 of I/10 missing; fols. 17–31 contain the toccatas and the intabulation of *Toccate* II, with the opening ornaments omitted in II/11. The canzonas from *Toccate* II are copied on fols. 31–36v, the hymns and Magnificats on fols. 36v–40v, minus the first verset in the Magnificat Secundi Toni. The manuscript ends with five variation sets from *Toccate* I: Aria detta Balletto, the Romanesca, Monica, Ruggiero, and Follia. Another hand has added an anonymous Ballo di Mantova on fols. 51–52. The manuscript is marked "Acquisto Canal 1928" and is dated in the late seventeenth or early eighteenth century, probably of Venetian provenance, by Silbiger; the Marciana catalogue dates it "sec. XVII.°."

Literature: Silbiger, p. 145.

Verona, Biblioteca Capitolare, Cod. MCXXIX

A manuscript containing copies of compositions from the 1626 *Capricci,* the *Fiori,* and the *Canzoni* of 1645 and signed "Copia fatta da me N.L.M. 1703."

Literature: Silbiger, p. 145.

Vicenza, Biblioteca Civica Bertoliana, Mus. Ms. FF 2.7.17.
A manuscript probably copied in the eighteenth century, containing excerpts from the 1615 *Recercari* and the *Fiori musicali.*
Literature: Silbiger, p. 146.

Vienna, Minoritenkonvent, Musikarchiv XIV, 713
p. 113: Fuga *Frescobaldi* (an eight-measure fragment in a hand differing from the main one of the manuscript).
Literature: Friedrich W. Riedel, *Quellenkundliche Beiträge zur Geschichte der Musik für Tasteninstrumente in der zweiten Hälfte des 17. Jahrhunderts* (Kassel: Bärenreiter, 1960), pp. 45–47; Riedel, *Das Musikarchiv im Minoritenkonvent zu Wien* (Kassel, 1963), p. 46.

Vienna, Minoritenkonvent, Musikarchiv XIV, 717–722
C / Varia Praeludia, Toc: / :catae, Fugae, et Versiculi, / ex C♮ dur et C b mol.
D / Varia Praeludia, / Toccatae, Fugae et / Versiculi, ex D♮ dur / et d b mol
E / Varia Praeludia, / Toccatae, Fugae, et Ver: / :siculi, ex E♮ dur et E mol
F / Varia Praelu: / :dia, Toccatae, Fugae, / et Versiculi, ex f.
G / Varia Praeludia, Toccatae, Fugae, et / Versiculi ex G♮ dur et G b mol
B et H / Varia Praeludia, / Toccatae, ex B et H / cum aliqvibus Fugis, et Versiculis
A collection of versets in various keys, belonging to P. Alexander Giessel (1694–1766) but not copied by him. It contains works attributed to Frescobaldi, short versets like those published in *Orgelstücke in den alten Kirchentonarten,* ed. B. Kothe (Cincinnati, 1870, Dr. 444 in the Santini Collection in Münster) and *Organon: Sammlung von Fughetten und Versetten in alten und neuen Tonarten,* ed. Karl Wüstefeld (Augsburg, n.d.).
Literature: Riedel, *Quellenkundliche Beiträge,* p. 90; *Das Musikarchiv,* pp. 73–75.

Vienna, Minoritenkonvent, Musikarchiv XIV 723
fol. 9v: Frescobaldi Preludia omnium Tonorum
A manuscript dated c. 1717.
Literature: Riedel, *Das Musikarchiv,* pp. 75–77.

Vienna, Oesterreichische Nationalbibliothek, Ms. 18491, "Regina Clara Im Hoff anno 1629"
fol. 23: "Couranta Frescobaldi. 57." (*Toccate* II), Corrente prima
Literature: Schierning, p. 111.

II. OTHER INSTRUMENTAL WORKS

1. 1608f: BASSO / CANZONI PER / Sonare Con Ogni / Sorte Di Stromenti / A Quattro, Cinque & Otto / Con il suo Basso generale per l'Organo, /

Nouamente raccolte da diuersi Eccellentissimi / Musici, & date in luce. / LIBRO PRIMO. / Con Privilegio. / [printer's mark] / IN VENETIA / Appresso Alessandro Rauerij. / M.D.CVIII. Q

Nine fascicles in quarto, C.A.T.B.5.6.7.8. Bc. On the verso of the title page, dedication to Conte Scipio Nasica Fantagucci, dated Venice, 20 June 1608. Index on verso of fol. 35:

TAVOLA DELLE CANZONI

De diuersi Eccellentissimi Auttori.

	A Quattro	
Canzon 1	Giovanni Gabrieli	1
Canzon 2	Del ditto	2
Canzon 3	Del ditto	3
Canzon 4	Del ditto	4
Canzon 5	Claudio Merulo da Correggio	5
Canzon 6	Gioseppe Guami	6
Canzon 7	Florentio Maschera	7
Canzon 8	Dei ditto	8
Canzon 9	Constanzo Antegnati	9
Canzon 10	Luzasco Luzaschi	10
Canzon 11	Pietro Lappi	11
Canzon 12	Del ditto	12
Canzon 13	Girolamo Frescobaldo	13
Canzon 14	Capriccio di Gio: Battista Grillo	14
Canzon 15	Del ditto	15
Canzon 16	Del ditto	16
Canzon 17	Gioseppe Guami	17
	A Cinque	
Canzon 18	Claudio Merulo da Correggio	18
Canzon 19	Gioseppe Guami	19
Canzon 20	Costanzo Antegnati	20
Canzon 21	Girolamo Frescobaldo	21
Canzon 22	Bastiano Chilese	22
Canzon 23	Claudio Merulo da Correggio	23
	A Otto	
Canzon 24	Gioseppe Guami	24
Canzon 25	Del ditto	25
Canzon 26	Pietro Lappi	26
Canzon 27	Giovanni Gabrielli	27
Canzon 28	Del ditto	28
Canzon 29	Girolamo Frescobaldo	29
Canzon 30	Orindo Bartolini	30
Canzon 31	Bastiano Chilese	31

Canzon 32	Del ditto	32
Canzon 33	Tiburtio Massaino	33
Canzon 34	Del ditto	34
Canzon 35	Del ditto à 16	35
Canzon 36	Claudio Merulo da Correggio à 5.	36

IL FINE.

RISM 1608[24].

Augsburg, Staats- und Stadtbibliothek (complete); Berlin, Oeffentliche Wissenschaftliche Bibliothek (5. Bc.); Bologna, Civico Museo Bibliografico Musicale (6. 7. 8.); Cesena, Biblioteca Comunale (5.); Frankfurt, Stadt- und Universitätsbibliothek (C.A.T.B.6.7.8.); Helmstadt, Bibliothek des Kantorats zu St. Stephani (C.T.); Lausanne, Collection Cortot [? not in the Chambure Collection; see Sartori vol. 2, 48] (Bc.); Munich, Bayerische Staatsbibliothek (complete); Oxford, Bodleian Library (ex-Coll. Harding) (T.); Rome, Biblioteca del Conservatorio di Santa Cecilia (5.); Wolfenbüttel, Herzog August Bibliothek (C.T.).

Literature: Leland Bartholomew, "Alessandro Rauerij's Collection of 'Canzoni per sonare' " (Ph.D. dissertation, University of Michigan, 1963); John Harper, "The Instrumental Canzonas of Girolamo Frescobaldi: A Comparative Edition and Introductory Study" (Ph.D. dissertation, University of Birmingham, England, 1975), pp. 44–48.

Modern edition: Bartholomew, vol. 2; Harper, pp, 924–967. The three Frescobaldi canzonas were published as *3 Canzoni (1608)* (Musica Rara, vols. 19–21, London, 1970), and the eight-part canzona was also issued in *Zwei doppelchorige Kanzonen zu acht Stimmen* (Consortium, Wilhelmshaven, 1963) and the four-part work in *Venezianische Canzonen zu vier Stimmen* (Antiqua, Mainz, 1958), which are to be preferred to the Musica Rara editions, transcriptions for modern brass instruments.

2. 1628i: IN PARTITVRA / IL PRIMO LIBRO / DELLE CANZONI / A VNA, DVE, TRE, E QVATTRO VOCI. / Per sonare con ogni sorte di Stromenti. / Con dui Toccate in fine, vna per sonare con Spinettina / sola, ouero Liuto, l'altra Spinettina è Violi- / no, ouero Liuto, è Violino. / DEL SIG. GIROLAMO FRESCOBALDI. / ORGANISTA IN S. PIETRO DI ROMA. / DATE IN LVCE DA BARTOLOMEO GRASSI / Organista in S. Maria in Acquirio di Roma. / CON PRIVILEGIO. / [arms of Mons. Bonvisi] / IN ROMA. / Appresso Paolo Masotti. M.DC.XXVIII. / CON LICENZA DE' SVPERIORI.

Folio, 152 pp., pp. 30–31 numbered 28–29.
On p. (3) the dedication to Mons. Girolamo Bonvisi, dated Rome, 1628. On p. (151) "ALLI STVDIOSI DELL'OPERA." and index:

TAVOLA

IN ROMA, Appresso Paolo Masotti. / MDCXXVIII.

RISM F 1869.

Bologna, Civico Museo Bibliografico Musicale; London, British Library (King's Music Library); Lüneburg, Ratsbücherei; Wolfenbüttel, Herzog August Bibliothek.

Literature: Harper, *The Instrumental Canzonas,* pp. 95–96.

Modern editions: Harper, pp. 786–792, 892–909. The last three works are printed in Shindle, III, 57–71; the two for violin and spinettina appear in the series *Diletto Musicale* (Vienna: Doblinger, 1962), 49, ed. Friedrich Cerha.

2a. 1628j: CANTO PRIMO / IL PRIMO LIBRO / DELLE CANZONI / Ad vna, due, trè, e quattro voci. / Accomodate, per sonare ogni sorte / de stromenti. / DI GIROLAMO / FRESCOBALDI, / Organista in S. Pietro di Roma. / [Medici arms] / In Roma, Appresso Gio. Battista Robletti. 1628. / Con Licenza de' Superiori.

Five part-books in quarto: C. I 55 pp., C. II 31 pp., B. I 39 pp., B. II 39 pp., Basso generale 61 pp. On p. (3) the dedication to Ferdinando II, Grand Duke of Tuscany, undated. Index from the end of the basso continuo (the first four items according to C. I):

TAVOLA, DELLE CANZONI,
della presente Opera.

IL FINE.

RISM F 1868.

Berkeley, University of California (C. I, B. I); Bologna, Civico Museo Bibliografico Musicale (C. I, C. II, B. I, B); Lüneburg, Ratsbücherei (C. I, C. II, B. I, B); Pistoia, Archivo del Duomo (B. generale, pp. 9–40); Washington, D.C., Library of Congress (C. I, B. I, B., B. generale); Wroclaw, University Library (C. I, B. I, B., B. generale [the edition listed as 1623e in Sartori's first volume does not exist]).

Literature: Harper, pp. 94–95.

Modern editions: Harper, pp. 361–365, 421–426, 567–575, 685–706, 773–785, 794–891, 910–922. An edition based on the 1628 *partitura* conflated with the part-books of 1628 and 1634 is being issued under the editorship of Bernard Thomas (*The Ensemble Canzonas of Frescobaldi,* London: London Pro Musica Edition, 10 vols., 1975–1977). Other editions of selections from the *Canzoni* include those of Friedrich Cerha (*Diletto Musicale,* Vienna: Doblinger, 1966), vols. 87–89; *Canzoni per sonar* (five canzonas for 2 cantos and bc.), ed. Hans David (Antiqua, Mainz: Schott, 1933), and 6 *Canzoni (1628),* ed. Gustav Leonhardt (Vienna, 1956); these editions also suffer from attempts to provide a synoptic reading of the 1628 and 1634 texts (see Harper, pp. 13–14). For a frankly modern approach with dynamics, phrasing, instrumentation, and so on, see *Girolamo Frescobaldi, musiche strumentali dalle canzoni da sonare 1608 e 1634;* messe in partitura da Riccardo Neilsen (Bologna: Bongiovanni, 1954).

3. 1634: BASSO PER L'ORGANO / CANZONI / DA SONARE / A VNA DVE TRE, ET QVATTRO / Con il Basso Continuo / DI / GIROLAMO FRESCOBALDI / ORGANISTA IN SAN PIETRO DI ROMA / LIBRO PRIMO. / CON PRIVILEGIO. / [arms of Cardinal Desiderio Scaglia] / IN VENETIA, / Appresso Alessandro Vincenti. / MDCXXXIV.

Five part-books in quarto: C. I 49 pp., C. II 41 pp., B. I 32 pp., B. II 44 pp., BASSO PER L'ORGANO 61 pp. On the verso of the title page, the dedication (missing in the B. Per l'Organo) to Desiderio Scaglia, Cardinal of Cremona, dated Venice, 10 January 1635. On the verso of p. 61 the index:

TAVOLA DELLE CANZONI

Canto solo.

Basso Solo.

A due Bassi.

A 2 Canto, e Basso.

Canzon prima.	20
Canzon seconda.	22
Canzon terza.	23
Canzon quarta.	25
Canzon quinta.	26
Canzon sesta.	28

A 2 Canti.

Canzon prima.	30
Canzon seconda.	31
Canzon terza.	32
Canzon quarta.	33

A 3. due Bassi, e Canto.

Canzon prima.	34
Canzon seconda.	53
Canzon terza.	27
Canzon quarta.	38

Due Canti, e Basso.

Canzon prima.	40
Canzon seconda.	41
Canzon terza,	43
Canzon quarta	44
Canzon quinta.	45

A 4. due Canti, e due Bassi.

Canzon prima.	47
Canzon seconda.	48
Canzon terza.	50
Canzon quarta.	52

Canto Alto Tenor, e Basso.

Canzon prima sopra Rugier.	53
Canzon seconda,	54
Canzon terza.	56
Canzon quarta.	57
Canzon quinta.	59
Canzon Sesta.	61

IL FINE.

RISM F 1870.

Bologna, Civico Museo Bibliografico Musicale (complete); Kassel, Landesbibliothek (C. I, Basso per l'Organo); London, Royal College of Music (complete); Wroclaw, University Library (B. I, minus title page and last page).

Literature: Harper, pp. 96–97, 106–113.

Modern editions: Harper, pp. 335–360, 366–389, 396–420, 427–566, 576–684, 707–772. See II.2a.

III. VOCAL WORKS

A. Works with Italian Text

1. 1608: DI GIROLAMO / FRESCO-BALDI / IL PRIMO LIBRO DE / MADRIGALI / A CINQVE VOCI / Nuouamente Composti & dati luce. / CANTO. / IN ANVERSA / Appresso Pietro Phalesio / M DC VIII.

Five part-books: Canto, Alto, Quinto, Tenore, Basso, (ii) plus 21 numbered pages. On the verso of the title page, the dedication to Mons. Guido Bentivoglio, dated Antwerp, 13 June 1608. On the verso of p. 21 the index:

TAVOLA.

AHi bella si	2
Amor ti chiama il mondo	6
Amor mio perche piangi	15
Cor mio chi mi t'inuola	17
Come perder poss'io	21
Da qual sfera	4
Fortunata per me felice aurora	1
Giunto e pur Lidia il mio	11
2. parte. Ecco l'hora	12
3. parte. Lidia ti lasso	13
Lasso io languisco e moro	16
Perche spesso a verder	5
Perche fuggi tra salci	10
Qui dunque oime	19
Se la doglia e'l martire	3
S'a la gelata mia timida lingua	8
S'io miro in te m'vccidi	14
So ch'aueste in lasciarmi	18
Se lontana	20
Tu pur fuggi ancora	7
Vessosissima Filli	9

IL FINE.

RISM F 1852, Vogel 1023.

Oxford, Bodleian Library (C, T, 5., B); Paris, Bibliothèque Nationale (formerly Collection Mme de Chambure) (complete).

Modern edition: *Sei madrigali,* ed. F. Boghen (Florence: Casa Editrice Musicale Italiana, [1920]).

2. 1621[14]: CANTO PRIMO / GHIRLANDETTA / AMOROSA, / Arie, Madrigali, e Sonetti, / Di diuersi Eccellentissimi Autori, / A Vno, à Due, à Tre, & à Quattro, / Poste in luce / DA FABIO COSTANTINI ROMANO / Maestro di Cappella dell'Illustrissima / Città d'Oruieto. / OPERA SETTIMA. LIBRO PRIMO / [arms of Adriano Canali and Caterina Avveduti] / IN ORVIETO, Per Michel'Angelo Fei, & / Rinaldo Ruuli. 1621

   Four part-books: C, C II, B, Bc. On pp. 3–4 of C I, pp. 4–5 of Bc, "CANTO Solo, ouer Tenore. Alla Gloria alli honori" of Frescobaldi. Title of Bc.: "Basso Steso per il Cimbalo, ouero altri Stromenti."

   Vogel Sammlung 1621[1].

   Bologna, Civico Museo Bibliografico Musicale (complete); London, British Library (C I, C II, Bc).

3. 1621[15]: GIARDINO / MVSICALE / DI VARII ECCELLENTI / AVTORI, / DOVE SI CONTENGONO SONETTI, / Arie, & Vilanelle, à vna, e due voci. Per cantare / con il Cimbalo, & altri stromenti simili, con l'alfabeto per la Chitarra Spagnola, in / quelle più a proposito. / Dedicate Al Molt'Illustre, e Reuerendiss. Sig. Il Sig. / PAOLO QVAGLIATI / PRONOTARIO APOSTOLICO, &c. / [printer's mark] / IN ROMA, / Appresso Gio. Battista Robletti. 1621. / Con licenza de' Superiori.

   On pp. 8–10 "O bell'occhi che guerrieri, 1 p., del Sig. Gironimo Frescobaldi"; "Lumi vaghi, ch'amorosi, 2 p."; "Stelle amate, alme pupille, 3 p."

   Vogel Sammlung 1621[2].

   Rome, Cappella Giulia (pp. 5–6, 19–20 missing).

4. 1622[10]: CANTO PRIMO. / L'AVRATA CINTIA / ARMONICA, / ARIE, MADRIGALI, DIALOGHI, E VILLANELLE, / Di diuersi Eccelentissimi Autori, à 1. à 2. à 3. & à 4. / Posta in luce / DA FABIO COSTANTINI ROMANO / *Opera Ottua, Libro Secondo. Con la Partitura* / IN ORVIETO, Per Michel'Angelo Fei, e Rinaldo Ruuli 1622.

   C I, C II, "Basso steso per il Cimbalo, o uero altri Stromenti." On p. 34 (C I), pp 27–28 (C II), p. 11 (Bc): "A 2. Canti. Era l'anima mia" of Frescobaldi.

   Vogel Sammlung 1622[1].
   Bologna, Civico Museo Bibliografico Musicale (C I, C II); London, British Library (complete).

5. 1630: PRIMO LIBRO / D'ARIE MVSICALI / PER CANTARSI / Nel Grauicimbalo, e Tiorba. / A VNA, A DVA, E A TRE VOCI. / Di / GIROLAMO FRESCOBALDI / ORGANISTA / DEL SERENISSIMO / GRAN DVCA / DI TOSCANA. / [Medici arms] / IN FIRENZE Per Gio: Batista Landini. MDCXXX. / Con licenza de' SS. Superiori.

Octavo, 48 pp. On p. 3 the dedication to Ferdinando II, Grand Duke of Tuscany. Imprimatur 25, 27 September 1630 on index, p. 48:

TAVOLA

D'ARIE, E CANZONE DEL PRESENTE LIBRO.

Signor, c'hora frà gli ostri Canto solo 4
  [Sonetto in stile recitativo]
Degnati ò gran Fernando Canto solo 6
  [Canto in stile recitativo]
Ardo, e taccio il mio mal Canto solo 8
  [Canto in stile recitativo]
Doue, doue Signor quieto ricetto Canto solo 11
  [Sonetto spirituale in stile recitativo]
Dopo si lungo error Canto solo 13
  [Canto spirituale]
A piè della gran Croce Canto solo 15
  [Sonetto spirituale. Maddalena alla Croce]
Dunque dourò del puro seruir mio Canto solo 17
  [Aria di Romanesca]
 [seconda parte: O Tradite speranze 17
 Te, te, Amor, te odo hora (terza parte) 18
 Te, te incolpar degg'io (quarta parte) 18]
Se l'onde, ohime, che da quest'occhi Canto solo 19
  [Aria]
 [seconda parte: Cercherò col morir tornar 20
 Se per amar chi tand'odia (terza parte) 21]
Donna siam rei di morte Basso solo 22
  [Sonetto]
Entro naue dorata Canto solo 24
  [Aria]
Troppo sotto due stelle Basso solo 25
  [Aria]
 [Ciò ben prov'io, ch'invan sospiro (seconda parte) 26
 Ed io più l'amo, e mentre gli occhi (terza parte) 27]
Non me negate, ohime Canto solo 28
  [Aria]
Di Licori un guardo solo Canto solo 29
  [Canto]

RISM F 1854.

Vogel 1021

Bologna, Civico Museo Bibliografico Musicale (pp. 13–16 missing); Florence, Biblioteca Nazionale Centrale (presentation copy).

6. 1630: SECONDO LIBRO / D'ARIE MVSICALI / PER CANTARSI / Nel Grauicimbalo, e Tiorba. / A VNA, A DVA, E A TRE VOCI. / DI / GIROLAMO FRESCOBALDI / ORGANISTA / DEL SERENISSIMO / GRAN DVCA / DI TOSCANA. / [Obizzi arms] / IN FIRENZE, / Per Gio: Batista Landini. M.DCXXX. / Con licenza de' Superiori.

Octavo, 40 pp. On p. 3 the dedication to Marchese Roberto Obizi, Cavallerizzo Maggiore to the Grand Duke of Tuscany. On p. 40 the Imprimatur 25, 29 September 1630 and the index:

TAVOLA

D'ARIE, E CANZONE DEL PRESENTE LIBRO.

RISM F 1854.

Vogel 1022.

Bologna, Civico Museo Bibliografico Musicale.

Modern editions: ed. Felice Boghen [Florence, 1933]; Helga Spohr, ed., *Arie Musicali (Florenz 1630), Musikalische Denkmäler* IV (Mainz: Schott, 1960), both volumes; selections ed. Alessandro Peroni (Milan: Ricordi, 1909).

B. Works with Latin Text

1. 1616[1]: BASSVS AD ORGANVM. / SELECTAE CANTIONES / EXCELLENTISSIMORVM / AVCTORVM, / Binis, Ternis, Quaternisq; Vocibus concinendae. / A FABIO CONSTANTINO ROMANO / insignis Basilicae S. Mariae Tras-Tyberim / Musices moderatore, simul collectae. / Liber Primus. Opus Tertium. / [arms of Cardinal Aldobrandini] / ROMAE, Apud Bartholomæum Zannettum MDCXVI.

C I, C II, B, B ad organum. In the dedication Costantini notes his service with Cardinal Aldobrandini: "quia eduntur a me, hoc est ab eo, quem tuo famulorum numero adscriptum." On p. 27 of C I, p. 20 of C. II, p. 23, B, p. 27 Bc, "a 3. Doi Soprani, e Tenore. Peccaui" of Frescobaldi.

Bologna, Civico Museo Bibliografico Musicale (complete); Brussels, Bibliothèque Royale (C I, B, Bc); London, British Library (complete); Lucca, Biblioteca del Seminario (complete); Regensburg, Bischöfliche Zentralbibliothek (C I); Rome, Conservatorio di Santa Cecilia: complete (2 copies).

Literature: Testi, *La musica italiana,* vol. 2, 203–204, who points out that the collection is a virtual anthology of composers connected with the Crocifisso.

Modern editions: *Il nuovo Frescobaldi,* ed. Van Den Eerenbeem (Rome, 1907); ed. Julius Bas (Düsseldorf: Schwann, 1908); ed. E. Maggini, *Musica Sacra* 9 (1964), no. 1, pt. 1.

2. 1618[3]: Scelta di motetti di diversi eccellentissimi autori à 2, à 3, à 4 et à 5 POSTI IN LVCE / DA FABIO COSTANTINI ROMANO / Maestro di Cappella dell'Illustrissima Città d'Oruieto. / Libro Secondo, Opera Quarta. / [printer's mark] / IN ROMA, / Appresso Bartholomeo Zannetti. M.DC.XVIII. / CON LICENZA DE' SVPERIORI.

Octavo, four part-books: C I, C II, B, Bc. On the verso of the title page, the dedication to Conte Cesare Bentivogli, Orvieto, 1 July 1618. On p. 8 of C II "Angelus ad pastores, a 2 Canto e Tenore di Girolamo Frescobaldi."

Lucca, Biblioteca del Seminario (complete); Regensburg, Bischöfliche Zentralbibliothek (C I); Rome, Conservatorio di Santa Cecilia (complete).

Literature: index in Maggini, *Biblioteca . . . Lucca,* pp. 18–19; see Testi, *La musica italiana,* vol. 2, 203.

3. 1621[3]: CANTVS I. / LILIA CAMPI / BINIS, TERNIS, / Quaternisq; vocibus concinnata. / A IO. BAPTISTA ROBLETTO / excerta atque luce donata. / CVM BASSO AD ORGANVM. / [arms of Cardinal Ludovisi] / ROMAE, / Apud Io. Baptistam Roblettum. M.DC.XXI.

Quarto, three part-books: C I, C II, Bc. On p. 21 of C I, pp. 20–21 of C II, p. 14 of Bc, "Ego sum panis vivus" "A 3. Due Soprani, & vn Tenore."

Bologna, Civico Museo Bibliografico Musicale (complete); Regensburg, Bischöfliche Zentralbibliothek (C II).

Modern edition: ed. Enrico Capaccioli, *Musica Sacra* 11 (1966), no. 2, pt. 1.

Again, a typically Roman collection containing works by Quagliati, Giovannelli, Catalani, Anerio, Allegri, Severi, Zoilo, Landi, A. Costantini, Ugolini, Tarditi, and Boschetti.

4. 1625[1]: SACRI AFFETTI, / CON TESTI DA / DIVERSI ECCELEN- / TISSIMI AVTORI, RACCOLTI / DA FRANCESCO SAMMARVCO / ROMANO A 2 A 3. A 4. / è Aggiuntui nel fine le letanie della B.V. / ORGA- [arms of Cardinal Madruzzo] -NO / Apud Lucam Antonium Soldum. / SVPERIORVM PERMISSV. / IN AEdibus sanctus Spiritus in Saxia. Anno Iubbilei. 1625

Quarto, five part-books: C, A, T, B, organo. On p. 15 (C), 13 (A), 12 (T), 20 (Bc) "A 3. due Canti è Tenore Iesu rex admirabilis Gironimo Frescobaldi."

Ancona, Biblioteca Comunale "Benincasa" (B); Bologna, Civico Museo Bibliografico Musicale (complete).

Modern edition: J. Bas (Düsseldorf: Schwann, 1908).

5. 1627: CANTVS / Primus. / LIBER SECVNDVS / DIVERSARVM MODVLATIONVM / Singulis, Binis, Ternis, Quaternisque vocibus. / AVCTORE / HIERONYMO FRESCOBALDO / In Vaticana Principis Apostolorum Basilica / Organista. / [arms of Cardinal Scipione Borghese] / ROMAE, Apud Andream Phaeum. 1627. Superiorum permissu.

Five part-books: C I (27 pp.), C II (lost), T (26 pp.), B (24 pp.), BASSVS ad Organum (31 pp.). On the verso of the title page, the dedication to Cardinal Scipione Borghese, Archpriest of the Vatican, 1 June 1627:

ILL.MO ET REVER.MO PRINCIPI / SCIPIONI / CARD. BVRGHESIO / Vaticanae Basilicae Archipresbytero. / HIERONYMVS FRESCOBALDVS F. / SACRAS modulationes, ad Ecclesiae concen- / tum, & vsum pietatis, à me nuper expressas vul- / gò editurus, non vulgari patrocinio indigebam, / Cardinalis Amplis. imò veriùs, quaesituro illis / lucem, non alius mihi sese obtulit splendor, / quàm tuae amplitudinis clientela. Ergo, vt vel / isto nomine, mihi, rerumque mearum tenuitati / consulerem, ipse fortuna exiguus, & Psaltes iam- / diu Vaticanus, Musici porrò laboris iugiter aman - / tissimus, opus meum nulli alii inscribere debui, / quàm tibi; qui & magnitudine inter Principes / Romanos praecellis, & Templi Pręsul es Vaticani / & liberalium artium (Musices olim tu quidem imprimis) liberalissimus propaga- / tor. Iàm, quod mihi praestandum erat, id exequor, vt oculis, vt auribus tuis / mea subijciantur obsequia, tantae (quod possum) altitudini consonantia. Tu, / quę tuae sunt partes, munere libenter accepto delectari te fines; illudque / in me tuendo perficies, vt qui potentia, & gratia praeluces singulis, benignita- / te praeluceas vniversis. Vale. Calen. Iunij M D C X X V I I. / Imprimatur si videbitur Reuerendiss. P. M. Sac. Pal. Apostolici. / A. Episcopus Hieracen. Vicesgeren. / Imprimatur. Fr. Paulus Palumbara Socius Reuerendiss. P. F. Nicolai Rodulfij Sac. / Pal. Apost. Magist. Ord. Praed.

On p. (32) of the basso continuo the index (+ = incomplete):

TAVOLA.

Aspice Domine,	pag. 3	Canto solo.
Ipsi sum desponsata.	4	Canto solo.
Deus noster refugium, & virtus.	5	Canto solo.
Exultauit cor meum.	6	Tenore solo.
O Iesu mi dulcissime.	7	Tenore solo.
+Vidi speciosam sicut columbam.	8	a due Canti.
+De ore prudentis procedit mel.	9	a due Canti.
+Sicut mater consolatur filios.	10	a due Canti.
Beatus vir qui suffert tentationem	11	a due Canto, e Basso.
O mors illa quam amara.	12	a due Canto, e Basso.
Benedicta tu Mater sanctissima.	13	a due Canto, e Basso.
Viri sancti.	14	a due Tenori.
Tempus est.	15	a due Alto, e Tenore.
Benedicite Deum.	16	a due Tenori.

+Tota pulchra es amica mea.	17	a due Canto, e Tenore.
Decantabat populus Israel.	18	a due Canto, e Tenore.
Exurge Domine.	19	a due Bassi.
Reminiscere	20	a due Bassi.
+O bone Iesu	21	a due Canto, e Tenore.
+O sacrum Conuiuium.	22	a tre due Canti, e Tenore.
+Vox dilecti mei pulsantis.	23	a tre due Canti, e Tenore. Prima Pars.
Quam pulchra es, & speciosa Virgo.	24	a tre due Canti, e Tenore. Secunda pars.
+Sic amantem diligite	26	a tre Alto, e due Tenori.
+Ego flos Campi.	25	a tre due Canti, e Basso.
+Iesu Rex admirabilis.	26	a tre due Canti, e Tenore.
+Exaudi nos Deus	25	a tre Alto, Tenore, e Basso.
+Ego clamaui.	27	a quattro Canto, Alto, Tenore, e Basso.
+Ciuitas Hierusalem noli flere.	28	a quattro Canto, Alto, e due Tenori.
+Ego sum qui sum.	29	a quattro Canto, Alto, Tenore, e Basso.
+Corona aurea super caput eius.	29	a quattro Canto, Alto, Tenore, e Basso.
+Iesu flos mater Virginis.	30	a quattro Canto, Alto, Tenore, e Basso.
+Aue Virgo gloriosa.	30	a quattro Canto, Alto, Tenore, e Basso.

RISM F 1853.

London, British Library (C I, T, B, Bassus ad organum).

6. Rome, Basilica of San Giovanni in Laterno, musical archive (Archivo Generale del Vicariato), Mazzo XI no. 8. Nine part-books: C, A, T, B, P.o Choro; C, A, T, B, 2° Choro, Organo. On p. (2) the index:

Diversorum Autorum
Missae Quinque
a 8.

Missa sopra l'aria della Monaca	car. 1.
Missa sopra l'aria di Fiorenza	car. 5.

Missa primi Toni	car. 9.
Missa Portae nitent margaritis	car. 13.
Missa a 8.	car. 18.

Casimiri's ascription of the first two masses in this collection to Frescobaldi is based on the notation "G. F.di" at the beginning of the organ part for the first mass; since the second is in the same hand and forms part of the same fascicle, he further hypothesized that it was also to be attributed to Frescobaldi.

Literature: Raffaele Casimiri, "Girolamo Frescobaldi autore di opere vocali sconosciute ad otto voci," *Note d'Archivio* 10 (1933), 1–31; Oscar Mischiati and Luigi Ferdinando Tagliavini, eds., *Girolamo Frescobaldi: Due Messe.*

Modern edition: Mischiati and Tagliavini, *Due Messe.*

7. Bologna, Civico Museo Bibliografico Musicale, Ms. Q 43, fols. 7–10: "Feriae. V. in Coena *Domi*ni Lectio iii. S.r Frescobaldi. Jod Manu*m* suam" for C, Bc. Other Lamentation settings in the manuscript include works by Carissimi, Marazzoli, Gratiani, and Foggia—Roman *maestri di cappella* and organists of the 1630s—and the settings may have been performed at S. Maria in Vallicella.

   Literature: Hans Joachim Marx, "Carlo Rainaldi 'Architetto del Popolo Romano'," *Rivista Italiana di Musicologia* 4 (1969), 48–76; Marx, "Monodische Lamentationen des Seicento," *Archiv für Musikwissenschaft* 28 (1971), 1–23.

8. Bologna, Civico Museo Bibliografico Musicale, ms. Z 259
   Ps. 30, vs. 1–6, "In Te Domine Speravi" for two four-part choruses. This is a modern copy of the manuscript owned by Haberl, who considered it an autograph, a judgment disputed by Benvenuti.

   Literature: Haberl, "Girolamo Frescobaldi," p. 148; G. Benvenuti, "Frescobaldiana," *Bollettino Bibliografico Musicale* 6 (1931), n. 2, pp. 16–36, n. 3, pp. 15–34.

   Modern edition: ed. Ettore Ravegnani (Padua: Zanibon, 1938).

IV. DOUBTFUL, LOST, AND SPURIOUS WORKS

1629^5: ALTO / QVARTA / RACCOLTA / DE SACRI CANTI / A VNA, DVE, TRE, ET QVATTRO VOCI / Con il Basso per l'Organo. / De Diuersi Eccellentissimi Autori. / FATTA / DA DON LORENZO CALVI / Musico nella Cathedrale di Pauia. / Nouamente composta, & data in luce. / CON

PRIVILEGIO. / [printer's mark] / IN VENETIA, / Appresso Alessandro Vincenti. 1629.

Five part-books: C, A, T, B, Basso per l'Organo. Dedication (Venice, 28 September 1629) to D. Francesco Lazari, Canon of Broni: "questi Musicali Concerti, raccolti da me da segnalati Autori del secolo nostro (mercè del loro fauore)." Basso per l'Organo, verso of p. 65:

TAVOLA.

A VOCE SOLA

A DVE VOCI.

Naples, Biblioteca Oratoriana dei Filippini (4 vols); Oxford, Christ Church (complete); Piacenza, Archivo del Duomo (complete).

The ascription of the motet "O vere digna Hostia" to Frescobaldi is conjectural but is supported by the fact that one other composer in the collection identified by initials (O. B.) might also be a Roman composer, Orazio Benevoli.

The *Nova Instructio* of Bertoldo Spiridio (1669–1683) includes an unidentified Balletto 3 attributed to Frescobaldi and a version of the Cento Partite.

The keyboard manuscripts in the possession of Domenico Frescobaldi and the "many Madrigals and innumerable Church works, which circulate in manuscript" mentioned by Superbi as early as 1620 have disappeared. Among these may have been the "Magnificat a 4 Chori del 2.do tono" in the 1655 inventory of Schloss Ambras and the motets *Misericordias Domini* à 18 and *Plaudite Jubilate Deo* à 12 mentioned by Padre Martini (see the preface to the edition of III.B.6). Frescobaldi's first book of *Diversarum Modulationum*, probably published shortly before the second book of 1627, is his only known lost printed collection. A letter to Padre Martini from Girolamo Chiti (2 December 1746) mentions a collection of solfeggi including examples by Frescobaldi, and a letter from Mauro Magnani (22 January 1782) announces the dispatch of a manuscript containing psalms and hymns with Girolamo's name on the first blank page (see Anne Schnoebelen, *Padre Martini's Collection of Letters in the Civico Museo Bibliografico Musicale in Bologna*, New York: Pendragon Press, 1979, items 1277 and 2837). François Roberday claimed to have included a work by Frescobaldi in his *Fugues, et caprices* of 1660. Girolamo is credited by Bennati with the unlikely authorship of *Trattati sulla tonalità*.

In his reconstruction of the Franzini catalogue, Othmar Wesseley lists prints of the 1624 *Capricci*, the part-book edition of the 1628 *Canzoni*, *Toccate* II (1627), the *Liber Secundus Diversarum Modulationum* (1627), the 1615 *Recercari*, *Toccate* I (1615), the 1634 *Canzoni*, the 1626 *Capricci et recercari*, the *Fiori musicali*, and two unknown volumes, identified as "Sonate da Camera" and "Arie, Toccate, Ricercarj per l'organo" ("Der Indice der Firma Franzini in Rom," pp. 467–468). The catalogue by C. Gotwald of the Staats- und Stadtbibliothek in Augsburg mentions an *exemplum* by Frescobaldi in a mathematical/musical manuscript of 1649 (in 4° cod. 185).

The organ versets attributed to Frescobaldi in South German manuscripts are probably spurious, as is a vocal work ascribed to him in the manuscript Biblioteca Apostolica Vaticana, Barb. lat. 4156, fols. 355–362v. The pages have been cropped for binding, and under the remnant of the original composer's name (which seems to have begun with "Cav."), "baldi" has been added in another hand and different ink.

Ironically, Frescobaldi is most often represented to the general public by two blatantly spurious works, a toccata for violoncello and piano (also arranged for orchestra and for band), probably concocted by Gaspar Cassadó, and a keyboard fugue in g minor. In the second volume of his *Practical Harmony* (1802) Muzio Clementi printed eight pieces "by the celebrated GIROLAMO FRESCOBALDI" (pp. 138–157). Nos. 1 (*Toccate* II, Canzona I); 2 (*Toccate* II, Canzona III); 6 (*Toccate* II, Canzona IV); 7 (*Toccate* I, Corrente II); and 8 (*Toccate* II/8) are all authentic. As nos. 3–5 Clementi printed without acknowledgment the canzonas 8, 7, and 11 of Gottlieb Muffat as found in a set of nineteen canzonas whose earliest source is a manuscript copy by Muffat's friend Giessel ca. 1733 (Vienna, Minoritenkonvent XIV 172), although Clementi's immediate source seems to have been a later copy, Minoritenkonvent B 15780, where the three canzonas are interspersed among other works of Muffat. (See Mischiati and Tagliavini, preface to the edition of III.B.6; G. Benvenuti, "Notarella circa tre fughe attribuite al Frescobaldi," *Rivista Italiana di Musicologia* 27 (1920), 133–138; and Susan Wollenberg, "A Note on Three Fugues Attributed to Frescobaldi," *Musical Times* 116 (1975), 133–135.)

Frescobaldi's music appeared in Hawkins' *General History of the Science and Practice of Music* (1776), Clementi's *Practical Harmony* (1802), and from then on in a variety of collections: for a list of these see Alberto Basso, "Repertorio generale dei 'Monumenta Musicae'," *Rivista Italiana di Musicologia* 6 (1971), 3–135.

Notes

1. Ferrara

1. The principal sources of materials concerning Frescobaldi's family and his birth are F. X. Haberl, "Hieronymus Frescobaldi: Darstellung seines Lebensganges und Schaffens, auf Grund archivalischer und bibliographischer Dokumente," *Kirchenmusikalisches Jahrbuch* 2 (1887), 67–82, and Haberl, "Girolamo Frescobaldi: esposizione della sua vita e delle sue creazioni a base di documenti bibliografici ed archivistici," in *Ferrara a Gerolamo Frescobaldi nel terzo centenario della sua prima pubblicazione,* ed. Nando Bennati (Ferrara, 1908), pp. 133–155, in which a facsimile of Girolamo's baptismal act appears on p. 134: "Adi 15 7bre . . . Girolimo Alissandro di ms filippo frescobaldo cp̄ ms. pier' Jac.mo bianchetta com m.a Malgarita di paolj." The date has been variously read as 9 September (Haberl), 13 (Bennati), and 15 (Cametti, Casimiri); the latter was selected by the most recent writer, Anthony Newcomb, in his article "Girolamo Frescobaldi," *The New Grove Dictionary of Music and Musicians,* ed. Stanley Sadie (London: Macmillan, 1980), 20 vols., vol. 6, 824–835. Filippo Frescobaldi's second wife was Caterina Bianchetti, who became the mother of Girolamo's half-sister, Vittoria, and half-brother, the Cistercian monk Cesare of San Bartolomeo. (Nando Bennati, "Notizie inedite intorno alla famiglia di Gerolamo Frescobaldi e alla sua casa in Ferrara," *Ferrara a Gerolamo Frescobaldi,* pp. 37–43, and Margarete Reimann, "Frescobaldi," *Die Musik in Geschichte und Gegenwart* 4 (1955), cols. 912–926.)

2. D. Gaetano Cavallini, *Cenni storici intorno all'arte musicale in Ferrara,* Ferrara, Biblioteca Comunale Ariostea, Ms. Classe I, 695, p. 50, states that Filippo "fu egli pure organista," citing notary acts of 29 January 1592 (notary Antonio Colerino) and 31 August 1615 (notary Curzio Paccaroni) from the ex-monastery of San Guglielmo which refer to Filippo as "organista." See also Alberto Cametti, "Girolamo Frescobaldi in Roma. 1604–1643," *Rivista Musicale Italiana* 15 (1908), 701, n. 1.

3. Antonio Libanori, *Ferrara d'oro imbrunito,* part 3 (Ferrara: Stamperia Camerale, 1674), writes, "Girolamo Frescobaldi, Cittadino Ferrarese, disceso

dalla nobil Casa de Frescobaldi di Fiorenza . . ." (p. 168), and gives as Girolamo's coat-of-arms an inaccurate woodcut of the arms of the Florentine Frescobaldi. Later, however (III, 306), Libanori describes Girolamo's arms as consisting "in due Campi, quello di sopra è d'oro, quello di sotto è fatto a scacchi neri, e d'oro con tre pedine d'oro, che formano un triangolo"—a far cry from the red and gold shield with three silver objects like grappling-hooks borne by the Frescobaldi of Florence. This latter description is confirmed by the seal on a letter of Frescobaldi to the Duke of Mantua (Mantua, Archivio di Stato, Archivio Gonzaga E.xxv.3, busta 1010, 245).

Filippo's standing is indicated by the title "Illustrissimus" applied to him in the notary act of 11 May 1584, by which he acquired from Alessandro Caldori the house located in "la contra delle Petegole dal Cantone della zouecha sino all contra del mascararo," the "casa mezzana" of Girolamo's youth, now number 40 of the present Via Frescobaldi in Ferrara. The Frescobaldi paid an annual lease of four *baiocchi* and eight *danari* to the nuns of San Guglielmo, who owned the freehold. On 16 November 1615 a part of the house was assigned to Giulia Frescobaldi on her marriage to Francesco Rossetti, and on Filippo's death Rossetti purchased the shares of the widow, Caterina, and her daughter, Vittoria (see Bennati, "Notizie inedite," and the ensuing correspondence in "Sulla casa di Girolamo Frescobaldi lettere due dell'Ing. Comm. Eugenio Righini e del dott. Nando Bennati," *Atti della Deputazione Ferrarese di Storia Patria* 24 (1919), 115–129).

Even this minimal amount of family history is subject to complications and confusion, as there existed another Girolamo Frescobaldi in Ferrara, born in 1587 to Frescobaldo Frescobaldi (Raffaele Casimiri, "Tre 'Girolami Frescobaldi' coetanei negli anni 1606–1609," *Note d'Archivio* 14 (1937), 1–10; the "Girolami" are reduced to two, however, by the identification of the author of a letter concerning a certain "angiola" as our Girolamo—see Casimiri, "Girolamo Frescobaldi e un falso autografo," *Note d'Archivio* 19 (1942), 130–131.

4. From a 1575 account by the Venetian Emiliano Manolesso given in Angelo Solerti, *Ferrara e la corte estense nella seconda metà del secolo decimosesto; i discorsi di Annibale Romei* (Città di Castello: S. Lapi, 1900), p. ii (n. 1 of p. i). Unless otherwise noted, all translations are mine. It is impossible to give a detailed bibliography of the immense literature on Renaissance Ferrara. I have relied most heavily for the political history of the period on Agostino Faustini, *Libro delle historie ferraresi* (second part of Gasparo Sardi, *Libro delle historie ferraresi*) (Ferrara, 1646; reprinted Bologna: Forni, 1967); Carlo Olivi, *Annali della Città di Ferrara,* 1790, Ferrara, Biblioteca Comunale Ariostea, Ms. Classe I, 105; Marco Antonio Guarini, *DIARIO di tutte le cose accadute nella Nobilissima Città di Ferrara principiando da tutto l'Anno M.D.LXXX sino à questo di et Anno M.D.LXXXXVIII,* Modena, Biblioteca Estense, Ms. α H.2.16; P. Antolini, *Manoscritti relativi alla storia di Ferrara,* index (Argenta, 1891); and Antonio Frizzi, *Memorie per la storia di Ferrara* (Ferrara, 1847–1848). For the artistic history of the city I have drawn on the

bottomless riches of Solerti; Gustave Gruyer, *L'art ferrarais à l'époque des princes d'Este* (Paris, 1897, 2 vols.); Felton Gibbons, *Dosso and Battista Dossi: Court Painters at Ferrara* (Princeton: Princeton University Press, 1968); *Ferrara,* ed. Renzo Renzi (Bologna, 1969, 2 vols.); Anthony Newcomb, *The Madrigal at Ferrara 1579–1597* (Princeton: Princeton University Press, 1980, 2 vols.); and Glenn Watkins, *Gesualdo: The Man and His Music* (Chapel Hill: University of North Carolina Press, 1973).

5. From the *Relazione* of Orazio della Rena, secretary of the Florentine legation at Ferrara in 1589 (quoted at length in Solerti, *Ferrara,* pp. lviii–lxiv). Della Rena's account of the Ferrarese character is so detailed and succulent (and accords so well with what we know of Girolamo's own personality) that the interested reader should savor it in full.

6. On the *delizie* see Solerti, *Ferrara* , pp. xi–xix, and A. F. Trotti, "Le delizie di Belvedere illustrate," *Atti della Deputazione Ferrarese di Storia Patria* 2 (1889), 1–33.

7. Ercole Bottrigari, *Il desiderio overo, de' concerti di uarij strumenti musicali* (Venice, 1594). Translation by Carol MacClintock, Musicological Studies and Documents 9 (American Institute of Musicology, 1962), 50–52.

8. The list of keyboard instruments is taken from Modena, Archivio di Stato, Archivio Segreto Estense, Archivi per Materie, Musica e Musicisti, busta 3a, filza "instrumenti": "Dimanda fatta da noi Pagliarini per accomodar gli organi é Cembali del s. Duca." The same file also contains an inventory dated 18 December 1600 of the instruments in the Palazzo de' Diamanti and an inventory of harpsichords and organs "di V Altezza," dated 1640.

9. Modena, Archivio di Stato, Archivio Segreto Estense, Archivi per Materie, Musica e Musicisti, busta 4a, "Nota de' libri di musica," 25 January 1625. For an extended discussion of the collection see Newcomb, *The Madrigal,* vol. 1, 213–250.

10. Bottrigari, *Il desiderio,* trans. MacClintock, pp. 52–53.

11. Adriano Cavicchi, preface to Luzzasco Luzzaschi, *Madrigali per cantare e sonare a uno, due e tre soprani* (Brescia, 1965), p. 9. See also Solerti, *Ferrara,* pp. cxxix–cxl, and Newcomb, *The Madrigal,* vol. 1, 7–52.

12. The identification was suggested by Adriano Cavicchi. The performances are described in accounts quoted by Solerti, *Ferrara,* pp. cxxiv–cxxxviii. In summer they lasted from the nineteenth to the twenty-first hour (about half-past four to six in the afternoon), in winter from the first hour of night to past the third hour (approximately six to eight p.m.). On at least one occasion Laura Peverara prolonged the concert for four hours (Solerti, *Ferrara,* p. cxxxviii).

13. Anthony Newcomb, "Girolamo Frescobaldi," *The New Grove Dictionary.*

14. Agostino Superbi, *Apparato degli huomini illustri della città di Ferrara* (Ferrara, 1620), p. 133; what appears as a citation in Haberl's article is in fact a paraphrase.

15. Antonio Libanori, *Ferrara d'oro imbrunito,* 3 vols. (Ferrara, 1665–1674), III, 168–169.

16. From a manuscript Latin poem in praise of Frescobaldi attributed to the Vallombrosan monk and musician Don Gregorio Rasi (1585–1658), Abbot of Vallombrosa 1638–1642 and teacher of Don Onorato Maggi (one of the two musicians with whom Frescobaldi is documented as performing at the Florentine court). For the attribution see D. Torello Sala, *Dizionario storico biografico di scrittori, letterati ed artisti dell'Ordine di Vallombrosa* (Florence, 1929), II, 175–177. The poem is preserved in Florence, Biblioteca Riccardiana, Ms. Moreni 256, pp. 136–138: "Hieronymus Frescobaldus / Chori delicium, / Alter nostri seculi Apollo. / Qui, ut omnium Musicorum gloriam non degeneri imitatione expressit: / ita summa artis praestantia citra livorem superavit. / Cuius ingenij acumen, ac Genij suavitas, / Animum harmonica ratione compositum, atque ad melodiam natum declarant. / Quem xvij aetatis annum vix attingentem / Corde magis, quam chorda / organa miro pulsantem artificio / Urbs audijt, et obstupuit. / Ecquis [*sic*] non stupeat? / Musicis instrumentis sonans humanos affectus, ac voces in illis / metiebatur, et mentiebatur. / Quid suum Thebis Amphionem, aut cur suum / Thracibus Orpheum / invideat Italia? / FRESCOBALDUS UNUS / Quoscumque emunctae [*sic*] naris, vel erecti supercilij viros / Numero ac sonoro concentu allectos / Immobiles ac pene lapideos reddit. / Pulsanti / Charites, et Musae certatim articulos aptare / Suavitatem indere, atque harmoniam digitis / ita videntur instillare / Ut quo numeris omnibus adstrictior / hoc [numeris *canceled*] omnibus numeris absolutior / numerosus pereffluat sonus. / Aeternis Famae clangoribus immortalitate sacrandus. / Eia sui Nepos Franciscae Rasi / Animum erige. / Atque hunc unum, quem ut solem inter stellas / reliquorum omnium praestantissimum / admirantur universi, / imitandum tibi proponas. / Sic enim celeberrimi illius Francisci Rasij Patrui tui, / cuius tibi nomen haud ab re impositum est; / Quem apud Serenissimos Mutinenses Duces Musicae artis principem, / nedum Italia, sed tota prorsus Europa venerata est; / Virtutem, et gloriam consequeris / Sapere ergo aude, incipe / Ac numeros modulosque tuos canoros iucunditas, et suavitas, sed mage / Sanctitas exornet. / D. Gregorius Rasius Abbas Vallumbrosanus de musica olim benemeritus / Et quamquam aetate longaevus, tanti viri tamen discipulus esse non / dedignatur: / Patruus dulcissimo Nepoti / Vovet. [S.]" (I am greatly indebted to MaryAnn Bonino for the communication of this material.)

Rasi's statement that "when [Frescobaldi] had scarcely attained the seventeenth year of his age the City heard him playing the organ with wondrous art" is susceptible of two interpretations. If by "the City" he means Florence (and Florentine writers used the unqualified "la Città" to mean Florence), at any rate it supports Libanori's assertion that the young Girolamo traveled as a performer in Italy. If, on the other hand, Rasi's "Urbs" is used in its Classical meaning, he implies that at barely seventeen (that is, in the fall of 1600) Girolamo played in Rome, to the wonder of the City.

17. Faustini, *Historie,* II, 89.

18. The fullest account of Luzzaschi's life and career is contained in Cavicchi's preface to the *Madrigali;* see also Newcomb, *The Madrigal,* vol. 1, 169, 175. Rore's esteem for Luzzaschi is evident in his gift of the manuscript, now in Milan, Biblioteca Ambrosiana, Ms. A.10.Sup., and a cartella, presented by Luzzaschi to Cardinal Francesco Borromeo in 1606.

19. Bottrigari described the arcicembalo as "a large Clavicembalo . . . with all three harmonic genera and divided into twenty-six diatonic tones with more than 130 strings. It has two keyboards full of semitones, or black keys, double and split." He observed that "there is no skillful master tuner or practical and experienced organist of worth who is not almost terrified at being confronted with such a number of strings, and with the keys separated, as I have said, into two keyboards with the usual black semitones divided in two and others added. Besides, to overcome such difficulties, the player must many times press and hold down with one hand some keys of both keyboards at the same time, and occasionally do this with both hands at once." Nonetheless, the instrument rendered "new harmonies to the ears" and a "new sight for the eyes" when Luzzaschi "touches it delicately in several compositions of music composed by him for this instrument only" (Bottrigari, *Desiderio,* p. 51). Luzzaschi published at least three books of ricercars for four parts; the second of these was issued before 1578 (Cavicchi, preface to the *Madrigali,* p. 10, n. 15; Trabaci, ricercar on the seventh tone with three subjects, *Ricercate,* Naples, 1615; Howard M. Brown, *Instrumental Music Printed before 1600: A Bibliography,* Cambridge, Mass.: Harvard University Press, 1965, $[158?]_4$, p. 359; Padre Martini, *Zibaldone,* Bologna, Civico Museo Bibliografico Musicale H 67, f. 45, n. 64). Neither these nor the "Toccate, Sinfonie, e simili" mentioned by Libanori (*Ferrara d'oro,* III, 199) have survived, but Diruta's *Il Transilvano* (Venice, I, 1593; II, 1609) preserves a toccata and two ricercars of Luzzaschi, and an extended ricercar is included in one of the Foà manuscripts. (For more on Luzzaschi's keyboard works see Cavicchi, preface to the *Madrigali,* pp. 8–10, and Anthony Newcomb, "Il modo di far fantasia: An Appreciation of Luzzaschi's Instrumental Style," *Early Music* 7 (1979), 34–38.) Although most of his contemporaries praised Luzzaschi's playing, Lelio Guidiccioni told Pietro della Valle that Luzzaschi "did not know how to make a trill and that he played only by skill [*arte*] the finest subtleties of his counterpoints, without any accompaniment of elegance" (Cavicchi, preface to the *Madrigali,* p. 19, n. 56).

20. Faustini, *Historie,* II, 90.

21. This letter is given in translation in Watkins, *Gesualdo,* pp. 44–66. For the original see Anthony Newcomb, "Carlo Gesualdo and a Musical Correspondence of 1594," *Musical Quarterly* 54 (1968), 414.

22. This evolution is described in detail in Newcomb, *The Madrigal,* vol. 1, 29–52, 113–153. See also Newcomb's "Carlo Gesualdo," and his "Alfonso Fontanelli and the Ancestry of the Seconda Pratica Madrigal," in *Studies in Renaissance*

and Baroque Music in Honor of Arthur Mendel, ed. Robert Marshall (Kassel: Bärenreiter, 1974), pp. 47–68; and Watkins, *Gesualdo,* pp. 37–72.

23. The Duke of Bavaria to Alfonso II d'Este, 7 December 1585: Lasso "non si sazia di decantare la musica rarissima udita" and "non può più lodare la musica mia" (Solerti, *Ferrara,* p. cxix). On the visits of the Florentines, see Newcomb, *The Madrigal,* vol. 1, 191–194, 199–203.

24. According to Superbi, *Apparato,* p. 132, Ercole Pasquini "for many years played the principal organs in his native city." Despite his "delicate and rapid hand," Pasquini did not serve at court because of his youth and went to Rome, where he was admitted organist of the Cappella Giulia at St. Peter's in October 1597 and dismissed on 19 May 1608 for "just cause" (the ruling of the Chapter of San Pietro is given in Cametti, "Girolamo Frescobaldi," p. 710)—probably insanity, since already in 1605 his monthly salary was assigned to the *maestro di casa* of the Ospedale dei Pazzi for Pasquini's maintenance (Haberl, "Girolamo Frescobaldi," p. 151, n. 24). See Oscar Mischiati, "Ercole Pasquini," *Die Musik in Geschichte und Gegenwart,* vol. 10, col. 868. On at least two occasions Pasquini performed in the Este city of Modena, already displaying some signs of mental instability (Gino Roncaglia, *La cappella musicale del duomo di Modena* (Florence, 1957), pp. 38–39, 57). Pasquini's surviving keyboard works were edited by W. Richard Shindle, *Ercole Pasquini: Collected Keyboard Works* (Corpus of Early Keyboard Music 12, American Institute of Musicology, 1966). See also Alexander Silbiger, *Italian Manuscript Sources of 17th Century Keyboard Music* (Ann Arbor: UMI Research Press, 1980), pp. 178–186.

25. On Brumel see Willi Apel, *The History of Keyboard Music to 1700,* trans. and rev. Hans Tischler (Bloomington: Indiana University Press, 1972), pp. 112–115, 170–171.

26. Watkins, *Gesualdo,* p. 43. Stella was so impressed by Luzzaschi's performance on the arcicembalo that he ordered one for himself. See G. B. Doni, *Compendio,* 1635, p. 20, and Newcomb, "Carlo Gesualdo," p. 418.

27. Newcomb, *The Madrigal,* vol. 1, 196.

28. Ibid., pp. 166, 179.

29. Ferrara, Archivio di Stato, Archivio Bentivoglio, letters to Enzo Bentivoglio, scaffale 9, mazzo 49/402: letter from the Marchese Martinengo, 23 June 1609: "et adesso il S.r Alessandro ha finito di dare un Ruggiero et una toccata stupenda alla Napolitana . . ."; 54/438: letter from Alessandro Piccinini, 7 August 1610: "e *per* uenire ale Curte auendo io fatto certe partite di romanesca le mando a giorgio in sieme una Corente. . . ." See Anthony Newcomb, "Girolamo Frescobaldi, 1608–1615," *Annales Musicologiques* 7 (1964–1977), 140.

30. Ferrara, Biblioteca Comunale Ariostea, coll. Antonelli 22, *Catalogo dei maestri di Cappella dell'Accademia della Morte dal 1596* [*recte* 1594] *al 1683 e catalogo dei musicanti di essa Accademia.* See also Cavicchi, "Contributo alla bibliografia di

Arcangelo Corelli," *Ferrara* 2 (1961), 4–5, and Newcomb, *The Madrigal,* vol. 1, 167, 173.

31. The account of the devolution of Ferrara is based, in the main, on Faustini's *Historie,* books III–IV; Guarini's *Diario,* I, 310–350; the *Memorie* of Guido Bentivoglio (*Opere storiche del Cardinal Bentivoglio,* V, Milan, 1807); and Ludwig Freiherr von Pastor, *Geschichte der Päpste seit dem Ausgang des Mittelalters,* 40 vols. (Freiburg in Breisgau, 1886–1889), which I have consulted in a variety of editions and translations. More restricted studies include E. Callegari, "La devoluzione di Ferrara alla S. Sede," *Rivista Storica Italiana* 12 (1895), 1–57; V. Prinzivalli, "La devoluzione di Ferrara alla S. Sede secondo una relazione inedita di Camillo Capilupi," *Atti della Deputazione Ferrarese di Storia Patria* 10 (1898), 119ff.; G. Pardi, "Sulla popolazione del Ferrarese dopo la devoluzione," *Atti della Deputazione Ferrarese di Storia Patria* 20 (1911), 1–132; Ferrara, Biblioteca Comunale Ariostea Ms. Classe I, 26: Scalabrini, *Metropolitana di Ferrara,* 1766; Alberto Gasparini, *Cesare d'Este e Clemente VIII* (Modena: Società Tipografica Editrice Modenese, 1959); Luciano Chiappini, *Gli Estensi* (Varese: Dall'Oglio, 1967).

32. The account of Clement VIII's entry is taken from Bentivoglio, *Memorie,* pp. 25–26. On the Bentivoglio family see Solerti, *Ferrara,* pp. lxvi–lxvii. Cornelio Bentivoglio had four sons and two daughters by Leonora d'Este, and by his second marriage with Isabella Bendidio he fathered five more sons. Guido was the second of these, and Solerti gives his birth date as 4 October 1579, which agrees with Guido's statement in the *Memorie,* p. 9 ("l'anno del Signore 1594 e della mia età il quintodecimo"), and conflicts with the date 4 October 1577 in the *Dizionario biografico degli Italiani* (Rome, 1960–), vol. 8 (1966), 634.

33. On the Accademia dello Spirito Santo see Adriano Cavicchi, "Il primo teatro d'opera moderno," in *Ferrara,* vol. 1, 65.

34. Solerti, *Ferrara,* p. lxvii, n. 1; Bentivoglio, *Memorie,* pp. 18–21; see also G. M. Artusi, *L'Artusi* (Venice, 1600; reprinted Bologna: Forni, 1968), fols. 1–2.

35. On the terms of the cessation of Ferrara, see Guarini, *Diario,* I, 333–334; on the rape of the city and the fate of the Belvedere, see Faustini, *Historie,* V, 10–12, and Solerti *Ferrara,* p. xviii and n. 2; on the dispersal of the Este collections, see Gibbons, *Dossi,* pp. 198–199.

36. Faustini, *Historie,* III, 133.

37. Luzzaschi's visit to Rome is documented by Claude V. Palisca, "Musical Asides in the Diplomatic Correspondence of Emilio de' Cavalieri," *Musical Quarterly* 49 (1963), 339–355. On 6 April 1601 Cavalieri reported the arrival in Rome of Cardinal Pietro Aldobrandini, who brought Luzzaschi. "They say he came for two months but he may well stay in Rome. I have not yet heard him play." On 25 May Cavalieri wrote: "I have been here in Rome with Claudio [Merulo] da Correggio and now with Lucciasco and everyone says in unison great things about me" (p. 353).

2. Rome and Flanders, 1607–1608

1. See Alessandro Piccinini, *Intavolatura di liuto e di chitarrone* (Bologna, 1623; facsimile edition, Antiquae Musicae Italicae Monumenta Bononiensia, Bologna, 1962), vol. 1, 8. Girolamo Piccinini was apparently dead by late August 1610 (Newcomb, "Girolamo Frescobaldi, 1608–1615," pp. 140–141).

2. The assertion that Frescobaldi became a member of Santa Cecilia in 1604 is based not on original documentation (which is largely lacking before 1651), but on a *Stato nominativo generale* of the Congregation compiled by its secretary, Luigi Rossi, between 1830 and 1849 after nearly twenty years of "laborious research" (the dates of Rossi's investigations are given according to Remo Giazotto, *Quattro secoli di storia dell'Accademia Nazionale di Santa Cecilia* (Rome: Accademia Nazionale di Santa Cecilia, 1970), vol. 1, 119; Cametti, "Girolamo Frescobaldi," p. 702, gives 1833–1851.) While Cametti saw no reason to doubt Rossi's information, Giazotto has found that for the years 1584–1640 the Stato shows "incongruities, inexactitudes . . . and . . . ingenuous judgments as well as inexplicable and unpardonable lacunae" (*Quattro secoli,* vol. 1, 121).

3. Dedication of *IL PRIMO LIBRO / DELLE FANTASIE / A QVATTRO, / DI GERONIMO FRESCOBALDI / Ferrarese, Organista* (Milan, 1608, dated "Di Ferrara li 8. Nouembre 1608"; Catalogue I.A.1). Printed in Claudio Sartori, *Bibliografia della musica strumentale italiana,* vol. 1 (Florence: Olschki, 1952), 159. The dedication itself presents a few problems. Francesco Borghese had little influence with his brother, Paul V (incorrectly identified as his uncle in Newcomb, "Girolamo Frescobaldi, 1608–1615," p. 116), especially by comparison with their nephew Scipione, and was rather isolated from the papal circle. Further, the title Duca di Regnano, which Frescobaldi applies to Francesco in 1608, does not in fact seem to have been his until after the death of another brother in 1609.

4. Rome, San Giovanni in Laterano, Archivio Storico del Vicariato di Roma: Santa Maria in Trastevere, Sagrestia 1573–1616, Armadio XII, 9, fols. 224–225. "Girolimo" was paid sc. 1.50 per month. (The scudo was a silver coin weighing about thirty grams, a bit less than seven and a half dollars at current exchange rates.) His name does not appear in the Chapter records of the Basilica, presumably because a decree of 1607 gave the head sacristan the right to change organists at will (*Liber Decretorum Capituli S.tae Mariae Transtiberim* 1600–1612, Armadio III, 3, fol. 51r). Girolimo's immediate predecessors as organist were Sebastiano Bilancetti (August 1598–December 1601), Alessandro Costantino (later Frescobaldi's rival for the post of organist of the Cappella Giulia and his eventual successor, January–September 1602), Jacomo Mainardi (October 1602–January 1603), D. Geronimo Melcarne (February–June 1603), Arnoldo Moretti (July 1603–August 1605) (*Sagrestia* 1573–1616, fols. 210–224). For September Moretti was replaced by a nameless "organista," after which Gio. Battista Ricchi took over the post until Girolimo's advent in January of 1607.

Although Ricchi seems to have been readmitted in March, he did not resume his post from Girolimo until June of 1607 (*Liber Decretorum,* fol. 53; *Sagrestia,* fol. 225).

5. As a general guide to Rome at this period I have employed Cesare D'Onofrio, *Roma nel seicento* (Florence: Vallecchi, 1969), which reproduces the manuscript guide to the city written by Fioravante Martinelli between 1660 and 1663 and annotated by Borromini. The 1624 inventory of Santa Maria in Trastevere is given in Beekman Cannon, "Music in the Archives of the Basilica of Santa Maria in Trastevere," *Acta Musicologica* 41 (1969), 201. For a drawing of the organ buffet see Renato Lunelli, *L'arte organaria del rinascimento in Roma* (Florence: Olschki, 1958), plate II.

6. In March 1607 the Chapter of Santa Maria in Trastevere assigned thirteen scudi per month to be paid to the *maestro di cappella* and the eight extra singers (*Liber Decretorum,* fol. 53), and a priest, Pellegrino (presumably the head sacristan of that name), was deputed to act as *maestro* (ibid., fol. 53v), while Venturo Cristallini received a half-month's salary for the same post and a full salary for the next month (*Sagrestia,* fol. 224v). In May Luca Sabbatelli was paid as *maestro* (ibid., fol. 225), and in June the turnover seems to have been halted through the election by the Chapter of Gio. Battista Alessio as *maestro* and Ricchi as organist (at a salary of two scudi a month) (*Liber Decretorum,* fol. 54). The choir included boys, presumably for the performance of polyphonic music (ibid., fol. 53), and payments are recorded for "large books for the Music" (presumably chant-books) (*Uscita di S. Maria in Trastevere* 1594–1624, "esattore," Armadio XIII, 12, fol. 54, April 1607) and for extra singers on Low Sunday, when the basilica's principal relics were displayed (ibid.; see also D'Onofrio, *Roma,* p. 135). During Girolimo's tenure the basilica had a procession, presumably for singing the Rogation litanies, on St. Mark's day, 25 April (*Uscita,* "esattore," fol. 54v).

7. See Stephen Bonta, "The Uses of the Sonata da Chiesa," *Journal of the American Musicological Society* 22 (1969), 84, n. 62. The account of the organist's functions at mass is a compendium of Adriano Banchieri, *L'organo suonarino* (Venice, 1605; reprinted with additions 1611, 1622, 1638; facsimile, Bologna: Forni, 1969), pp. 2–38; Banchieri, *Conclusioni nel suono dell'organo* (Bologna, 1609; facsimile, Bologna: Forni, 1968), pp. 18–19, 22–23; and Fra Bernardino Bottazzi, *Choro et organo* (Venice, 1614; facsimile, Bologna: Forni, 1980), pp. 14–83.

8. On the history and performance of organ masses see Apel, *Keyboard Music,* pp. 109–128, 418–419.

9. On the performance of organ music in the offices see Banchieri, *L'organo suonarino,* pp. 39-[125], his *Conclusioni,* pp. 20–21, and Bottazzi, *Choro,* pp. 86–136.

10. Banchieri, *L'organo suonarino,* p. 38; *Conclusioni,* p. 16.

11. *Conclusioni,* p. 17.

12. The musical library of Santa Maria in Trastevere is fortunately still

largely preserved, having been transferred recently from the basilica to the Archivio Storico del Vicariato di Roma at San Giovanni in Laterano. (For an account of the collection before its removal see Cannon, "Music in the Archives.") The surviving material from Girolimo's period of service includes four Passions, a Holy Week book, and the Palestrina hymn-settings. Among the composers of the first quarter of the century we find Abundio Antonello (*Cantiones,* a collection of mass-propers), G. F. Anerio, represented by the *Responsoria Nativitatis* of 1614, and Gio. Maria Sabino's *Psalmi de Vespere* à 4 (Naples, 1607), along with the *Selectae Cantiones* (1614) of Fabio Costantini (Archivio Storico del Vicariato, Santa Maria in Trastevere, Archivio Musicale, Armadio VII, 1, 2, 16; VIII, 9).

13. On small sacred concertos, Banchieri, *Conclusioni,* p. 18. On p. 61 Banchieri describes a mass of his own for four choirs. On the manner of employing the organ with such combinations of instruments and voices, Agostino Agazzari contributed a letter, dated from Rome 25 April 1606, describing the practice of "questi Signori Musici Romani": "when the organist is used as the basis in ensembles, he must play with great judgment, having regard to the quantity and quality of the voices and instruments, using few registers and doublings when they are few, adding and subtracting as the occasion demands" (*Conclusioni,* pp. 68–70).

14. From a manuscript diary of Pietro Boncore (d. 1741), cited by Giazotto, *Quattro secoli,* vol. 1, 48. Whether or not Frescobaldi was a member of Santa Cecilia, the oscillation between St. Peter's and the Oratorian movement is apparent in his career. His first surviving sacred vocal work, for example, appeared in a collection published by Fabio Costantini in 1616 that also included music by many of the composers of the *Gioie.* (see Flavio Testi, *La musica italiana nel seicento,* vol. 2 (Milan: Bramante, 1972), 203–204, for the relation of Costantini's publications of 1616 and 1618—both containing works by Frescobaldi—with the Oratorio del Crocifisso.)

15. On the conclaves and their aftermath see Ludwig Freiherr von Pastor, *The History of the Popes from the Close of the Middle Ages,* trans. Dom Ernest Graf, vol. 25 (St. Louis: Herder, 1937), 1–38.

16. See n. 1. It is indicative of the Ferrarese love of splendor and of the responsibility of Bentivoglio's position that he—the younger son of a second marriage—supported a musical retinue the equal in size of that brought to Ferrara by the *capostipite* Gesualdo.

17. *Lettere del Cardinal Bentivoglio,* ed. G. Biagioli, 3d ed. (Milan, 1828), pp. 22–23, letter of 21 July 1607 to Mons. di Modigliana, Bishop of Borgo S. Sepolcro, describing the journey from Ferrara to Lucerne. Guido recounted the trip from Rome to Ferrara in a letter of 24 June (pp. 15–16) and his arrival in Brussels in a letter of 11 August (pp. 32–35). Bentivoglio's unpublished correspondence with Cardinal Scipione Borghese (preserved in the Archivio Segreto Vaticano, Fondo Borghese, ser. II, nos. 98, 100, 103, 111, 115, for 1607–1608) gives few details of his household.

18. Bentivoglio, *Lettere,* pp. 32–35, letter of 11 August 1607 to Mons. di Modigliana.

19. See Bentivoglio's account of Flanders in his *Relationi fatte dall' Ill.mo, e Reu.mo Sig.or Cardinal Bentivoglio in tempo delle sue nuntiature di Fiandra, e di Francia* (Antwerp, 1629), I, 121.

20. For some reason the series *Analecta Vaticano-Belgica,* 2d ser., *Nonciature de Flandre,* skips Bentivoglio's nunciature. For accounts of this period see Hendrik J. Elias, "La nonciature de Guido Bentivoglio, archevêque de Rhodes, à Bruxelles (1607–1615)," *Bulletin de l'Institut Historique Belge de Rome,* 8 (1928), 273–281; also Raffaele Belvederi, *Guido Bentivoglio e la politica europea del suo tempo 1607–1621* (Padua, 1962), 51–52.

21. Letter of 7 June 1608 to Enzo Bentivoglio, *Memorie,* III, 20. Bentivoglio also described the occasion in a letter of the same date to Cardinal Borghese (Borghese II, 115, fols. 221v–222; other details of the regents' devotions are given on fols. 119, 132). A number of paintings still attest the active participation of Albert and Isabella in the splendid, if fatiguing, religious life of Flanders.

22. Cavicchi, preface to Luzzaschi, *Madrigali,* p. 14 and n. 31, whose original names Fiorini as "Lodovico."

23. Newcomb, "Girolamo Frescobaldi, 1608–1615," p. 113, suggests that Frescobaldi in fact left Flanders by mid-May.

24. Dedication to Guido Bentivoglio of *DI GIROLAMO / FRESCOBALDI / IL PRIMO LIBRO DE / MADRIGALI / A CINQVE VOCI* (see Catalogue III.A.1). Girolamo's journey to Antwerp is perhaps more significant in light of the fact that the nuncio and his suite resided in Brussels rather than following the peripatetic court of the regents (letter of Guido Bentivoglio to Cardinal Borghese, 1 December 1607, Borghese II, 100, fol. 311).

25. On Cornet and Philips see Apel, *History of Keyboard Music,* pp. 338–344, 296–300 (the works of Cornet, ed. Apel, appear as no. 26 of the Corpus of Early Keyboard Music). On Sweelinck see Alan Curtis, *Sweelinck's Keyboard Music* (Leiden: University Press, 1969).

26. For example, Robert L. Tusler, *The Organ Music of Jan Pieterszoon Sweelinck* (Bilthoven, 1958), pp. 93–94.

27. See n. 30.

28. Sir Dudley Carleton to John Chamberlaine, Hagh [The Hague], 5/15 September 1616, quoted by Frank Hubbard in *Three Centuries of Harpsichord Making* (Cambridge, Mass.: Harvard University Press, 1965), p. 76. Carleton continues: "In ye whole time we spent there I could never sett my eyes in the whole length of a streete uppon 40 persons at once: I never mett coach nor saw man on horseback: none of owr companie (though both were workie dayes) saw one pennie worth of ware ether in shops or in streetes bought or solde."

29. Newcomb, "Girolamo Frescobaldi, 1608–1615," p. 121, n. 2.

30. Superbi's statement (*Apparato,* p. 133) is simply that Girolamo "Fu

condotto nella Fiandra ove diede gran saggio di lui molt'anni," which is probably the source of a statement by Johann Mattheson (who seems to have been misinformed about virtually every aspect of Frescobaldi's career) that "Frescobaldi . . . spent many years in Flanders" (quoted in *The Bach Reader,* ed. Hans T. David and Arthur Mendel (New York: Norton, 1945), p. 233). This was expanded by F. J. Fétis, in an account of Frescobaldi published in Farrenc's *Trésor des pianistes* (Paris, 1868, vol. 13), into the assertion that Girolamo was organist at Malines in 1607, which was carefully refuted by Cametti ("Girolamo Frescobaldi in Roma," pp. 705–707).

31. Quoted by Cametti, p. 708. Enzo had traveled to Rome on other occasions, partly for the purpose of combating influences hostile to the Bentivoglio family in the circle of Cardinal Borghese (Archivio Segreto Vaticano, Borghese II, 100, fol. 305, letter of 24 November 1607 from Guido Bentivoglio to Cardinal Borghese; see also 115, fol. 96, a letter of 8 March 1608 in which Guido thanks Borghese for the "dimostrationi, che s'è degnata di fare ultimam.te uerso mio fratello Entio e uerso tutta la nostra Casa"—presumably Enzo's appointment).

32. A letter of Guido to Enzo Bentivoglio, 9 February 1608, pictures the straitened circumstances of the nuncio's household at this time: "Indeed I don't know how I have maintained my reputation up until now, since from the very beginning I have had to take on credit bread, beer, wood, and a thousand other necessities; Your Lordship can well understand that in this period that I have been penniless I have not been able to live on air, with so many mouths to feed" (*Memorie,* III, 14–15).

33. Letter of Frescobaldi to Enzo Bentivoglio from Sant'Ambrogio Maggiore, Milan, 25 June 1608, transcribed and translated in Newcomb, "Girolamo Frescobaldi, 1608–1615," pp. 112–113. In a letter written the following day Girolamo adds, "And if I resolve to remain in Milan, since I am much in request, I shall not lack the opportunity of earning; thus in order not to refuse the opportunity and the singular courtesy of Your Most Illustrious Lordship, I know what usefulness and repute it would be for me not to refuse the opportunity to serve Your Most Illustrious Lordship, praying you that to give satisfaction to these gentlemen that I remain until August in Milan, thus I will be most ready to serve Your Most Illustrious Lordship, and if you will do me the kindness to let me know when will be your departure for Rome you will do me a favor" (pp. 114–115). The letter, whose present location Newcomb describes as unknown, is now in the Mary Flagler Cary Collection in the Pierpont Morgan Library in New York City and is reproduced in the catalogue of the collection. While the date can be read as 1605, from the evidence of ensuing letters it clearly was written in 1608, the date given in the catalogue of the Heyer Collection.

34. Letter to Enzo Bentivoglio from Milan, 29 July 1608 (now in the Munich State Library) reproduced in Cametti, "Girolamo Frescobaldi in Roma," facing p. 709; Newcomb, pp. 115–116).

3. Rome, 1608–1614

1. Lino Bianchi and Karl Gustav Fellerer, *Giovanni Pierluigi da Palestrina* (Turin, 1971), pp. 32, 38–46.

2. On the development of the Cappella Giulia, ibid., pp. 38–42. The bull of Sixtus V is given in Llorens, *Le opere musicali della Cappella Giulia,* p. vii. For the membership of the Cappella, see Cametti, "Girolamo Frescobaldi in Roma," pp. 713–714. For salaries, Biblioteca Apostolica Vaticana, Cappella Giulia 61, fol. 40; the payments to Alessandro Costantini, as interim organist between Ercole Pasquini and Frescobaldi from June through October of 1608, are given on fols. 45–49.

3. The records of the election are cited by Cametti, "Girolamo Frescobaldi in Roma," pp. 709–710.

4. Ferrara, Archivio di Stato, Archivio Bentivoglio, 9, M 45, fol. 118: letter of 9 August 1608 from Mons. Estense Tassoni at Rome to Enzo Bentivoglio: "Tanto più gusto mi si accresce nell'hauere fauorito m Gir.mo Frescobaldi per il luogo di organista qui di S. Pietro quanto che ueggo hauer fatto cosa grata a V.S. I11.ma alla *qu*ale e per obligo, e per mia propria dispositione desid*e*ro seruire in ogni conto. Gia ho scritto ancorio a Milano a lui stesso, hauendo presente che trouasi colà, e uò trattendo il R.mo Capi*tol*o sino alla sua risposta che però necessario sarebbe hauerla q*uale* r*isposta* p*er* li rispetti auuisati all'Aless:ro, però sarà bene, ch'ella lo tenga solicitato, almeno p*er* la resolutione."

5. Archivio Bentivoglio, M 45, fol. 247: letter of 20 August 1608 from Bernardo Bizzone at Rome to Enzo Bentivoglio (partly illegible owing to the corrosion of the paper): "I11.mo sig.re p*a*trone oss.mo: Ms Ger.o mi scriue sotto il di 13 del corrente, nell istesso giorno, e tenore, ch*e* mi scriue anco VS. I11.ma A lui et da me et da altri fù dato il p*rimo* auuiso a Milano et hanno mandato li tre altri frati di S. Ambrogio di d*et*ta città li gli l'hanno riceuuto, et haurei caro ch*e* Ger.mo . . . con d*etti* frati ch*e* gli mandassero la mia l*ett*era p*er* . . . riscritti. Io mi rallegro co*n* lui che q*uesta* occasione sia anco p*er* continuare la seruitia sua co*n* l'I11.ma Casa, e particola*r*m*ente* co*n* la p*er*sona e sotto la p*ro*tettione di V.S. I11.ma l'elettione fatta dal capitolo d*e*lla p*er*sona di Ger.o [è] stabilitata e confirmata, e ridotta à p*er*fettione senza dubbio e difficoltà niuna; Io loderei bene, p*erche* qui è op*inion*e ch*e* VS. I11.ma no*n* sia p*er* essere qui sino alla fine d'octobre, che egli . . . se p*er*ò VS Ill.ma no*n* primo di hauerlo p*er* viaggio appresso la sua VS I11.ma p*er* . . . s'inviarse a q*uest*a uolta subb*it*o, ch*e* uede essere bene ripresento ma non già perch*e* sia vera questa e sicura . . . sr Frescobaldi . . . che non saria cosa no*n* bene di scriuere una l*ett*era ri*n*gratiatoria [fol. 247v] alli Ill.mi sig.ri canonici e capitolo di s. pietro et inuiare d*ett*a l*ett*era all'Ill.mo C*anonic*o Ottauio Tassoni ch*e* la presenti in capitolo, se però così giudicarà bene V.S. Ill.ma e cosi abbondare in cautela . . . Mi fauorisce anco di far leggere la p*resen*te à Geronimo, al quale no*n* serue per esser . . . tardi, e farli hauere subb*ito* . . . soprascritte, ch'egli mi riesca dell'ecc.ma Francesca Berglucci [?]".

6. Archivio Bentivoglio, M 45, fol. 253: letter of 20 August 1608 from Mons. Tassoni at Rome to Enzo Bentivoglio: "Per il luogo di organista qui di San Pietro in persona di ms Girolamo non ci è hora piu difficultà ueruna, giache sono sicuro, ch'egli habbia accettata la carica, poiche per assicurare il negotio, farò far il decreto in Capitolo che quando egli uolesse uenire . . . altro . . . accettarli; non ho uisto però ancora *que*sti SS.ri Canonici, doppo *que*sto auuiso, mà conforme à l'occasione, che haurò di andare a San Pietro, me darò loro conto, Intanto sarà bene che egli si trattenga costi, sino che se renfreschi per che il uolerlo far uenire adesso, sarebbe ua farlo porre a pericolo della Vitta."

7. Archivio Bentivoglio, M 46, fol. 395: letter from Mons. Tassoni at Rome to Enzo Bentivoglio, 4 October 1608 (badly corroded): "De Frescobaldi di cui V.S. Ill.ma mi scrisse non posso dir altro, se non come ho significato a lui med*esimo*, che mentre ella hà per uenire a questa uolta p*er* li xi del corrente può . . . egli trattenersi sin'all'hora, mà mentre diuerse . . . più oltre direi che fosse bene, che serà . . . dato per soddisfattione di *que*sti SS.ri Canonici."

8. Archivio Bentivoglio M 45, f. 249: letter of Camillo della Torre at Milan to Enzo Bentivoglio, 20 August 1608: "rimetto à VS Ill.ma il pieghetto che la . . . con la sua de*l* 4 per il Frescobaldi, che no*n* egli para... à cotesta volta, per quanto dicono quelli dou'era alloggiato, poiche à me non ha fatto moto alcuno." M 45, fol. 652: the same to the same, 23 July 1608: "ho poi hauuta la *lette*ra del p.re [priore?] con quella per il Frescobaldi, al quale l'ho fatta hauere, ma mi di . . . d'hauerlo à dire cha mancato a lei, et à me della parola data, non vna uolta ma diuerse, di uenire con V.S. Ill.ma a Roma, et specialm*ente* me lo ratifico ultimam*ente*, hauendolo poi mandato à domandare hoggi per incaminarlo con buona compagnia mi ha liberam*ente* detto di non ci uoler più fare altro, et di non ci uoler partire da Milano, onde può V.S. Ill.ma considerare quale io hò restato uedendomi mancare della parola tante uolte data, et con tutto ch'io le habbia messo in consideratione il male che potria auenire per l'inoseruanza della promessa fatta a lei, et a me, non ho potuto remouerlo dal suo proponim*ento* quanto io sia restato offeso da simile modo di procedere, lascio che lei lo giudichi, et se hauesse mancato à me solo sarei in gran pensiero [?], ma poiche lei ancora ci è interessato, lasciarei che la comandi quello le sarà di giusto, sicura ch'io la seruirò sempre à tutto mio potere in qual si uoglia cosa."

9. Letter of 5 November 1608 from Bernardo Bizzone at Rome to Enzo Bentivoglio; transcription and translation in Newcomb, "Girolamo Frescobaldi, 1608–1615," pp. 118–119.

10. Libanori, *Ferrara d'oro,* III, 169. Payments receipted by Frescobaldi himself or by an agent show that he drew his salary at irregular intervals and suggest that he may have been absent from Rome at times, as some of the receipts are signed by the *facchino* Nicolo Cocchi as "secondo [*or* soto] organista." Since the Cappella Giulia had no appointed second organist, it seems that Nicolo substituted for Frescobaldi. Girolamo receipted his salary for November and December of 1608. In 1609 he was paid for January, February plus March, April, May plus

June, and by single months for the rest of the year. In 1610 Girolamo signed for January, Nicolo for February through May, Girolamo for June-July and August-September, Nicolo for October-November, and Girolamo for December. All the receipts for 1611 are signed by Frescobaldi, who drew his salary month by month except for May-June and September-October. In 1612 he was paid monthly through June, then bimonthly through November. The *Entrata e Uscita* book for 1613 records payments for January-July, August-September, October-December. In 1614 Frescobaldi was paid bimonthly through June and again in November-December. The payments are recorded in the *censuali* of the Cappella Giulia: 1608: Biblioteca Apostolica Vaticana, Archivio Capitolare di San Pietro, Cappella Giulia Censuale 61: payments to Pasquini, January-May, fols. 40–44; Costantini, June-October, fols. 45–49; Frescobaldi, November-December, fols. 50–51; 1609: CG 62, fol. 75; 1610: CG 63, fol. 74; 1611: CG 64, fol. 28; 1612: CG misc. 427, filza 25, CG 65, *Entrata e Uscita,* fol. 52, *Esito delli denari et dell'intrata della Cappella Giulia,* fols. 11v–21; 1613: CG 66, fols. 49, 73; 1614: CG 67, fol. 70; *Libro Mastro Generale* A (armadio 64), 1612–1615, c. 20, 25, 28, 38, 60, 78.

11. See n. 9.

12. See Bonta, "Uses of the Sonata da Chiesa," p. 71; and above, chap. 2, n. 7.

13. The bills for the platforms and for moving the organ are found in the *censuali* of the Cappella Giulia, collections of *giustificazioni*, and so on: Cappella Giulia 163, nos. 15, 28 (1608); CG 164, *Libro di Mandati . . . 1609*, nos. 13, 20, 21; CG 165, *Liber Mandatorum . . . 1610,* no. 14: "per quando si guasto il choro per hauere calato à basso l'organo", no. 22: "Fu messo due organi dentro al teatro per intonarli insieme che vennero dà fuora . . . per hauere portato il nostro organo per intonarlo insieme coll'altri messi tutti tre insieme"; CG 64 (1611), fol. 63; fol. 67 mentions dust-covers for the organs; CG 66, *Libro dell'Entrata et Uscita* (1612, an especially complete listing); CG 66 (1613–1614).

14. On the history of the organs in St. Peter's see Renato Lunelli, *L'arte organaria del rinascimento in Roma,* pp. 37–98; for Maccioni's rebuilding, pp. 79–80. For a divergent account see Leopold M. Kantner, *"Aurea Luce": Musik an St. Peter in Rom 1790–1850,* (Vienna: Oesterreichische Akademie der Wissenschaften, 1979), pp. 26–29.

15. For 1608 there is a "Lista de Musici da Pagarsi per la festa di S. Pietro" (CG 163, 1608, no. 4) and payments for the Dedication at n. 24; for 1609, CG 164, no. 20; 1610, CG 165, no. 17; 1611, CG 64, fol. 63.

16. CG 163, no. 15; CG 165, no. 22. For the duties and ceremonies of the choir, see Biblioteca Apostolica Vaticana, Archivio Capitolare di San Pietro, Miscellanea 426, *Ordini da osservarsi dai cantori, et cappellani della Cappella Giulia* (Rome, 1600).

17. On the musical library of the Cappella Giulia see Llorens, *Le opere musicali della Cappella Giulia.*

18. Cf. Llorens, *Le opere,* no. 56, p. 116.

19. Llorens, *Le opere,* pp. 221–226. For a study of Anerio's collection see James Armstrong, "The *Antiphonae, seu Sacrae Cantiones* (1613) of Giovanni Francesco Anerio: A Liturgical Study," *Analecta Musicologica* 14 (1974), 89–150.

20. See James H. Moore, *Vespers at St. Mark's: Music of Alessandro Grandi, Giovanni Rovetta and Francesco Cavalli* (Ann Arbor: UMI Research Press, 2 vols., 1981), pp. 172 and 361, n. 345, quoting Venice, Archivio di Stato, Procuratia de Supra, busta 88, processo 195, fol. 58, an inquest of October 1589: "et quando non si trovava salmi che fossero statti composti li faceva cantar in falso bordon, il che è con gran vergogna della Chiesa."

21. Herman-Walther Frey, "Die Gesänge der sixtinischen Kapelle an den Sonntagen und hohen Kirchenfesten des Jahres 1616," *Mélanges Eugène Tisserant,* VI, Biblioteca Apostolica Vaticana Studi e Testi 236 (Vatican City, 1964), 395–437; Llorens, *Capellae Sixtinae Codices,* Biblioteca Apostolica Vaticana Studi e Testi 202 (Vatican City, 1960), pp. 152–153, no. 107.

22. See Newcomb, "Girolamo Frescobaldi, 1608–1615," pp. 120–122, and above, chap. 1, n. 29. By 1612 the ensemble included a second generation of the Piccinini family, the son of Girolamo, presumably a lute player like his father and uncles (see n. 42 below).

23. Archivio Bentivoglio, M 80, fols. 9, 12: letter from Girolamo Fioretti to Enzo Bentivoglio, Rome, 8 June 1615: "Il S.r Cav.re ha fornito d'insegnarli il sonetto, sebene tuttavia attende a farglilo esercitare per ridurlo totalmente a perfettione; et intanto và componendo un aria nuova per insegnarglila. Il S.r Nanini anch'esso continua d'insegnarli con ogni diligenza, . . . et oltre le solite lettioni che da al Baldassare di cantare, é comporre gl'insegna anche à sonare sù la parte . . . farò anche l'uffizio col S.r Frescobaldi, sicome hò fatto con la S.a Ippolita." M 80, fols. 25–26: the same to the same, Rome, 13 June 1615: "Baldassare, il quale continua di andare à pigliar lettioni dal S.r Nanini, accompagnandolo sempre il Ghenizzi, sicome fà quando va à scuola di sonare dal S.r Girolamo. Il S.re Cav.re Marotta hà risoluto di darli lettioni tre, e quattro volte al giorno." M 80, fols. 45, 48, 46, 47: the same to the same, Rome, 20 June 1615: "Nel resto continua di andare dal Nanini ogni giorno, dove io mi trovo ogni mattina, e gli dà due buon'hore lettioni dispensandone una in far lo cantare, ed intonar bene, e l'altra in farlo attendere allo studio del Contrapunto alla mente e Composi*z*ione . . . Il S.r Cav.re continua di farlo cantare più volte il giorno . . . Va similmente à pigliar lettione dal S.r Girolamo Frescobaldi ogni giorno alle 16. hore." M 80, fols. 236–238: the same to the same, Rome, 8 July 1615: "Starà hora alla disposi*z*ione della S.ra Hippolita l'insegnarli di sonare la Chitarra, . . . Nel resto và continuando gli soliti studi ed io l'ho raccomandato di nuovo al S.r Cav.re, et al S.r Nanini, come anche al S.r Frescobaldi, il quale dice, che gl'insegnerà à sonare sù la parte . . . Sebene il S.r Nanini ancora gli fa esercitare questo medesimo studio." (I am indebted to John Hill for the communication of

this material.) The strength of this Roman tradition is evident from Giovanni Andrea Angelini Bontempi's account of his training as a singer under Virgilio Mazzocchi a few years later (*Historia Musica,* Perugia: Costantini, 1695, p. 170).

24. Letter of 8 July 1609 from Cosimo Bandini in Rome presumably to Enzo Bentivoglio, Newcomb, "Girolamo Frescobaldi, 1608–1615," p. 125. Financial transactions between Filippo Frescobaldi and Enzo Bentivoglio are mentioned in a letter of 24 June 1609 from Alfonso Verati at Rome to Bentivoglio (Archivio Bentivoglio, M 49, fol. 414): "Ieri ho riceuuto sc*u*di setanta del Frescobaldi, il quale dice che V.S. Ill.ma ha fati pagar a suo padre in Ferrara."

25. On Angiola Zanibelli see Stuart Reiner, "La vag'Angioletta (and others)," *Analecta Musicologica* 14 (1974), 26–88. The letter quoted on pp. 61–62 may refer to Frescobaldi in the phrase "the teacher from whom I [Angiola] shall be learning."

26. Letter of Cosimo Bandini at Rome to Enzo Bentivoglio, 11 July 1609; Newcomb, "Girolamo Frescobaldi, 1608–1615," pp. 125–126.

27. Ibid., pp. 122–123.

28. Letter of 15 July 1609, ibid., pp. 123–124.

29. Ibid., pp. 126–127. Settimia Caccini eventually married Alessandro Ghivizzani, whom her father later called "both crazy and evil." See M. A. Bacherini Bartoli, "Giulio Caccini. Nuove fonti biografiche e lettere inedite," *Studi Musicali* 9 (1980), 59–72.

30. Letter of 9 September 1609; Newcomb, "Girolamo Frescobaldi, 1608–1615," pp. 128–129.

31. Archivio Bentivoglio, M 50, fol. 716: letter to Enzo Bentivoglio from Rome, 27 August 1609 (not in Newcomb): "Girolamo della spinetta ua dicendo ch*e* non si uol maritare con l'anzolla per che suo padre li ascritto che li dara la sua maledicione a tutti doi . . . [*illegible*] lo feci a trouare in capra...ca et lo feci una grand*issi*ma brauatta, lui non sa che rispondere se non che fara . . . sara ragioneuelle ma che pensaua che lanzolla auesse piu dotte et chal suo parentado fosse meglio. li risposti *que*sta risposta et li dissi che VS aurebbe parlatto a suo padre; VS li parli et li facia [fol. 716v] una brauata sul saldo et lo induca a corricarli che Girolamo la sposi et VS li prometta graui cose et facia che li scriua p*er* che altrimente auremo fastidio assai con questa bestia p*er* ch*e* siamo a roma et non lo posso piliar per forza a farlola sposare; lo faro ancora fare una parlatta dal To . . . io non posso menac*i*arlo per che mi . . . di non offendello VS a fare pur suo padre ascriuerli che è contento perche altrimente auremo de disgusti."

32. Continuation of letter cited in n. 31. On the concealment hypothesis see Newcomb, "Girolamo Frescobaldi, 1608–1615," p. 134. The thousand scudi are mentioned in the letter of Cavalier Giovanni Bentivoglio (Rome, 2 September 1609) quoted by Newcomb, p. 127.

33. Letter of Caterina Martinengo Bentivoglio to Enzo Bentivoglio, Rome, 9 September 1609. To Newcomb's text (p. 128) may be added the opening sentences: "Sig.r mio VS. non a ragione di dirmi che io uadi in colera per puoco

puoiche non e cosa che io desideri più che di auer sue li cose in questa sua cosi longa absenza et uedendomene priua et non saper la cagione mi fa timore quanto ho saputo che il magnanimo se hora . . . scordata io non ho piu parlato."

34. Archivio Bentivoglio, M 50, fols. 287–289, letter of Francesco Calcetti (who had been sent to Frescobaldi with a letter from Enzo) at Rome to Enzo Bentivoglio, 23 September 1609, fol. 287v (not in Newcomb): "Parlai Dom*en*ica matt*in*a d'ordine del s.r Cau*ali*ere e sig.ra Marchesa à ms. Gir*ola*mo dandoli la *lett*er*a* di V.S. Ill.ma poiche prima non l'haueuo potuto trouare in luoco al*cun*o e proponendoli tutte quelle ragioni per le quali io mi pensai di poterlo persuadere à prender l'Anzola per sua moglie conforme alla promessa fatta prima à Dio e poi a V.S. Ill.ma ed à questi sig.ri lo trouai più ostinato che mai, e perche mi disse che suo P*ad*re non si contentaua, io le mostrai una lettera doue V.S. Ill.ma scriueua al s.r Cau*ali*ere che suo P*ad*re haueua dato parola à V.S. Ill.ma di douersene contentare, e di douerlo scriuere à lui, mà egli mi rispose che suo P*ad*re non [fol. 288] gl'haueua scritto di questo tenore, ma gl'haueua scritto che non ne uoleua saper altro, e che se facesse male sarebbe suo il danno, e finalm*en*te mi disse ch'auendole promesso la s.ra Marchesa che l'Anzola era nata di parenti onorati, che trouandola altrom*en*te per la madre, e per le sorelle; non intendeua d'essere obbligato ad osseruare la sua promessa, se non gl'era osseruato questo capo, [e finalmente mi disse *canceled*] dicendomi anco di più che haueua scritto a V.S. Ill.ma ed al s.r Goretti il suo pensiero, e che attendeua la risposta. La s.ra Marchesa dice che non è uero che gl'habbi promesso cos'alcuna, e soggiunge ch'egli stesso senza recercar altro fece la promessa libera, ond'io non hò mancato di mettere in considerazione . . . di d*ett*o m. Gir*ola*mo il danno che glie ne può succedere, ond' à lui starà il pensarci bene, perche mostra di non ne uoler far altro."

35. Letter in Newcomb, "Girolamo Frescobaldi, 1608–1615," pp. 130–131.

36. On the subsequent history of Enzo's *musica* see Newcomb, "Girolamo Frescobaldi, 1608–1615," pp. 134–142.

37. Archivio Bentivoglio, letters of Caterina Bentivoglio at Rome to Enzo Bentivoglio, M 53, fol. 470 (June 1610): the marriage of the "Napuolitana" to "quel giouane che uene qui a sonar distromento"; M 53, fol. 641 (23 June 1610): "non solo la musica e finita ma e piu in fiore che mai puoiche a pigliato in casa il marito."

38. See Archivio Bentivoglio, M 62, fol. 122, M 63, fols. 305, 313. The "Gironimo" in question seems to have been a secretary.

39. Cametti, "Girolamo Frescobaldi in Roma," p. 715, n. 2.

40. Ibid., p. 716 and notes.

41. Ibid., p. 716.

42. See Newcomb, "Girolamo Frescobaldi, 1608–1615," pp. 136–140, who is unaware of Frescobaldi's return to the service of Enzo Bentivoglio. The continuing importance of the musical establishments of both Bentivoglio brothers is emphasized in a letter from Vincenzo Landinelli in Rome to Enzo Bentivoglio in

Ferrara (Archivio Bentivoglio, M 63, fol. 313). The original, not in Newcomb's article, is given complete and the relevant portion in translation. The letter is dated 21 January 1612.

"Hieri pregato condusse [-i?] il s.r Amb.re di Fiandra con tre, o quattri altri ss.ri principalissimi fiamminghi à sentir sonare la Napolitana, et gli piaque in estremo, e uolse sapere il nome, e cognome di lei, e del Marito, e lo noto sul libro, desiderando anco sentire la sig.ra Hippolita, ma perche il s.r Cesare si truoua à letto per un poco di male ch'ha in una gamba, e gli conuiene domandar licenza al s.r Cardinal Montalto non sarranno compiaciuti cosi presto, ho detto à questi Ss.ri che in mandando [=mantenendo?] questa Napoletana con fratello e sorelle importa a VS Ill.ma più di mille scudi all'anno, e spende altro tanto in mantenere altri simili uirtuosi che cantano, et il Piccinino di Gironimo molto bene conosciuto da loro, accio che sono certificati che sorte di persona hanno per Nontio in Fiandra se bene non gli è parso nuouo; sapendo molto bene la qualità di questa Casa." (Yesterday evening, being asked, I brought the Ambassador of Flanders with three or four other most important Flemish gentlemen to hear the Neapolitan play, and she pleased him extremely, and he wished to know the names of her and her husband, and noted them in a book . . . I told these gentlemen that maintaining this Neapolitan with brother and sisters costs Your Most Illustrious Lordship more than one thousand scudi a year, and that you spend as much again in maintaining other similar virtuosi who sing, and Piccinino the son of Gironimo well known by them, so that they are satisfied about what sort of person they have as Nuncio in Flanders, if indeed it did not seem new to them, knowing well the merit of this House.)

Clearly, the performances of Girolamo Piccinini in Guido's *musica* must have been impressive enough for the Flemish ambassador to remember him upon meeting his son two years after Girolamo's death.

43. Archivio Bentivoglio, M 70, fol. 128: letter of Ercole Provenzale (not Province, as in Newcomb) at Rome to Enzo Bentivoglio, 29 May 1613 (not in Newcomb): "Nel partire che fece V.S. Ill.ma da Roma non mi comisse cosa con magiore effetto che si dese conto come si portaua la s.ra Francesca, et li suoi maestri pero ogni ordinario ne daro conto à V.S.Ill.ma et sapra di giorno in giorno chi li da lecione et chi no— dopo la partita di V.S. Ill.ma il Caualiere Marotta non lià datto altro che due uolte lecione è uero che non c'è statto il Cimballo se non da 8 Giorni in qua il qual Cimballo sié piliatto à pigione et e di sodisfacione alla detta s.ra Francesca per che si conforme alla sua uoce e poi statto le feste di pasqua ma questa matina il detto Caualiere mi detto che li dara lezione ogni giorno dalle feste in fora il S.re Girollimo le a datto poche uolte lezione per che si purga ma mià detto che adeso a finitto la purga et che li dara lecione ogni giorno il s.re Anibale li a datto ogni giorno lezione et la detta S.ra Francesca si porta benissimo, et fa ottima musicista." See also M 70, fol. 65.

44. Archivio Bentivoglio, M 70, fol. 490, letter of Provenzale at Rome to Enzo Bentivoglio, 3 July 1613: "il S.r Girolimo li ueneua pero à deso non li uiene

niente con tutto che lo sia andatto à trouare molte uolte et dettoli che à torto a trat*tare* con V.S. Ill.ma in questo modo mi promete sempre di ben fare ma il Pouero uomo é mezo pazo *per* quanto pare à me il Gobo [fol. 490v] é di sodisfacione del Caualiere et limpara di sonare il Cimballo si che abiamo poco bisogno di Girolimo." Provenzale's letters to Enzo Bentivoglio are one long litany of Girolamo's failures to appear. M 70, fol. 154, 1 June 1613: [Francesca] "non é *per* far profitto alcuno sotto di lui . . . il S.re Girolimo lia datto lecione uenero et mia detto che non [f. 155] mancara da qui à uante di darelli lecione ogni giorno." M 70, fol. 207, 5 June 1613: "il s.re Girolimo non sie stato ne sabato ne domenica ne lunedi ne martedi ne oge che mercor." M 70, fol. 234, 8 June 1613: "Giouedi non ci fu ne il S.re Girolimo ne il s.re Caualiere." M 70, fol. 327, 18 June 1613: "e girolamo cie stato martedi sola mente." M 70, fol. 415, 26 June 1613: "girollimo non ci uiene mai; et quando uiene li mostra 2 botte curando sene ua uia ma adeso che li uiene il Gobo non ci state *per* che lui limpara ancor il Cimbalo mi creda V.S. Ill.ma questo Girollimo è mezo pazo-."

45. Ercole Provenzale in Rome to Enzo Bentivoglio, 21 July 1613: "Girollimo non li uiene piu à mostrare con tutto che io labbia pregato piu uolte" (M 70, fol. 532).

46. Newcomb, "Girolamo Frescobaldi, 1608–1615," p. 142 (Alessandro Costantini, letter of 9 November 1622).

47. Ibid., p. 141.

48. Ibid., p. 145.

49. Giacinto Gigli, *Diario romano,* p. 39 (1617).

50. Archivio Doria-Pamphilj, Fondo Aldobrandini, busta 28, no. 87: "Rollo della Famiglia dell'Ill.mo et R.mo s. Card.e Aldobrandino restata à Roma *per* la sua partita *per* Rauenna questo di xbre 1620 . . . D. Gironimo Organista." For information on this archive see Renato Vignodelli Rubrichi, "Il 'Fondo Aldobrandini' dell'Archivio Doria Landi Pamphili," *Archivio della Società Romana di Storia Patria* 92 (1969).

51. Frascati, Archivio Aldobrandini, Libro Mastro Generale H (1620), ccxxxxiiij: "E adi 18 detto [giugno] sc. 24 m*one*ta pag*a*ti à Girolamo fescobaldi, che tanti deue pag*are*, cioè sc. 21 a 7 musici che andorno alla Villa di Frascati c*on* l'occa*sione* del Banchetto che si fece al s.re Card*ina*le di Sauoia, *per* la musica da loro cantata è sc. 3 dati à un M*aestro* che accordò il clauecenbalo hauer la d*etta* sera sc. 24."

52. Archivio Doria-Pamphilj, Fondo Aldobrandini, no. 19: RIGISTRO DEI MANDATI / H, v. 2 (b. 19, 59a, 1621–1628), fol. 7: "5 sett. 1621: A Girolimo Frescobaldi musico sc. 6 mancia *per* pagare a cinque musici che uennero a seruire all'ultimo banchetto sc. 6."

4. Mantua, 1614–1615

1. Monteverdi's performance of the same service for the Gonzaga court is well documented, as witness his letter of 18 December 1627 to Alessandro Striggio

in *Claudio Monteverdi: lettere, dediche e prefazioni,* ed. Domenico de' Paoli (Rome: De Santis, 1973), pp. 295–297.

2. The letters are in Mantua, Archivio di Stato, Archivio Gonzaga, buste 1006 and 1010. These were communicated by the archivist Davari to Alberto Cametti, who published portions of them in "Girolamo Frescobaldi in Roma," pp. 717–722, not always accurately. The correspondence was reexamined by Newcomb in "Girolamo Frescobaldi, 1608–1615," pp. 145–157; Newcomb's article does not include Girolamo's letter of 5 September 1615 (see n. 24 below).

3. "Principe più che mezzanamente erudito nella musica," G. B. Doni, *Opere* II, lezione 5, cited by Pietro Canal in "Della musica in Mantova," *Memorie del Reale Istituto Veneto di Scienze, Lettere ed Arti* 21 (1879), 735.

4. On the relation between the two academies, see James H. Moore, "Marco da Gagliano's 'La Dafne': A Critical Edition" (M.A. thesis, University of California, Los Angeles, 1972), pp. 5–9.

5. Marco da Gagliano, preface to *La Dafne,* in Emil Vogel, "Marco da Gagliano: zur Geschichte der florentiner Musiklebens von 1570–1650," *Vierteljahrsschrift für Musikwissenschaft* 5 (1889), 396–442, 509–568; see documents 9, 11, 28. See also Jacopo Peri's letters to Ferdinando of April 1608 in Angelo Solerti, *Gli albori del melodramma* (Milan, 1904–1905), vol. 1, 88–89, and Alessandro Ademollo, *La bell'Adriana ed altre virtuose del suo tempo alla corte di Mantova* (Città di Castello, 1888), pp. 59–60, 63–64, concerning settings of Ferdinando's poetry by Caccini.

6. Claudio Monteverdi, letter of 28 December 1610 to Cardinal Ferdinando Gonzaga, *Lettere,* p. 52 (see also p. 57).

7. On music at the Mantuan court, in addition to the works of Ademollo, Solerti, and Vogel, see Antonio Bertolotti, *Musici alla corte dei Gonzaga in Mantova dal secolo XV al XVIII* (Milan, 1890). The description of Ferdinando's musical establishment is based on unpublished material kindly supplied by Susan Parisi.

8. On sacred music at Mantua see Pierre M. Tagmann, *Archivalische Studien zur Musikpflege am Dom von Mantua (1500–1627),* Publikationen der Schweizerischen Musikforschenden Gesellschaft, ser. 2, vol. 14 (Bern, 1967).

9. Text in Newcomb, "Girolamo Frescobaldi, 1608–1615," pp. 145–146.

10. Letter of 22 November 1614 from Facconi to Ferdinando Gonzaga (ibid., pp. 146–147). For Luzzaschi's settlement see Modena, Archivio di Stato, Archivio Segreto Estense, Archivi per Materie, Musica e Musicisti: compositori (sec. XV–XVIII), cass. 1/A, 43, and *The Letters of Claudio Monteverdi,* translated and introduced by Denis Stevens (Cambridge: Cambridge University Press, 1980), pp. 55–61.

11. Monteverdi, letter of 13 March 1620 to Alessandro Striggio, *Lettere,* pp. 148–154.

12. Text in Newcomb, "Girolamo Frescobaldi, 1608–1615," pp. 146–147.

13. Ibid., pp. 148–149; the letter has also been redated 13 December.

14. Ibid., p. 148: Newcomb translates "che questi scudi 300 siano di Roma" as "to make these *scudi* Roman ones." On the Mantuan scudo see *The Letters of Claudio Monteverdi,* trans. Stevens, p. 59.

15. Newcomb, "Girolamo Frescobaldi, 1608–1615," p. 149. The original appears to read "lotava della *Pasqua,*" that is, the Epiphany, which in Rome is called "Prima Pasqua."

16. Ibid., pp. 149–150.

17. Ibid., pp. 150–151; this is confirmed in a letter from Facconi to Magni, 14 February 1615 (ibid., pp. 151–152).

18. Letter of 16 February 1615, ibid., pp. 152–153.

19. Cametti, "Girolamo Frescobaldi in Roma," p. 721.

20. Monteverdi, *Lettere,* pp. 68, 71.

21. See Adẹmollo, *La bell'Adriana,* p. 123, and *The Letters of Claudio Monteverdi,* pp. 56–57.

22. Newcomb, "Girolamo Frescobaldi, 1608–1615," pp. 154–155; the date should be added.

23. Ibid., pp. 155–156.

24. Mantua, Archivio di Stato, Archivio Gonzaga, busta 1010, 439: "Ser.mo et R.mo Sig.re Il S.r Pauolo Faconi mi ha significato la mercede che V.A. R.ma s'è compiaciuta farmi con li 300 scudi la cui generosa attione si non m'e stata nuoua dalla innata sua reale magnanimita: che si come non è ordinaria, cosi con modi straordinari abbracia e fauorisce i suoi serui ben mi è stata e sara sempre per tuti i rispetti cariss.mi e s'a me fosse cosi facile il sapernela ringratiare come non è difficile il saper conoscere l'obligo, che le ne debbo, sodisfarei hora in qualche parte a questo nuouo debito, il quale con indissolubil catena di perpetua obligat*io*ne m'ha stretto al serui*zi*o dell'A.V. et aceso maggiormente il desiderio che tengo di poterlo effetuare conforme alla diuotione mia particolare uerso la seren:ma sua persona la quale supplico tratanto restar seruita di gradir questa piccola dimostratione di gratitudine di parole, finche mi sia conceduto poterla meglio dimostrare con miei effetti e qui all'AV. Rma con profonda riuerenza inchinato auguro felicissimi auenimenti. Di Roma il di 5 setemb*re* 1615 Di Vostra Altezza serenissima e Rma Humilisimo et deuotisimo ser.re Girolimo Frescobaldi." (Most Serene and Most Reverend Lord Sig. Pauolo Faconi has communicated to me the kindness that Your Most Reverend Highness has been pleased to do me with the 300 scudi, which generous action has not surprised me because of your inborn royal magnanimity, which, as it is not common, thus in unusual ways embraces and favors your servants, for me it has been and always will be good in every dearest respect. And if it were as easy for me to know how to thank you for it, as it is easy to feel the obligation which I owe you, I would satisfy now this new debt in some part, which with an unbreakable chain of perpetual obligation has bound me to the service of Your Highness and more inflamed the desire that I have to be able to carry it out as fits my particular devotion to your

most serene person which I beg meanwhile to be pleased by the small verbal show of gratitude, until I can better show it with my deeds [*effetti*] and here, deeply bowing before your Most Reverend Highness, I wish you a most happy future. From Rome the 5th of September 1615. Your most serene and Most Reverend Highness' Most humble and devoted servant Girolimo Frescobaldi.)

As a pendant to Girolamo's Mantuan flirtation we find a letter from Alessandro Costantini, whose career so curiously shadows Frescobaldi's, dated from Rome, 12 December 1615, asking Ferdinando's brother and successor to find Costantini a place among the Duke's servants, "nella mia professione di sonar cimbalo, e cantar basso" (Mantua, Archivio di Stato, Archivio Gonzaga, busta 1010, 678).

5. Rome, 1615–1628

1. It is noteworthy that Frescobaldi did not trouble to obtain a leave of absence from the Chapter of St. Peter's for his Mantuan visit, as he was to do in 1628 for his trip to Florence. The organist's salary for 1615 was paid in his name. Soriano received the January and February stipends, out of which he presumably paid a substitute. Girolamo drew his salaries for March and April together, and after his return the payments continued as before. The organist drew his salary in monthly or bimonthly installments that were sometimes receipted by Nicolo Cocchi, the *facchino* in charge of moving the platforms for musical performances in the basilica and apparently the mysterious "soto organista" of earlier payments. These signatures may indicate absences from Rome on Girolamo's part—in 1616 he himself signed only twice, and in 1618 once—but it is more likely that Nicolo was simply a convenience. From August 1625, when the salary was divided between Cocchi and Frescobaldi, until the latter's departure in 1628, the receipts are generally in Girolamo's own hand (Biblioteca Apostolica Vaticana, Cappella Giulia, censuali 68–81). Frescobaldi was last paid for October through December of 1628, "E in fede ho fatta la presente riceuta di mia propria mano questo di 18 Novembre 1628," (Cappella Giulia, Censuale 81, fol. 29).

2. On Mellan, Salianus, and Sas see the entries in Ulrich Thieme and Felix Becker, *Allgemeines Lexikon der bildenden Künstler von der Antike bis zur Gegenwart* (Leipzig, 1907–1950). On the Mellan drawing see Jean Vallery-Radot, *Le dessin français au XVIIe siècle* (Lausanne: Editions Mermod, 1953), pp. 191–192. Vallery-Radot dates the drawing as "one of the first portraits drawn by Mellan at the beginning of his Roman stay (1624–1637) under the influence of Vouet" and considers it more likely that in the engraving Mellan was mistaken about the sitter's age than that he was in Rome in 1619. The original copper plate of Mellan's engraving is reproduced in *Collection musicale André Meyer: manuscrits autographes, iconographie* (Abbeville: F. Paillart, 1973), plate 113, where it is dated 1613. The caricature attributed to Bernini is found in the Biblioteca Apostolica Vaticana, Cod. Chigi P.VI.4, fol. 9, an album dated ca. 1640–1645. An oil portrait in Bologna is clearly derived from the engravings.

3. Superbi, *Apparato*, III, 133.

4. Alexander Silbiger, "The Roman Frescobaldi Tradition," *Journal of the American Musicological Society* 33 (1980), p. 53 and n. 25.

5. Bennati, "Notizie inedite," pp. 39–40. There is some confusion on this point, as Girolamo's marriage act named him as the son of the *quondam* Filippo Frescobaldi in 1613, while late in 1614 Facconi relayed to the Duke of Mantua Girolamo's request for a house large enough for his family and his father (perhaps a confusion with Orsola del Pino's uncle, who accompanied Girolamo to Mantua?). (See Cametti, "Girolamo Frescobaldi in Roma," p. 716, and Newcomb, "Girolamo Frescobaldi, 1608–1615," p. 147.) According to the marriage contract of Giulia Frescobaldi, Filippo was still alive in November 1615 (Bennati, "Notizie," p. 39).

6. Cametti, p. 716 and nn. 3–4.

7. Jörg Garms, *Quellen aus dem Archiv Doria-Pamphilj zur Kunsttätigkeit in Rom unter Innozenz X*, Publikationen des oesterreichischen Kulturinstituts in Rom, 1 (Rome 1972), nos. 479–495 (pp. 117–119), purchases of houses by Cardinal Aldobrandini. No. 486: "Palazzo ò Casa grande in Colonna nel Corso . . . dalli Fossani" (apparently the nucleus of the present Palazzo Chigi; 1616); no. 490, 14 July 1618: "Casa che confinava con il detto Palazzo verso il vicolo de Verospi," purchased from the Ven. Arciconfraternita della Carità di S. Geronimo for sc. 661.15; no. 491, 22 May 1618: "Et piu per un altra casa in detto loco, che fu comprata da Geronimo Friscobaldo et Orsola del Pino sua moglie per prezzo di s. 689.27." The Doria-Pamphilj materials are in Rome, Archivio Doria-Pamphilj, scaffale 88, no. 45, int. 7, while the notary act of the sale is preserved in Rome, Archivio di Stato, Boccamattius notaio, Tribunale acque e strade no. 51 (*olim* 27), 1618, fols. 493–498. See also Renato Lefevre, "Il patrimonio romano degli Aldobrandini nel '600", *Archivio della Società Romana di Storia Patria* 82 (1959), 1–24.

8. Archivio Storico del Vicariato di Roma, S. Stefano del Cacco, *Status animarum* 1623–1625, fol. 33, no. 211; f. 57; *Stato di anime* 1626–1631, fols. 6, 36 (fol. 30, no. 78, shows that the organ builder Ennio Bonifatij also resided in the parish). See Cametti, "Girolamo Frescobaldi in Roma," p. 717.

9. See chap. 3, n. 23, above. On 11 July 1615 Ercole Provenzale wrote from Rome to Enzo Bentivoglio that "il S.re Girolamo in tutti li modi voria mandare uno contralto a V.S. Ill.ma" (Ferrara, Archivio di Stato, Archivio Bentivoglio, M 80, fol. 206).

10. Letter of 14 September to Cardinal Alessandro d'Este, in Newcomb, "Girolamo Frescobaldi, 1608–1615," pp. 143–144.

11. On Santo Spirito, Antonio Allegra, "La cappella musicale di S. Spirito in Saxia di Roma: appunti storici (1551–1737)," *Note d'Archivio* 17 (1940), 26–38, and Pietro De Angeles, *Musica e musicisti nell'Arcispedale di Santo Spirito in Saxia dal quattrocento all'ottocento* (Rome, 1950). Girolamo's entry is recorded in Rome, Archivio di Stato, Archivio dell'Ospedale di S. Spirito, Copie di Mandati

1921 (1620), c. 136, no. 967, 28 July: "Gerolimo Frescobaldi organista dalle 7 giugno a tutto luglio a giu. 25 il mese—sc. 4.50." Copie 1921, c.197, no. 1383: "Sr Gerolimo Frescobaldi *per* suo sal*ario* di *questo* mese a sc. 3 per so*pplimento* del *primo* mese che comincio a seruire che gli fu fatto il conto a *giuli* 25 e doueua dire a sc. 3 come in esso si uede—sc. 3.90." For a drawing of one of the organs, see Lunelli, *L'arte organaria,* plate III.

12. Archivio di S. Spirito, documenti inediti no. 1414, quoted by Allegra, "La cappella musicale," p. 30: "Vi è l'organista a cui si dà sc. 2,50 il mese senz'altro solo nelle solennità se li dà da mangiare la mattina al Refettorio dei preti ed è obbligato tutte le feste a Messa e vespro, tutti li sabbati all'espozitione del Santissimo Sacramento alle Lettanie della Madonna. Alle hore 23 è obligato anche alli mattutini di Pasqua di Resurretione con li due giorni seguenti nella Pentecoste ed altre solennità di tutto l'anno che si tralasciano per brevità."

13. Allegra, "La cappella musicale," p. 29. See a letter of Cesare Zoilo (Ferrara, Archivio di Stato, Enzo Bentivoglio, M 71, fol. 209), Rome, 23 August 1613, in which he states that at Santa Maria in Sassia "I am obliged [to play] every day perpetually at the sung mass and at vespers, and similarly every day I must teach counterpoint to some of the children of the Chapel."

14. Payments to Frescobaldi are recorded in Copie 1921, nos. 1509, 2658, 1726 [*sic*]; Copie 1922 (1621), nos. 71, 177, 311: "gerolamo Frescobaldi organista per mezo mese—sc. 1.50," after which he was succeeded by Sigismundo Arsille or Arselli, perhaps a consequence of Annibale Zoilo's return to the post of *maestro di cappella;* he replaced Giovanni Boschetti, a composer associated with Frescobaldi in Robletti's *Giardino musicale* and *Lilia Campi* of 1621 (Catalogue III.A.3, B.3). As at St. Peter's, soon after Girolamo's appointment at S. Spirito the instruments of the church were put in order; a payment of sc. 19 was made to Armodio Mazzoni (= Maccione) for "taking apart both organs of the aforesaid church and redoing some pipes and other work" and for tuning the organs (Copie 1921, no. 983). The 1626 payments to Girolamo are recorded in Copie 1925, nos. 994, 1162, 3280 [*sic*], 1403, 1484, 1621. The *mandati* for 1627 are missing, but Copie 1926 (1628), no. 768, 17 June, shows Girolamo's presence at Pentecost: "A Dom Matteo scudi ventidua *baiocchi* 50 *moneta* si li fanno pagare *per* che li dia alli Infrascritti a Ciascuno la sua nota *per* la musicha fatta in la *nostra* Chiesa la domenica e lunedi della Pente Costa che son quattro." Among the "Infrascritti" are: "Al mastro di Cappella di S. Pietro sc. 2 / A Girolamo organista di S. Pietro sc. 2." On Frescobaldi's service at San Luigi dei Francesi see the forthcoming article of Jean Lionnet in *Les fondations françaises dans la Rome pontificale: collection de l'Ecole Française de Rome;* the relevant accounts are Rome, San Luigi, box 48 (1625) and box 49 (1627).

15. Gigli, *Diario romano*, p. 57.

16. Ibid., pp. 72–73: the Bolognese Pope's laissez-faire attitude is epitomized in his words to his relatives, "Governeme, et fè vù."

17. On the election see Gigli, *Diario romano,* pp. 74–78, and Pastor, *History of the Popes,* vol. 27 (1938), 1–54.

18. Gigli, *Diario romano,* p. 37.

19. For 1614–1616 the two extra organists were G. F. Anerio and Gio. Batta. Ricchi (Cappella Giulia 167, nos. 11 (1615), 6, 22 (1616), 1617, nos. 6, 9). CG 167 (1618), no. 4: sixteen singers and Ruggiero and Vincenzo "per la batuta"; no. 8; CG 167 (1619; documents not numbered), Heredia and Ricchi, organists. For the Dedication in 1620 twenty-one singers were employed, with s. Lorenzo "for the beat," Heredia and Ricchi as extra organists, with organs rented from Ruggiero Giovanelli and s. Ludovico and a third provided gratis by Maccione according to the terms of his contract (CG 167, 1620). By 1623 there were twenty-six singers, plus three organs and a violone (CG 168, 1622, no. 7; CG 76, 1623: "Ss.ri Musici ch'hanno seruito *per* il 2o Vesp.ro di s Pietro quest'anno. 1623," signed by Ugolini).

20. The Holy Year prompted the acquisition of a number of music prints by the Cappella Giulia and the copying of works intended for functions in the four greater basilicas (Llorens, *Le opere musicali,* nos. 37–38, and CG 78). The forces for the Dedication were augmented by three trombones and three cornetts (CG 78). On the projects for the baldacchino see Heinrich Thelen, *Zur Entstehungsgeschichte der Hochaltar-Architektur von St. Peter in Rom* (Berlin, 1967), and Irving Lavin, *Bernini and the Crossing of St. Peter's* (New York, 1968).

21. CG 80, unnumbered; the instruments included trombones, cornetts, a violin, and four organs.

22. CG 81, ff. 70–73v: "In nomine Dñi amen Jesus: / Nota de Ssig.ri Musici che hanno seruito *per* il / secondo vespero di SS. Pietro et Paolo nel / 1628 / Esendo fatta vna musica a dodici Chori da / me Paolo Augustini Maestro di Cappella / esendo Card*inal*e Prefetto Ill.mo et R.mo sig. Antonio / Magalotto in honore de dodici Apostoli / Deo Gratias."

23. Giazotto, *Quattro secoli,* vol. 1, 90–108.

24. See Catalogue III.B.5. The Libro Mastro A of the Chapter (1616–1632), c. 57, contains expenses connected with Cardinal Borghese's *possesso* as Archpriest.

25. See Catalogue III.A.2–4.

26. Printed in Sartori, *Bibliografia,* vol. 1, 328–329.

27. Quoted by Oscar Mischiati and L. F. Tagliavini, preface to Sandro Dalla Libera, *Girolamo Frescobaldi: nove toccate inedite* (Brescia: L'Organo, 1962), pp. vi–vii and n. 4. In his *Discorsi e regole sopra la musica et il contrappunto,* completed about 1650, Don Severo Bonini speaks of "the universal reputation and renown that [Frescobaldi] enjoys, and by his manuscripts and published works containing toccatas, *ruggieri, romanesche, monache,* passacaglias, *canzone francesi,* and solemn ricercars scored for four parts" (*Severo Bonini's Discorsi e Regole,* trans. and ed. MaryAnn Bonino, Provo, Utah: Brigham Young University Press, 1979, p. 155).

28. Letter of Frescobaldi to Alfonso d'Este, Rome, 4 June 1624, Modena, Archivio di Stato, Archivio Segreto Estense, Archivi per Materie, Musica e Musicisti: Compositori, cass. no. 1/A, no. 23: "Ser.mo sig.re Prendo ardire di presentare à V.A. compositioni di Musica, non solo perche ella condescende tal'uolta à sentir con diletto questi armonici tratteni*menti* Mà perche mi rendo anche sicuro, che tanto più le saranno care, quanto più grande riconosco la proportione frà l'dono, e l'animo di V.A. perche, se in esso la diuersità di molti suoni con ordinata confusione uà unità à formar' gratioso concerto, nell'animo di V.A. la magnanimità, la gentilezza, il valore, et altre belle doti con gloriosa uarietà concorrano à formar' quella uirtuosa armonia, che risulta dalle sue nobili operationi, oltreche ella è generoso figlio di quella Ser.ma Casa, che è stata sempre il ricouero all'arti più belle, e spetialm.te à questa, per la quale si rese così caro ser*uito*re il Luzzasco, ch'io piglio animo, sotto questo titolo solo d'esser stato suo discepolo, di gir' ricoprendo le mie imperfettioni, come egli sotto si gran' protettione hebbe fortuna di far più ragguardeuole la merauiglia dell'arte. Supplico però V.A. a gradire questo mio picciolo dono, e con quell *animo* suo grande destinato al godimento dell'armonie superiori, si contenti hora godere almeno l'ombra di quelle celesti in queste Musiche terrene: mentre io con profonda humiltà l'inchino, e prego dal Cielo à V.A. il compimento de suoi magnanimi pensieri. Roma li di 4 Giugno 1624. Di V.A.S. Humiliss:mo e Deuot:mo Ser:re Girolamo Frescobaldi."

For Monteverdi's letter, see *Lettere,* pp. 217–219. Newcomb's statement in *The New Grove Dictionary* that Alfonso was about fifteen at the time is incorrect; he was in fact thirty-three.

29. Catalogue I.A.5a, 5b.

30. Pier Francesco Paoli of Pesaro, whose name recalls that of Girolamo's godmother, contributed the sonnet. He also wrote the texts for three *Serenate* in the first book of Frescobaldi's pupil Bartolomeo Grassi (Othmar Wessely, "Aus römischen Bibliotheken und Archiven," in *Symbolae Historiae Musicae: Hellmut Federhofer zum 60. Geburtstag,* ed. F. W. Riedel and Hubert Unverricht, Mainz, 1971, pp. 82–83; see also Llorens, *Le opere musicali,* no. 123, CG XV 59). See also A. D'Angeli, "Un laudatore pesarese di G. Frescobaldi," in *Ferrara a Gerolamo Frescobaldi,* ed. Nando Bennati, pp. 91–95. The 1637 edition of Paoli's *Rime* was dedicated to Cardinal Antonio Barberini.

31. Catalogue I.A.6.

32. Florence, Archivio di Stato, Compagnie religiose soppresse (Conventi soppressi) 2029 (unnumbered: second *filza* of letters to Ippolito and Francesco Nigetti, 1616–1654), Francesco Toscani in Rome to Francesco Nigetti in Florence, 21 October 1623: "Quanto al Frescobaldi, non à stampato nulla di nuouo se non quatro madrigali da cantare sopra al'organo, senza sonare, il quale dice non essere cosa buona da mandare fuora. Ma tuttauia ma [va] mettendo in ordine il libro per mandare a Venetia a stampare, chè questi stampatori qui stanno con il prezzo rigoroso. Basta, quando ci sarà cosa nuoua ue lo farò sapere."

33. The same to the same, Rome, 24 February 1624: "Ho parlato di nuouo questa setimana al Frescobaldi per conto del libro. Dice che fra 10 giorni sarà in ordine, et io ve lo manderò." 2 March 1624: "Quanto al libro del Frescobaldi, ancora non l'à finito di fare stampare [*in marg.*: cioè non è finito], et io gli ò domandato del prezzo di esso libro: mi ha detto che saremo d'accordo. Quanto al' amicitia, non ci ò punto di conoscenza di chi lo possa disporre. Basta, lui mi à detto saremo d'acordo. Vedrò subito sarà in ordine ve lo manderò." 16 March 1624: "Ancora il libro non è finito di stanpare et mi dispiace fino al quore non sia finito, che proprio a me ne sa male. Subito che sarà finito, ve lo manderò acciò ve ne possiate servire nelle vostre occorenze ec." 27 April 1624: "Mi ero scordato di*r*gli che ancora non è finito il libro, ma è al'u*l*timo foglio, et il Frescobaldi mi à detto che per tutta questa setimana che viene sarà finito di stampare, et io subito ve lo manderò." 11 May 1624: "Ancora non è finito di stanpare il libro, e subito sarà finito ve lo manderò."

34. 14 June 1625: "Quanto al libro del Frescobaldi, sono stato a trovallo et mi à detto che l'à finito, ma al presente non me l'à possuto dare. Mi à detto che io vadia uno giorno di questa settimana che mi servirà, et io questa altra setimana lo consegnerò al procaccio ouero a qualche amico che venissi costì, e rispiarmerei il porto."

35. 28 June 1625: "Vi promessi di mandarvi il libro del Frescobaldi, ma non fur possibile, chè lui è huomo tanto lungo nelli sua negoti che non lo potresti credere, et questa setima*na* vi sono stato ugni giorno. Fina*l*mente me l'à dato. Ebbi a stare da lui dua ore buone a 'spettare che lo rico*re*gessi, come vedrete, chè la stampa à fatto qualche errore, ma è ricorretto. Inperò andate dal presente procaccio che non so il nome, che ve lo consegnerà involto et sopra scritto 'Di*asi* al Mag*nifi*co S.r Francesco Nigetti, franco di porto'. Et abbiate pacienza se siate stato troppo a disagio."

36. 19 July 1625: "Quanto al libro del Frescobaldi, habbi*a*m auto caro sia a suo gusto. Quanto al costo, pocho inporta et sono stato per pigliarne uno overo dua et mandarvegli, acciò possiate servir qualche vostro amico. Ma non sono ricorretti: mi à detto che gli rivedrà et uno giorno di questa setimana me gli darà, et io gli manderò a V.S." A letter dated "Di Roma li 25 di novembre" without year may refer to the same volume or, if it is to be dated 1625, may concern some further publication: "Quanto al Frescobaldi, non ha messo cosa nuoua alla stampa, ma uno altro libro in ordine per mandare a Venetia a stampallo, et quando sarà stampata subito l'averete."

6. Florence, 1628–1634

1. Much of the material in this chapter has appeared in Frederick Hammond, "Girolamo Frescobaldi in Florence 1628–1634," *Essays Presented to Myron P. Gilmore,* 2 vols., ed. Sergio Bertelli and Gloria Ramakus (Florence: La Nuova Italia, 1978), vol. 2, 405–419. Banchieri's letter to Frescobaldi was published in

the *Lettere armoniche* (Bologna, 1628; reprinted Bologna: Forni, 1968), pp. 63–64; see also p. 105. Giustiniani is cited according to Carol MacClintock's translation of his *Discorso sopra la musica de' suoi tempi,* Musicological Studies and Documents 9 (American Institute of Musicology, 1962), p. 78. On the transcription of the corrente, see Catalogue I.B, Vienna, Oesterreichische Nationalbibliothek.

2. *Avvisi di Roma,* Biblioteca Apostolica Vaticana, cod. Vat. lat. 7850, c. 209, quoted by Cametti, "Girolamo Frescobaldi in Roma," p. 726. The assumption that Frescobaldi and the Grand Duke met through the Aldobrandini is unconfirmed by the noncommittal letters of the Archduchess Maria Maddalena (Florence, Archivio di Stato, Mediceo del Principato 127, fols. 169, 202). The expense accounts of the trip record only unspecified gifts to the *guardaroba* and gardeners of Villa Aldobrandini and a sum for the ambassador Niccolini to present to the musicians (Florence, Archivio di Stato, Depositeria Generale 1017, nos. 17–18, 22). Further on the Grand Duke's trip see Riguccio Galluzzi, *Storia del Granducato di Toscana* (Florence, 1822), vol. 7, 80–82. It seems curious that Ferdinando should take the initiative in hiring Frescobaldi inasmuch as the Grand Duke had the reputation of considering music "a mere step away from buffoonery" (Bonini, *Discorso,* ed. Bonino, p. xviii, n. 51).

3. The documents are given in Cametti, "Girolamo Frescobaldi in Roma," p. 728.

4. See Angelo Solerti, *Musica, ballo e drammatica alla Corte Medicea dal 1600 al 1637* (Florence, 1905); Pietro Gori, *Le feste fiorentine attraverso i secoli* (Florence, 1926); and Eric Cochrane, *Florence in the Forgotten Centuries 1527–1800* (Chicago: University of Chicago Press, 1973), pp 163–228, although the references on p. 221 to Doni as a friend of Girolamo and to Girolamo as organist of St. Peter's until 1632 are inaccurate.

5. See Solerti, *Musica,* pp. 157–158.

6. An undated document transcribed and translated in Frederick Hammond, "Musicians at the Medici Court in the Mid-Seventeenth Century," *Analecta Musicologica* 14 (1974), 151–169.

7. *Correspondance du P. Marin Mersenne, religieux Minime,* ed. Cornélis de Waard (13 vols., Paris: Beauchesne, 1933–1977), vol. 4, 346, quoting Mersenne's *Harmonicorum Libri II,* Lib. II, Prop. 20, p. 109. The emphasis on Frescobaldi's skill in playing the organ of Cardinal Borghese suggests that, like Cardinal d'Este's harpsichord (see chap. 5, n. 10), it probably had an unusual, complex keyboard. Fantini joined the Grand Duke's service in 1630 (Sartori, *Bibliografia*, vol. 1, 361).

8. For the performance of Marco da Gagliano's *La Flora* at the wedding of Odoardo Farnese and Margherita de' Medici in 1628 the castrato Cavalier Loreto and the keyboard player Andrea Falconieri were brought from Rome (Hammond, "Girolamo Frescobaldi in Florence," p. 416, n. 20). Adriana Basile and her daughter visited in May of 1630 and performed several times at court, and in 1634 "Paolina the Venetian" and a French lute player performed (Solerti, *Musica,* p. 196; Florence, Archivio di Stato, Miscellanea Medicea 11, fols. 244v, 251v, 298).

9. Summaries of account-rolls from 1540 to 1692 are contained in Florence, Archivio di Stato, Manoscritti 321, *Cariche d'onore . . . , Tomo secondo.* Here Frescobaldi is listed at a salary of 25 scudi a month beginning in 1628 (which means that he arrived in Florence before March 1628/9) and is described as "musico." The same source lists him at the same salary for 1631–1632 and describes him as "maestro di cappella" in 1633. The payment-book (the only one of this period I was able to find) is Depositeria Generale 1524, *Libro dei Salariati da S.A.S.*, September 1631–August 1632.

10. Florence, Archivio di Stato, Ms. 321, *Cariche d'onore,* pp. 509–512. On Tacca see Rudolf Wittkower, *Art and Architecture in Italy 1600 to 1750,* 3d rev. ed. (Penguin Books, 1973), pp. 133, 523.

11. Florence, Archivio di Stato, Mediceo 135, no. 41: "Il Gran Duca Ad Alvise Gaetano, Maestro di Mosaico della Republica de Venezia. 3 Settembre 1630. Girolamo Frescobaldo mi ha presentato il mio ritratto di mosaico fabricato da voi come opera di dotta mano."

12. Florence, Biblioteca Nazionale Centrale, Mss. Grandi Formati 133, *DESCRIZIONE DEL NVMERO DELLE CASE E DELLE PERSONE DELLA CITTA DI FIRENZE . . .* MDCXXXII (pages not numbered); see Cochrane, *Florence,* p. 196.

13. Libanori (*Ferrara d'oro,* III, 169) says: "Stanco poi il Frescobaldi, di stare â Roma, chiamato dal gran Duca Ferdinando II. si ritirò à Fiorenza, e per molt'anni seruì la Corte, & hebbe l'Organo di S. Croce, e vi sueglio i soliti stupori, amato generalmente dà tutti, e dà pochi anco inuidiato." Girolamo has also been claimed as organist at the ducal church of San Lorenzo, but investigation in the archives of both churches supports neither assertion. The Entrata e Uscita books in Florence, Archivio del Capitolo di San Lorenzo for these years (1945^{9}, 1945^{10}, 1949^{1}, 1949^{2}, 2519, 2520, 2521) show that the organist was Cesare Ferri. The archive of Santa Croce, *Memoriale E partitj* / DEL OPERA SANTA CROCE / 428, contains a *ristretto* "del Libro de Partiti dall'anno 1589 in qua" which indicates that the priest Antonio di Santi Guelfino was elected organist on 13 December 1632 to succeed Bartolomeo Bettini (fol. 15).

14. Manuscript *Diario* of Cesare Tinghi, quoted in Solerti, *Musica,* p. 196.

15. Biblioteca Apostolica Vaticana, Benedetto Buonmattei, *Descrizion delle feste fatte in Firenze per la canonizzazione di S.to Andrea Corsini* (Florence, 1632); see also Clemente Terni, "Girolamo Frescobaldi a Firenze (1628–1633)," *Paragone* 20 (1969), 12, and Riccardo Gandolfi, "La cappella musicale della corte di Toscana (1539–1859)," *Rivista Musicale Italiana* 16 (1909), 511–512. Raffaele Casimiri, "Girolamo Frescobaldi autore di opere vocali sconosciute ad otto voci," *Note d'Archivio* 10 (1933), 1–31. For an account of these works see Appendix II.B.2 and Catalogue II.B.6.

16. Florence, Archivio di Stato, Archivio dell'Arte de' Mercatanti di Calimala, vol. 69, *Partiti, 1627–1631,* fol. 77v: "Adì 15 di ottobre 1630 . . . sentite come per la morte di Pierantonio di Pagolo Parigi era vacato il luogo de l'organista

de l'oratorio di San Giovanni . . . elesseno et deputarono detto M Girolamo Frescobaldi per [*inserted*: un anno] organista di San Giovanni in luogo del Parigi . . . "; fol. 86 [2 gennaio 1630/31]: "Havendo visto l'electione di [Frescobaldi] addì 15 di ottobre 1630 . . ." I am indebted to Professor Frank A. D'Accone for this information.

17. Roberto Fioravanti, *La musica a Prato dal duecento al novecento* (Prato, 1973), pp. 58–59. The construction of the organ at San Domenico was underwritten by the Grand Duke.

18. See the inventories in Frederick Hammond, "Musical Instruments at the Medici Court in the Mid-Seventeenth Century," *Analecta* 15 (1975), 202–219.

19. Pitoni, "Notizie de contrapuntisti," cited by Silbiger, "The Roman Frescobaldi Tradition," pp. 53–54; Mario Fabbri, "Francesco Feroci nella scuola organistica fiorentina del XVIII secolo," in *Musiche italiane rare e vive da Giovanni Gabrieli a Giuseppe Verdi* (Siena: Accademia Musicale Chigiana, 1962), p. 147; Fabbri, "Giovanni Maria Casini, 'Musico dell'umana espressione'," *Studien zur Musikwissenschaft* 25 (1962), 137.

20. Florence, Archivio di Stato, Compagnie religiose soppresse 2030: letter of Alberto del Vivaio to Francesco Nigetti, 20 January 1640: "Per l'Apportatura della presente mando per il primo libro delle Toccate del Frescobaldi della prima stampa di che hiermattina ne parlaij a V.S. è compiacendosi fauorirmi potrà consegnarlo al detto che fra pochi giornj la restituerò a VS. Ho curiosità di uederlo . . . "

21. "Signora Lucia Coppi plays the *cembalo* gracefully. A Roman and the student of Signor Girolamo Frescobaldi, she imitates her teacher so well that every foreign gentleman who enjoys the sound of that instrument attempts to hear her. Thus, on account of her excellence, she has been employed by the Most Serene Cardinal Gian Carlo de' Medici" (*Discorsi,* trans. Bonino, p. 156).

22. In 1652 Scipione Giovanni, organist and *maestro di cappella* of the Florentine Mont'Oliveto, noted that the Florentine Alberto del Vivaio delighted in teaching children music, "whence I rejoice, as did Sig.r Girolamo Frescobaldi of happy memory, in obliging this Gentleman with my manuscript works for the use of these children" (preface to his *Partitura di cembalo, et organo,* Venice, 1652, in Sartori, *Bibliografia,* vol. 1, 414).

23. Cochrane, *Florence,* p. 196.

24. Florence, Archivio di Stato, Miscellanea Medicea 439, fol. 143, 31 January 1633: "Poi andarono in Casa di Agnolo Galli à sentire una Commedia In Musica con molto gusto."

25. Misc. med. 439, fol. 146: "e dalla sua Venuta il male comincio à cedere." On the plague see Cochrane's account, *Florence,* pp. 195–200, and Carlo Cipolla, *Cristofano e la peste* (Bologna: Il Mulino, 1976). Florence, Archivio di Stato, Mediceo 125 contains considerable correspondence concerning the plague.

26. See Giorgio de Santillana, *The Crime of Galileo* (Chicago: University of Chicago Press, 1955), and Cochrane, *Florence,* especially pp. 181–182, 528–535.

27. Misc. med. 11, *Diario di Etichetta,* III, fol. 250v.

28. On Obizzi see Hammond, "Girolamo Frescobaldi in Florence," pp. 411–412 and notes.

29. See Claudio Gallico, "Discorso di G. B. Doni sul recitare in scena," *Rivista Italiana di Musicologia* 3 (1968), 286–302.

30. This stylistic change is evident in Domenico Anglesi's *Libro primo d'arie musicali* of 1635, the next published Florentine monody collection (see Nigel Fortune, "Solo Song and Cantata," in *New Oxford History of Music,* vol. 4, ed. Gerald Abraham (London, 1968), 178).

31. Doni to Mersenne, *Correspondance,* vol. 8 (1963), 17–18 (letter of 7 August 1638).

32. Biblioteca Apostolica Vaticana, Cod. Barb. 1782; see also Cametti, "Girolamo Frescobaldi in Roma," pp. 739–740.

7. Rome, 1634–1643

1. The documentary material concerning Frescobaldi's service with Cardinal Francesco Barberini is presented in Frederick Hammond, "Girolamo Frescobaldi and a Decade of Music in Casa Barberini," *Analecta Musicologica* 19 (1979), 94–124. On the Barberini family see pp. 96–97.

2. See Gigli, *Diario romano,* 142–143; Filippo Clementi, *Il Carnevale Romano* (Rome, 1899), pp. 379–404; and Francis Haskell, *Patrons and Painters* (New York: Harper & Row, 1971), pp. 55–56.

3. Biblioteca Apostolica Vaticana, Archivio Barberini, Cardinal Francesco senior, mandati 1630–1636, n. 3670: "pagare al s.r Geronimo Frescobaldi sc. 100 moneta per souentione del Viaggio che deue fare da Firenze à Roma con la sua famiglia."

4. Rome, Archivio Storico del Vicariato, San Lorenzo ai Monti, *Status animarum,* 1635–1643. According to Cametti the Frescobaldi family occupied the first of four apartments in the third house from the bottom of the salita on the left ("Girolamo Frescobaldi in Roma," pp. 730–732). For the rent payments see Hammond, "Girolamo Frescobaldi and a Decade," p. 99 and n. 16.

5. Ibid., pp. 98–99 and notes.

6. Biblioteca Apostolica Vaticana, Cappella Giulia, censuale 88 (1635), p. 86, 30 January 1635: Frescobaldi adds to his receipt, "E più ho riceuuto scudi ventiquatro monetta sono per lo cresimento delli due scudi al mese fattomi dal Rmo Capitolo." Cardinal Francesco Barberini had been installed as Archpriest of the basilica in 1633 (see Cappella Giulia, censuale 86, 1633, p. 100, a payment to Virgilio Mazzocchi for "il nolo di 3. organi tenuti per la musica del possesso dell'ementiss.o Card.le Barberino pigliò dell'Arcipretato di S. Pietro").

7. Hammond, "Girolamo Frescobaldi and a Decade," p. 99.

8. Frescobaldi's presence in Rome is documented by his salary receipts in the *censuali* of the Cappella Giulia. His salary began in May 1634 and was drawn in

monthly or bimonthly payments through January 1635, when he signed for sc. 30 for five months. On 26 April he receipted sc. 24 for the increase made him by the Chapter of two scudi per month, to begin 1 May and end the following April (Cappella Giulia, censuale 87, 1634, p. 75; CG, Libro Mastro Generale B, 1633–1690, 1634, c. 48; CG, censuale 88, 1635, p. 86). The supplement was renewed annually until Frescobaldi's death. Domenico Frescobaldi, now a beneficed cleric of St. Peter's, occasionally received his father's salary, as in July and August of 1635, October and November of 1636, April of 1637, June through December of 1638, and May through June of 1639 (CG, censuale 89, 1636, p. 89, Libro Mastro Generale B, c. 58 (1635) and c. 70 (1636); censuale 90, 1637, p. 88, Libro Mastro B, c. 84; censuale 91, 1638, p. 79; censuale 92, 1639, p. 79, Libro Mastro B, c. 92 (1638), c. 98 (1639). Girolamo and Domenico also received payments for Ennio Bonifatij, "maestro d'organi" of the basilica. Girolamo signed the receipts for most of his payments in 1640, all of those of 1641 (the first five months in a lump sum), all of those in 1642, and those for January and February of 1643 (CG, censuale 93, 1640, p. 79, Libro Mastro B, c. 104; censuale 94, 1641, p. 79, Libro Mastro B, c. 109; censuale 95, 1642, p. 79, Libro Mastro B, c. 115; censuale 96, 1643, p. 79: "Signor Alessandro Costantino / Fu accettato adi 15 Marzo"; Libro Mastro B, c. 122.)

9. On Mazzocchi's role in the household of Cardinal Francesco Barberini see Hammond, "Girolamo Frescobaldi and a Decade," pp. 111–124.

10. Pietro Della Valle, *Della musica dell'età nostra . . .*, quoted by Flavio Testi, *La musica italiana nel seicento,* vol. 2 (Milan: Bramante, 1972), 246–247 and n. 27. See the unnumbered *giustificazioni* in CG, censuali 87 (1634) and 88 (1635). The records for Peter and Paul of 1636 are contained in CG, censuale 89 (not numbered): "organista / Frescobaldi di chiesa / Franceschino / Pelegrino / Cau.r Costantino / Leonardo / organi cinque . . . Rettori de i chori / del 2.o cho: Martino è frà i cantori / del 3.o cho: D. Luca è frà i cantori / del 4.o cho: Domenico Mazzocchi / del 5.o cho: Massentio." "Franceschino" was apparently Girolamo's pupil Francesco Muti. For the Dedication the organists were Frescobaldi, Franceschino, and Leonardo, while Massenzio conducted the third choir. Censuale 90 (1637, unnumbered): "Cornetti 3. per la Cuppula / . . . Violoni 3 / . . . organi 6 / organisti / Frescobaldi di chiesa / Franceschino / Cavalier Cons*tantino* / Gio: Batta. / Pellegrino / Leonardo / m*aes*tri di Capp*ell*a / Martino / Sabbatelli / Simone / Mazzocchi / Massentio."

11. Ibid. The organists were Costantino, Pellegrino, Leonardo, Margarino, and Allegri; the spinet players, Gio. Batta [Ricchi?] and Franceschino.

12. CG, censuale 87, 1634, p. 77, 18 May 1634: sc. 4 to Francesco Antonio Rossi "per hauer accordato et segato in due parti, e messe pelle chiodi al organetto, et hauer haccomodato li Mantici di detto organetto, accordato, et spolverato."

13. The platform was designed by Luigi Bernini and the woodwork was entrusted to G. B. Soria, who also worked for the Barberini; see Lunelli, *L'arte organaria,* pp. 95–98.

14. See Haskell, *Patrons and Painters,* chap. 2, "Pope Urban VIII and His Entourage," pp. 24–62.

15. Hammond, "Girolamo Frescobaldi and a Decade," pp. 100–103.

16. Ibid., pp. 107–111.

17. Mersenne, *Harmonie universelle* (Paris, 1636), *Traité des instruments à chordes,* VIII, 65; Doni, letter to Mersenne, 7 August 1638, *Correspondance du P. Marin Mersenne,* vol. 8, 17–18.

18. Letter of Doni to Mersenne, 22 July 1640, *Correspondance,* vol. 9, 486–490.

19. Doni, *De Praestantia Musicae Veteris,* in *Lyra Barberina* (Florence: 1763), vol. 1, 97–98.

20. Doni, *Lyra Barberina,* vol. 2, 252–253.

21. See Sartori, *Bibliografia,* vol. 1, 380–382, 395–397.

22. Hammond, "Girolamo Frescobaldi and a Decade," p. 109, n. 55.

23. See Silbiger, "The Roman Frescobaldi Tradition," pp. 66–71.

24. See the entries on Kerll and Tunder in *Die Musik in Geschichte und Gegenwart;* the pretension of having studied with Frescobaldi was ridiculed by Christian Weise, *Der politische Quacksalber* (ca. 1687), quoted by Andrea della Corte, *Satire e grotteschi di musiche e di musicisti d'ogni tempo* (Turin, 1946), pp. 172–174.

25. André Maugars, *Response faite à un curieux sur le sentiment de la musique d'Italie, escrite à Rome le premier octobre 1639* (printed probably at Paris, late 1639 or 1640), ed. E. Thoinan (Paris, 1865; reprinted London, 1965), p. 29. On the origin and early history of the Arciconfraternita del Crocifisso I have consulted Josephine von Henneberg, "An Early Work by Giacomo della Porta: The Oratorio del Santissimo Crocifisso di San Marcello in Rome," *Art Bulletin* 52 (1970), 157–171. Material from the archive of the Oratorio (now in the Archivio Segreto of the Biblioteca Apostolica Vaticana) was published by Domenico Alaleona, *Studi su la storia dell'oratorio musicale in Italia* (Turin, 1908, reprinted in Milan, 1945, as *Storia dell'oratorio musicale in Italia*), pp. 325–362. Testi, *La musica italiana nel seicento,* vol. 2, 201, suggests that, since music is not mentioned in the statutes of the Società, the subsequent development of the Latin oratorio there was a response to the vernacular works presented at the Chiesa Nuova by the followers of St. Philip Neri. See Howard E. Smither, *A History of the Oratorio,* vol. 1 (Chapel Hill: University of North Carolina Press, 1977), 209–215.

26. Rome, Archivio Segreto Vaticano, San Marcello, Arciconfraternita del Santissimo Crocifisso, P I 61, p. 81, 24 February 1640, for example, records the choice of preachers for Lent of that year. A XI 56, *Entrata et Vscita del Camerlengo* A, 1601–1614, c. 89, no. 303: sc. 176.50 to Paolo Quagliati " . . . cioe li cinque Venerdi di Quadragesima" (Quagliati was also *maestro di cappella* of the parent church of San Marcello al Corso; see c. 112, no. 711); c. 123, no. 871, 6 May 1611: "et scudi trenta à Stefano Landi per mercede delli musici che hanno cantato li uenerdi di quad.ma nel oratorio et li offitii della settimana santa." (An undated

remonstrance in F XIX 20, *Conti, e Riceuute diuerse antiche 1508–1638,* protests that "Noi infrascritti Musici" have been paid only part of their salary by Landi. The signers include Lorenzo Sances and Alessandro Costantini "per sei seruitij, cioè tre oratorij e li tre giorni della settimana santa.") In A XI 56, c. 128, no. 960, 1 December 1612, sc. 66 to Ruggiero Giovannelli for the Lenten music; c. 133, no. 1032: sc. 131.40 for "diuersi musici" in Lent of 1613; c. 136, no. 1081: the same for 1614. These are supplemented by A XII 101, *REGISTRO De MANDATI PER LA COMPAGNIA DEL SMO CRVCIF.*, 1509–1610. In 1621 the music was drastically curtailed (Testi, *La musica italiana,* vol. 2, 201, n. 3).

27. F XIX 25 (unnumbered bills for 1635–1654), bill of Bonifatij, 26 May 1636, for "la portatura del'organo portatile *per* li seruiti del oratorio di uenerdi di marzo prossimo passato et scudi quindici *per* l'accomodatura del organo di legnio alla octaua a bassa nel oratorio." An undated bill in F XIX 20 is headed "Lista delli lauori fatti al Organo di 14 Piedi che sta Nell' Oratorio di S.o Marcello." The pipes were cleaned and "remessoci il pionbo che serue *per* acchordare richolare quelle che erano scolate, è rechomposto et achordato a tono delli altri organi che stanno in detto Oratorio / Rifatto à cinque Canne Le magiore di 14 piedi li fonelli di Noce / . . . / Rifatto una Redotione di fero sotto la tastatura *per* fare sonare li Contrabassi." Inventories of the Oratorio in C XVIII 22, *Libro di Inuentario, delle Robbe, dell'Oratorio, della Compagnia, dell'SS.mo Crocifisso, in San Marcello* (taken in 1653, 1687, and 1696) list "Vn Organo con Cane di Legno Grande nel Coro sopra Pionbe con Bandinela di tela" (1653, c. 31), "Dui Organi nelli Coretti piccoli" (presumably the portable platforms which Maugars describes as reserved for the best of the instrumental musicians: "eschaffaux de huit à neuf pieds de haut," described in the 1687 inventory, p. 13, as "Dui Coretti da Musica intagliati, dorati con pittura Vasi simili nell'Oratorio con sue coperte di tela verde / Vn'altro Coro grande con Gelosie con tre quadri di pittura nell'Oratorio") and "Vn Organo fatto à Cassa nella stanza sopra la tribuna," unusable by 1696 (p. 36).

28. P I 61, p. 175; the Libro Mastro Generale Z X 4 (1637–1660) records a payment of sc. 35 for the instrument (1643, c. 252).

29. A XI 56, c. 123, no. 871, 6 May 1611: "scudi sei à stefano biagi organista; *per* aconciatura del organo et cimbalo *per* ser*v*itio del *oratorio*"; c. 128, no. 960, 1 December 1612: "sc. 6 a m stefano Bagi organista, *per* conciatura del organo et grauicimbalo."

30. F XIX 26, "Lista della spese che ci sonno fatte per seruitio delli uenardi di quaresima . . . del anno . . . 1641 . . . E piu per portatura di doi cimboli et una spinetta . . . E piu per fare portare et riportare doi cimboli et una spineta del Cortona." As early as 1619 Boni was tuning harpsichords for performances at the German College.

31. F XIX 21, 25 March 1639: "il cimbolo da S. Pietro et la spinetta con il cimbolo dal sig.re Marchese [Cesi]."

32. F XIX 25, 1636, nos. 4, 43.

33. P I 61, p. 21, 16 January 1637; Z X 4, c. 128; for 1638 there is a receipt of 5 March (F XIX 21).

34. F XIX 21, 12 June 1639.

35. F XIX 26. Loreto and Pasqualini may have performed in Lent of 1639 as well, since Maugars singles them out for special praise (*Response,* pp. 35–36).

36. F XIX 26, fol. 1 (1641): "E piu per portatura di doi cimboli et una spinetta -25 [f. 2] E piu per fare portare et riportare doi cimboli et una spineta del Cortona sc. -25."

37. In December of 1640 the guardians chose Foggia, maestro of San Giovanni, to direct the Lenten music for 1641 (P I 61, p. 106). The payment records for 1642 and 1643 are uninformative, but ironically those for 1644 are quite detailed (A XII 102, *REG.ro DE MANDATI,* 1641–1647, and F XIX 26).

38. Maugars, *Response,* pp. 29–30. For the repertory of dialogues and the oratorio see Howard E. Smither, "The Latin Dramatic Dialogue and the Nascent Oratorio," *Journal of the American Musicological Society* 20 (1967), 403–433, and *History of the Oratorio,* vol. 1, 77–257; Alaleona, *Studi,* pp. 163–185; and Testi, *La musica italiana,* vol. 2, 200–221. That the introduction of castrati and newer styles into church music was not universally appreciated is demonstrated in a satire by Salvator Rosa, composed probably in the autumn of 1640 and bearing a suspicious resemblance to descriptions of the Crocifisso (Della Corte, *Satire e grotteschi,* p. 151).

39. F XIX 25, a bill of 1654, mentions an "Arcibasso al coretto."

40. One of the earliest surviving compositions for two keyboard instruments is a setting of the Bergamasca, Giles Farnaby's *For Two Virginals* in the Fitzwilliam Virginal Book. A Bergamasca of Scheidt (ms. 26 of the Bartfelder Sammlung in the Music Division of the Szechenyi Landesbibliothek, Budapest, fols. 42v–44, in the Scheidt *Werke,* ed. G. Harms and C. Marenholz, Hamburg, vol. 5 (1937), 28–30) includes as its last four measures the harmonic scheme of the Bergamasca in a low register, marked "Cimbaln in discant"—clearly not a final variation, but an accompaniment to the preceding variations.

41. Maugars, *Response,* pp. 30–31.

42. Gigli, *Diario romano,* pp. 199–223.

43. Florence, Archivio di Stato, Compagnie religiose soppresse 2029, Ippolito Toscani at Rome to Francesco Nigetti in Florence, 2 November 1641.

44. The same to the same, 4 October 1642; 11 October 1642.

45. Bentivoglio, *Memorie,* p. 64.

46. Cappella Giulia, Censuale 96, p. 79.

47. On Girolamo's death and funeral see Cametti, "Girolamo Frescobaldi in Roma," pp. 735–738. According to Pitoni (1847), Frescobaldi was interred in the chapel of the Santo Spirito in Santi Apostoli (Armand Machabey, *Gerolamo Frescobaldi Ferrarensis (1583–1643)* (Paris: La Colombe, 1952), p. 37).

48. Gigli, *Diario,* p. 258.

49. "Signor Girolamo Frescobaldi, who has made an 'anatomy,' as they say, of music by having discovered a new manner of playing *gravicembali* in particular." Trans. Bonino, p. 155.

50. Liberati, *Lettera scritta in risposta ad una del Signor Ovidio Persapegi . . .* (Rome, 1685), quoted in *Girolamo Frescobaldi: Due Messe,* ed. Oscar Mischiati and L. F. Tagliavini (Milan: Suvini Zerboni, 1975), p. vi.

51. See the discussion in Silbiger, "The Roman Frescobaldi Tradition," pp. 68, 77–87. Paul Hainlein commented on the lack of good organists in Rome after Frescobaldi's death (letter of 13 December 1647 in Wilibald Gurlitt, "Ein Briefwechsel zwischen Paul Hainlein und L. Friedrich Behaim," *Sammelbände der Internationalen Musikgesellschaft* 14 (1912–1913), 497).

52. Ralph Kirkpatrick, *Domenico Scarlatti* (Princeton: Princeton University Press, 1953), p. 27. Penna states: "Nor need I teach here, how the student of this Profession should guide himself, in responding to the Choir in Masses, Vespers, Compline, & other matters of Plainsong; since there are in print so many fine Ricercari, Toccate, Canzoni, Capricci &c. of Masters, such as an Urbino of Bologna [Girolamo Cavazzoni], a Luzasco Luzaschi, a Girolamo Frescobaldi, & Others, I have no need to be prolix; therefore I leave the Beginners, to look at the aforesaid Authors, & in particular Girolamo Frescobaldi, who was the Wonder of his times in this profession; in addition with the knowledge of the second book, the Student will be able to form by himself Versets, Toccate, Canzoni, &c." (*Li primi albori musicali,* Bologna, 1684; reprinted 1969, pp. 145–146).

53. See Christoph Wolff, *Der Stile antico in der Musik Johann Sebastian Bachs: Studien zu Bachs Spätwerk* (Wiesbaden: Franz Steiner Verlag, 1968). On the "Adiunctum Frescobaldicum" to Bertoldo Spiridio's *Nova instructio* (1670 ff.), see Apel, *History of Keyboard Music,* pp. 578–579. On Frescobaldi's influence in Germany, see F. W. Riedel, *Quellenkundliche Beiträge zur Geschichte der Musik für Tasteninstrumente* (Kassel: Bärenreiter, 1960).

54. On Heather see A. Hyatt King, *Some British Collectors of Music c. 1600–1960* (Cambridge: Cambridge University Press, 1963), p. 8. On the Blow attributions see Catalogue I.A.3c, 6.

55. See Catalogue IV.

8. Frescobaldi's Instruments

1. Maugars, *Response,* p. 27.

2. Lunelli, *L'arte organaria,* pp. 39, 86–88. The description is from a proposal made in 1720 for the renovation of the instrument.

3. Ibid., pp. 79–81.

4. See Pollak, *Die Kunsttätigkeit,* vol. 2, 232, 240–248, 294, 297–299; Lunelli, *L'arte organaria,* p. 86.

5. Ibid., pp. 53–55; see also Cametti, "Organi, organari e organisti della basilica vaticana nel secolo XVII," pp. 741–751.

6. Lunelli, *L'arte organaria,* pp. 92–94.

7. Ibid., p. 86.

8. *L'arte organica,* fol. 7.

9. *Il Transilvano,* part 2, book 4, p. 22.

10. *L'arte organica,* fols. 7–9v.

11. Banchieri marks the closing measures of a *Sonata in dialogo* "ripieno" (*L'organo suonarino,* 1605, p. 64); another dialogue bears the indications "principale & Ottaua" and "Leuasi l'Ottaua" (1611, p. 32); the sections of *La battaglia* are marked "Ottaua & Flauto," "Giungasi Principale adagio," "Presto & pieno," "Adagio & vuoto," "Ottaua & Flauto; allegro," "Pieno & allegro" (1611, pp. 38–39).

12. Mersenne, quoted by Frank Hubbard, *Three Centuries of Harpsichord Making* (Cambridge, Mass.: Harvard University Press, 1965), pp. 97–98; Raymond Russell, *The Harpsichord and Clavichord* (London: Faber & Faber, 1959), pp. 28–29.

13. Hubbard, *Three Centuries,* pp. 97–98. The device described by Mersenne survives in an eighteenth-century Italian polygonal spinet in the Yale Collection of Musical Instruments (see Sibyl Marcuse, *Check-List of Western Instruments in the Yale Collection of Musical Instruments,* no. 110); for a similar device, see Santiago Kastner, "Le 'clavecin parfait' de Bartolomeo Jobernardi," *Anuario Musical* 8 (1953), 193–209.

14. Hubbard, *Three Centuries,* p. 6. The tone quality of the instrument also could be altered by closing the lid, and Doni even proposed a device for raising the lid gradually which foreshadowed the eighteenth-century machine stop (*Annotazioni sopra il Compendio* (Rome: Andrea Fei, 1640), p. 367). Much as one dislikes the sound of a harpsichord played with the lid closed, it is necessary to admit that the practice is well documented, from the woodcut on the title page of Andrea Antico's *Frottole* of 1517 through the portraits of musicians at the Florentine court by A. D. Gabbiani (1652–1726) reproduced in Hammond, "Musical Instruments," plates 1 and 2, and beyond. On the practice of playing the organ with the shutters closed, see chap. 2.

15. Hubbard, *Three Centuries,* pp. 17–18.

16. Ibid., p. 25. The instrument is dated 1631 by Hubbard, 1637 by Edwin Ripin, "The Surviving Oeuvre of Girolamo Zenti," *Metropolitan Museum Journal* 7 (1973), 76.

17. On spinets and their probable pitches see Sibyl Marcuse, *A Survey of Musical Instruments* (New York: Harper & Row, 1975), p. 295.

18. Hubbard, *Three Centuries,* p. 24.

19. Banchieri described hearing in Milan an "Arpicordo Leutato," on the model of which he commissioned an instrument at lower pitch to simulate the chitarrone (*L'organo suonarino,* Quinto Registro [1611], pp. 3–4).

20. See Hubbard, *Three Centuries,* pp. 49–51.

21. Marcuse, *Survey,* p. 304. Doni suggested tuning the harpsichord a quarter-tone high, as the stage lights caused the strings to fall below the organ in pitch.

22. Modena, Archivio di Stato, Archivio Segreto Estense, Archivi per Materie, busta 3a, filza "instrumenti": "Dimanda fatta da noi Pagliarini per accomodar gli organi é cembali del s. Duca."

23. An inventory dated 18 December 1600 contained in the same file.

24. Hubbard, *Three Centuries,* p. 71.

25. Klaas Douwes (1699) and Quirinus van Blankenburg (1739), quoted by Hubbard, *Three Centuries,* pp. 72–73; on Italian spinets and virginals see pp. 24–25. For a rather more enthusiastic view see Gustav Leonhardt, "In Praise of Flemish Virginals of the Seventeenth Century," in *Keyboard Instruments: Studies in Keyboard Organology 1500–1800,* ed. Edwin M. Ripin (New York: Dover, 1977), pp. 45–48.

26. See Diruta's remarks in *Il Transilvano,* quoted in chap. 15, below.

27. See chap. 3, n. 43, above.

28. Frascati, Villa Aldobrandini, Archivio Aldobrandini, INVENTARIO / GENERALE DELLA CASA / dell' / Illustriss.mo et Reuer.mo Sig.re Pietro Cardinale / Aldobrandino . . . MDCIII, c. 175: "Instromenti Musici. / Vn'Organetto piccolo fatto à modo di Studiolo coperto di Velluto negro e trina d'oro attorno, con suoi Cassettini dentro à tre registri, col suo piede doue stanno i mantici. / Due Cimbali grandi Napolitani con i semitoni spezzati, et sue casse, e piedi bianchi. / Vn'altro Cimbalo di forma ordinaria Napolitano con sua Cassa coperta di corame rosso, et dentro nel coperto depintoui la Creatione del mondo, con suoi piedi depinti di rosso, et indorati, con l'Arme del S.re Diego b*ona* m*emoria* / Vn'altro Cimbalo della sopradetta forma con un filo d'Ebano attorno, et bottoncini d'osso, con sua cassa di corame Turchesco rosso, con bollette fatte à stelle indorate, con suoi piedi depinti et indorati à fogliami, con l'Arme del s.r Card.le / Vn'altro Cimbalo Venetiano à due registri, con pittura di buona mano dentro al coperchio. Vecchio / Vn Regale con le Canne di Legno et la Cassa di Noce intersiata di legno bianco, e rosso / Vn'altro Regaletto con le Canne d'ottone, et cassa depinta di rosso, con suoi pionbi. / Vn Clauiorgano ordinario mal in essere. / Vna Spinetta Francese / Vn liuto tutto d'Auorio con cassa foderata di rouerso. / Vna Chitarra d'Ebano incauata, à cinque ordini, con cassa foderata di rouerso. / Vna Chitarra di Noce incauata à q*u*attro ordini, Napolit*a*na, con cassa foderata di rouerso"; c. 176: "Vn'Organo grande con le canne quadri fatte tutte di legno; era del Card.le Aragona."

29. Garms, *Quellen aus dem Archiv Doria-Pamphilj,* pp. 271, 286, 301, 308, 329, 386, 417, 421, 426, 438–440. On Zenti see Ripin, "The Surviving Oeuvre."

30. See Hammond, "Musical Instruments."

31. Hubbard, *Three Centuries,* pp. 35–37.

32. See the article "Trasuntino" by Donald Boalch and Peter Williams, *The New Grove Dictionary*, vol. 19, 122–123.

33. Printed in Marilyn Aronberg Lavin, *Seventeenth-Century Barberini Documents and Inventories of Art* (New York: New York University Press, 1975), pp. 155–156.

34. Biblioteca Apostolica Vaticana, Barb. lat. 5635, fols. 9v, 22v; Archivio Barberini, Cardinal Francesco senior, *Inuentario* (in full in Hammond, "Girolamo Frescobaldi and a Decade," pp. 103–104, n. 40).

35. Mersenne, cited by Hubbard, *Three Centuries*, p. 36. In 1634 Nicolò Borbone was paid for repairing a Grauiorgano (Archivio Barberini, Cardinal Francesco senior, Libro Mastro B (1630–1634), c. 359).

36. Hammond, "Girolamo Frescobaldi and a Decade," p. 104 and n. 42.

37. Ibid., n. 43.

38. The "maistre de Chappelle de S. Pierre" to whom Doni refers in letters to Mersenne (see, for example, 22 July 1640) is not Frescobaldi, as the editor of Mersenne's *Correspondance* has identified him, but Virgilio Mazzocchi. On Doni's instruments and Della Valle's employment of them see Angelo Solerti, "Lettere inedite sulla musica di Pietro Della Valle a G. B. Doni," *Rivista Musicale Italiana* 12 (1905), 271–338, and Agostino Ziino, "Pietro Della Valle e la 'musica erudita': nuovi documenti," *Analecta Musicologica* 4 (1967), 97–111. Michael Thomas, in "The Development of the Tuning and Tone Colour of an Instrument Made in Venice about 1500," *English Harpsichord Magazine* 1 (1975), 145–155, states (p. 152) that in 1640 Frescobaldi "was nearly persuaded to tune an organ in a church in Damascus in equal temperament." The statement, whose source is unknown to me, presumably refers in fact to Cardinal Francesco's titular church of San Lorenzo in Damaso, for which two organs were being built at that time (see Hammond, "Girolamo Frescobaldi and a Decade," pp. 123–124, n. 100).

39. See chap. 7, n. 19, above.

40. Bontempi, *Historia musica*, p. 95.

41. Gagliano to Cardinal Ferdinando Gonzaga from Florence, 6 October 1612, in Vogel, "Marco da Gagliano," p. 563.

42. Cappella Giulia, censuale 80 (1627, unnumbered): "Lista della fattura dell'organo portabile di S. Pietro . . . Ho giuntate tutte le Canne per abbassarlo mezzo tono ò poco meno, ricompostolo, Intonato, et Accordato con darlo sonare."

43. Maugars, *Response*, p. 27.

44. Arthur Mendel, "Pitch in the 16th and Early 17th Centuries," *Musical Quarterly* 34 (1948), 28–45, 199–221, 336–357, 575–593. The passage from Doni (*Annotazioni sopra il compendio*, pp. 181–182) is given on p. 236. See also Mendel, "Pitch in Western Music since 1500: A Re-examination," *Acta Musicologica* 50 (1978), 1–93. The authors of the article on "Pitch" in the *New Grove Dictionary* note that Mendel's determination of Praetorius' *Cammer-Thon*, which they employ as their standard and place at A = ca. 430, was nearly four semitones higher than

Ellis's estimate and is not necessarily final. Their estimation of Roman pitch as A = 395.2 on the basis of a pitchpipe purchased there in 1720 is, however, inconclusive for a century earlier (Mark Lindley et al., "Pitch," *The New Grove Dictionary,* vol. 14, 779–786).

45. Doni, *Annotazioni,* pp. 181–182.

46. Renato Lunelli, "Un trattatello di Antonio Barcotto colma le lacune dell' 'Arte Organica'." *Collectanea Historiae Musicae* 1 (1953), 153.

47. On indications for performing media given on title pages see the table in Silbiger, *Italian Manuscript Sources,* p. 27.

48. Trabaci, *Secondo libro di ricercate* (Naples: Carlino, 1615), p. 117.

49. The claviorganum in the Kunst- und Wunderkammer in Salzburg is described and illustrated by Gerhard Croll and Gerhard Walterskirchen in the liner notes for the record *Claviorganum: Musik in der Salzburger Residenz* (Harmonia Mundi 414).

9. The Art of Counterpoint

1. For a bibliography of some of the controversies arising from the work of Luigi Ronga, proponent of the "grandezza e solitudine" approach to Frescobaldi, see *Girolamo Frescobaldi: Due Messe,* ed. Mischiati and Tagliavini, p. v, nn. 3–4. What might be called the determinist view of Frescobaldi's artistic formation—especially in attempts to link it with the keyboard tradition of southern Italy and, by extension, Spain—is represented in such studies as Willi Apel's "Neapolitan Links between Cabezón and Frescobaldi," *Musical Quarterly* 24 (1938), 419–437, and Roland Jackson's "On Frescobaldi's Chromaticism and Its Background," *Musical Quarterly* 57 (1971), 255–269. More recent investigation, such as James Ladewig's dissertation, "Frescobaldi's *Recercari et canzoni franzese* (1615): A Study of the Contrapuntal Keyboard Idiom in Ferrara, Naples, and Rome, 1580–1620" (University of California, Berkeley, 1978), has begun to concentrate more logically on influences closer to Frescobaldi: the musical culture of Ferrara at the end of the sixteenth century and that of Rome in the early seventeenth century (see n. 4 below).

2. In Chapters 9–15, Frescobaldi's keyboard works are quoted according to *Girolamo Frescobaldi: Orgel- und Klavierwerke,* ed. Pierre Pidoux, 5 vols. (Kassel: Bärenreiter, 1957–1963), the version most easily accessible to the general reader; all citations have been verified from the original editions and corrected where necessary. Both books of toccatas, however, are cited from a more recent critical edition, the second and third volumes in a projected *opera omnia* of Frescobaldi: *Girolamo Frescobaldi: Il primo libro di toccate d'intavolatura di cembalo e organo 1615–1637* (Milan: Suvini Zerboni, 1977) and *Il secondo libro di toccate d'intavolatura di cembalo e organo 1627–1637* (1979), ed. Etienne Darbellay. In general, I have referred to the contents of these two books as, for example, *Toccate*

I/1 = the first toccata of the first book, except in the single chapters devoted to each book, where unless otherwise indicated a Roman numeral designates the number of the toccata and for brevity the number of the collection is assumed.

The Luzzaschi ricercar in the Turin manuscript is quoted from James Ladewig's dissertation. The keyboard works of Andrea Gabrieli were consulted in the edition of Pidoux, 5 vols. (Kassel: Bärenreiter, 1953). The ricercars, canzonas, capriccios, and *canti fermi* of Giovanni Maria Trabaci's *Libro primo* of 1603 were edited by Oscar Mischiati, 2 vols. (Monumenti di Musica Italiana I/3–4; Brescia: L'Organo, 1964, 1969) and the *Secondo libro* of 1615 by J. Bonfils (L'Organiste Liturgique 54, 57; Paris: Schola Cantorum, 1965, 1966). Ascanio Mayone's *Secondo libro di diversi capricci* was edited by Macario Santiago Kastner (Orgue et Liturgie 63, 65; Paris: Schola Cantorum, 1964, 1965).

The identifying numbers for instrumental collections printed before 1600 refer to Howard M. Brown, *Instrumental Music Printed before 1600: A Bibliography* (Cambridge, Mass.: Harvard University Press, 1965); those for printed collections after 1600 refer to Claudio Sartori, *Bibliografia della musica strumentale italiana* (Florence: Olschki, I, 1952; II, 1968).

3. Adriano Banchieri, *Lettere armoniche* (Bologna: Mascheroni, 1628; reprinted Forni, 1968), p. 86 (to Diruta): "When I sent the two Ricercate à 4 in score in the Authentic Fifth mode, and Plagal Sixth mode to Your Reverence as requested of me . . ."

4. The Macque ricercars are preserved in Florence, Biblioteca Nazionale Centrale, Ms. Magl. XIX, 106 bis. See Silbiger, *Sources*, pp. 101–102, 165–170.

5. Quoted in Roland Jackson, "The *Inganni* and the Keyboard Music of Trabaci," *Journal of the American Musicological Society* 21 (1968), 204.

6. See Gioseffo Zarlino, *Le istitutioni harmoniche*, III (1558), trans. Guy A. Marco and Claude V. Palisca as *The Art of Counterpoint* (New York: Norton, 1976), chap. 63: "Some practitioners write on a cantus firmus or other subject with a certain set condition (*obligo*)."

7. Apel, *History of Keyboard Music*, p. 417.

8. See James Ladewig, "Luzzaschi as Frescobaldi's Teacher: A Little-Known Ricercare," *Studi Musicali* 10 (1981), 241–264. For an elegant demonstration of the role played by *inganni* in the formation of thematic material, see John Harper, "Frescobaldi's Early *Inganni* and Their Background," *Proceedings of the Royal Musical Association* 105 (1978–1979), 6–9.

10. Songlike *Affetti* and Diversity of *Passi*

1. See Chapter 15 for fuller interpretations of Frescobaldi's indications for performance of the toccatas.

2. For a list of Fedele settings, see E. Apfel, *Entwurf eines Verzeichnisses* (Saarbrücken, 1977), pp. 56–57.

11. Various Subjects and Airs

1. On traditional arie, balli, and tenori, see Silbiger, *Sources,* pp. 39–41. For "Brunsmedelijn" see Howard M. Brown, *Instrumental Music Printed before 1600,* items 1569_6, 1570_3, 1578_8, 1583_7. Praetorius' observations on the Spagnoletta are found in his preface to *Terpsichore* (1612), which contains three settings of the tune; see also Agazzari, *Musica ecclesiastica* (Siena, 1638), p. 6, where the subject is a *scemo,* not a *scimmia.* See also Dragan Plamenac, "An Unknown Violin Tablature of the Early 17th Century," *Papers of the American Musicological Society* (1941), 144–157. "Or che noi rimena," identified as More Palatino by Silbiger, *Sources,* p. 123, n. 81, is also related to the *Aria detto Balletto* to *Toccate* II. The capriccios are cited according to the numbering of the 1626 and subsequent editions.

2. For the text of Frescobaldi's preface see Sartori, *Bibliografia,* I, 295–296. On its meaning see Irmgard Herrmann-Bengen, *Tempobezeichnungen* (Münchner Veröffentlichungen zur Musikgeschichte 1; Tutzing: H. Schneider, 1959), pp. 52–53. See also Chapter 15.

12. A New Manner

1. Apel, *History of Keyboard Music* , p. 415 and n. 13; but Antegnati in 1608 already mentioned playing the organ at the Elevation (*L'arte organica,* fol. 7v).

2. See, for example, variation 3–4 of Byrd's *The Bells,* or variation 7 of *Hugh Aston's Ground.*

3. *Il Transilvano,* II, book IV, p. 22.

4. See, for example, the instrumental dances from Naples, Conservatorio di San Pietro a Majella, ms. 4.6.3, published in *A Neapolitan Festa a Ballo,* ed. Roland Jackson (Recent Researches in the Music of the Baroque Era 25; Madison: AR Editions, 1978).

5. Detailed instructions for improvising on *cantus firmi* are given by Bottazzi (1614): "If the Organist wishes to play on some Cantus-firmus subject, such as a Kyrie, Sequence, Hymn, Gradual, Alleluia, or the like, he must take a part of the plainsong, & make the parts progress (as if playing, and one striving with another) imitating that part of the chant, on which he wishes to play, with imitations now above, & now below, so that the parts imitate the other parts, and not the cantus firmus; because such imitations of the cantus firmus are so often practised, & employed, that they can be made rarely or never, that they are not commonplace, and often heard: it is true nonetheless, that in Hymns, and in Sequences the imitation of the cantus firmus is greatly necessary; but concerning the other canti fermi one can observe the above order, making one part imitate the other" (p. 9).

6. On the history of these patterns see Richard Hudson, *Passacaglio and Ciaccona: From Guitar Music to Italian Keyboard Variations in the Seventeenth Century* (UMI Research Press: Ann Arbor, 1981).

13. A Variety of Inventions

1. A "ghost" edition of 1623 is a misreading of the 1628 title page; see Sartori, *Bibliografia,* vol. 1, 293, and vol. 2, 6. A listing of available editions of the canzonas is given in Catalogue II.2,2a,3. The existence of three original editions, the third a drastic reworking of the first two in repertory and one of the first two in unbarred parts, the other in barred score, already poses problems for quoting the canzonas. These are compounded in the modern editions, which attempt to amalgamate two or even all three versions. To spare the reader who wishes to follow using a printed score, I have quoted according to the best printed edition available—the editions of Cerha and Thomas—or my own transcriptions, where I have adopted Grassi's measures for the numbering of bars in the canzonas he prints (the part-books, of course, are unbarred). The modern editions often halve bars in duple meter, so there may be an apparent discrepancy in measure numbers.

2. Sartori, *Bibliografia,* vol. 2, 68.

14. Last Works

1. See Apel, *History of Keyboard Music,* pp. 109–128, 408–447.

2. Bottazzi, *Choro et organo,* pp. 14–18, gives the chant for the first Kyrie before the organ version, the chant for the second Kyrie alone, and the chant for the third Kyrie again before the organ version. As the Gloria makes clear, however, the Primus Chorus is not intended for performance but rather for presenting the chant on which the organist is to improvise, contrary to Apel's hypothesis (*History,* pp. 418–419).

3. Petrarch, Canzone 105, lines 16–17: "I' die' in guarda a san Pietro; or non più, no. / Intendami chi pò, ch'i' m'intend'io"—which one commentator calls "verso inesplicabile."

4. Bonini, *Discorsi,* ed. Bonino, p. 43.

5. For the history and employment of the Girometta and related tunes see Warren Kirkendale, "Franceschina, Girometta, and Their Companions," *Acta Musicologica* 44 (1972), 181–235; on these tunes in the Barberini operas see Hammond, "Girolamo Frescobaldi and a Decade," pp. 115–116. A keyboard Bergamasca is attributed to Scheidt (see chap. 7, n. 40), but his "Canzon Bergamasca à 5," ed. Heiner Garff (Hortus Musicus 96; Kassel: Bärenreiter, 1952), is based on another tune that seems to have no relation to the Bergamasca melodies or their underlying I-IV-V-I structure. The treatment of this material as a basis for an extended independent work is to be distinguished from the simple settings in anonymous manuscripts of keyboard arie and balli. Further on the Bergamasca see Lawrence Moe, "Dance Music in Printed Italian Lute Tablatures from 1507 to 1611" (Ph.D. dissertation, Harvard University, 1956), pp. 30, 172–173, 251–253.

6. See Silbiger, *Sources,* p. 109 and note.

7. Hammond, "Girolamo Frescobaldi and a Decade," pp. 113–114.

8. On the Chigi manuscripts see Silbiger, *Sources,* pp. 128–129.

9. A detailed study of their changes and a reconstruction of the stages in the composition of the *Cento partite,* together with their relation to the Chigi passacagli, is to appear in Darbellay's *Revisionsbericht* for his edition of *Toccate* I.

10. The erosion of the proportional meaning of time signatures is at least apparent by 1673, when Giovanni Maria Bononcini published his *Musico prattico:* "the lower number denotes which values make up the bar, and the upper how many of these there will be" (quoted by William Klenz, *Giovanni Maria Bononcini of Modena: A Chapter in Baroque Instrumental Music,* Durham, N.C.: Duke University Press, 1962, p. 116).

15. The Performance of Frescobaldi's Keyboard Music

1. Honorable exceptions to this are Darbellay's "Liberté, variété et 'affetti cantabili' chez Girolamo Frescobaldi," *Revue de Musicologie* 61 (1975), 197–243; Darbellay's preface to *Toccate* I; and Luigi Ferdinando Tagliavini, "L'arte di 'non lasciar vuoto lo strumento': appunti sulla prassi cembalistica italiana nel Cinque- e Seicento," *Rivista Italiana di Musicologia* 10 (1975), 360–378. Christopher Hogwood's "Frescobaldi on Performance," *Italian Music and the Fitzwilliam* (Cambridge, 1976), pp. 14–22, is a useful compendium, although occasionally a translation is open to question.

2. Antegnati, *L'arte organica,* fol. 8; Grassi, Sartori, *Bibliografia,* vol. 1, 328.

3. Sartori, *Bibliografia,* vol. 1, 184.

4. Ibid., pp. 395–396.

5. Ibid., pp. 349, 412.

6. The apposition of *affetto,* "a passion of the soul," and *effetto,* "that which receives the being of the cause" (*Vocabolario degl'Accademici della Crusca,* Venice: Alberti, 1612; reprinted Florence: Licosa, 1976, pp. 25, 312), and by extension the particular means of arousing the *affetto,* seems to have been frequent in seventeenth-century Italian (Bottazzi, *Choro et organo,* p. 5: "supplisca vi prego l'affetto il difetto dell'effetto"; Monteverdi, *Lettere,* p. 108).

7. See Ottavio Durante, *Arie devote,* 1608: "*passaggi* and other *affetti*"; Caccini, *Nuove musiche e nuova maniera di scriverle,* 1614: "*trilli,* and *gruppi,* & other new *affetti.*"

8. David Boyden, *The History of Violin Playing from Its Origins to 1761* (London: Oxford University Press, 1965), p. 171.

9. Ottavio Durante, preface to *Arie devote:* "Nel principio di qualsivoglia composizione affettuosa, e grave si deve principiare con gravità senza passaggi ma non senza affetti, ed i passaggi farli in luoghi che non impediscano l'intelligenza delle parole."

10. Trabaci, *Ricercate* (1603), pp. 40, 110: "Allarga la battuta."

11. See *Toccate* II/9, Fantasia II, and the capriccio "Fra Jacopino," for example.

12. The examples of major and minor sesquialtera and major and minor hemiola are taken from Zarlino, trans. Marco and Palisca, pp. 260–261; the example of three semiminims is supplied by analogy. This interpretation also occurs in Doni (*IO. BAPTISTAE DONI / . . . / COMMERCIVM / LITTERARIVM*, Florence, 1754, letter to Albertus Bannius, cols. 136–141): " $\frac{3}{1}$ Suprapositus numerus 3. significat, tres notulas semibreves, unam mensuram absolvere, quarum unica mensuram ordinariam temporis aequalis implebat . . . sesquiterti $\frac{3}{2}$ . . . Numerus 3. suprascriptus, ostendet, tres notulas semiminimas, mensuram facere, quarum duae tempori aequali serviunt. Haec proportio fere duplicat velocitatem triplae, quoad durationem mensurae: hoc est, una tertia parte velociorem exigit mensuram $\frac{3}{4}$ . . . Haec proportio duplicat velocitatem sesquialterae."

13. Compare the views advanced by Michael Collins in "The Performance of Coloration, Sesquialtera, and Hemiolia (1450–1750)" (Ph.D. dissertation, Stanford University, 1963), and subsequent articles.

14. Sartori, *Bibliografia*, vol. 1, 396. Francesco Severi's directions for the performance of passages with dotted notes (*Salmi passeggiati*, Rome: Borbone, 1615) reveal that the performance of dotted notes was flexible rather than measured: "Third. When singing eighth notes of which the first is dotted, let them be sung with liveliness but not very fast, and the dots not struck too hard. Fourth. When you find eighth notes which have the second dotted, let them be sung not very fast, and for ease in singing them one must pass rapidly the first eighth, and stop on the second."

15. See Putnam Aldrich, *Rhythm in Seventeenth-Century Italian Monody* (New York: Norton, 1966), pp. 85–92.

16. *Il Transilvano*, I, fol. 5v.

17. Ibid., fol. 6.

18. *L'organo suonarino*, 1611, p. [42].

19. Penna, *Li primi albori*, pp. 149, 197: "2. In ascending in the Right Hand, the fingers are moved one after the other, and first the middle, then the ring finger, and then the middle & so on but the fingers should not play together; but in descending they are changed, the middle, then the index then the middle &c, but ascending in the left hand do the contrary, that is first the middle, then the index, &c. and descending, the middle, then the ring finger, &c." On Bis-Mantova see Adriano Cavicchi, "Prassi strumentale in Emilia nell'ultimo quarto del seicento: flauto italiano, cornetto, archi," *Studi Musicali* 2 (1973), 111–143, and Maria Boxall, "Girolamo Diruta's 'Il Transilvano' and the Early Italian Keyboard Tradition," *English Harpsichord Magazine* 1 (1976), 168–172.

20. Banchieri, *L'organo suonarino*, 1611, p. [42].

21. Thomás de Sancta Maria, *Libro llamado arte de tañer fantasia* . . . (Valladolid: Fernandez, 1565; reprinted Gregg International Publishers, 1972), fol. 38.

22. *Il Transilvano,* I, fol. 8.

23. Praetorius, *Syntagma Musicum,* II (Wolfenbüttel, 1619; reprinted Kassel: Bärenreiter, 1958), p. 44.

24. Etienne Darbellay, "Peut-on découvrir des indications d'articulation dans la graphie des tablatures de clavier de Claudio Merulo, Girolamo Frescobaldi et Michel-Angelo Rossi?" International Musicological Society, *Report of the Eleventh Congress* (Copenhagen, 1972), pp. 342–350. The discussion of beamings in *Italienische Diminutionen,* ed. Richard Erig and Veronika Gutman (Zurich: Amadeus, 1979), pp. 44–48, shows that articulation was at most one consideration in the beaming or separation of notes in printed music.

25. Michel de St. Lambert, *Les principes du clavecin* (Paris: Ballard, 1702; reprinted Geneva: Minkoff, 1972), p. 61: "There are those who maintain that these two different manners of forming the eighth notes establish a difference in the manner of expressing them; that when they are attached together by the line that makes them eighths, they must be played unevenly; & that when on the contrary they are separated & each one flagged separately, on the contrary one must play them equally; But this is a rule to which one must pay no attention: since it is not the shape of the eighths which decides the manner of playing them."

26. In his *Intavolatura* (1623), Chapter III, Piccinini remarks, "and where the music is full of dissonances, for variety it succeeds very well to play sometimes, as they do at Naples that at the dissonances they repeat the same dissonance now loud & now soft, and the more dissonant it is the more they repeat it." See also Fasolo's directions for Elevations.

27. For a summary of these see Tagliavini, "L'arte di 'non lasciar vuoto lo strumento'."

28. The principal sources consulted are: Thomás de Sancta Maria, *Arte de tañer fantasia* (1565_5), Elias Nicholas Ammerbach, *Orgel oder Instrument Tablatur* (1571_1), Antonio Valente, *Intavolatura de cimbalo* (1576_3), Girolamo della Casa, *Il vero modo di diminuir* (1584_2), Richardo Rogniono, *Passaggi* (1592_{10}), Lodovico Zacconi, *Prattica di musica* I (1592), Giovanni Luca Conforti, *Breve et facile maniera* (1593_2), Giovanni Battista Bovicelli, *Regole, passaggi* (1594_3), Girolamo Diruta, *Il Transilvano* (1597_3), Emilio de' Cavalieri, *Rappresentazione* (1600), Aurelio Virgiliano, *Il dolcimelo* (ca. 1600), Adriano Banchieri, *Cartella musicale* (1601 et seq.), Giulio Caccini, *Le nuove musiche* (1602), Giovanni Maria Trabaci, *Ricercate* (1603c), Ottavio Durante, *Arie devote* (1608), Diruta, *Il Transilvano* II (1609–1610), Bernardino Bottazzi, *Choro et organo* (1614b), Trabaci, *Ricercate* II (1615c), Michael Praetorius, *Syntagma Musicum* III (1619), Alessandro Piccinini, *Intavolatura* (1623), Vincenzo Bonizzi, *Alcune opere . . . passaggiate* (1626c), Girolamo Fantini, *Modo per imparare a sonare di tromba* (1638b), Johann Hiero-

nymus Kapsberger, *Intavolatura di chitarrone* IV (1640), Lorenzo Penna, *Li primi albori musicali* (1672), Bartolomeo BisMantova, *Compendio musicale* (1677).

29. Zacconi, *Prattica,* I, fol. 56v.

30. *Il Transilvano,* fols. 10–12.

31. Bottazzi, *Choro et organo,* p. 13. See also Penna: "If you wish to do Trills, these are formed on two keys, that is the one of the Note, or number written, and the neighboring key above, stopping at the end on the Note, or number written, noting, that if they are played with the left hand, they are generally done with the middle, and Index [fingers]; but with the right, for the most part they must be done with the Ring, and Middle [fingers]" (*Li primi albori,* p. 152). For BisMantova's vocal trill, see Cavicchi, "Prassi," pp. 120–121.

Appendix I. Other Keyboard Works Attributed to Frescobaldi

1. See Silbiger, *Italian Manuscript Sources,* p. 8, n. 6.

2. Ibid., p. 153.

3. One such candidate, twice published as a Frescobaldi autograph, has been debunked; see n. 5 below.

4. Silbiger, *Italian Manuscript Sources,* pp. 111–112, 159–160.

5. See Etienne Darbellay, "Un manuscrit frescobaldien à Genève," *L'Organo* 13 (1975), 49–69.

6. Personal communication from Alexander Silbiger.

7. See Chapter 15, n. 3; it is Darbellay's view that some of the Passacagli variations in the Chigi manuscripts are authentic works of Frescobaldi.

Appendix II. Vocal Works

1. I am indebted to Lorenzo Bianconi for tracing the greater part of the attributions of texts in the *Madrigali* and *Arie musicali.*

2. Texts for music are attributed to Bentivoglio in Biblioteca Apostolica Vaticana, mss. Barberini lat. 4201, 4219, 4222, and 4223 ("Deh non più mi ferite" and "Quanto poco durate").

3. *Opere scelte di Giovan Battista Marino e dei Marinisti,* ed. Giovanni Getto (Turin, 1962), vol. 1, 58–60. On Marino's departure from the Cardinal's entourage see Newcomb, "Girolamo Frescobaldi, 1608–1615," p. 141.

4. On Balducci see Smither, *History of the Oratorio,* vol. 1, 179–182.

5. Printed in Federico Ghisi, *Alle fonti della monodia* (Bologna, 1970), p. 47, from the *Maschere di bergiere* of 1590.

6. See chap. 7, n. 52.

7. Superbi, *Apparato,* p. 133.

8. Franz Waldner, "Zwei Inventarien aus dem XVI. und XVII. Jahrhundert über hinterlassene Musikinstrumente und Musikalien am Innsbrucker Hofe," *Studien zur Musikwissenschaft* 4 (1916), 134. On Goretti see Chapter 1.

9. Quoted by Mischiati and Tagliavini in the preface to Frescobaldi, *Due Messe,* p. v and nn. 6–8.

10. Anne Schnoebelen, *Padre Martini's Collection of Letters in the Civico Museo Bibliografico Musicale in Bologna* (New York: Pendragon Press, 1979); see Catalogue IV.

11. Raffaele Casimiri, "Girolamo Frescobaldi autore di opere vocali sconosciute ad otto voci," *Note d'Archivio* 10 (1933), 1–31.

12. Silbiger, *Italian Manuscript Sources,* pp. 164–165.

Bibliography

ARCHIVAL MATERIALS

Bologna, Civico Museo Bibliografico Musicale, Carteggio Martiniano, I.22.85 (Tomo XXVI).

Ferrara, Archivio di Stato, Archivio Bentivoglio, letters to Enzo Bentivoglio: scaffale 9, mazzi 39–55, 55*bis*–56; scaffale 10, mazzi 57–72 (1607–1613).

Ferrara, Archivio di Stato, Atti notarili di Antonio Porti, 1584, matr. 682.

Ferrara, Biblioteca Comunale Ariostea

Ms. Classe I, 22, Coll. Antonelli: catalogue of maestri and musicians of the Accademia della Morte.

Ms. Classe I, 26: Giuseppe Antenore Scalabrini, *Metropolitana di Ferrara*, 1766.

Ms. Classe I, 105: Carlo Olivi, *Annali della Città di Ferrara*, 1790 (2 vols.).

Ms. Classe I, 456: G. A. Scalabrini, *Sacrestia della Cattedrale.*

Ms. Classe I, 472: Girolamo Merenda, *Memorie intorno alla Città di Ferrara.*

Ms. Classe I, 664–666: D. Gaetano Cavallini, *Pro memoria.*

Ms. Classe I, 695: D. G. Cavallini, *Cenni Storici.*

M. F. 138. 10: [Carlo Festini] ORDINI / STABILITI PER LO BVON GOVERNO / Dell' Accademia della Compagnia della / MORTE IN FERRARA / . . . IN FERRARA, Per Giuseppe Gironi. / Stampatore Episcopale. 1648.

Florence, Archivio del Capitolo di San Lorenzo: *entrata* and *uscita* 1945^9, 1945^{10}, 1949^1, 1949^2, 2519, 2520, 2521.

Florence, Archivio di Santa Croce

Libro 426 (giustificazioni).

Memoriale E partitj / DEL OPERA SANTA CROCE / 428.

Florence, Archivio di Stato

Conventi soppressi: 2029, 2030.

Depositeria Generale: 418, 1017, 1524.

Guardaroba Mediceo: 448, 664.

Manoscritti: 321.
Mediceo del principato: 125, 126, 127, 135, 179, 1430, 1431.
Miscellanea Medicea: 11, 434, 437–441, 6379.
Florence, Biblioteca Nazionale Centrale: Ms. Grandi formati 113.
Florence, Biblioteca Riccardiana: Ms. 2218 (Bonini, *Discorsi e regole*).
Ms. Moreni 256.
Frascati, Villa Aldobrandini, Archivio Aldobrandini
Giornale del Libro Mastro D (1603–1605).
INVENTARIO / GENERALE DELLA CASA / dell' / Ilustriss.mo et Re-uer.mo Sig.re Pietro Cardinale /Aldobrandino . . . MDCIII.
Libri mastri E, F, G, H, M.
Mantua, Archivio di Stato, Archivio Gonzaga
E.xxv.3, buste 1006, 1010.
E.xxxi.3, buste 1264, 1265.
Modena, Archivio di Stato, Archivio Segreto Estense
Archivi per Materie, Musica e Musicisti, buste 1–4.
Modena, Biblioteca Estense
Ms. α H.2.16: Marco Antonio Guarini, DIARIO.
Münster, Bibliothek des Bischöfliches Priesterseminar
Santini Collection.
Rome, Archivio Capitolino
Index Testamentorum Rogatorum á Notarijs Vrbis Ab Anno 1645 ad Annum 1651.
Testamenti 1630 al 1645.
Testamenti degl'Huomini 1625.
Rome, Archivio Doria-Pamphilj, Fondo Aldobrandini: busta 28, no. 19: REGI-STRO DEI MANDATI.
Rome, Archivio di Stato, Notaii Acque e Strade: 51 [*olim* 27].
Rome, Archivio di Stato, Ospedale di Santo Spirito in Sassia: Copie di mandati 1912–1926 (1608–1628), 1932–1941 (1634–1643).
Rome, Archivio Segreto del Vaticano
Fondo Borghese, ser. II, nos. 98, 100, 103, 111, 115.
San Marcello, Arciconfraternita del Santissimo Crocifisso: A XI 56; A XII 101, 102; C XVIII 22; F XIX 20–22, 25, 26; P I 61; Z X 4.
Rome, San Giovanni in Laterano: Archivio Storico del Vicariato di Roma
Catalogo delle Parrochie di Roma.
San Lorenzo ai Monti: *Status animarum* 1634–1649.
Santa Maria in Trastevere: musical archive, Armadi VII–VIII; Liber Decretorum Capituli, Arm. III, 3; Sagrestia 1573–1616, Arm. XII, 9; Uscita, Arm. XIII, 12.
Santa Maria in Via: *Status animarum* 1610–1613.
Santo Stefano del Cacco: *Status animarum* 1623–1625, 1626–1631.

Rome, Biblioteca Apostolica Vaticana

Archivio Barberini, Cardinal Antonio junior: GIORNALE/C/, 1636–1644.

Archivio Barberini, Cardinal Francesco senior: GIORNALE/A/, 1624–1629; GIORNALE/B/, 1630–1634; GIORNALE/C/, 1635–1640; Giornale 1635–1644 (in fact a *guardaroba* book), III/7/29; *filze* of giustificazioni 1101–1300 (1629), 2001–3675 (1634–1640), 3848–4070 (1641), 4183–4500 (1642–1643). Libro mastro generale A, 1623–1629; B, 1630–1634; C, 1635–1640; Mastro di casa, 1631–1634, III/1/3; Registro de mandati, 1630–1636, III/3/109; 1637–1641, III/3; 1642–1648, II/3; Salari e companati, 1633–1636, 1637–1642.

Archivio Capitolare di San Pietro: Decreti 10–13; Entrata e uscita, 1607–1612; Inventari 19; Misc. 426; Sacrestia mandati 52.

Archivio capitolare di San Pietro, Cappella Giulia: Censuali 61–81 (1608–1628), 86–96 (1633–1643); Introitus et Exitus Libro Mastro A, 1612–1615; Libro mastro A, 1616–1632; Libro mastro B, 1633–1690; Mandati 163–170; Miscellanea 427, 429, 431.

Ms. Barb. lat: 4145, 4156, 4386, 5635.

Ms. Chigi: Q. IV. 4, 25–29, 35; Q. VIII. 188, 205–206.

Ms. Ottoboni: 3339, 3394.

Ms. Urb. lat.: 1076 (*Avvisi di Roma*).

Ms. Vat. lat.: 12292–98; 12320; 12327; 13363.

Ms. Vat. mus.: 569.

PRINTED SOURCES AND LITERATURE

Adami, Andrea. *Osservazioni per ben regolare il Coro dei Cantori della Cappella Pontificia.* Rome, 1711.

Adams, Ruth. "The *Responsoria* of Carlo Gesualdo." M.A. thesis, University of California, Los Angeles, 1957.

Ademollo, Alessandro. *La bell'Adriana ed altre virtuose del suo tempo alla corte di Mantova.* Città di Castello, 1888.

——— *I teatri di Roma nel secolo decimosettimo.* Rome, 1888.

Agazzari, Agostino. *Musica ecclesiastica.* Siena, 1638.

Agostini, Lodovico. *Canzoni alla napolitana a cinque voci, libro primo,* ed. Adriano Cavicchi and Riccardo Neilsen. Monumenti di Musica Italiana, 2d ser., 1. Brescia, L'Organo, 1963.

Alaleona, Domenico. *Studi su la storia dell'oratorio musicale in Italia,* 1908; reprinted as *Storia dell'oratorio musicale in Italia.* Milan: Fratelli Bocca, 1945.

Aldrich, Putnam. *Rhythm in Seventeenth-Century Italian Monody.* New York: Norton, 1966.

Allegra, Antonio. "La cappella musicale di S. Spirito in Saxia di Roma: appunti storici (1551–1737)." *Note d'Archivio* 17 (1940), 26–38.

Antegnati, Costanzo. *L'arte organica.* Brescia, 1608; reprinted Bologna: Forni, 1971.

Antolini, Patrizio. *Manoscritti relativi alla storia di Ferrara.* Argenta, 1891.

Apel, Willi. "Die handschriftliche Ueberlieferung der Klavierwerke Frescobaldis." In *Festschrift Karl Gustav Fellerer,* ed. Heinrich Hüschen, pp. 40–45. Regensburg: Bosse, 1962.

——— *The History of Keyboard Music to 1700,* trans. and rev. Hans Tischler. Bloomington: Indiana University Press, 1972.

——— "Neapolitan Links between Cabezón and Frescobaldi." *Musical Quarterly* 24 (1938), 419–437.

——— "Studien über die frühe Violinmusik." *Archiv für Musikwissenschaft* 30 (1973), 153–174; 31 (1974), 185–213; 32 (1975), 272–297.

Apfel, Ernst. *Entwurf eines Verzeichnisses aller Ostinato-Stücke zu Grundlagen einer Geschichte der Satztechnik.* Saarbrücken: Apfel, 1977.

Armstrong, James. "The *Antiphonae, seu Sacrae Cantiones* (1613) of Giovanni Francesco Anerio: A Liturgical Study." *Analecta Musicologica* 14 (1974), 89–150.

Arnold, Denis. "A Background Note on Monteverdi's Hymn Settings." In *Scritti in onore di Luigi Ronga,* pp. 33–44. Milan: Ricciardi, 1973.

——— "Alessandro Grandi, A Disciple of Monteverdi." *Musical Quarterly* 43 (1957), 171–186.

——— "Luzzasco Luzzaschi." In *Die Musik in Geschichte und Gegenwart,* 16 vols., vol. 8, cols. 1354–56. Kassel: Bärenreiter, 1949–1979.

Arnold, Denis, and Fortune, Nigel, eds. *The Monteverdi Companion.* New York: Norton, 1972.

Arnold, F. T. *The Art of Accompaniment from a Thorough-Bass,* 2 vols. New York: Dover, 1965.

Artusi, G. M. *L'Artusi.* Venice, 1600; reprinted Bologna: Forni, 1968.

Bacherini Bartoli, M. A. "Giulio Caccini. Nuove fonti biografiche e lettere inedite." *Studi Musicali* 9 (1980), 59–72.

Baini, Giuseppe. *Memorie storico-critiche della vita e delle opere di Giovanni Pierluigi da Palestrina,* 2 vols. Rome, 1828; reprinted Hildesheim: G. Olms, 1966.

Balilla Pratella, F. "Ancora dell' '*Aria della Monicha*' e dell' '*Aria di Fiorenze*'." *Note d'Archivio* 11 (1934), 214–219.

Banchieri, Adriano. *Cartella musicale.* Venice, 1614; reprinted Bologna: Forni, 1968.

——— *Conclusioni nel suono dell'organo.* Bologna, 1609; reprinted Bologna: Forni, 1968.

——— *Lettere armoniche.* Bologna, 1628; reprinted Bologna: Forni, 1968.

——— *Moderna armonia di canzoni alla francese.* Venice, 1612.

——— *L'organo suonarino.* Venice, 1605, 1611, 1622, 1638; reprinted Bologna: Forni, 1969.

——— *Prima parte del primo libro al direttorio monastico di canto fermo.* Bologna, 1615.

Barblan, Guglielmo. "Sui rapporti italo-tedeschi nella musica strumentale del Settecento." *Analecta Musicologica* 4 (1967), 1–12.

Barblan, Guglielmo; Gallico, Claudio; and Pannain, Guido. *Claudio Monteverdi.* Turin: Edizioni RAI Radiotelevisione Italiana, 1967.

Barnes, John. "The Specious Uniformity of Italian Harpsichords." In *Keyboard Instruments: Studies in Keyboard Organology 1500–1800,* ed. Edwin Ripin, pp. 1–10. New York: Dover, 1977.

Bartholomew, Leland. "Alessandro Rauerij's Collection of 'Canzoni per sonare'." Ph.D. dissertation, University of Michigan, 1963.

Basso, Alberto. "Repertorio generale dei 'Monumenta Musicae'." *Rivista Italiana di Musicologia* 6 (1971), 3–135.

Becherini, Bianca. *Catalogo dei manoscritti musicali della Biblioteca Nazionale di Firenze.* Kassel: Bärenreiter, 1959.

Beck, Hermann. "Lorenzo Allegris 'Primo Libro Delle Musiche' 1618." *Archiv für Musikwissenschaft* 22 (1965), 99–114.

Belvederi, Raffaele. *Guido Bentivoglio e la politica europea del suo tempo 1607–1621.* Padua: Liviana Editrice, 1962.

Bennati, Nando. "Musicisti ferraresi: note biografiche." *Atti della Deputazione Ferrarese di Storia Patria* 12 (1901), 287–340.

——— "Notizie inedite intorno alla famiglia di Gerolamo Frescobaldi e alla sua casa in Ferrara." In *Ferrara a Gerolamo Frescobaldi,* ed. Nando Bennati, pp. 37–43. Ferrara: Stabilimento Tipo-Litografico Ferrarese, 1908.

Bentivoglio, Guido. *Lettere del Cardinal Bentivoglio,* ed. G. Biagioli, 3rd ed. Milan, 1828.

——— *Memorie* (vol. V of *Opere storiche del Cardinal Bentivoglio*). Milan, 1807.

——— *Relationi fatte dall Ill.mo, e Reu.mo Sig.or Cardinal Bentivoglio in tempo delle sue nuntiature di Fiandra, e di Francia.* Antwerp, 1629.

Benvenuti, G. "Frescobaldiana." *Bollettino Bibliografico Musicale* 6 (1931), no. 2, 16–36; no. 3, 15–34.

——— "Notarella circa tre fughe attribuite al Frescobaldi." *Rivista Italiana di Musicologia* 27 (1920), 133–138.

Bertelli, C., and Galeassi Paluzzi, C. *S. Maria in Via Lata.* Rome: Marietti, 1971.

Bertolotti, Antonio. *Musici alla corte dei Gonzaga in Mantova dal secolo XV al XVIII.* Milan, 1890; reprinted in *La musique à Mantoue aux XVe et XVIIIe siècles.* Geneva: Minkoff, 1978.

Bevignani, A. "L'Arciconfraternita di S. Maria dell'orazione e morte in Roma e le sue rappresentazioni sacre." *Archivio della Reale Società Romana di Storia Patria* 33 (1910), 1–176.

Bianchi, Lino. *Carissimi, Stradella, Scarlatti, e l'oratorio musicale.* Rome: De Santis, 1969.

Bianchi, Lino, and Fellerer, Karl Gustav. *Giovanni Pierluigi da Palestrina.* Turin: Edizioni RAI Radiotelevisione Italiana, 1971.

Bianconi, Lorenzo. "Weitere Ergänzungen zu Emil Vogels 'Bibliothek der gedruckten weltlichen Vocalmusik Italiens, aus den Jahren 1500–1700' aus italienischen Bibliotheken." *Analecta Musicologica* 9 (1970), 142–202; 12 (1973), 370–397.

BisMantova, Bartolomeo. *Compendio musicale,* 1677. Facsimile of the manuscript, Archivum Musicum 1. Florence: Studio per Edizioni Scelte, 1978.

Bjurström, Per. *Giacomo Torelli and Baroque Stage Design.* Nationalmusei Skriftserie 7. Stockholm, 1961.

Blunt, Anthony. "The Palazzo Barberini: The Contributions of Maderno, Bernini and Pietro da Cortona." *Journal of the Warburg and Courtauld Institutes* 21 (1958), 256–287.

Boalch, Donald. *Makers of the Harpsichord and Clavichord, 1440–1840,* 2d ed. Oxford: Clarendon Press, 1974.

Boalch, Donald, and Williams, Peter. "Trasuntino." In *The New Grove Dictionary of Music and Musicians,* 20 vols., vol. 19, 122–123. London: Macmillan, 1980.

Bonino, MaryAnn. *Severo Bonini's Discorsi e Regole.* Provo, Utah: Brigham Young University Press, 1979.

Bonnefoy, Yves. *Rome 1630: l'horizon du premier baroque.* Milan, 1970.

Bonta, Stephen. "The Uses of the Sonata da Chiesa." *Journal of the American Musicological Society* 22 (1969), 54–84.

Bontempi, Giovanni Andrea Angelini. *Historia musica.* Perugia, 1695.

Borsetti, Ferrante. *Historia Almi Ferrariae Gymnasii,* 2 vols. Ferrara, 1735.

Borzelli, Angelo. *Storia della vita e delle opere di Giovan Battista Marino.* Naples: Artigianelli, 1927.

Bottazzi, Fra Bernardino. *Choro et organo.* Venice, 1614; reprinted Bologna: Forni, 1980.

Bottrigari, Ercole. *Il desiderio.* Venice, 1594; reprinted Bologna: Forni, 1969.

——— *Il desiderio.* trans. Carol MacClintock. Musicological Studies and Documents 9. American Institute of Musicology [n.p.], 1962.

Bouchard, J. J. *Un parisien à Rome et à Naples en 1632: d'après un manuscrit inédit,* ed. Lucien Marcheix. Paris, n.d.

Bovicelli, Giovanni Battista. *Regole, passaggi di musica.* Venice, 1594; reprinted Kassel: Bärenreiter, 1957.

Boxall, Maria. "Girolamo Diruta's 'Il Transilvano' and the Early Italian Keyboard Tradition." *English Harpsichord Magazine* 1 (1976), 168–172.

——— "New Light on the Early Italian Keyboard Tradition." *English Harpsichord Magazine* 2 (1977), 71–72.

Boyden, David. *The History of Violin Playing from Its Origins to 1761.* London: Oxford University Press, 1965.

Boyer, Ferdinand. "Les Orsini et les musiciens d'Italie au début du XVIIe siècle." *Mélanges de philosophie, d'histoire et de littèrature offerts à Henri Hauvette,* pp. 301–310. Paris: Presses Françaises, 1934.

Bradshaw, Murray. *The Origin of the Toccata.* Musicological Studies and Documents 28. American Institute of Musicology [n.p.], 1972.

Brown, Howard Mayer. *Instrumental Music Printed before 1600: A Bibliography.* Cambridge, Mass.: Harvard University Press, 1965.

——— *Sixteenth-Century Instrumentation: The Music for the Florentine Intermedi.* Musicological Studies and Documents 30. American Institute of Musicology [n.p.], 1973.

Buonmattei, Benedetto. *Descrizion delle feste fatte in Firenze per la canonizzazione di S.to Andrea Corsini.* Florence, 1632.

Bussi, Francesco. "La produzione sacra di Cavalli e i suoi rapporti con quella di Monteverdi." *Rivista Italiana di Musicologia* 2 (1967), 229–254.

Caccini, Giulio. *Le nuove musiche.* Florence, 1602.

——— *Nuove musiche e nuova maniera di scriverle.* Florence, 1614.

Caetani, L. "Vita e diario di Paolo Alaleone de Branca maestro delle cerimonie pontificie 1582–1638." *Archivio della Reale Società Romana di Storia Patria* 16 (1893), 5–39.

Caggese, Romolo. *Firenze dalla decadenza di Roma al risorgimento d'Italia,* vol. III: *Il Principato.* Florence, n.d.

Callegari, E. "La devoluzione di Ferrara alla S. Sede." *Rivista Storica Italiana* 12 (1895), 1–57.

Cametti, Alberto. "Alcuni documenti inediti su la vita di Luigi Rossi compositore di musica (1597–1653)." *Sammelbände der Internationalen Musikgesellschaft* 14 (1912–13), 1–26.

——— "Frescobaldi, Girolamo Alessandro." *I musicisti italiani,* proof, Rome, 1919. (Venice, Fondazione Cini, coll. Rolandi).

——— "Girolamo Frescobaldi in Roma. 1604–1643." *Rivista Musicale Italiana* 15 (1908), 701–740.

——— "I musici di Campidoglio." *Archivio della Reale Società Romana di Storia Patria* 48 (1925), 95–135.

——— "Organi, organari e organisti della basilica vaticana nel secolo XVII." *Rivista Musicale Italiana* 15 (1908), 741–751.

Canal, Pietro. *Della musica in Mantova.* Venice, 1879; reprinted in *La musique à Mantoue.* Geneva: Minkoff, 1978.

Cannon, Beekman. "Music in the Archives of the Basilica of Santa Maria in Trastevere." *Acta Musicologica* 41 (1969), 199–212.

Caradente, Giovanni. *Il Palazzo Doria Pamphilj.* Milan: Electa, 1975.

Carfagno, Simon. "The Life and Dramatic Music of Stefano Landi." Ph.D. dissertation, University of California, Los Angeles, 1960.

Casimiri, Raffaele. " 'Disciplina musicae' e 'mastri di cappella' nel Seminario Romano (sec. XVI–XVII)." *Note d'Archivio* 15 (1938), 1–14, 49–64, 97–112, 145–156, 225–247.

——— "Girolamo Frescobaldi autore di opere vocali sconosciute ad otto voci." *Note d'Archivio* 10 (1933), 1–31.

——— "Girolamo Frescobaldi e un falso autografo." *Note d'Archivio* 19 (1942), 130–131.

——— "Il sepolcro dei Cantori Pontificii nella Chiesa Nuova di Roma." *Note d'Archivio* 3 (1926), 221–232.

——— "Tre 'Girolami Frescobaldi' coetanei negli anni 1606–1609." *Note d'Archivio* 14 (1937), 1–10.

Castagnoli, Ferdinando, et al., eds. *Topografia e urbanistica di Roma.* Bologna: Istituto di Studi Romani, 1958.

Cauchie, A., and Maere, R. *Recueil des instructions générales aux nonces de Flandre (1596–1635).* Brussels: Kiesseling, 1904.

Cavalieri, Emilio de'. *Rappresentazione di anima e di corpo.* Rome, 1600; reprinted Bologna: Forni, 1967.

Cavicchi, Adriano. "Contributo alla bibliografia di Arcangelo Corelli." *Ferrara* 2 (1961), 3–7.

——— "Lettere di musicisti ferraresi: Ludovico Agostini (1534–1590)." *Ferrara Viva* 4 (1962), 185–210.

——— "Prassi strumentale in Emilia nell'ultimo quarto del seicento: flauto italiano, cornetto, archi." *Studi Musicali* 2 (1973), 111–143.

——— "Il primo teatro d'opera moderno." In *Ferrara,* ed. Renzo Renzi, pp. 59–66. Bologna: ALFA, 1968.

——— "Il teatro e la musica." In *Ferrara,* ed. Renzo Renzi, pp. 316–332. Bologna: ALFA, 1968.

Celani, E. "I cantori della Cappella Pontificia nei secoli 16–18." *Rivista Musicale Italiana* 14 (1907), 83–104, 752–790; 16 (1909), 55–112.

Ceremoniale Episcoporum Clementis VIII. Primum Nunc Denuo Innocentii Papae X. Auctoritate Recognitum. Rome, 1651.

Cerone, Pedro. *El melopeo y maestro.* Naples, 1613; reprinted Bologna: Forni, 1969.

Cervelli, Luisa. "Brevi note sui liutai tedeschi attivi in Italia dal secolo XVIo al XVIIIo." *Analecta Musicologica* 5 (1968), 299–337.

Ceseri, Carlo; Pastore, Michele; and Scannavini, Roberto. *Il centro storico di Ferrara,* ed. Pier Luigi Cervellati. Modena, 1976.

Chiappini, Luciano. *Gli Estensi.* Varese: Dall'Oglio, 1967.

Ciaconius, Alphonsus. *Vitae et Res Gestae Pontificum Romanorum.* Rome, 1630.

Cipolla, Carlo. *Cristofano e la peste.* Bologna: Il Mulino, 1976.

Cittadella, L. N. *Notizie relative a Ferrara.* Ferrara, 1864.

Clementi, Filippo. *Il Carnevale Romano nelle cronache contemporanee.* Rome: 1899.

Cochrane, Eric. *Florence in the Forgotten Centuries 1527–1800.* Chicago: University of Chicago Press, 1973.

Collection Musicale André Meyer. *Catalogue.* Abbeville: F. Paillart, [1961].

——— *Collection manuscrits autographes, iconographie.* Abbeville: F. Paillart, 1973.

Collins, Michael. "The Performance of Coloration, Sesquialtera, and Hemiolia (1450–1750)." Ph.D. dissertation, Stanford University, 1963.

Colombani, Ernesto. *Catalogo della collezione d'autografi lasciata alla R. Accademia Filarmonica di Bologna.* Bologna, 1881.

Conforti, Giovanni Luca. *Breve et facile maniera.* Rome, 1593 or 1603.

Cordans, Bartolomeo. "La cappella musicale del duomo di Udine." *Note d'Archivio* 7 (1930), 87–201.

Corte, Andrea della. "Ferrara." In *Die Musik in Geschichte und Gegenwart,* vol. 4, cols. 55–71. Kassel: Bärenreiter, 1949–1979.

——— *Satire e grotteschi di musiche e di musicisti d'ogni tempo.* Turin: Unione Tipografico-Editrice Torinese, 1946.

Croll, Gerhard, and Walterskirchen, Gerhard. Liner notes for *Claviorganum: Musik in der Salzburger Residenz.* Harmonia Mundi 414.

Culley, Thomas. "The Influence of the German College in Rome on Music in German-Speaking Countries during the Sixteenth and Seventeenth Centuries." *Analecta Musicologica* 7 (1969), 1–35.

——— *A Study of the Musicians Connected with the German College in Rome during the 17th Century and of Their Activities in Northern Europe.* Sources and Studies for the History of the Jesuits. St. Louis, Mo.: Jesuit Historical Institute, St. Louis University, 1970.

Curtis, Alan. *Sweelinck's Keyboard Music: A Study of English Elements in Seventeenth-Century Dutch Composition.* Leiden: University Press, 1969.

Dalla Casa, Girolamo. *Il vero modo di diminuir.* Venice, 1584; reprinted Bologna: Forni, 1970.

D'Angeli, A. "Un laudatore pesarese di G. Frescobaldi." In *Ferrara a Gerolamo Frescobaldi,* ed. Nando Bennati, pp. 91–95. Ferrara, 1908.

Darbellay, Etienne. "Liberté, variété et 'affetti cantabili' chez Girolamo Frescobaldi." *Revue de Musicologie* 61 (1975), 197–243.

——— "Un manuscrit frescobaldien à Genève." *L'Organo* 13 (1975), 49–69.

——— "Peut-on découvrir des indications d'articulation dans la graphie des tablatures de clavier de Claudio Merulo, Girolamo Frescobaldi et Michel-Angelo Rossi?" In International Musicological Society, *Report of the Eleventh Congress* [Copenhagen, 1972], 342–350. Copenhagen, 1974.

De Angeles, Pietro. *Musica e musicisti nell'Arcispedale di Santo Spirito in Saxia dal quattrocento all'ottocento.* Rome, 1950.

Deffner, O. "Ueber die Entwicklung der Fantasie für Tasteninstrumente." Ph.D. dissertation, Kiel, 1927.

Diruta, Girolamo. *Il Transilvano.* Vol. I, Venice, 1593; vol. II, Venice, 1609; reprinted Bologna: Forni, 1969.

Dizionario biografico degli Italiani. Rome: Istituto della Enciclopedia Italiana, 1960–

Dolmetsch, Arnold. *The Interpretation of the Music of the 17th and 18th Centuries.* London: Novello, 1915.

Donà, Mariangela. *La stampa musicale a Milano fino all'anno 1700.* Biblioteca di Bibliografia Italiana 39. Florence: Olschki, 1961.

Doni, Giovanni Battista. *Annotazioni Sopra il Compendio.* Rome, 1640.

——— *Commercium Litterarium.* Florence, 1754.

——— *Compendio del trattato de' generi e de' modi.* Rome, 1635.

——— *Lyra Barberina,* 2 vols. Florence, 1754.

D'Onofrio, Cesare. "Inventario dei dipinti del Cardinal Pietro Aldobrandini compilato da G. B. Agucchi nel 1603." *Palatino* 8 (1965), 15–20.

——— *Roma nel seicento.* Florence: Vallecchi, 1969.

——— *La Villa Aldobrandini di Frascati.* Rome: Staderini, 1963.

Durante, Ottavio. *Arie devote.* Rome, 1608.

Eggebrecht, Hans Heinrich. "Arten des Generalbasses im frühen und mittleren 17. Jahrhundert." *Archiv für Musikwissenschaft* 14 (1957), 61–82.

Eitner, Robert. *Biographisch-bibliographisches Quellenlexikon der Musiker und Musikgelehrten der christlichen Zeitrechnung bis zur Mitte des 19. Jahrhunderts,* 10 vols. Leipzig, 1899–1904.

Elias, Hendrik J. "La nonciature de Guido Bentivoglio, archevêque de Rhodes, à Bruxelles (1607–1615)." *Bulletin de l'Institut Historique Belge de Rome* 8 (1928), 273–281.

Engel, Hans. *Luca Marenzio.* Florence: Olschki, 1956.

Erig, Richard, and Gutman, Veronika, eds. *Italienische Diminutionen: die zwischen 1553 und 1638 mehrmals bearbeiteten Sätze.* Prattica Musicale 1. Zurich: Amadeus, 1979.

Eubel, Conrad, et al. *Hierarchia Catholica Medii et Recentioris Aevi,* 6 vols. Regensburg: Patritius Gauchat, 1913–1958.

Evelyn, John. *The Diary of John Evelyn,* ed. E. S. de Beer, 6 vols. Oxford: Oxford University Press, 1955.

Fabbri, Mario. "Francesco Feroci nella scuola organistica fiorentina del XVIII secolo." In *Musiche italiane rare e vive da Giovanni Gabrieli a Giuseppe Verdi,* pp. 145ff. Siena, 1962.

——— "Giovanni Maria Casini, 'Musico dell'umana espressione': contributo su documenti originali." *Studien zur Musikwissenschaft* 25 (1962), 135–159.

Fanfani, Amintore. *Storia del lavoro in Italia: dalla fine del secolo XV agli inizi del XVIII,* 2d ed. Milan: Giuffrè, 1959.

Farrenc, Louise. *Trésor des pianistes,* vol. 13. Paris, 1868.

Fasolo, Fra Giovanbattista. *Annuale.* Venice, 1645.

Faustini, Agostino, and Sardi, Gasparo. *Libro delle historie ferraresi.* Ferrara, 1646; reprinted Bologna: Forni, 1967.

Felini, Pietro Martire. *Trattato nuovo delle cose maravigliose dell'alma Città di Roma.* Rome, 1610.

Fellerer, Karl Gustav. "Zur Kontrapunktlehre im 17. Jahrhundert." In *Scritti in onore di Luigi Ronga,* pp. 179–189. Milan: Ricciardi, 1973.

Ferand, Ernest T. "Didactic Embellishment Literature in the Late Renaissance: A Survey of Sources." In *Aspects of Medieval and Renaissance Music,* ed. Jan LaRue, pp. 154–172. New York: Norton, 1966.

——— "Improvvisazioni e composizioni polifoniche." *Rivista Musicale Italiana* 54 (1952), 128–138.

Ferrara, Biblioteca Comunale. *Catalogo delle opere musicali.* Bollettino dell'Associazione dei Musicologi Italiani, ser. 9, 1917.

Fétis, F. J. *Biographie universelle des musiciens,* 2d ed., 8 vols. Paris, 1860–1865.

Fiorani, Luigi, ed. *Biblioteca Apostolica Vaticana, Archivio Barberini, Indexes,* 4 vols. Vatican City, 1978–1980.

Fioravanti, Roberto. *La musica a Prato dal duecento al novecento.* Prato: Azienda Autonomo Turismo, 1973.

Florence, Accademia della Crusca. *Vocabolario.* Venice, 1612; reprinted Florence: Licosa, 1976.

Florence, Archivio di Stato. *Archivio Mediceo del Principato: inventario sommario.* Ministero dell'Interno: Pubblicazioni degli Archivi di Stato I. Rome, 1966.

Fortune, Nigel. "A Florentine Manuscript and Its Place in Italian Song." *Acta Musicologica* 23 (1951), 124–136.

——— "A Handlist of Printed Italian Secular Monody Books 1602–1635." *Royal Musical Association Research Chronicle* 3 (1963), 27–50.

——— "Italian Secular Monody from 1600 to 1635: An Introductory Survey." *Musical Quarterly* 39 (1953), 171–195.

——— "Sigismondo d'India." *Proceedings of the Royal Musical Association* 81 (1954–1955), 29–48.

——— "Solo Song and Cantata." In *New Oxford History of Music,* vol. 4, ed. Gerald Abraham, pp. 125–217. London: Oxford University Press, 1968.

[Franzini, Girolamo]. *Les merveilles de la ville de Rome.* Rome, 1646.

Frescobaldi, Girolamo. (Only editions of general importance are listed here; for others, see the listings following the individual items in the Catalogue of Works.)

——— *Arie Musicali (Florenz 1630),* ed. Helga Spohr. Vol. 4 of *Musikalische Denkmäler.* Mainz: Schott, 1960.

——— *Due Messe,* ed. Oscar Mischiati and L. F. Tagliavini. *Opere Complete,* I. Milan: Suvini Zerboni, 1975.

——— *Keyboard Compositions Preserved in Manuscripts,* ed. W. R. Shindle, 3 vols. Corpus of Early Keyboard Music 30. American Institute of Musicology [n.p.], 1968.

——— *Orgel- und Klavierwerke*, ed. Pierre Pidoux, 5 vols. Kassel: Bärenreiter, 1957–1963.

——— *Il primo libro di toccate d'intavolatura di cembalo e organo 1615–1637,* ed. Etienne Darbellay. *Opere Complete*, II. Milan: Suvini Zerboni, 1977.

——— *Il secondo libro di toccate d'intavolatura di cembalo e organo 1627–1637,* ed. Etienne Darbellay. *Opere complete,* III. Milan: Suvini Zerboni, 1979.

Frey, Herman-Walther. "Die Gesänge der sixtinischen Kapelle an den Sonntagen und hohen Kirchenfesten des Jahres 1616." In *Mélanges Eugène Tisserant,* 7 vols., vol. 6, pp. 395–437. Biblioteca Apostolica Vaticana Studi e Testi 236. Vatican City, 1964.

Frizzi, Antonio. *Memorie per la storia di Ferrara,* 5 vols. Ferrara, 1796; 2d ed., 1847–1848.

Frutaz, A. P., ed. *Le piante di Roma,* 3 vols. Rome: Istituto di Studi Romani, 1962.

Gabrieli, Andrea. *Orgel- und Klavierwerke,* ed. Pierre Pidoux. Kassel: Bärenreiter, 1953–1963.

Gallico, Claudio. "Discorso di G. B. Doni sul recitare in scena." *Rivista Italiana di Musicologia* 3 (1968), 286–302.

——— "Monteverdi e i dazi di Viadana." *Rivista Italiana di Musicologia* 1 (1966), 242–245.

Galluzzi, Riguccio. *Storia del Granducato di Toscana.* Florence, 1822.

Gandolfi, Riccardo. "La cappella musicale della corte di Toscana (1539–1859)." *Rivista Musicale Italiana* 16 (1909), 506–530.

Garms, Jörg. *Quellen aus dem Archiv Doria-Pamphilj zur Kunsttätigkeit in Rom unter Innozenz X.* Quellenschriften der Barockkunst in Rom 4. Rome: Austrian Cultural Institute, 1972.

Garofalo, C. G. "Una scoperta importante di musiche inedite e ignorate." *Rivista Nazionale di Musica* 3 (1922), 307–309.

Gaspari, Gaetano. *Catalogo della Biblioteca del Liceo Musicale di Bologna,* 5 vols. Bologna: Romagnoli, 1890–1943.

Gasparini, Alberto. *Cesare d'Este e Clemente VIII.* Modena: Società Tipografica Editrice Modenese, 1959.

Gasparini, Francesco. *L'armonico pratico al cimbalo.* Venice, 1708.

Geck, Martin. "Franz Tunder." In *Die Musik in Geschichte und Gegenwart,* vol. 13, cols. 975–979. Kassel: Bärenreiter, 1949–1979.

Ghisi, Federico. *Alle fonti della monodia.* Turin, 1940; reprinted Bologna: A.M.I.S., 1970.

——— " 'Il mondo festeggiante': balletto a cavallo in Boboli." In *Scritti in onore di Luigi Ronga,* pp. 233–240. Milan: Ricciardi, 1973.

Ghislanzoni, Alberto. *Luigi Rossi (Aloysius de Rubeis): biografia e analisi delle composizioni.* Milan: Fratelli Bocca, 1954.

——— "Luigi Rossi (un musicista dimenticato del seicento)." *Studi Romani* 2 (1954), 663–668.

Giazotto, Remo. "Un inedito contributo di Benedetto Croce (documenti sui teatri di Roma nel XVII secolo)." *Nuova Rivista Musicale Italiana,* 2 (1968), 494–500.

——— "Pietro Della Valle alla festa fatta in Roma il 25 febbraio 1634." *Nuova Rivista Musicale Italiana* 3 (1969), 121.

——— *Quattro secoli di storia dell'Accademia Nazionale di Santa Cecilia,* 2 vols. Rome: Accademia Nazionale di Santa Cecilia, 1970.

——— "Il testamento di Pietro della Valle." *Nuova Rivista Musicale Italiana* 3 (1969), 96–100.

Gibbons, Felton. *Dosso and Battista Dossi: Court Painters at Ferrara.* Princeton: Princeton University Press, 1968.

Gigli, Giacinto. *Diario romano (1608–1670),* ed. Giuseppe Ricciotti. Rome: Tumminelli, 1958.

Giovanni, Don Scipione. *Intavolatura di cembalo, et organo.* Perugia, 1650.

——— *Partitura di cembalo, et organo.* Venice, 1652. [Only manuscript copies of the title pages and dedications survive in Bologna, Civico Museo Bibliografico Musicale.]

Giustiniani, Vincenzo. *Discorso sopra la musica* (1628), trans. Carol MacClintock. Musicological Studies and Documents 9. American Institute of Musicology [n.p.], 1962.

Gläsel, Rudolf. "Zur Geschichte der Battaglia." Ph.D. dissertation, Leipzig, 1931.

Glover, Jane. *Cavalli.* New York: St. Martin's Press, 1978.

Golzio, Vincenzo. *Documenti artistici sul seicento nell'Archivio Chigi.* Rome: Reale Istituto d'Archeologia e Storia d'Arte, 1939.

Gori, Pietro. *Le feste fiorentine attraverso i secoli: le feste per San Giovanni.* Florence: Bemporad, 1926.

Grotefend, Hermann. *Taschenbuch der Zeitrechnung des deutschen Mittelalters und der Neuzeit.* Hannover: Hahnsche Buchhandlung, 1960.

Gruyer, Gustave. *L'art ferrarais à l'époque des princes d'Este,* 2 vols. Paris, 1897.

Gundersheimer, Werner. *Ferrara: The Style of a Renaissance Despotism.* Princeton: Princeton University Press, 1973.

Gurlitt, Wilibald. "Ein Briefwechsel zwischen Paul Hainlein und L. Friedrich Behaim aus den Jahren 1647–48." *Sammelbände der Internationalen Musikgesellschaft* 14 (1912–13), 491–499.

Gustafson, Bruce. *French Harpsichord Music of the 17th Century,* 3 vols. Ann Arbor, Mich.: UMI Research Press, 1979.

Haas, Robert. *Die Estensischen Musikalien.* Regensburg: Bosse, 1927.

Haberl, F. X. "Girolamo Frescobaldi: esposizione della sua vita e delle sue creazioni a base di documenti bibliografici ed archivistici." In *Ferrara a Gerolamo Frescobaldi,* ed. Nando Bennati, pp. 133–155. Ferrara, 1908.

——— "Hieronymus Frescobaldi: Darstellung seines Lebensganges und Schaffens, auf Grund archivalischer und bibliographischer Dokumente." *Kirchenmusikalisches Jahrbuch* 2 (1887), 67–82.

Hammond, Frederick. "Girolamo Frescobaldi and a Decade of Music in Casa Barberini." *Analecta Musicologica* 19 (1979), 94–124.

——— "Girolamo Frescobaldi in Florence 1628–1634." In *Essays Presented to Myron P. Gilmore,* ed. Sergio Bertelli and Gloria Ramakus, 2 vols., vol. 2, pp. 405–419. Florence: La Nuova Italia, 1978.

——— "Musical Instruments at the Medici Court in the Mid-Seventeenth Century." *Analecta Musicologica* 15 (1975), 202–219.

——— "Musicians at the Medici Court in the Mid-Seventeenth Century." *Analecta Musicologica* 14 (1974), 151–169.

Harper, John. "Frescobaldi's Early *Inganni* and Their Background." *Proceedings of the Royal Musical Association* 105 (1978–1979), 1–12.

——— "The Instrumental Canzonas of Girolamo Frescobaldi: A Comparative Edition and Introductory Study." Ph.D. dissertation, University of Birmingham, England, 1975.

Harris, Ann Sutherland. *Andrea Sacchi: Complete Edition of the Paintings with a Critical Catalogue.* Princeton: Princeton University Press, 1977.

Haskell, Francis. *Patrons and Painters: A Study in the Relations between Italian Art and Society in the Age of the Baroque.* New York: Harper & Row, 1971.

Heartz, Daniel. "Les styles instrumentaux dans la musique de la Renaissance." In *La musique instrumentale de la Renaissance,* ed. Jean Jacquot, 61–76. Paris: Centre Nationale de la Recherche Scientifique, 1955.

Henneberg, Josephine von. "An Early Work by Giacomo della Porta: The Oratorio del Santissimo Crocifisso di San Marcello in Rome." *Art Bulletin* 52 (1970), 157–171.

Herrmann-Bengen, Irmgard. *Tempobezeichnungen.* Münchner Veröffentlichungen zur Musikgeschichte 1. Tutzing: Schneider, 1959.

Hibbard, Howard. *Bernini.* New York: Penguin Books, 1965.

——— *Carlo Maderno and Roman Architecture 1580–1630.* University Park: Pennsylvania State University Press, 1971.

Hilmar, Ernst. "Ergänzungen zu E. Vogels 'Bibliothek der gedruckten weltlichen Vocalmusik Italiens'." *Analecta Musicologica* 4 (1967), 154–206; 5 (1968), 295–298.

——— "Die Musikdrucke im Dom von Faenza." In *Symbolae Historiae Musicae: Hellmut Federhofer zum 60. Geburtstag,* ed. F. W. Riedel and Hubert Unverricht, pp. 68–80. Mainz: Schott, 1971.

Hodge, Brian. "A New Frescobaldi Attribution." *Musical Times* 122 (1981), 263–265.

Hogwood, Christopher. "Frescobaldi on Performance." In *Italian Music and the Fitzwilliam,* pp. 14–22. Cambridge: Fitzwilliam Museum, 1976.

Horsley, Imogene. *Fugue: History and Practice.* New York: Free Press, 1966.

Hubbard, Frank. *Three Centuries of Harpsichord Making.* Cambridge, Mass.: Harvard University Press, 1965.

Hudson, Richard. *Passacaglio and Ciaccona: From Guitar Music to Italian Keyboard Variations in the Seventeenth Century.* Ann Arbor, Mich.: UMI Research Press, 1981.

Hughes-Hughes, Augustus. *Catalogue of Manuscript Music in the British Museum,* 3 vols. London, 1906–1909.

Huys, Bernard. *Catalogue des imprimés musicaux des XVe, XVIe, et XVIIe siècles.* Brussels: Bibliothèque Royale de Belgique, 1965.

Incisa della Rocchetta, Giovanni. "Notizie inedite su Andrea Sacchi." *L'Arte* 27 (1924), 60–76.

Jackson, Roland. "The *Inganni* and the Keyboard Music of Trabaci." *Journal of the American Musicological Society* 21 (1968), 204–208.

——— "On Frescobaldi's Chromaticism and Its Background." *Musical Quarterly* 57 (1971), 255–269.

——— , ed. A *Neapolitan Festa a Ballo*. Recent Researches in the Music of the Baroque Era 25. Madison, Wisc.: AR Editions, 1978.

——— , ed. *Neapolitan Keyboard Composers Circa 1600*. Corpus of Early Keyboard Music 24. American Institute of Musicology [n.p.], 1967.

Kämper, Dietrich. "Studien zur instrumentalen Ensemblemusik des 16. Jahrhunderts in Italien." *Analecta Musicologica* 10 (1970).

Kantner, Leopold. *"Aurea Luce": Musik an St. Peter in Rom 1790–1850*. Vienna: Oesterreichische Akademie der Wissenschaften, 1979.

Kast, Paul. "Biographische Notizen zu römischen Musikern des 17. Jahrhunderts." *Analecta Musicologica* 1 (1963), 38–69.

——— "Unbekannte Dokumente zur Oper 'Chi soffre speri' von 1637." In *Helmuth Osthoff: zu seinem siebzigsten Geburtstag*, ed. Ursula Aarburg and Peter Cahn, pp. 129–134. Tutzing: Schneider, 1969.

Kastner, Santiago. "Le 'clavecin parfait' de Bartolomeo Jobernardi." *Anuario Musical* 8 (1953), 193–209.

Kaufmann, Henry W. *The Life and Works of Nicola Vicentino (1511–c. 1576)*. Musicological Studies and Documents 11. American Institute of Musicology [n.p.], 1966.

Killing, Joseph. *Kirchenmusikalische Schätze der Bibliothek des Abbate Fortunato Santini*. Düsseldorf, n.d.

King, A. Hyatt. *Some British Collectors of Music c. 1600–1960*. Cambridge: Cambridge University Press, 1963.

Kinkeldey, Otto. "Luzzasco Luzzaschis Solo-Madrigale mit Klavierbegleitung." *Sammelbände der Internationalen Musikgesellschaft* 9 (1907–1908), 538–565.

——— *Orgel und Klavier in der Musik des 16. Jahrhunderts*. Leipzig, 1910; reprinted Hildesheim: Georg Olms, 1968.

Kinsky, Georg. *Musikhistorisches Museum von Wilhelm Heyer in Cöln: Katalog*, 4 vols. Cöln: Breitkopf, 1910–1916.

Kirkendale, Warren. *L'Aria di Fiorenze, id est il Ballo del Gran Duca*. Florence: Olschki, 1972.

——— "Franceschina, Girometta, and Their Companions." *Acta Musicologica* 44 (1972), 181–235.

Kirkpatrick, Ralph. *Domenico Scarlatti*. Princeton: Princeton University Press, 1953.

Klenz, William. *Giovanni Maria Bononcini of Modena: A Chapter in Baroque Instrumental Music*. Durham, N.C.: Duke University Press, 1962.

Kothe, B. *Orgelstücke in den alten Kirchentonarten*. Cincinnati, 1870.

Krummel, Donald. "Musical Functions and Bibliographical Forms." *The Library*

(Transactions of the Bibliographical Society), ser. 5, vol. 31, no. 4 (December 1976), 327–350.

Ladewig, James L. "Frescobaldi's *Recercari et canzoni franzese* (1615): A Study of the Contrapuntal Keyboard Idiom in Ferrara, Naples, and Rome 1580–1620." Ph.D. dissertation, University of California, Berkeley, 1978.

——— "Luzzaschi as Frescobaldi's Teacher: A Little-Known Ricercare." *Studi Musicali* 10 (1981), 241–264.

La Fage, J. A. L. de. *Essais de dipthérographie musicale,* 2 vols. Paris, 1864.

Lavin, Irving. *Bernini and the Crossing of St. Peter's.* College Art Association Monograph 18. New York, 1968.

——— "Lettres de Parme (1618, 1627–28) et débuts du théatre baroque." In *Le lieu théatral à la Renaissance,* ed. Jean Jacquot, pp. 105–158. Paris, 1964.

Lavin, Marilyn Aronberg. *Seventeenth-Century Barberini Documents and Inventories of Art.* New York: New York University Press, 1975.

Lazzari, Alfonso. *La musica alla corte dei duchi di Ferrara.* Ferrara, 1928.

Ledbetter, Steven. "Luca Marenzio: New Biographical Findings." Ph.D. dissertation, New York University, 1971.

Lefèvre, Renato. *Il palazzo degli Aldobrandini e dei Chigi a Piazza Colonna.* Vol. 14 of *Quaderni di Storia d'Arte.* Rome: Istituto di Studi Romani, 1964.

——— *Palazzo Chigi.* Rome, 1973.

——— "Il patrimonio romano degli Aldobrandini nel '600." *Archivio della Società Romana di Storia Patria* 82 (1959), 1–24.

Leonhardt, Gustav. "In Praise of Flemish Virginals of the Seventeenth Century." In *Keyboard Instruments,* ed. Edwin Ripin, pp. 45–48. New York: Dover, 1977.

——— "Johann Jacob Froberger and His Music." *L'Organo* 6 (1968), 15–40.

Leppert, Richard. "Musical Instruments and Performing Ensembles in Flemish Paintings of the Seventeenth Century." Ph.D. dissertation, Indiana University, 1973.

——— *The Theme of Music in Flemish Paintings of the Seventeenth Century,* 2 vols. Munich: Katzbichler, 1977.

Lewine, Milton. "An Inventory of 1647 of a Roman Art Collection." *Arte Antica e Moderna* 20 (1962), 306–315.

Libanori, Antonio. *Ferrara d'oro imbrunito,* 3 vols. Ferrara, 1665–1674.

Liber Usualis. Tournai: Desclée, 1962.

Libera, Sandro Dalla. *L'arte degli organi a Venezia.* Venice: Istituto per la Collaborazione Culturale, 1962.

Liess, Andreas. "Materialien zur römischen Musikgeschichte des Seicento: Musikerlisten des Oratorio San Marcello 1664–1725." *Acta Musicologica* 29 (1957), 137–171.

Ligi, B. "La cappella musicale del duomo d'Urbino." *Note d'Archivio* 2 (1925), 1–368.

Lincoln, Harry B. "I manoscritti chigiani di musica organo-cembalistica della Biblioteca Apostolica Vaticana." *L'Organo* 5 (1967), 63–82.

———, ed. *Seventeenth-Century Keyboard Music in the Chigi Manuscripts of the Vatican Library,* 3 vols. Corpus of Early Keyboard Music 32. American Institute of Musicology [n.p.], 1968.

Lindley, Mark, et al. "Pitch." In *The New Grove Dictionary of Music and Musicians,* 20 vols., vol. 14, 779–786. London: Macmillan, 1980.

Llorens, José M. *Capellae Sixtinae Codices.* Biblioteca Apostolica Vaticana Studi e Testi 202. Vatican City, 1960.

——— "The Musical Codexes of the Sistine Chapel Written through the Generosity of the Pauline Popes." In *Studies in Musicology: Essays in the History, Style, and Bibliography of Music in Memory of Glen Haydon,* ed. James W. Pruett, pp. 18–50. Chapel Hill: University of North Carolina Press, 1969.

——— *Le opere musicali della Cappella Giulia I: manoscritti e edizioni fino al '700.* Biblioteca Apostolica Vaticana Studi e Testi 265. Vatican City, 1971.

Lunelli, Clemente. "Una raccolta manoscritta seicentesca di danze e partite per cembalo nella Biblioteca Comunale di Trento." *L'Organo* 16 (1978), 55–75.

Lunelli, Renato. *L'arte organaria del rinascimento in Roma e gli organi di S. Pietro in Vaticano dalle origini a tutto il periodo frescobaldiano.* "Historiae Musicae Cultores" Biblioteca 10. Florence: Olschki, 1958.

——— *Der Orgelbau in Italien in seinen Meisterwerken.* Mainz: Rheingold, 1956.

——— "Un trattatello di Antonio Barcotto colma le lacune dell' 'Arte Organica'." *Collectanea Historiae Musicae* I (1953), 135–155.

Luzio, Alessandro. *La Galleria dei Gonzaga venduta all'Inghilterra nel 1627–28.* Milan: Cogliati, 1913.

Luzzaschi, Luzzasco. *Madrigali per cantare e sonare a uno, due e tre soprani (1601),* ed. Adriano Cavicchi. Brescia: L'Organo, 1965.

MacClintock, Carol. *Giaches de Wert, 1535–1596; Life and Works.* Musicological Studies and Documents 17. American Institute of Musicology [n.p.], 1966.

Machabey, Armand. *Gerolamo Frescobaldi Ferrarensis (1583–1643).* Paris: La Colombe, 1952.

Maggini, Emilio. *Lucca, Biblioteca del Seminario. Catalogo delle musiche stampate e manoscritte del fondo antico.* Milan: Istituto Editoriale Italiano, 1965.

Manfroni, C. "Nuovi documenti intorno alla legazione del Cardinal Aldobrandini in Francia." *Archivio della Reale Società Romana di Storia Patria* 13 (1890), 101–150.

Marcuse, Sibyl. *Musical Instruments: A Comprehensive Dictionary.* New York: Norton, 1975.

——— *A Survey of Musical Instruments.* New York: Harper & Row, 1975.

Marino, Giambattista. *Epistolario,* ed. A. Borzelli and F. Nicolini, 2 vols. Bari: Laterza, 1911–1912.

——— *Opere scelte,* ed. Giovanni Getto. Turin: Unione Tipografico-Editrice Torinese, 1962.

Maroni Lumbroso, Matizia, and Martini, Antonio. *Le confraternite romane nelle loro chiese.* Rome: Fondazione Marco Besso, 1963.

Marsolo, Pietro Maria. *Secondo libro dei madrigali à quattro voci,* ed. Lorenzo Bianconi. Rome: De Santis, 1973.

Marx, Hans Joachim. "Carlo Rainaldi 'Architetto del Popolo Romano' come compositore." *Rivista Italiana di Musicologia* 4 (1969), 48–76.

——— "Monodische Lamentationen des Seicento." *Archiv für Musikwissenschaft* 28 (1971), 1–23.

Masson, Georgina. "Papal Gifts and Roman Entertainments in Honour of Queen Christina's Arrival." In *Queen Christina of Sweden: Documents and Studies, Analecta Reginensia* I, pp. 244–261. Stockholm, 1966.

——— *Queen Christina.* New York: Farrar, Straus and Giroux, 1968.

Maugars, André. *Response faite à un curieux sur le sentiment de la musique d'Italie,* ed. E. Thoinan. Paris, 1865; reprinted London: Stephen Austin, 1965.

Mayone, Ascanio. *Secondo libro di diversi capricci per sonare,* ed. M. S. Kastner. Orgue et Liturgie 63, 65. Paris: Schola Cantorum, 1964–1965.

Mazzoldi, Leonardo, et al. *Mantova: la storia,* vol. III. Mantua: Istituto Carlo d'Arco per la Storia di Mantova, 1963.

Mendel, Arthur. "Pitch in the 16th and Early 17th Centuries." *Musical Quarterly* 34 (1948), 28–45, 199–221, 336–357, 575–593.

——— "Pitch in Western Music since 1500: A Re-examination." *Acta Musicologica* 50 (1978), 1–93.

Mendel, Arthur, and David, Hans T. *The Bach Reader.* New York: Norton, 1945.

Mersenne, Marin. *Correspondance du P. Marin Mersenne, religieux Minime,* ed. Cornélis de Waard, 13 vols. Paris: Beauchesne, 1933–1977.

——— *Harmonicorum Libri.* Paris, 1635.

——— *Harmonie universelle.* Paris, 1636; reprinted Paris: Centre Nationale de la Recherche Scientifique, 1963.

Mirollo, James V. *The Poet of the Marvelous: Giambattista Marino.* New York: Columbia University Press, 1963.

Mischiati, Oscar. "Adriano Banchieri (1568–1634), profilo biografico e bibliografia delle opere." In *Annuario 1965–70,* Conservatorio di Musica "G. B. Martini," Bologna, 39–208. Bologna, 1971.

——— "Un elenco romano di cembalari redatto nel 1741." *L'Organo* 10 (1972), 105–106.

——— "Ercole Pasquini." In *Die Musik in Geschichte und Gegenwart,* vol. 10, col. 868. Kassel: Bärenreiter, 1949–1979.

——— "L'intavolatura d'organo tedesca della Biblioteca Nazionale di Torino." *L'Organo* 4 (1963), 1–154.

Mischiati, Oscar, and Tagliavini, Luigi Ferdinando. "L'arte organistica in Emilia." In *Musicisti lombardi ed emiliani,* ed. A. Damerini and G. Roncaglia, pp. 97–115. Siena: Accademia Musicale Chigiana, 1957.

——— "La situazione degli antichi organi in Italia: problemi di censimento e di tutela." *L'Organo* 7 (1969), 3–61.

Moe, Lawrence. "Dance Music in Printed Italian Lute Tablatures from 1507 to 1611." Ph.D. dissertation, Harvard University, 1956.

Montagu, Jennifer. "Antonio and Gioseppe Giorgetti: Sculptors to Cardinal Francesco Barberini." *Art Bulletin* 52 (1970), 278–298.

Montaigne, Michel de. *Journal de Voyage,* ed. Louis Lautrey. Paris, 1909.

Monteverdi, Claudio. *Lettere, dediche e prefazioni,* ed. Domenico de' Paoli. Rome: De Santis, 1973.

——— *The Letters of Claudio Monteverdi,* translated and introduced by Denis Stevens. Cambridge: Cambridge University Press, 1980.

Moore, James H. "Marco da Gagliano's 'La Dafne': A Critical Edition." M.A. thesis, University of California, Los Angeles, 1972.

——— *Vespers at St. Mark's: Music of Alessandro Grandi, Giovanni Rovetta and Francesco Cavalli,* 2 vols. Ann Arbor: UMI Research Press, 1981.

Morel, Fritz. *Gerolamo Frescobaldi: Organista di San Pietro di Roma 1583–1643.* Winterthur: "Organist," 1945.

Moroni, Gaetano. *Dizionario di erudizione storico-ecclesiastico.* Venice, 1890.

Murata, Margaret. *Operas for the Papal Court 1631–1668.* Ann Arbor: UMI Research Press, 1981.

Neumann, Frederick. *Ornamentation in Baroque and Post-Baroque Music.* Princeton: Princeton University Press, 1978.

Newcomb, Anthony. "Alfonso Fontanelli and the Ancestry of the Seconda Pratica Madrigal." In *Studies in Renaissance and Baroque Music in Honor of Arthur Mendel,* ed. Robert L. Marshall, pp. 47–68. Kassel: Bärenreiter, 1974.

——— "Alfonso Fontanelli and the Seconda Pratica in Ferrara: Some Newly Uncovered Music and Letters." In International Musicological Society, *Report of the Eleventh Congress* [Copenhagen, 1972], 576–580. Copenhagen, 1974.

——— "Carlo Gesualdo and a Musical Correspondence of 1594." *Musical Quarterly* 54 (1968), 409–436.

——— "Girolamo Frescobaldi." In *The New Grove Dictionary of Music and Musicians,* 20 vols, vol. 6, 824–835. London: Macmillan, 1980.

——— "Girolamo Frescobaldi, 1608–1615." *Annales Musicologiques* 7 (1964–1977), 111–158.

——— *The Madrigal at Ferrara 1579–1597,* 2 vols. Princeton: Princeton University Press, 1980.

——— "Il modo di far fantasia: An Appreciation of Luzzaschi's Instrumental Style." *Early Music* 7 (1979), 34–38.

——— Review of Luzzaschi, *Madrigali,* ed. Cavicchi. *Journal of the American Musicological Society* 21 (1968), 222–226.

Oldham, Guy. "Louis Couperin: A New Source of French Keyboard Music of the

Mid-17th Century." "*Recherches*" *sur la musique française classique* 1 (1960), 51–59.

Orbaan, J. A. F. *Documenti sul barocco in Roma.* Miscellanea della Reale Società Romana di Storia Patria 6. Rome, 1920.

——— "Un viaggio di Clemente VIII nel Viterbese." *Archivio della Reale Società Romana di Storia Patria* 36 (1913), 113–145.

Osthoff, W. *Das dramatische Spätwerk Claudio Monteverdis.* Monteverdistudien 1. Tutzing: Schneider, 1960.

Palisca, Claude V. "The 'Camerata fiorentina': A Reappraisal." *Studi Musicali* 1 (1972), 203–236.

——— "Musical Asides in the Diplomatic Correspondence of Emilio de' Cavalieri." *Musical Quarterly* 49 (1963), 339–355.

Pardi, G. "Sulla popolazione del Ferrarese dopo la devoluzione." *Atti della Deputazione Ferrarese di Storia Patria* 20 (1911), 1–132.

Pasquini, Ercole. *Collected Keyboard Works,* ed. W. Richard Shindle. Corpus of Early Keyboard Music 12. American Institute of Musicology [n.p.], 1966.

Pastor, Ludwig Freiherr von. *Geschichte der Päpste seit dem Ausgang des Mittelalters,* 40 vols. Freiburg in Breisgau, 1886–89.

Pecchiai, P. *I Barberini.* Rome, 1959.

Penna, Lorenzo. *Li primi albori musicali.* Bologna, 1684; reprinted Bologna: Forni, 1969.

Pergola, Paula della. "Gli inventari Aldobrandini." *Arte Antica e Moderna* 1960, 425–444; 1962, 316–322; 1963, 61–87.

Pesenti, Michele. *Il secondo libro delle correnti alla francese.* Venice, 1630.

Piccinini, Alessandro. *Intavolatura di liuto e di chitarrone* (1623), 2 vols. Facsimile edition and transcription by Mirko Carfagni, 2 vols. Antiquae Musicae Italicae Monumenta Bononiensia. Bologna, 1962.

Pirro, André. "Frescobaldi et les musiciens de la France et des Pays-Bas." *Bulletin Français de la Société Internationale de Musicologie,* 1908, 1127–53.

Pirrotta, Nino. *Li due Orfei: da Poliziano a Monteverdi.* Turin: Edizioni RAI Radiotelevisione Italiana, 1969.

——— "Note su Marenzio e il Tasso." In *Scritti in onore di Luigi Ronga,* pp. 557–571. Milan: Ricciardi, 1973.

Plamenac, Dragan. "An Unknown Violin Tablature of the Early 17th Century." *Papers of the American Musicological Society,* 1941, 144–157. [1946.]

Pohlmann, Ernst. *Laute, Theorbe, Chitarrone: Die Lauten-Instrumente, ihre Musik und Literatur von 1500 bis zur Gegenwart,* 3d edition. Bremen: Eres, 1975.

Pollak, O. *Die Kunsttätigkeit unter Urban VIII.* Vol. 1, *Kirchliche Bauten und Paläste,* Vienna, 1927. Vol. 2, *Die Peterskirche in Rom,* Vienna, 1931.

Praetorius, Michael. *Syntagma Musicum,* vol. 1, Wittenberg, 1614/1615; vol. 2, Wolfenbüttel, 1618/1619; vol. 3, Wolfenbüttel, 1619; reprinted Kassel: Bärenreiter, 1958–1959.

Prinzivalli, V. "La devoluzione di Ferrara alla S. Sede secondo una relazione inedita di Camillo Capilupi." *Atti della Deputazione Ferrarese di Storia Patria* 10 (1898), 119ff.

Prunières, Henry. "Les musiciens du Cardinal Antonio Barberini." *Mélanges de musicologie offerts à M. Lionel de la Laurencie,* pp. 117–122. Publications de la Société Française de Musicologie. Paris, 1933.

——— *L'opéra italien en France avant Lulli.* Paris: E. Champion, 1913.

Racek, Jan. *Stilprobleme der italienischen Monodie: ein Beitrag zur Geschichte des einstimmigen Barockliedes.* Prague: Státní Pedagogické Nakladatelstvì, 1965.

Redlich, Hans. "Girolamo Frescobaldi." *The Music Review* 14 (1953), 262–274.

Reese, Gustave. "An Early Seventeenth-Century Italian Lute Manuscript at San Francisco." In *Essays in Musicology in Honor of Dragan Plamenac,* ed. Gustave Reese and Robert V. Snow, pp. 253–280. Pittsburgh: University of Pittsburgh Press, 1969.

Regesti di Bandi, editti, notificazioni e provvedimenti diversi relativi alla città di Roma ed allo stato pontificio. Rome, 1932.

Reimann, Margarete. "Girolamo Frescobaldi." In *Die Musik in Geschichte und Gegenwart,* vol. 4, cols. 912–926. Kassel: Bärenreiter, 1949–1979.

Reiner, Stuart. "La vag'Angioletta (and others), Part I." *Analecta Musicologica* 14 (1974), 26–88.

——— "Preparations in Parma—1618, 1627–28." *Music Review* 25 (1964), 273–301.

Répertoire international des sources musicales (RISM). A/I/3, *Einzeldrücke vor 1800,* ed. Karlheinz Schlager, 1971– . Kassel: Bärenreiter. *Recueils imprimés 16e–17e siècles,* ed. François Lesure. Munich: Henle, 1960.

Riedel, Friedrich Wilhelm. "Der Einfluss der italienischen Klaviermusik des 17. Jahrhunderts auf die Entwicklung der Musik für Tasteninstrumente in Deutschland während der ersten Hälfte des 18. Jahrhunderts." *Analecta Musicologica* 5 (1968), 18–33.

——— *Quellenkundliche Beiträge zur Geschichte der Musik für Tasteninstrumente in der zweiten Hälfte des 17. Jahrhunderts (vornehmlich in Deutschland).* Schriften des Landesinstituts für Musikforschung Kiel 10. Kassel: Bärenreiter, 1960.

——— "Ein Skizzenbuch von Alessandro Poglietti." In *Essays in Musicology: A Birthday Offering for Willi Apel,* ed. Hans Tischler, pp. 145–152. Bloomington: Indiana University Press, 1968.

Ripin, Edwin. "On Joes Karest's Virginal and the Origins of the Flemish Tradition." In *Keyboard Instruments: Studies in Keyboard Organology, 1500–1800,* ed. Edwin Ripin, pp. 67–76. New York: Dover, 1977.

——— "The Surviving Oeuvre of Girolamo Zenti." *Metropolitan Museum Journal* 7 (1973), 71–87.

Roche, Jerome. "Anthologies and the Dissemination of Early Baroque Italian Sacred Music." *Soundings* (University of Cardiff) 4 (1974), 6–12.

Rogniono, Richardo. *Passaggi per potersi essercitare nel diminuire.* Venice, 1592.

Rognoni Taegio, Francesco. *Selva de varii passaggi.* Milan, 1620; reprinted Bologna: Forni, 1970.

Roncaglia, Gino. *La cappella musicale del duomo di Modena.* "Historiae Musicae Cultores" Biblioteca 5. Florence: Olschki, 1957.

Ronga, Luigi. *Gerolamo Frescobaldi.* Turin: Fratelli Bocca, 1930.

——— "Grandezza e solitudine di Gerolamo Frescobaldi." *Rivista Musicale Italiana* 56 (1954), 28–44.

——— "Inediti frescobaldiani." *Rivista Musicale Italiana* 57 (1955), 151–156.

Rovighi, Luigi. "Prassi esecutiva barocca negli strumenti ad arco." *Rivista Italiana di Musicologia* 8 (1973), 38–112.

Russell, Raymond. *The Harpsichord and Clavichord*. London: Faber & Faber, 1959.

Saint Lambert, Michel de. *Les principes du clavecin.* Paris, 1702; reprinted Geneva: Minkoff, 1972.

Sala, D. Torello. *Dizionario storico biografico di scrittori, letterati ed artisti dell'Ordine di Vallombrosa.* Florence, 1929.

Sancta Maria, Thomás de. *Libro llamado arte de tañer fantasia.* Valladolid, 1565; reprinted Gregg International Publishers [n.p.], 1972.

Sandberger, Adolf. "Johann Kaspar Kerll." In *Ausgewählte Aufsätze zur Musikgeschichte,* 2 vols., 181–187. Munich: Drei Masken, 1921.

Santillana, Giorgio de. *The Crime of Galileo.* Chicago: University of Chicago Press, 1955.

Santoro, Elia. *La famiglia e la formazione di Claudio Monteverdi: note biografiche con documenti inediti.* Annali della Biblioteca Governativa e Libreria Civica di Cremona 18/1. Cremona: Athenaeum Cremonese, 1967.

Sartori, Claudio. *Bibliografia della musica strumentale italiana stampata in Italia fino al 1700.* Florence: Olschki; vol. 1, 1952; vol. 2, 1968.

——— *Dizionario degli editori musicali italiani.* Biblioteca di Bibliografia Italiana 32. Florence: Olschki, 1958.

——— "Milleville." In *Die Musik in Geschichte und Gegenwart,* vol. 9, cols. 337–338.

——— "Le 7 edizioni delle *Toccate* di Girolamo Frescobaldi." *La Bibliofilia* 50 (1948), 198–214.

Scharlau, Ulf. *Athanasius Kircher (1601–1680) als Musikschriftsteller.* Studien zur Hessischen Musikgeschichte 2, ed. Heinrich Hüschen. Marburg: Görich and Weiershaüser, 1969.

Scheidt, Samuel. *Werke,* ed. G. Harms and C. Marenholz. Hamburg: Ugrino, 1923– .

Schierning, Lydia. *Die Ueberlieferung der deutschen Orgel- und Klaviermusik aus der ersten Hälfte des 17. Jahrhunderts: eine quellenkundliche Studie.* Schriften des Landesinstituts für Musikforschung Kiel 12. Kassel: Bärenreiter, 1961.

Schmid, Hans. "Una nuova fonte di musica organistica del secolo XVII." *L'Organo* 1 (1960), 107–113.

Schnoebelen, Anne. *Padre Martini's Collection of Letters in the Civico Museo Bibliografico Musicale in Bologna.* New York: Pendragon Press, 1979.

Seelkopf, Martin. "Das geistliche Schaffen von Alessandro Grandi." Ph.D. dissertation, Würzburg, 1973.

Selfridge-Field, Eleanor. *Venetian Instrumental Music from Gabrieli to Vivaldi.* New York: Praeger, 1975.

Severi, Francesco. *Salmi passeggiati.* Rome: Borbone, 1615.

Silbiger, Alexander. *Italian Manuscript Sources of 17th Century Keyboard Music.* Ann Arbor: UMI Research Press, 1980.

——— "The Roman Frescobaldi Tradition, c. 1640–1670." *Journal of the American Musicological Society* 33 (1980), 42–87.

Smith, Logan P. *The Life and Letters of Sir Henry Wotton,* 2 vols. Oxford: Oxford University Press, 1907.

Smither, Howard. "The Latin Dramatic Dialogue and the Nascent Oratorio." *Journal of the American Musicological Society* 20 (1967), 403–433.

——— *A History of the Oratorio I: The Oratorio in the Baroque Era; Italy, Vienna, Paris.* Chapel Hill: University of North Carolina Press, 1977.

——— "Romano Micheli's 'Dialogus Annuntiationis' (1625): A Twenty-Voice Canon with Thirty 'Obblighi'." *Analecta Musicologica* 5 (1968), 34–91.

Solerti, Angelo. *Gli albori del melodramma,* 3 vols. Milan, 1904–1905.

——— *Ferrara e la corte estense nella seconda metà del secolo decimosesto; i discorsi di Annibale Romei,* 2d ed. Città di Castello: Lapi, 1900.

——— "Lettere inedite sulla musica di Pietro Della Valle a G. B. Doni ed una veglia drammatica-musicale del medesimo." *Rivista Musicale Italiana* 12 (1905), 271–338.

——— *Musica, ballo e drammatica alla Corte Medicea dal 1600 al 1637.* Florence: Bemporad, 1905.

Stanghetti, G. "La scuola di canto nel Pontificio Collegio Urbano di Roma (1627–1925)." *Note d'Archivio* 3 (1926), 46–57.

"Sulla casa di Girolamo Frescobaldi lettere due dell'Ing. Comm. Eugenio Righini e dell dott. Nando Bennati." *Atti della Deputazione Ferrarese di Storia Patria* 24 (1919), pp. 115–129.

Superbi, Agostino. *Apparato degli huomini illustri della città di Ferrara.* Ferrara, 1620.

Tagliavini, Luigi Ferdinando. "L'arte di 'non lasciar vuoto lo strumento': appunti sulla prassi cembalistica italiana nel Cinque- e Seicento." *Rivista Italiana di Musicologia* 10 (1975), 360–378.

——— "Un' importante fonte per la musica di J. K. Kerll." *Collectanea Historiae Musicae* 4, pp. 283–293. Florence: Olschki, 1966.

Tagmann, Pierre M. *Archivalische Studien zur Musikpflege am Dom von Mantua (1500–1627).* Publikationen der Schweizerischen Musikforschenden Gesellschaft, ser. 2, vol. 14. Bern: Haupt, 1967.

Terni, Clemente. "Girolamo Frescobaldi a Firenze (1628–1633)." *Paragone* 20 (1969), 3–20.

Testi, Flavio. *La musica italiana nel seicento,* 2 vols. Milan: Bramante, 1970–1972.

Teti, Girolamo. *Aedes Barberinae ad Quirinalem.* Rome, 1642.

Thelen, Heinrich. *Zur Entstehungsgeschichte der Hochaltar-Architektur von St. Peter in Rom.* Berlin, 1967.

Thieme, Ulrich, and Becker, Felix. *Allgemeines Lexikon der bildenden Künstler von der Antike bis zur Gegenwart,* 37 vols. Leipzig: W. Engelmann, 1907–1950.

Thomas, Michael. "The Development of the Tuning and Tone Colour of an Instrument Made in Venice about 1500." *English Harpsichord Magazine* 1 (1975), 145–155.

Trabaci, Giovanni Maria. *Composizioni per organo e cembalo,* ed. Oscar Mischiati. Monumenti di Musica Italiana, ser. 1, vols. 3–4. Brescia: L'Organo, 1964, 1969.

——— *Secondo libro di ricercate* (1615), ed. J. Bonfils. L'Organiste Liturgique 54, 57. Paris: Schola Cantorum, 1965, 1966.

Trotti, Anton Francesco. "Le delizie di Belvedere illustrate." *Atti della Deputazione Ferrarese di Storia Patria* 2 (1889), 1–33.

Tusler, Robert L. *The Organ Music of Jan Pieterszoon Sweelinck.* Bilthoven: A. B. Creyghton, 1958.

Valdrighi, Luigi Francesco. *Nomocheliurgografia antica e moderna.* Modena, 1884.

Valente, Antonio. *Intavolatura de cimbalo.* Naples, 1576.

Vallery-Radot, Jean. *Le dessin français au XVIIe siècle.* Lausanne: Mermod, 1953.

Valsecchi, Franco. *L'Italia nel seicento e nel settecento.* Società e Costume 6. Turin: Unione Tipografico-Editrice Torinese, 1967.

Van den Borren, Charles. "A proposito de l' 'Aria della monicha'." *Note d'Archivio* 10 (1933), 200.

Van der Meer, John Henry. "Flämische Cembali in italienischen Besitz." *Analecta Musicologica* 3 (1966), 114–121.

Veroli, Claudio di. *Unequal Temperaments and Their Role in the Performance of Early Music.* Argentina [no city], 1978.

Via del Corso. Rome: Cassa di Risparmio, 1961.

Vignodelli Rubrichi, Renato. "Il 'Fondo Aldobrandini' dell'Archivio Doria Landi Pamphili." *Archivio della Società Romana di Storia Patria* 92 (1969), 15–40.

Virgili, L. "La cappella musicale della chiesa metropolitana di Fermo dalle origini al 1670." *Note d'Archivio* 7 (1930), 1–86.

Virgiliano, Aurelio [pseud.]. *Il dolcimelo,* ed. Marcello Castellani. Facsimile edition of the manuscript. Archivum Musicum 11. Florence: Studio per Edizioni Scelte, 1979.

Vogel, Emil. *Bibliothek der gedruckten weltlichen Vocalmusik Italiens aus den Jahren 1500 bis 1700,* 2 vols. Berlin, 1892. Revised edition, *Bibliografia della musica italiana vocale profana pubblicata dal 1500 al 1700,* ed. Alfred Einstein, François Lesure, Claudio Sartori, 3 vols. Pomezia: Minkoff, 1977.

——— "Marco da Gagliano: zur Geschichte der florentiner Musiklebens von 1570–1650." *Vierteljahrsschrift für Musikwissenschaft* 5 (1889), 396–442, 509–568.

Völkl, Gerhard. "Die Toccaten Claudio Merulos." Ph.D. dissertation, Ludwig Maximilians-Universität, Munich, 1969.

Waldner, Franz. "Zwei Inventarien aus dem XVI. und XVII. Jahrhundert über hinterlassene Musikinstrumente und Musikalien am Innsbrucker Hofe." *Studien zur Musikwissenschaft* 4 (1916), 128–147.

Watkins, Glenn. *Gesualdo: The Man and His Music.* Chapel Hill: University of North Carolina Press, 1973.

Wendland, John. " 'Madre non mi far Monaca': The Biography of a Renaissance Folksong." *Acta Musicologica* 48 (1976), 185–204.

Wessel, Stephen. "The Claviorganum in England." *English Harpsichord Magazine* 2 (1977), 226–233.

Wessely, Othmar. "Aus römischen Bibliotheken und Archiven." In *Symbolae Historiae Musicae: Hellmut Federhofer zum 60. Geburtstag,* ed. F. W. Riedel and Hubert Unverricht, pp. 81–102. Mainz: Schott, 1971.

——— "Der Indice der Firma Franzini in Rom." In *Beiträge der Musikdokumentation : Franz Grasberger zum 60. Geburtstag,* ed. Günter Brosche, pp. 439–492. Tutzing: Schneider, 1975.

Wessely-Kropik, Helene. *Lelio Colista: ein römischer Meister vor Corelli, Leben und Umwelt.* Vienna: Böhlaus, 1961.

Williams, Peter. *The European Organ 1450–1850.* London: Batsford, 1966.

Wittkower, Rudolf. *Art and Architecture in Italy 1600–1750.* Pelican History of Art, 3d rev. ed. Harmondsworth, Eng.: Penguin, 1973.

Witzenmann, Wolfgang. "Autographe Marco Marazzolis in der Biblioteca Vaticana." *Analecta Musicologica* 7 (1969), 36–86; 9 (1970), 203–294.

Wolff, Christoph. *Der Stile antico in der Musik Johann Sebastian Bachs: Studien zu Bachs Spätwerk.* Beihefte zum Archiv für Musikwissenschaft 6. Wiesbaden: Steiner, 1968.

Wollenberg, Susan. "A Note on Three Fugues Attributed to Frescobaldi." *Musical Times* 116 (1975), 133–135.

Wüstefeld, Karl, ed. *Organon: Sammlung von Fughetten und Versetten in alten und neuen Tonarten.* Augsburg, n.d.

Zacconi, Lodovico. *Prattica di musica.* Vol. 1, Venice, 1592; vol. 2, Venice, 1622; reprinted Bologna: Forni, 1967.

Zarlino, Gioseffo. *Le istitutioni harmoniche,* vol. 3 (1558). Trans. Guy A. Marco and Claude V. Palisca as *The Art of Counterpoint.* New York: Norton, 1976.

Ziino, Agostino. " 'Contese letterarie' tra Pietro della Valle e Nicolò Farfaro sulla musica antica e moderna." *Nuova Rivista Musicale Italiana* 3 (1969), 101–120.

——— "Pietro Della Valle e la 'musica erudita': nuovi documenti." *Analecta Musicologica* 4 (1967), 97–111.

Index

An asterisk (*) indicates a page with a music example from the work cited.

HIEBERT LIBRARY
3 6877 00150 4413